GOVERNING WITH

THE NEWS

STUDIES IN COMMUNICATION, MEDIA,
AND PUBLIC OPINION

A series edited by Susan Herbst
and Benjamin I. Page

TIMOTHY E. COOK

GOVERNING WITH THE NEWS

The News Media as a

Political Institution

THE UNIVERSITY OF CHICAGO PRESS

CHICAGO & LONDON

6/98

3711 5952

TIMOTHY E. COOK is professor of political science at Williams College. He is most recently a coauthor of *Crosstalk: Citizens, Candidates, and the Media in a Presidential Campaign,* also published by the University of Chicago Press.

The University of Chicago Press, Chicago 60637
The University of Chicago Press, Ltd., London
© 1998 by The University of Chicago
All rights reserved. Published 1998
Printed in the United States of America
07 06 05 04 03 02 01 00 99 98   1 2 3 4 5

ISBN: 0-226-11499-6 (cloth)
ISBN: 0-226-11500-3 (paper)

Library of Congress Cataloging-in-Publication Data

Cook, Timothy E., 1954–
    Governing with the news : the news media as a political institution / Timothy E. Cook.
        p. cm. — (Studies in communication, media, and public opinion)
    Includes bibliographical references and index.
    ISBN 0-226-11499-6 (alk. paper). — ISBN 0-226-11500-3 (pbk. : alk. paper).
        1. Government and the press—United States—History.   2. Press and politics—United States—History.   I. Title.   II. Series.
PN4738.C66   1997
070.4′49324′0973 — dc21   97-23716
                                                                  CIP

⊛ The paper used in this publication meets the minimum requirements of the American National Standard for Information Sciences—Permanence of Paper for Printed Library Materials, ANSI Z39.48-1984.

To the memory of my mother,

Audrey J. Cook

1913–1972

and to the memory of her mother, my Gran,

Hilda Jackson

1891–1987

CONTENTS

ACKNOWLEDGMENTS

The origin for this book was perhaps fortuitous. Marvin Kalb, director of the Joan Shorenstein Center on the Press, Politics, and Public Policy at the Kennedy School of Government at Harvard, and Gary Orren met with me in late 1988 and invited me to add to their curriculum by teaching a class to be entitled "The Press and Government." Having just completed my study of media strategies in the U.S. House of Representatives, it seemed a natural opportunity to extend and develop the thesis I examined there about the increasing connection of media strategies and governing strategies. It turned out—both from preparing for and from teaching the course in the spring of 1990—that there was more potential in this thought than I had anticipated. The Political Communication section of the American Political Science Association was formed shortly thereafter, and, in part to ensure that the panels would not be populated largely by yet more research on elections, I gave a convention paper at the 1990 meetings exploring the possibility of the news media as a political institution situated among other political institutions. Editors expressed interest in my developing this into a book, and before I knew it I had agreed to write one. Several years later, the manuscript is finally finished; I am grateful to many for help along the way.

In one sense, my preparation for the book began much earlier, when, as a graduate student at the University of Wisconsin, I took two classes taught by Murray Edelman: one on organizational theory and practice, the other on political communication. This manuscript builds on putting those literatures together and, in general, owes much to the example of Murray's inquisitive and interdisciplinary mind. I also owe much to the abiding questions and fruitful methods of my other teachers, most notably the late Barbara Hinckley, Dan Mazmanian, Dick Merelman, Ben Page, Gina Sapiro, and the mentor who influenced me the most, my eighth-grade English and social studies teacher, Harold Golden (wherever he may be).

When I originally set out to write this book, I had thought that I would proceed largely by "soaking and poking" in newsbeats in Washington, but it soon became clear, as I plowed into the literature, that the problem with the field of political communication was not a dearth of information but instead the lack of a larger scheme to make sense of it all. I am indebted to the many fine scholars—whose names will be copiously found in the endnotes—in political science, communication, sociology, history, psychology, anthropology, economics, and beyond; without their research, this book certainly could not have been written.

My year at the Shorenstein Center in 1989–90 provided an ideal incubation for this idea. I learned much from my fellow fellows, particularly through long and thought-provoking conversations with my office mate, Jim Lederman. The administrators of the center (Marvin Kalb, Gary Orren, and Ellen Hume) helped make the center a welcoming and stimulating place, and I will always be obliged to my good friends on the center staff for going out of their way to help me out. Thanks to all as well who have continued since that time to make the Shorenstein Center an intellectual home for me away from Williams. Most of all, I must thank my students in that Kennedy School class on "The Press and Governing" for their enthusiasm and good humor, their willingness to tolerate as yet unformed arguments, and their thoughts and insights. I also am grateful to my students at Williams, and, in the spring of 1995, at Yale, who have also greatly helped me to develop my ideas.

I have been fortunate to labor in two most collegial subfields of political science (legislative studies and political communication). I benefited from comments on the preliminary versions of some of these chapters as presented at conventions, particularly from Ron Berkman, Kurt Lang, David Mayhew, Bert Rockman, and Pamela Shoemaker. I was also privileged to have a number of gracious telephone conversations with the late Douglass Cater; although we never met face-to-face, his encouragement and thoughts—as well as a continuing belief that "the fourth branch" was worth studying—were invaluable. My once (and I hope, future) co-authors, David Colby and Lyn Ragsdale, generously allowed me to borrow from previous collaborative work. Robert Picard helped to sort through the confusing mass of public policies toward the news. Doug Arnold, Lance Bennett, Doris Graber, Dan Hallin, Susan Herbst, Steve Hess, David Mayhew, Ben Page, Michael Schudson, and Bat Sparrow gave constructive critiques of the penultimate manuscript; I appreciate how each of them pushed me in directions I needed to go, even if I may not have gone as far as they would have liked. At the University of Chicago Press, John Tryneski was a model editor. I benefited from his excellent advice, not to mention his well-calibrated balance of prodding and patience. Many others provided citations, ideas, feedback, encouragement, and the sense that these ideas were worth saying. My thanks to them all.

Much of the writing and research for the book was carried out during a sabbatical from Williams College. Division II grants and a Greenbaum Faculty Fellowship from Williams also funded the exemplary research assistance over two summers of Zachary Cook (who is, by the way, no relation, as far as we can tell).

On the more personal side, none can approach the intellectual engagement, deep convictions, unwavering support, and companionship of Jack Yeager. Jack may not have spirited me off to the Château de la Napoule to begin the book (as he did with my first), but a well-furnished study overlooking York Harbor in Maine, where much of the book was written, and a house in the woods in Eugene, Oregon, where I finished the conclusion, come awfully close. I hope that, with the completion of this project, the adventure of our lives together will be, at least momentarily, less cluttered with stacks of half-written chapters, library books, xeroxed articles, news clippings, and videotapes.

My father died not long after I agreed to write this study. I cannot say what he would have thought of my conclusions, but I am especially sorry he did not live to hold the book in his hands, because I know he would have been pleased to read the dedication.

Timothy E. Cook

March 21, 1997
Williamstown, Massachusetts

1

INTRODUCTION: WHY DON'T WE CALL

JOURNALISTS POLITICAL ACTORS?

To paraphrase Mark Twain's famous bon mot about the weather, all observers of American politics nowadays talk about the news media's power in government, but nobody does anything about it—or, at least, no one has yet figured out just how to make sense of that power. This is a bit of a puzzle, particularly given that, almost forty years ago, Douglass Cater wrote a slender volume entitled simply *The Fourth Branch of Government*. Here was his theme:

> The reporter is the recorder of government but he is also a participant. He operates in a system in which power is divided. He as much as anyone . . . helps to shape the course of government. He is the indispensable broker and middleman among the subgovernments of Washington. . . . He can illumine policy and notably assist in giving it sharpness and clarity; just as easily, he can prematurely expose policy and, as with an undeveloped film, cause its destruction. At his worst, operating with arbitrary and faulty standards, he can be an agent of disorder and confusion. At his best, he can exert a creative influence on Washington politics.[1]

In the essay-writing tradition of another journalist-intellectual, Walter Lippmann, Cater pointed to the news media's power in the American political system. But his true insight was that he saw journalists as playing not only a political but a governmental role. He argued that a separation-of-powers system, where each institution controls significant resources, requires both communication between the branches and the imprimatur of public opinion if anything is to get done.

The news media, said Cater, provide a way to fulfill that task. Getting into the news provides a means to communicate quickly and directly across and within branches in a way otherwise denied to officials. Likewise, public opinion may be called upon to arbitrate between branches but is not readily available except through the surrogate of the news media. But because of the corporate sponsorship of their operations, the media are at least partially autonomous of the other three branches. With this independence, political actors in the three branches who wish to use the media's power for their own goals must accommodate themselves to the institutional needs of the news media—much as each branch must do when they wish to do the same with one of the other three established constitutional branches. The net effect, Cater warned, is that "government by publicity" may be an increasingly important focus for political actors in Washington who seek to accomplish policy goals, but that gain may be made at a high cost: further implicating journalistic standards of news into political standards of governance.

Cater did not set forth (and did not intend to set forth) a developed theoretical model; instead, his book is a series of discrete essays on a variety of topics related to the interaction of the press and government. Yet his idea deserves close attention as a spur to our attention and imagination. For one, Cater's notions presage, in the years before the dominance of television and before the rise of a media-savvy political class, our contemporary preoccupation with mass-mediated politics.

Most important, although we might quibble with the notion of a "fourth branch,"[2] Cater's sketch of the news media acting as an intermediary institution in Washington provides us with a new and productive way to make sense of the place of journalism in today's American political life. It is particularly beneficial, because for all the bounty of scholarship in political science, sociology, communication, and beyond on the news media and politics, no one has yet come up with an overarching model that would take all this enormously useful work and place it into a larger context that tells us something about the news media's political role. Instead, while there is controversy, confusion, and combat, scholars have tended to speak past each other. Some have proceeded from different definitions of "politics." Others have chosen case studies that cover only one part of the process of newsmaking or that deal with only certain kinds of news content and then extrapolate incorrectly to statements about the news media and politics.

In particular, our ability to make sense of the political power of the American news media has foundered on difficulties we have encountered in thinking productively of the news media as a "political institution." Many scholars have pointed to political and governmental roles for reporters and newspersons. But none has set forth, as I will attempt to do, a clear model that sees the news media as a coherent intermediary institution without which the three branches established by the Constitution could not act and could not work. This book seeks to show how the news media are recognizable as a political institution: because of their historical development, because of shared processes and predictable products across news organizations, and because of the way in which the work of newspersons is so intertwined with the work of official Washington that the news itself performs governmental tasks.

And not only is the news a "coproduction" of the news media and government, but policy today is likewise the result of collaboration and conflict among newspersons, officials, and other political actors. And none of this requires expanding the definition of "politics" past its customary definition in scholarship. Indeed, I will claim that the American news media today are not merely part of politics; they are part of government.

This book will develop, clarify, and refine a new model of the reporter as a key participant in decision making and policy making and of the news media as a central political force in government. It seeks to fill out an empirical theory of the news media as a political institution that will bring together growing literatures: on the internal structures of news organization; on the development of press offices in every branch of government and every level of government; on the relationships of governmental officeholders and journalists inside and outside of the newsbeat system; and on the direct and indirect ways in which official federal policies and practices have, both historically and today, accommodated, regulated, and (above all) subsidized the news.

Given the wealth of information on the public record and the paucity of models that make sense of that evidence, I am more concerned with developing rather than testing an empirical theory of the news media as a political institution. Most of what follows is based on secondary analysis of published studies, with some attention to public speeches and published writings by journalists and political officials—and, of course, the news itself. By returning to this public record, the reader can see if the model makes sense. To the extent that it does, I hope that it will suggest hypotheses for future empirical research.

In that endeavor, I have been inspired by books such as David Mayhew's instant classic, *Congress: The Electoral Connection*. As every good student of Congress knows, Mayhew suggested that the behavior of members of Congress and its institutional structure could be explained by the single-minded pursuit of reelection. But what is less remembered is that Mayhew did not demonstrate this point as much as he posited it. This book resembles Mayhew's in its willingness to push the argument to the very limits of its ability to explain. "Perforce it will raise more questions than it answers. As is the custom with monocausal ventures, it will no doubt carry arguments to the point of exaggeration; finally, of course, I shall be satisfied to explain a significant part of the variance rather than all of it."[3]

Explanation is one of my goals; evaluation is another. If indeed we can term the news media a "political institution," then we must begin to ask questions about their structure, function, and responsibilities much as political scientists have already done (exhaustively) for the other three branches. In particular, the ascent of the news media as an unelected intermediary institution raises problems of capacity and accountability.

Stated differently, I pose three questions. Does the growth of the media's influence in American politics empower an institution that is poorly equipped to assist in governance, given the prominence of journalistic rather than overtly political goals therein? Who elected reporters to represent them in government and politics, and can we think of the news media as politically accountable for the political choices and impacts they have? Does this then mean that perhaps it is time to start thinking about creating a new, more coherent policy regarding the news media to ensure that the news we receive gets us toward the politics and toward the democracy we want?

Now, readers may well protest: But surely, if this is such a good idea, why hasn't anyone thought of it before? Why didn't anyone take a cue from Cater in all the time since 1959? The answer is twofold. First, journalists work hard to discourage people from thinking of them as political actors. Indeed, they may be so successful at this attempt that they have convinced even themselves. Second, the study of political communication developed amidst a tradition emphasizing "media effects," and the disciplines most involved in the study of the politics of the news media have held back from implications of their work. In particular, while political scientists have been quite comfortable referring to the media's political contribution, they have been less willing to see the news media as an institution; conversely, while sociologists have had little problem referring to the news media as a social institution, they have not been as persuasive in outlining the news media's political role.

Journalists' Self-Concepts and Public Personas

One reason we don't think of journalists as political actors is because journalists themselves are reluctant to think of themselves in those terms. In fact, they do quite a bit to discourage that conception—whether in their own minds or those of outside observers such as officials and audiences. This doesn't mean that journalists harbor personal political biases that they cleverly mask by going through the motions of objectivity. This is *not* a critique of individual journalists for failing to live up to the norms and standards of their profession. On the contrary: American journalists are faced with an impossible task of gathering all the most important and interesting news under the unremitting pressure of the deadline and with declining resources to do so. Moreover, journalists are conscientiously committed to high standards of impartiality and to excluding their own personal values from the newsmaking process.

But seemingly neutral news values include presumptions about what makes a quality story—most generally, the twin concerns that news should be important and it should be interesting. Neither concern is free from politics. As we shall see later on in this book, important news is most often certified as such by persons "in a position to know" based on their official position within government. Thus, powerful officials are best positioned to create news events, certify issues as newsworthy, and make news on their own terms.

But while such political actors are best able to certify importance, journalists are the final arbiter of what is likely to be interesting. Officials stage media events with particular coverage in mind, but the ultimate news product diverges, in whole or in part, from what they would prefer. Production values—such as drama, novelty, timeliness, vividness, color, easily described stories with two distinct sides, terseness, good visuals, pithy sound bites—often dictate the angle of the story or the "play" given it. Likewise, certain accounts are esteemed as quality stories, particularly when they follow the "enduring values" that the sociologist Herbert Gans identified in the news of the early seventies and that we still see in today's news: stories of rugged individuals fighting faceless bureaucracies, of threats to small-town Americana, of selfless leaders taking charge in government or business, and, above all, of the return of normal order after its natural or unnatural interruption. So much news is highly formulaic that it has been labeled "novelty without change."[4] The repetitive quality of the news generally offers access only to certain storylines—and to those political actors who anticipate the recurring preferences of the news media.

It is not in spite of, but because of, their commitment to norms of objectivity and impartiality that journalists are nowadays important political actors. By following standard routines of newsmaking, journalists end up hiding their influence not only from outside actors but also from themselves. In particular, they follow what the sociologist Gaye Tuchman aptly termed "objectivity as strategic ritual."[5] The notion of objectivity continues to have a powerful pull on journalists. Thus, disagreement over the ethical demands of their profession rarely produces conflict over the idea that, at base, they should and can be neutral observers of politics. A striking example arose in 1995 when the National Association of Black Journalists debated whether or not to pass a resolution asking for a new trial for Mumia Abu-Jamal, an African-American journalist sentenced to death for murdering a police officer in Philadelphia.[6] Journalists on both sides of the resolution noted their adherence to objectivity. A *Washington Post* reporter arguing against the resolution said, "If we get involved in calling for a new trial, that would threaten the integrity of the organization. I don't want to step out of ourselves and become part of the story." His statement was reinforced by a *Newsday* columnist, who said, "We are journalists, not activists and not lawyers." But those who spoke for the resolution advocated objectivity as well. A *New York Times* reporter contended that Abu-Jamal "was a journalist just like us. He tried to produce stories that made him infamous to a lot of people including those in law enforcement. To suggest that he get a new trial does not say he is guilty or innocent."[7]

Journalists, by adhering to the strategic ritual of objectivity, can persuade their readers and themselves that their report is as neutral as it can be. Reports present conflicting possibilities but rarely go beyond "both sides of the story." Narrowing a complex situation down to two and only two sides, however, already defines the politics and power that is likely to follow. Colorful judgments are usually found in quotes, not in the journalist's own language, even if reporters have sought out particular sources with the hope that they will say exactly what the reporters expect them to say. Passive voices abound ("It was learned today that . . ."), inanimate objects and concepts come to life ("Questions continued to dog President Clinton . . ."), and first-person pronouns are frowned upon ("When Mr. Gorbachev greeted a visitor today . . ."), as if journalists' presences, let alone their queries, had not affected what was learned and asked.

In short, the final news product gives little sense of the individual choices that reporters work hard to protect in their work; instead, reporters try to call attention to the skill and craft with which they interpret the inevitable facts of the outside world. The rise of news analysis and punditry, on one hand, or the palpable physical presence of television reporters, on the other hand, may mean that journalists are less able to obscure their individual power.[8] Yet all news in any medium undergoes strategic rituals. It is legitimized by quotes from official authoritative sources to provide the raw material of their stories. The separation of editorials and "news analysis" on one hand from straight news on the other suggests that only the former is subjective. And as Tuchman has noted, the camera framing of television journalists is a visual translation of the strategic ritual of objectivity, shot in "close social distance," which allows for discussion without intimacy. At its most famous—the *60 Minutes* exposé—the investigating journalist is shot at a respectful distance while the face of the person who is being grilled fills the screen with the emotion and power of an extreme close-up shot.[9] Not just the language of news in print but the implications of television framing are clear: journalists present themselves as coolly dispassionate in contrast to the intensity, color, and subjectivity of their subjects.

The daily strategic ritual can and does break down. Journalists sometimes are missing from the scene of a newsworthy occurrence (for instance, the assassination of President Kennedy, captured only by amateur photographers), thereby raising doubts about professional competence.[10] At other times, they inadvertently reveal that news would not have happened without their direct involvement; rather than merely channeling or reflecting it, they are perceived thereby to have interfered in politics and come in for criticism for their choices. But on occasions when one strategic ritual breaks down, another—"repair work"—goes into play.[11] Sometimes, internal investigations proceed; at other times, ombudsmen and media critics examine the evidence. But, almost inevitably, these failed stories become opportunities for the news media to reinforce the strategic ritual, by pointing the finger away from the standard methods of journalism that often contributed to the story and toward individual infractors, whether flawed journalists or devious sources. When the media themselves become newsworthy, the resultant soul-searching rarely restricts the power of journalists or the strategic rituals that help make it possible.

In short, journalists work hard to maximize their autonomy. But they also work hard to present a news account that seems largely beyond their individual control. This is not to doubt the many restrictions under which journalists work; indeed, I will describe a number of them later in this book. Yet these cannot justify protestations of journalists that they exercise little discretion and therefore have no political power in their own right.

But journalists' skillful elision of their power is not the only reason for scholarly inattention. We must note also how the disciplines most actively involved in the study of the news media's politics—particularly political science, sociology, and communication—developed so as to reinforce the journalists' self-concepts and public personas, and so as to occlude the possibility of the news media as a political institution.

THE ROADS NOT TAKEN

Let us begin with political science, which has been quite confused about whether, and to what extent, the news media are a political institution. Here are some quotes from distinguished political scientists who are among the leading scholars of the news media. Stephen Hess, senior scholar at the Brookings Institution, is best known for his *Newswork* series of insightful books about the Washington press corps that suggests we may have overestimated their influence. But Hess has had no problem in referring to the Washington press corps as "another public policy institution" to which he turned after studying the presidency.[12] By contrast, Thomas Patterson, Bradlee Professor of Government and the Press at Harvard's Kennedy School of Government, has written landmark works that charge that the news media are overly powerful in American politics. Yet in Patterson's two best-known studies of the media's role in American elections, he notes, "The campaign is chaotic largely because the press is not a political institution and has no capacity for organizing the election in a coherent manner."[13] Even political scientists who owe much to the sibling disciplines of sociology and communication are ambivalent. Thus, Daniel Hallin, a political scientist now in the communication department at the University of California at San Diego, wrote in an important essay about the potential contributions of critical theory in sociology to our understanding of the news: "The mass media are an institution with a dual social identity. They are both an economic (or, in Western Europe, often political) and a cultural institution; they are a profit-making business and at the same time a producer of meaning, a creator of social consciousness."[14]

This presents a quandary. Why is it that one author who doubts the media's power does see them as a political institution, while the reverse is true of other scholars warning about the media's role in politics? Is it important that Hess refers to a "public policy institution" rather than a "political institution"? Do Patterson and Hallin imply that nothing can be a political institution unless it has been explicitly "instituted" to pursue political aims?

It is hard to know the answers to any of these questions, given that none of these authors develop or even justify their rather bare evocation of the news media as being institutional or not. Numerous political scientists have pointed to the potential power of the news media, but from that it is equally tough to know whether this power is exercised by journalists, by officials (and other sources who have easy access to the news), or by some combination thereof.[15]

Sociologists—and communication scholars heavily influenced by the sociological tradition—have had less difficulty pointing to the news media as an institution. For instance, whether we refer to the Weberian tradition found in the writings of C. Wright Mills, or the lineages of neo-Marxist critical theory and cultural studies, sociologists have aptly depicted the news media as a social institution, perhaps a pivotal social institution.[16] Yet these scholarly insights break down in turn on partial or unconvincing or incomplete understandings of politics. Mills and critical theorists such as Max Horkheimer, Theodor Adorno, and Herbert Marcuse all saw the rise of the "culture industry" as creating a "mass society" that made it less possible for individuals to resist the messages thereby diffused.[17] Yet this key assumption has been greatly eroded by research that concludes that the audience can and does make unique individual sense of media content—which in turn raises questions about the political impact of "the culture industry."

Those sociologists who moved into cultural studies likewise pointed to the institutional aspects of the news media, operating to reinforce an ideological hegemony that constricted the range of possible political outcomes and emphasized a "common sense" approach to political problems that reinforced the status quo. In its subtlest version, best articulated by Stuart Hall and Todd Gitlin, scholarship provided evidence that "media institutions were both, in fact, free of direct compulsion and constraint, and yet freely articulated themselves systematically around definitions of the situations which favoured the hegemony of the powerful."[18] Yet such studies looked at only a limited albeit important sample of political news, usually those dealing with social movements, the definition of "deviance," crime, international security, and foreign policy. It is telling that students of hegemony have rarely taken their inquiries into domains of mainstream domestic politics. In other words, while these authors may well be right that "one 'function' of the media [is] reproducing dominant conceptions of the political world," they bypass "other possible functions such as giving information for elites to make decisions or serving as a forum for debate among elites."[19]

But not only has there been confusion about the news media's politics and their institutional dimension. The disciplines of political science and mass communication have been under the sway of what one recent book terms "the voter persuasion paradigm."[20] The standard focus in media studies on elections does provide a key entry point. But they do not and cannot tell us much about politics and government outside the electoral context. Studies of voting tend implicitly to favor a model going from political sources through the media to the public which responds, thereby influencing politicians to formulate and implement policy. Such a unidirectional model leads to two commonly made assumptions: first, if the public is not involved, the media cannot be said to have exerted influence; and second, the media, reflecting information obtained from sources, do not act as an independent influence. These assumptions usually go unchallenged (even unspoken), but they are seriously flawed. The news media have direct contact with and influence upon elites. And not only does information change as it passes through the filters of the media, but political actors respond to the agenda of the news and often anticipate the media's response even before they decide what to do and how to do it.

This paradigm emerged following the First World War and the rise of fascism in the 1920s and 1930s when social scientists were, not surprisingly, preoccupied with the potential of governmental propaganda.[21] In studying the impact of propaganda, social scientists drew upon expertise in marketing. But to use that knowledge, they needed to find a political decision comparable to those made by consumers selecting a product to purchase. Choosing a candidate fit the bill best, most powerfully in the work of Paul Lazarsfeld and his coauthors, starting with the 1940 Erie County study, *The People's Choice*,[22] which established the "effects tradition" as the initial paradigm for mass (including political) communication research. As it turns out, by selecting a homogeneous community for their survey, Lazarsfeld and his colleagues ended up being stymied in their attempts to find a persuasive impact of the news media on the vote. Yet their conclusion was judged so persuasive that the less sociologically minded set of election studies from the University of Michigan did not even bother to study the impact of the media; news consumption was regarded only as "vicarious participation in campaign activities available to practically every American."[23]

Even during the 1950s, not all scholars pointed to limited effects.[24] But the effects paradigm subtly and powerfully foreclosed certain answers by pushing research away from certain questions. In particular, it directed scholars away from any research that did not fit the larger assumption of the effects tradition: a linear and unidirectional understanding of the communication process, passing from a source who encodes the message by a given medium to a receiver who decodes it and acts upon it.[25]

Since the mid-1960s, of course, the effects tradition has slowly been eroded. First, effects were expanded to include setting the public's agenda; then, audience studies stressed the ways in which the public could creatively rework the messages in their own ways for their own purposes, even if they had little power over the initial formulation of those messages. But in either of these, the potential for interaction and interdependence is rarely considered. The effects paradigm, even when directly disputed and decried, has continued to limit investigation.

TROUBLE IN PARADIGMS

Take one question: If the public is not involved, then can the media have exerted power? Stephen Hess has provided a representative answer when discussing why senators should be expected not to exploit media strategies as part of their legislative work:

> Trying to use the media to get legislation through Congress is a Rube Goldberg design based on (A) legislator influencing (B) reporter to get information into (C) news outlet so as to convince (D) voters who will then put pressure on (E) other legislators. Given all of the problems inherent in successfully maneuvering through the maze, no wonder that legislative strategies are usually variations of (A) legislator asking (E) other legislators for their support.[26]

Yet the American news media can and do directly influence political elites: helping to highlight particular issues and alternatives, influence perceptions of public moods, and in other ways shape the context of one legislator asking another for support, whether or not the public was involved, had chosen sides, or was even aware of the issue.[27] It is often not remembered that only once did Ronald Reagan's much-vaunted communication skills succeed in pressuring Congress by mobilizing public opinion. Otherwise, when Reagan's public strategy at other times might have succeeded to move an otherwise recalcitrant legislature, public opinion was divided or confused. Far from following Hess's Rube Goldberg scenario, then, Reagan's presidency relied upon the news media not to convince voters but instead to set a context and a tone that raised the stakes of resistance or inaction.[28]

All right then: How can the media act as an independent influence if they gather information, usually obtained from powerful, governmental sources? A typical response is revealed in John Kingdon's otherwise superb pioneering study of agenda processes. Kingdon noted that the essential first step is defining problems worthy of public attention, consideration, and action. In policy realms that are already salient, empirical indicators are deemed most influential; less visible matters require what Kingdon terms "focusing events, crises and symbols."[29] Yet how do policy areas maintain, attain, or lose salience? How do occurrences become focusing events, or crises? One flaw in Kingdon's analysis is his neglect of one key actor: the media. He claimed that the media are less important than popular wisdom might predict because "the media report what is going on in government, by and large, rather than having an independent effect *on* governmental agendas."[30] Kingdon granted that the media might be important by allowing communication within policy communities, by magnifying (but not originating) issues, and by influencing public opinion. Yet his main point seems to be that the media have little independent effect upon agenda setting because they are largely passing along information from elsewhere.

Kingdon was partially right. To the extent that journalists wait for authoritative sources to do or say newsworthy things, their role in agenda setting is unlike those of other political actors. (Other political actors, however, wield power in reactive ways—most notably the Supreme Court, which can address legal and constitutional questions only in the context of cases that have arisen through the judicial system.)[31] And many studies of journalism, reviewed later in the book, reveal the power of sources in suggesting and shaping if not determining the news.

Yet the literature is asymmetrical, with many more journalist's-eye views of the process than perspectives from the politicians' side.[32] Leon Sigal has written that "sources make the news."[33] So why do these sources complain as much as they do about the coverage they garner? Simply put, the news media do more than reflect or merely pick and choose from among what others are doing.[34] Journalists are often reliant on sources, but news organizations reinforce journalists' notions of quality by superiors and peers who provide feedback, and such coworkers—who are the ones, after all, who pay the reporters' salaries—can help to counterbalance pressure from sources.[35]

Such a conclusion does not mean that the media call the political shots in the United States. Instead, newsmaking and its place in the political system is best conceived not as a linear, unidirectional process but as interactive and interdependent, the result of what I have elsewhere termed the *negotiation of newsworthiness*. Political actors and journalists (and only occasionally citizens) interact in a constant but implicit series of negotiations over who controls the agenda, what can be asked, where and how, and what a suitable answer will be.[36]

As I will develop the argument below, officials and journalists each control important resources because of the duality whereby news is to be both important *and* interesting. Politicians dictate conditions and rules of access and designate certain events and issues as important by providing an arena for them. Journalists, in turn, decide whether something is interesting enough to cover, the context in which to place it, and the prominence the story receives. A source's power may not be enough to get it in print or on the air in the absence of such interest. At other times, sources may provide access to journalists for a particular purpose only to find that they have unwittingly made themselves available to be questioned on other matters the reporters deem more newsworthy. So whether or not problems and issues can rise to the American political agenda through the media depends not only upon their connection with powerful "authoritative sources." Journalistic criteria for quality news are not only central to reporters but to sources, who make decisions in anticipation of those criteria, both in the short term (when figuring out what questions reporters are likely to pose) and over the long haul (when planning how to gain favorable and regular publicity).

To take the example I have developed elsewhere for Congress, the political agenda is set not by the media by themselves or by the members by themselves but by the two sides, whether working together or in competition.[37] Entrepreneurial members of Congress wishing to make a name for themselves in Washington will often latch onto issues that promise to be newsworthy, and in that sense the media's preferences will shape the congressional agenda. But at the same time, reporters trying to figure out what the "big story" is in Washington will attend to the sayings and doings of members that are deemed in positions to be influential. Insofar as institutional action is required for news and public salience is necessary for any such movement, the legislative process may maintain its momentum by alternating publicity with decisions, each of which reinforces the other.

In short, we cannot make simple interpretations of political effects *on* the news or of the media's effect *on* politics. The two are so intertwined that it is preferable to study, first, the news media's interactions with political actors, including the perspectives from both the political and the journalistic spheres in the process, and, second, the effects that those interactions and negotiations have on the kind of news that appears and the kind of policies and politics that are thereby encouraged.

THE PLAN OF THE BOOK

The news media are less formally constituted and less bounded as a political institution than those that political scientists customarily examine. Consequently, studying them is necessarily complex and requires diverse, eclectic methods. I begin in Chapters 2 and 3 by interpreting the historical record of the American news media. I follow the increasingly important approach of American political development, whereby political science uses historical data to trace the origins of contemporary institutional arrangements and to specify the political, social, and economic conditions under which they emerged. I will suggest that, far from being free from governmental involvement and intervention, the evolution of the American news media has always been and continues to be intimately tied to various versions of political sponsorship, subsidization, and protection.

Direct sponsorship prevailed up through the mid-nineteenth century. Newspapers were generally funded by a party, received patronage such as printing contracts and postmasterships, and provided an interventionist journalism. Likewise, access to politicians, especially in the most newsworthy branch of government (Congress), was highly selective and politicized.

Such direct kinds of political help have been gradually displaced by ones that are more indirect, beginning with the generous subsidies provided by the post office since the colonial era to deliver newspapers. As the news media became commercialized and politically independent, and as government's goals became more entwined with publicity, indirect institutional subsidies completely displaced the previous sponsorships, with the rise in the twentieth century of press offices and press officers that provide the raw (or, more correctly, predigested) material for journalistic accounts, authored by reporters working in limited newsbeats. There is by now a public policy toward the news media, but one that works very much to the profitability of the industry. The news media's structure, process, and output have been crucially shaped by government action throughout American history; one must question the interpretation of "freedom of the press" as referring to untrammeled and independent development.

In Chapter 4, I develop a model of the news media as institutional. This analysis has been inspired by the "new institutionalism" in the study of social and political organizations. Unlike traditional approaches in political science that studied formal mechanisms without seeing how these institutions worked in practice, today's institutionalism recognizes the central part of unquestioned forms, structures, and routines, as they interact with the everyday practice of these institutions. In particular, I focus here on a model of collective action that notes that explicit utility maximizing must be complemented by taken-for-granted notions of the way things have always been done and the way they should be done, notions that not merely constrain but enable the choices and interests of those operating within institutions.

Whereas much research on the purported bias of the news media end up examining individual journalists and their individually held values and attitudes, an institutional approach stresses the roles that journalists and political actors occupy within their respective political and social systems. I seek to establish two things. First, the news media are not simply distinct organizations but make up a collective institution—a site of systematized principles of action enduring across time and supervising a central area of social and political life. Second, journalists' activities are not merely constrained, they are enabled if not constituted by such an institutional framework. The historical developments sketched in the previous chapters show how the news media are treated as an institution by government, with subsidies and privileges available to a class of publications. The pressures of uncertainty as well as the rise of professionalism also push news organizations, even those across modalities of communication, to look alike. We can then speak not of the news media as organizations or as institutions in the plural, but as a single—and quite singular—institution.

Chapter 5 turns from the question of the news media as institutional to the notion of the news media as political. It addresses the implications of viewing newspersons as political actors in their own right. It turns from the examination of the total system of newsbeats to the interactions and negotiations within individual newsbeats. I study the centrality of governmental participation in the very process of newsmaking, and the impact of the political institution or agency itself on the organization of the newsbeat, on journalists' conceptions of news, and on the ultimate product itself. I argue that governmental processes provide the stages, the actors, and the lines for the accounts that journalists create. But the latter cut and paste these elements together according to their own standards of quality and interest, which may well diverge from the optimal "spin" of the politicians. Since politicians certify importance while journalists have the last say on interest, the built-in tension is never resolved but instead is always subject to renegotiation. Nonetheless, a bargain of sorts is struck at newsbeats; in the words of a plaque on the desk of President Reagan's White House spokesman Larry Speakes, "You don't tell us how to stage the news and we don't tell you how to cover it."

Having established how journalists and governmental officials jointly make the news, Chapter 6 outlines the uses of news for governmental actors. American government increasingly relies upon the news media to communicate among and within its disparate parts. Among national institutions, it is striking that *all* three branches now devote more time and energy to media relations and to "going public" than they did in the late 1950s when Cater discussed "the fourth branch." The entry of journalists into governing is not without cost, given their final control over the news product and their potentially divergent sense of what's news. But linking media strategies and governing strategies has become an attractive option for officials, whether to communicate to an ever more complex and dispersed political system, to influence the context in which other officials decide inside and outside their own institutions, or to make policy itself by the use of performative language. Officials have furthered the importance of newsmaking by hiring professional public information officers who bring the journalistic perspective into the governmental process. Chapter 6 concludes with a consideration of how the best-known mass-mediated official—the American president—can set up expectations for the other branches.

In Chapter 7, I develop a model further by positing that while every institution has some sort of concerted and consistent media strategy, the extent and kind of media strategy in each case depends on the disjuncture between the ambitions of the occupants of the institution and the resources available to them to accomplish those ambitions. In other words, working with and through the news media becomes attractive to officials in the three branches to counteract the central institutional weakness bequeathed to each by the Constitution. I note how the differing organization of the newsbeats and the understanding of the typical continuing stories at those newsbeats shape and constrain the potential for a media strategy to contribute to a governing strategy.

Chapter 8, the conclusion, draws these various strands together to reiterate the two problems of the rise of the news media as a political institution: political capacity and political accountability. The growth of the media's influence in American politics may empower an institution that is poorly equipped to assist in democratic governance, particularly if journalistic concerns predominate over explicitly political aims and create a politics of their own. And we must answer the question: If the media are now a key intermediary institution, who elected reporters to represent them in politics and how well is their power popularly checked? I will consider this problem of a potentially unaccountable political force in government, note the limits of popular control of the news media, and offer suggestions for how to deal with the rise of the news media as an intermediary political institution without undercutting the First Amendment's commitment to freedom of the press. We have a policy toward the news media that is partially explicit but mostly implicit; perhaps it is time to start talking directly about the news we wish to have and the policies we can implement to further that goal.

PART ONE

THE POLITICAL DEVELOPMENT

OF THE

AMERICAN NEWS MEDIA

In the next two chapters, I will point to a somewhat neglected interpretation of what produced the American news media system we have today. I will argue that politics and policy have been and are today central shapers of news organizations, practices, formats, and content. Such an assertion may, at first blush, be surprising. After all, consider the legacy of the First Amendment that prohibits the passage of laws that would "abridge" freedom of the press, the news media's formal independence from government, and public broadcasting that is much less widespread than in other countries. Far from being free from governmental involvement and intervention, however, the evolution of the American news media has always been and continues to be intimately tied to political sponsorship, subsidization, and protection. The change we see over American history is less *whether* the news media and news products are shaped by governmental practices and policies than *how*.

This political contribution to the current shape of the news media has been overlooked, in part because other hypotheses have gained attention instead. For instance, technological explanations are popular to use in an effort to make sense of how the American news media developed. Some credit the invention of the telegraph, and the subsequent establishment of wire services such as the Associated Press, in the 1840s, with provoking the news to move away from lengthy partisan opinion to neutral bare-bones political facts.[1] Innovations such as circular presses and later linotype machines helped speed up newspaper production and are noted for provoking large circulation, large issues, and more popular content. More recently, television is supposed to have transformed American journalism due to its preference for news that is personalized, interpretive, terse, and visual.[2]

Yet the technological explanation misses the mark. Even prior to the invention of the telegraph, the press had started valuing recency, relying on pony expresses or express steamships to get the news from colleagues in other towns. Rather than slow down the expresses with complete editions of bulky newspapers, editors began sending along "slips." These short items, often written on tissue paper, synopsized the latest news and were the precursor of what would be sent over the wires.[3] Television, too, built on already existing forms of news, picking up the modes that newspaper reporters had devised in the Progressive era, emphasizing color, drama, and the persona of a crusading journalist seeking to reform the failures of an otherwise admirable system. New technologies come into play amidst already established expectations of what was news; they do not create new forms from scratch.[4]

Economic explanations are also often cited but limited. Scholars have claimed how the "penny press" in the 1830s discovered a market that had been previously untapped in the days of an elite "six-penny press"; in pursuit of that larger mass audience, the argument goes, the penny press had to soft-pedal politics and partisanship and turn its attention toward politically neutral but lively subjects like local news and human interest stories.[5] Michael Schudson, in his very fine "social history of American newspapers," has convincingly argued that for the penny press to succeed, the idea of news could be transformed into an egalitarian ideal only with the Jacksonian redefinition of politics.[6] But in turn, Schudson's emphasis upon the development of social and political theories (at mass or elite levels) as the impetus for new forms of reporting does not tell us the mechanics of how such ideas became translated into political, let alone journalistic, practice.

In sum, the emphases upon technology, economics, or

ideas each seem to fall short of a full explanation for how America came to have the kind of news media it has today. The next two chapters, then, explore the possibility that political practices and governmental policies centrally shaped the development of the American news media. This is not to counterpose an exclusively political explanation against the others. Instead, how technology, economics, and social ideas affect the news is often accomplished itself through political decisions. Politics can, after all, encourage or discourage the development, reach, and availability of technology, influence the establishment of particular markets, and instigate the political applicability of political ideas. More completely, the historical record suggests that the relationship between the evolving news media and the developing governmental structure is interactive. Since government and the news media are (and always have been) at least partially independent of one another, changes in political practices and policies provoke alterations in journalism *and* vice versa.

These two chapters draw their inspiration from recent work in what has come to be known as "American political development," a comparative politics of institutions over time rather than across political systems. It allows an examination of political institutions in a variety of contexts, but it also enables a view of particular institutional arrangements as the result of politics as well as the other way around.[7]

What follows is undoubtedly more of a sketch for future hypotheses and future work. Nevertheless, from the evidence already available, *it is clear that, at any stage in American history, the production of news was centrally aided and abetted by political and governmental policies and practices.* Whether explicitly or implicitly, what government decided and what it did toward the news media helped to impel the media to take the shape they ultimately have today. But history is not constant. In particular, while there has indeed been a remarkable historical shift, it is not—contrary to most authors—from a regulated press through the mid-nineteenth century to a relatively unregulated news media today. Instead, the displacement of government's relations to the news media has been from *sponsorship* to *subsidies*.

2

THE DECLINE OF THE SPONSORED PRESS:

AMERICAN NEWSPAPERS IN THE EIGHTEENTH

AND NINETEENTH CENTURIES

From the infancy of the newspaper in North America in early eighteenth-century Boston all the way through the Civil War, politics infused and informed the production of news, in direct, conscious, and unsubtle ways. Support tended to consist of individual sponsorship. Newspapers most often were launched with the help of politically powerful sponsors—officials, factions, or, by the first years of the republic, parties. Continuing operations were supported by government patronage. In addition, reward was reinforced by punishment. Legal action policed newspapers' criticism initially by arrests for seditious libel and for violating parliamentary privilege; as these waned, they were replaced by attempts to deny access to governmental processes to offending reporters. Sometimes extralegal efforts arose, ranging from canceling subscriptions and advertising to violence and vigilantism against individual presses.

By contrast, fewer policies or practices existed as virtual governmental entitlements to newspapers or those who produced them, with one key exception: generous postal regulations that favored the rapid development of newspapers. By allowing printers to exchange their products with one another without charge prior to the Revolution, and by charging newspapers much lower rates for delivery than letters thereafter, public policy was squarely placed behind the growth and interdependence of a national news media system.

In the next chapter, I will outline how such subsidies—entitlements given either to anything that qualified as a news outlet or to specially targeted news media such as small local weekly papers—grew in importance, as individual sponsorship waned in the late nineteenth century. These subsidies took two forms: in explicit policies toward a range of news media, and in the practices of governmental and political figures assisting and giving automatic access to all "bona fide" journalists in their jobs. Most important, in contrast with the early years of the republic, when access was viewed as a privilege to be granted or taken away as reward or punishment for particular coverage, the practice a hundred years later was to recognize universalistic criteria by which one could assess whether reporters were entitled to that access or not. By the late nineteenth century, then, the press was officially recognized as an institution whose members had rights and privileges appertaining thereto, rather than a disparate collection of individual newspapers, reporters, and editors, to be dealt with one at a time.

Political sponsorship of the news media is pretty much a thing of the past. If one were to focus on its decline alone, it would lend credence to a notion of ever-growing independence from government for American news media. This, however, is only half of the story. Starting with the postal subsidies for newspapers, government has always subsidized the news media but now does so in several ways: in part by regulation on their own terms, in part by decisions to exempt news organizations from regulations under which they would otherwise have to operate, and in part by a governmental public relations infrastructure that aims to satisfy journalists' needs and to help them fill up the news. But before we get to the details of subsidies, sketched in Chapter 3, let's turn to the earlier tale of the rise and fall of a sponsored press.

THE CONTRADICTORY LEGACY OF COLONIAL AND REVOLUTIONARY AMERICA

In 1704, the first issue of the first regularly produced newspaper in the North American colonies—the *Boston News-Letter*—appeared, its masthead proclaiming, "Published by Authority."[1] Its only predecessor (the 1690 Boston newspaper, *Publick Occurrences*) had lasted but one issue before the authorities shut it down. The governor and his council, concluding that it was printed "[w]ithout the least Privity or Countenance of Authority," suppressed it, adding a reminder that all who wish to print must receive a license.[2]

Licensing was allowed by Parliament to expire in 1694 and would never again be exploited so effectively.[3] But laws forbidding "seditious libel" and protecting "parliamentary privilege" meant that authorities could arrest and prosecute, and occasionally convict, writers and printers for disseminating sentiments that the powers deemed defamatory to themselves and thereby (so they claimed) damaging to the public peace.[4]

True, seditious libel fell out of favor after the famous 1735 trial of John Peter Zenger, whose attorney convinced the jury to acquit the printer because he had printed the truth, whatever the consequences.[5] Breach of parliamentary privilege was still available, though. In Harold

Nelson's words, "Printers were forever being called before the bars of the legislative bodies to answer for 'affronts,' 'breach of privilege,' 'impudence,' 'indignities' upon authority, and 'libels.' "[6] Yet, there too convictions were rare, and charges were often dropped.[7] Nevertheless, both provided official avenues to harass and jail printers. Zenger himself was jailed for over a year prior to his acquittal; little wonder that sometime after having been freed he would happily become the official printer for New York.[8]

Subtler ties of newspapers with government also existed, not surprisingly, given their small elite circulation.[9] The *Boston News-Letter*'s publisher, John Campbell, was not first and foremost a newspaper publisher; his newspaper work was an extension of his position as Boston postmaster.[10] The norm by the middle of the eighteenth century was for newspaper publishers to be printers, but the production of newspapers, as well as the income obtained in that capacity, was only one part of their enterprises, which comprised printing books, religious tracts, political broadsides, blank forms, official announcements, and laws, in addition to many side jobs, such as serving as auctioneers (sometimes for slaves), and selling books, lottery tickets, and other goods.[11]

This diversity provided some independence from governmental and political patrons in the largest cities. Elsewhere, printers relied on obtaining the public business.[12] All benefited economically by printing on commission; newspapers were simply part of this overall business logic of diversification.[13] Such market logic provoked most printers to portray themselves as impartial intermediaries passing along what was provided to them.[14] "Freedom of the press" thus referred less to journalistic independence from government intervention than to the capacity of individuals to have free access to a printing press and thereby disseminate their views. Printers would simply play a part comparable to today's cable public access channels: provide technologies and resources for individuals to reach larger audiences, as long as they did not cross the line between "liberty" and "license."[15]

With newspapers only one part of printers' output, and with the often precarious financial survival of their shop,[16] government could and did assist as well as punish. Government provided much news content via official notices, announcements, proclamations, and brief items. The second support was more direct. Being postmaster not only provided a royal salary to Campbell; he was thereby well-placed to gather news, used the office's franking privilege to send his newspapers gratis through the mail, and petitioned for funds from the public treasury—allotted to him several times in his first years of business.[17] Other printers received patronage: postmasterships, printing contracts from governors and assemblies, appointments as clerks or secretaries. Such jobs rarely provided the bulk of printers' income, but they provided more stable cash flow than was received from subscriptions, and they also provided entrée into political circles to parlay into more news and more profit.[18]

With such official connections, most newspapers in the early 1700s were bland and meek. They focused on distant European affairs rather than local politics. The job of reporter, as we know it today, was nonexistent. Most news was directly lifted, albeit with acknowledgment, from London papers. The remainder consisted of official proclamations, letters from contacts in other cities (hence the origin of the term, "correspondent"), word-of-mouth accounts from captains of recently docked vessels, lists of newly arrived ships and of prices for goods in other ports, and a few items from local grapevines.[19] Even if, as historian Charles Clark has concluded, these newspapers' "support of the successive administrations . . . was usually implicit rather than explicit, characterized in the main by a simple refusal to recognize opposition voices and enter into local political disputes,"[20] official control of incentives apparently helped to cultivate a press that was generally on their side.

The colonial period does provide precursors of adversarial journalism. But since such newspapers arose in politically divisive times, their appearance supports rather than questions the thesis of a sponsored press. Take James Franklin's denunciation of the political forces urging inoculation against smallpox in his *New-England Courant* in the early 1720s, which is commonly noted as the first example of a journalistic political crusade. But this episode occurred amidst an elite divided along religious lines, with the lone medical doctor in the colonies writing for the *Courant*.[21] Likewise, Zenger emerged as a legend only because of a feud between the governor and the New York chief justice who thought he was owed the governor's job. Zenger was hauled into court for printing diatribes against the former in a newspaper written and funded by the latter. Such crusading journalism was not then independent of politics; indeed, it was made possible, if not necessary, by splits in the ruling elites.[22] Once those splits healed, printers found it more beneficial to try to work with all sides, as the later, establishment-minded careers of these two printers make clear.

Nevertheless, these crusading examples gave a new twist to the notion of "freedom of the press" by offering exemplars ready to criticize government and standing up to authorities who would squelch them.[23]

Yet such printers did not abandon the doctrine of impartiality.[24] "Freedom of the press" before the Revolution had different definitions, either of which could be mobilized depending on circumstances.

To be sure, the crusading approach became more visible after 1765 and the Stamp Act Crisis. Parliament had sought to pay the debts left by the French and Indian War by taxing paper in the North American colonies. Printers would bear its costs. The first historian of the American Revolution was to write in 1789, "It was fortunate for the liberties of America, that newspapers were the subject of a heavy stamp duty. Printers, when uninfluenced by government, have generally ranged themselves on the side of liberty, nor are they less remarkable for attention to the profits of their profession. A stamp duty, which openly invades the first, and threatened a great diminution of the last, provoked their united zealous opposition."[25]

Economics now pushed printers into political advocacy and into a new spot; the old stance of avoiding controversy only got them into trouble. Newspapers trying to bridge the divide between loyalists and patriots were suspected, fairly or not, to be Tory sympathizers. Historian Stephen Botein has recounted one 1774 example: "Following the neutral logic of pre-revolutionary printers, the *New-Hampshire Gazette* reprinted the opposing views of 'Novanglus' and 'Massachusettensis' in parallel columns, along with advice from the printers that people *'read both Sides with an impartial Mind.'* Daniel Fowle [the *Gazette*'s printer] was subsequently reprimanded by the New Hampshire legislature for his willingness to publish an argument against American independence."[26] Other printers with good patriot credentials could be besmirched simply by announcing plans to put out a loyalist pamphlet.[27] Mobs smashed the presses of the most openly loyalist printers (John Mein in Boston and James Rivington in New York) and pushed them into at least temporary exile.[28] In addition, the Committees on Observation and Inspection, which the Continental Congress in 1774 urged each town to establish, were not only means to publicize "infamy" but also to monitor and to denounce criticism of the cause.[29] In effect, the old concern with "licentiousness" had been extended to publications opposed to the revolutionary cause. As the crisis grew, the Tories' access to the press contracted; in Arthur Schlesinger Sr.'s famous phrase, patriots "simply contended that liberty of speech belonged to those who spoke the speech of liberty."[30]

The American Revolution thus tightened rather than loosened the ties of newspapers to politics and government. After 1765, newspapers were published with the assistance and sufferance of the rebellious Americans, who were directly involved in putting together the paper. For instance, in 1769, John Adams wrote in his diary of an evening spent with fellow patriots James Otis and Samuel Adams and printer John Gill, among others, "preparing for the next day's newspaper,—a curious employment, cooking up paragraphs, articles, occurrences, &c., working the political engine!"[31] If the revolutionary press was not entirely under the thumb of politicians, it was only because factions within and between legislatures took potshots at each other in print.[32] The end of the Revolution left a contradictory legacy—on one hand, stressing impartiality and the empirical collection of facts in newspapers deferential to officialdom, and on the other, independent crusades against corrupt authority on behalf of a political faction. Political and government sponsorship was critical in nurturing this legacy. Newspapers in the colonial and revolutionary eras were supported by political patronage, factional disputes, and the participation of politicians in the assembly of the newspaper. If the first hundred years of American newspapers saw government's punitive authority against newspapers wane somewhat, the press was far from independent: their ability to criticize government depended on powerful factions to provide copy, support, and political cover.

THE HEYDAY OF THE PARTISAN PRESS: JEFFERSON TO JACKSON

Legend has it that the founders of the American republic were a different breed of politician—favoring reasoned, principled, and disinterested deliberation in the manner of the debates in the Constitutional Convention and the *Federalist* papers thereafter. Such a legend is, to put it mildly, flawed. The Constitutional Convention came up with their Solomonic compromises only because it met in secret and Philadelphia newspapers stayed aloof from covering its meetings.[33] When Alexander Hamilton, James Madison, and John Jay engaged in political theorizing by publishing newspaper essays under the pen name of "Publius" to win ratification, this was just one level of the game; other Federalists were busy boycotting and pulling advertising from anti-Federalist newspapers to make them go bankrupt.[34] And after the Constitution was ratified, scholars agree that newspapers set new standards for vituperation and scurrility; even the sainted George Washington was a target for journalistic ambuscades.

When President Washington's administration split into factions behind Thomas Jefferson, secretary of state, and Alexander Hamilton, secretary of the treasury, so too did the American press. In 1789, Federalists had helped John Fenno to launch a semiweekly newspaper in the capital of Philadelphia called *The Gazette of the United States*. Initially, with no advertising and few subscribers, the *Gazette* was kept afloat by public patronage: Fenno received printing orders from the Treasury, commissions to publish the federal laws from the State Department, and other jobs from the Senate.[35] But as Fenno increasingly cast his lot with Hamilton, Jefferson became disquieted and, through Madison, urged Philip Freneau to come to Philadelphia to start a rival semiweekly. Jefferson lacked Hamilton's deep official pockets but arranged Freneau's appointment as clerk for foreign languages. Jefferson apologized for the minuscule annual salary of $250, but he added that "it gives so little to do, as not to interfere with any other calling the person may choose, which would not absent him from the seat of government."[36] Jefferson and Madison acted as subscription agents compiling names of supporters and urging likeminded friends to take the paper.[37]

The appearance of Freneau's *National Gazette* in 1791 aggravated the divide with Hamilton. The split went public the next year when Hamilton wrote pseudonymous letters to Fenno's *Gazette,* revealing Freneau's State Department employment and charging that Jefferson was "institutor and patron" of the new paper.[38] Freneau dryly noted in print that his compensation was paltry next to Fenno's, but he felt obliged to swear in an affidavit that "the Editor has consulted his own judgment alone in the conducting of it—free—unfettered—and uninfluenced."[39] Jefferson responded, to President Washington's dismay, asserting (technically correctly) that he had never written or provided any direction to Freneau. Nevertheless, when Jefferson resigned as secretary of state in 1793, Freneau lost his clerkship, and the paper expired.[40]

From this beginning, the party press would emerge. A new kind of newspaper developed, an extension and crucial tool of the party. After Hamiltonians and Jeffersonians split into two rival parties (the Federalists and the Republicans), party organizing included founding newspapers both to reach sympathetic electors and to mobilize them to support the party slate. Colonial printers first and foremost had started a journal as the best way to economic success; now politicians became editors to further their political ambition, sometimes holding simultaneous party, newspaper, and government positions. As Culver Smith expressed it, "It is indeed probable that many of the editors were not sure whether their interest was primarily journalism or politics. But it is certain that those who counted most were politicians wielding newspapers."[41] All of this produced a journalism that, in Gerald Baldasty's formulation, was segmented by partisanship and directed toward readers who controlled a vote, in contrast to the news media since the mid-nineteenth century, which aim at a larger audience of consumers, namely readers who control disposable income.[42] Not viewing the truth as best served by dispassionate, impartial coverage of both sides, those who ran party presses saw themselves as presenting the best case for their side—much as competing attorneys do today in trials.[43]

Such sponsorship was not merely beneficial to politicians. It was central for printers. Their financial situation—and the tools of their craft—were much the same as it had been during the Revolution, thus auguring a still precarious existence.[44] Since most of the population lived outside cities that were large and prosperous enough to support a press without patronage, sponsorship was essential to get most newspapers off the ground. Such a task had begun to shift from printers to editors, as printers' shops became more specialized and larger.[45] Those proposing a new journal would circulate a prospectus declaring their guiding principles, which, by the 1790s, entailed defending a given party and philosophy.[46] Government printing, combined with subscriptions, could cover the overhead; the income derived from advertisements furnished the profit.[47] Besides printing contracts, politicians could and did give loans (not always repaid) to printers, buy up papers that they would distribute free of charge, urge sympathetic partisans to advertise their wares, volunteer legal assistance, and submit information and essays as copy.[48] Printers assumed that efforts for the party would be rewarded by the party. One wrote the Republican leader Albert Gallatin in 1798: "Now that my friends and the friends of the principles we have professed have returned I look up to them for their friendly aid—not doubting that I shall receive it."[49]

To be sure, after 1792, all newspapers could and did take advantage of favorable postal rates (discussed in Chapter 3). But this subsidy on an equal basis to all newspapers contrasted with governmental support in the forms of appointments and government printing, meted out for past political performance and future political expectations. The criterion for desert was summed up early by Postmaster General Timothy Pickering, who wrote one applicant in 1790: "I should not think it expedient for you to receive [a post office] on account of [your] political sentiments."[50]

When the Jeffersonians ousted the Federalists in 1801, they changed the policy to prevent printers from being postmasters, but did so, in part, to purge the bureaucracy of Federalist printers.[51] They took full advantage of federal patronage for printing contracts and sought to coordinate the support the states provided as well. The laws enacted by Federalist Congresses instructed the secretary of state to name up to three newspapers in each state to publish the federal laws—enabling the Jeffersonians to dole out around $150 per Congress to each of a wide variety of supporters.⁵² Jefferson made his approach clear in his first year as president; he wrote to a Vermont printer who had complained about his state government's support for Federalists:

> I am sorry to learn . . . that the officers in the public employment still use the influence and the business of their offices to encourage presses which disseminate principles contrary to those on which our constitution is built. This evil will be remedied . . . Your press having been in the habit of inculcating the genuine principles of our constitution, and your sufferings for those principles, entitle you to any favors in your line which the public servants can give you; and those who do not give them, act against their duty. Should you continue in the business you will have the publications of the laws in your state . . .⁵³

Not only in the hinterlands was such patronage applied. Jefferson began an administration newspaper by inviting Samuel Harrison Smith to the new capital of Washington before his election to start the *National Intelligencer*.⁵⁴ As soon as Jefferson took power, Smith obtained printing from the State Department of around $2,000 per year, plus that of other departments, and by the end of 1801 he had also secured printing for the House which brought in about $4,000 annually.⁵⁵

An official organ gave the administration a chance to enter into debates without undermining the dignity of the executive, as many feared speeches and public controversy would do.⁵⁶ Jefferson routinely sent notes to Smith passing along recent developments or taking particular stances, sometimes accompanied by disingenuous cover letters that made it look as if Smith would exercise discretion: "The inclosed paper memo seems intended for the legislature as well as Executive eye; but certainly not to be laid before the former in a regular way. The only irregular one would be in the newspapers. But this must depend on it's [sic] merit and your opinion of it."⁵⁷ Smith routinely reprinted what Jefferson requested without listing him as a source. So when one representative asked Vice President Burr if the *Intelligencer* should be "relied on . . . [as] a useful guide to our country Papers," Burr replied, "The Washington paper edited by Smith has the countenance and support of the administration. His explanations of the Measures of Government and of the Motives which produce them are, I believe, the result of information and advice from high Authority."⁵⁸

Such patronage built networks of partisan newspapers that were centered in the official party organs in Washington. Already in the Federalist era there had been "a fraternity among Republican journals. They advertised for one another, accepted subscriptions for each other, and applauded the establishment of each new Jeffersonian paper."[59] The paucity of Washington reporters, the official subsidy of printers' exchanges, and the common practice of reprinting news from other newspapers further magnified the reach of papers such as the *Intelligencer*.[60]

The apogee of the party press came in the 1820s, following the demise of the Federalists and the split of the Republicans between four presidential candidates in 1824. Andrew Jackson received a plurality of both the popular and the electoral vote, but lost to John Quincy Adams when the election was thrown into the House of Representatives. Jackson and his troops spent the next four years preparing for the election of 1828, building a far-reaching network of partisan newspapers supported by party funds, heavy use of congressional franking privileges, and whatever local, state, and federal patronage could be scraped together.[61] The printers' exchanges that had worked to build a wide system of newspapers were now used to fashion a national party.

In this era, the franchise expanded, and the nation became far-flung. Wishing to mobilize voters without subjecting candidates to the charge of self-aggrandizement, newspapers were crucial partisan tools. "Party organization in the Jacksonian era usually began with the formation of a central committee to coordinate party activities. The next task was to establish political newspapers."[62] Any wall between journalistic and political enterprises was gone; editors were party leaders, served on party central committees, and gave speeches on behalf of the federal and state party slates.

When Jackson became president in 1829, he elevated patronage of the press to a new level. Jackson's first choice to run the administration press, Duff Green, had already received the Senate's printing in 1827; Green added that of the House in 1829. These jobs were lucrative; for instance, from 1831 to 1833, Green took in over $140,000 at an estimated profit of 24 percent. Green's agitation for Jackson to be succeeded by Vice President Calhoun caused the president to dump Green's organ for a new one, whose editor, Francis P. Blair, soon was handed over half of all of the executive printing worth around $25,000 per year.[63] As many as fifty-nine other editors received plush political appointments as postmasters, customhouse collectors, clerks, marshals, and even as librarian of Congress.[64]

Punishment still played a part. Seditious libel had one last federal appearance; the Sedition Act passed by the Federalists in 1798 made it a crime to "write, print, utter or publish . . . any false, scandalous and malicious writings" against the government, Congress, or the president.[65] The Sedition Act may have derived from a principled distinction of "liberty" and "licentiousness," but it was primarily exploited by Federalist officials against Jeffersonians.[66] Most of the eighteen libel prosecutions documented were successful.[67] The Sedition Act was already set to expire in 1801 at the end of Adams's first (and only) term, and Jefferson had successfully campaigned for president against the act; but the latter was never clear whether his opposition simply stemmed from an anti-Federalist belief that such libels should only be dealt with at the state level. In fact, as president, Jefferson would write to the governor of Pennsylvania, "Prosecutions of the most prominent offenders would have a wholesome effect in restoring the integrity of the press."[68] Seditious libel was not formally renounced in the law but largely disappeared; as parties became more organized, all sides had a stake in avoiding going to court.[69]

A more enduring sanction was to deny individual reporters access to governmental proceedings—particularly to the most newsworthy branch, Congress—when they offended officials or otherwise threatened the cozy relationship of politics and the press.[70] The Senate initially made no accommodations for reporters (what we would today call stenographers) to take down the debate. Senators presumed their chamber to be more august and accountable only to the state legislatures that had elected their members. They opened the Senate galleries to the public in 1795 only in response to petitions from anti-Federalist state legislatures, a decision presaging regular accommodation for reporters in 1802.[71] The House, popularly elected, was deemed worthier for public proceedings, but even there access was checkered. In the First Congress, reporters for one of the numerous privately printed predecessors of the *Congressional Record* came under attack for inaccuracies and bias; they ended up reporting the rest of the session from the public gallery when the House refused to readmit them to the floor.[72] After the government moved to Philadelphia, floor seats were reserved for reporters, but in 1797 the House accorded the Speaker power to decide access on a case-by-case basis. As a result, House members could and often did seek to deny access to reporters as a class, or, more frequently with time, to find a way to block the access of those whose coverage they found irksome. So just as patronage focused on specific newspapers, debates over access targeted individual reporters.

In December 1800, Samuel Harrison Smith showed up at the new Capitol to report on the House for the Jeffersonian *National Intelligencer*. Smith asked to be allowed within the bar of the chamber to better hear the proceedings. The Federalists, led by Speaker Theodore Sedgwick's tie-breaking vote, denied his petition. Smith did what he could from outside the bar. The next month, Sedgwick claimed that Smith, "either through incompetency, or intentionally . . . grossly misrepresented my conduct," and the sergeant-at-arms ordered him to leave his custom-ary spot. Smith retreated to the public gallery. Two days later, Sedgwick barred him from the House altogether, saying only that Smith would be given the papers that the House clerk "pleases to let you have," a decision twice backed by the House in full vote.[73] Only when the Jeffersonians came to power later in 1801 was Smith welcomed to Capitol Hill, but the House still decreed that the Speaker would give reporters places only "as shall not interfere with the convenience of the House."[74]

Smith's travails foreshadowed later occasions when one or another legislator, vexed about coverage, would seek revenge. Members of Con-gress could (and sometimes did) introduce a resolution barring access to specific individuals or reporters of a given paper, summon reporters to an investigation either of their charges or of the identity of the pseudony-mous authors of congressional coverage, or deny access to an entire class of reporters, such as when the Democrat-controlled Senate adopted a rule in 1838 that admitted only reporters to Washington papers to the floor, which conveniently blocked access to Whig papers.[75] Legislators may well have been suspicious of those committing their oral performances to print. Such sanctions ensured the publicity they wanted, as reporters took care to consult with orators and to help them rewrite their sometimes inchoate debate points for print.[76]

The policies and practices of the early republic all favored the devel-opment of a party press. Providing resources, it appears, was more relied upon to obtain the kind of publicity one wanted than punitive attempts to bring libel charges or to block access to governmental proceedings. The shift from a personally organized politics of the 1780s to the partisan organization of the early nineteenth century occasioned a shift in what newspapers did and said. But the centrality of the press for the party also suggests that the political system, too, was dependent upon the newspa-per system, to the point that if, for reasons largely beyond politics, the press were to change, so too would the political possibilities of newspa-pers, and so in turn would politics.

THE COMMERCIALIZATION OF THE PRESS AND THE DECLINE OF POLITICAL SPONSORSHIP

By the 1830s, political actors had developed many ways to, if not domi-nate the press, at least control its excesses. But these powers over the press were all eventually voluntarily discarded in the next forty-odd years. Consider the following:

1. The federal government got almost entirely out of the business of

patronage for printers. In particular, the establishment of the Government Printing Office in 1860 obviated contracting out most printing within Washington. The last vestiges were private printing of the congressional debates, which stopped with the establishment of the government-published *Congressional Record* in 1873, and the requirement that the laws be published in newspapers in every state and territory, repealed by Congress in 1875.[77] Patronage continued at the state and local level, especially in newly settled areas, and reporters might find a congressional sinecure to tide them over between sessions, but patronage was all but moribund as a matter of federal policy.[78]

2. The administration newspaper disappeared even prior to the expiration of public printing, when in 1860 lame-duck President Buchanan formally disavowed the official organ, the *Constitution,* for expressing secessionist views. Despite expectations to the contrary, the next president (Abraham Lincoln) declined to designate an official successor, and the tradition died. Newspapers' partisan affiliations were usually still easily identified, but parties provided little direct support.[79]

3. And finally both houses of Congress ceded the authority to decide access for reporters on a case-by-case basis. Instead, they turned over the job to the journalists themselves, whose Standing Committee of Correspondents adjudicated who was and who was not "a bona fide reporter with good standing in his profession."[80]

In short, by the last quarter of the nineteenth century, the sponsored press had vanished. But what happened? Why did political actors unilaterally abandon powers over the press that had worked to their benefit?

Some of the answer is certainly due to political shifts. Reformism rose in response to what became known as the "spoils system." Mass meetings and other forms of campaigning displaced the newspaper's centrality in elections of the Jacksonian era. Similarly, policies and practices toward the press tended to shift if they became political issues or were entangled in partisan battles. For example, seditious libel prosecutions had already become difficult to pursue after Jefferson had won office, in part, by running against the Sedition Act; the resultant shift to civil suits could not as effectively protect official actions from criticism.[81] Patronage and official publications were less useful when parties were internally riven. Thus, the picture was confused when Whig President William Henry Harrison died in 1841 and was succeeded by his less Whiggish running mate John Tyler; the latter, soon splitting with most of his inherited Cabinet and the Whigs in Congress, underwent a confusing four years of designating and then withdrawing from official newspapers.[82]

Probably the fullest explanation, however, lies with transformations in the press and in journalism that made political sponsorship clumsy to use and of limited value. In particular, the growth of mass circulation newspapers and the commercialization of the press as a big business over the nineteenth century meant that newspapers became big, complex, specialized, and hierarchical. Technology—notably the use of steam power, more powerful presses, and less expensive paper—was harnessed to churn out increasingly large numbers of issues. As the circulation of financially independent newspapers increased in both absolute terms and relative to the party press, patronage was no longer deemed as useful in crafting public opinion. Government printing itself was becoming vaster, more sophisticated, and pricier, to the point that the main federal patronage in the Buchanan presidency did not even go to a newspaper printer, but went instead to a crony of the president who had built a large printing plant just north of the Capitol for that purpose in expectations of huge profits. When, in the wake of congressional investigations, the Government Printing Office was established in 1860, the government simply purchased his plant.[83]

Moreover, the very definition of news began to shift away from the focus on ideology that dominated the party press and, indeed, away from the central concern of politics.[84] Many historians agree that the Civil War cemented a new relationship of journalism to the American public eager for up-to-date news and created new roles for officials, reporters, and editors.[85] It also delivered the coup de grâce to the old partisan system. In its place, amidst the rampant industrialization of the late nineteenth century, an industrial-scale mass media played by considerably different rules. By the close of the century, advertisers, not politicians, bankrolled newspapers. Little surprise that newspapers had by then shifted away from previous preoccupations with ideas and politics toward human interest stories and a lighter, breezier tone.[86] Most newspapers still claimed a party affiliation after the Civil War, but such party papers were disproportionately found in county seats where the last patronage survived; even then, their editors and publishers were quick to note loyalty to the principles of the party, not its politicians.[87]

The shifting dynamics of the relationship between government and newspapers can be seen not only in the demise of patronage, but also in Congress's evolving accommodation of the transformed press corps. A commercial newspaper approached politicians differently from its predecessors, both in terms of what was news and how it was gathered, and Congress was relatively powerless to move the emphasis back to the deferential synopses of debates.

Whether or not the first issue of the *New York Sun,* on September 3, 1833, touched off a revolution in the news,[88] the *Sun* was a pioneer. Not only was this penny paper cheaper and livelier than its six-penny counterparts. In order to address the perennial problem of collecting on subscriptions, the *Sun* was sold at a discount (67 cents per 100 issues) to delivery boys who collected the subscription amounts every week on their route. Instead of politics, the *Sun* stressed new kinds of stories—colorful but fact-filled narratives, more local occurrences and crime—and declared that they were politically independent. This did not mean that these journals had no strong opinions or that they did not generally support one party over another. They were usually as opinionated and even occasionally as partisan as party papers; the "independence" they proclaimed simply meant no reliance on patronage and spoils. This pursuit of large audiences and of independence followed two paths already broken in the 1820s. Christian evangelists, not newspaper publishers, "first dreamed the dream of a genuine mass medium—that is, they proposed to deliver the same printed message to everyone in America" by exploiting new technologies and devising new methods of distribution through Bible and tract societies.[89] Around the same time, workingmen's newspapers had arisen, stressing a common class interest that surpassed partisan divisions.[90] Such working-class newspapers did not long survive the rampant unemployment of the Panic of 1837, but their emphasis on a public good above partisan gain was borrowed and exploited by their commercial counterparts.

Methods of newsmaking changed as a result. Instead of clipping and reprinting from their party's Washington papers, penny papers began relying on their own staff for news, including sending reporters to Washington to write their own dispatches.[91] Already, in the 1820s, James Gordon Bennett had pioneered a new form of Washington correspondence: lively personal essays rather than terse stenographic reports on debates or other forms of intelligence. Bennett, after founding the *New York Herald* in 1835, sent regular correspondents from Washington who filed witty accounts. By 1841, the pages of the *Herald* proclaimed that "we have now organised, at vast expense, an efficient corps of the ablest reporters that this country can afford, who will furnish, at the close of every day's proceedings, a report of the debates."[92]

Bennett did not win access to congressional proceedings without a struggle. Indeed, the dispute over whether the Senate should make provisions to admit any reporters for newspapers outside of Washington and its ultimate resolution shows an intriguing shift in the relationship of politicians and reporters. Its dénouement recognized, apparently for the first time, the right of reporters to gain access to legislative floor proceedings from the special purview of a section reserved to them.[93]

In 1835, the Senate had passed a rule that gave access to the floor to reporters from Washington newspapers but to no one else. When Bennett's reporters arrived at the Senate in 1841, the president pro tempore, Samuel Southard, notified them that they would not be admitted to the floor. After Bennett lobbied Southard's fellow Whig, Henry Clay, and suggested that the *Herald*'s reporters could take down debate as efficiently as the publicly supported stenographers, the Senate repealed the previous language and bade the secretary to "cause suitable accommodations to be prepared in the eastern gallery for such reporters as may be admitted by the rules of the Senate." Southard specified that ten seats of the front row of that gallery be reserved for reporters, divided equally between Washington and out-of-town papers, and stipulated that "none [are] to be admitted within the reporters' rail except bona fide reporters, so certified by their editors."[94] The onetime ascendancy of the Washington papers, as conduits to news outlets throughout the country, was thus first challenged by the penny press *before* the first use of the telegraph to report events and the emergence of the Associated Press later in the 1840s.[95]

Note how the Senate had thus replaced the previous case-by-case approach with a general principle of the right of access for reporters to congressional proceedings. It is important to note that reporters would be certified as "bona fide" not by Congress but by their editors. This decision—neglected by too many journalism historians—is apparently the first official recognition of reporters as belonging to a distinct and valuable occupation, even a profession, well before the late nineteenth century when journalists formed professional organizations, built long-lasting careers, and began to discuss codes of ethics.[96] In that sense, even the profession of journalism is, at least in part, a creation of governmental decisions.[97]

To be sure, members of Congress continued to threaten, and sometimes to deny, such preferential treatment when they were angered at a newspaper's coverage, as in 1846, when one representative, furious at the *New York Tribune*'s coverage of his lunching habits on the House floor, successfully persuaded his colleagues to expel all *Tribune* reporters.[98] But whether this accomplished much is open to question. Not only could *Tribune* reporters eavesdrop on the House from the ladies' gallery or, when escorted by a sympathetic representative, from the members' gallery, but the representative was remembered for his lunches for the remainder of his checkered political career.

Other news items from the 1840s to the 1870s would provoke members of Congress to attempt to bar editors from the floor or reporters from the gallery.[99] Also, when leaks from secret sessions were published, reporters were imprisoned when they refused to cooperate with investigations into the sources of those leaks.[100] None produced a satisfactory result from the point of view of the aggrieved legislators. And apart from amending the rule about "bona fide reporters" in 1852 to make admission to the press gallery contingent on "the condition that you are not and will not become an agent for the prosecution of any claim pending before Congress,"[101] it became hard to gauge just who should and should not be given access, particularly with the huge influx of reporters and personnel during and following the Civil War.

Perhaps, then, it is no surprise to find that, after the Civil War, Congress got out of the business of adjudicating access to the press gallery and delegated the job to the swiftly professionalizing journalists themselves. The recognition of the Standing Committee of Correspondents, a group nowadays elected by all reporters admitted to the congressional press galleries, is a good indicator of how far the government-newspaper relationship had evolved near the end of the nineteenth century from the sponsorship that prevailed at its beginning.[102] For their part, journalists gladly took on the responsibility of policing themselves. After all, Capitol Hill correspondents had already taken the initiative to meet with the House Speaker in 1877 about the assignment of seats in the gallery, and then in 1879 to devise rules for admission, most notably by restricting access to those who filed stories over the telegraph to daily newspapers (which, whether intentionally or not, effectively threw out what few African-American and women journalists had been admitted). Members of Congress, in turn, were able to get out of a task which was increasingly rancorous, time-consuming, and inefficient.

The result was the final chapter of the system of sponsorship. By the close of the nineteenth century, then, the relationship of the news media to government was dramatically different than it had been at its beginning. In comparison with a motley group of short-lived newspapers propped up by government patronage and party support, newspapers in the 1890s had become enormous enterprises, free of political and financial sponsorship by government.

CONCLUSION

If we were to stop there with the evidence that we have thus far examined, it would seem as though the news media evolved Whiggishly from governmental sponsorship in its infancy to strapping independence. This, of course, is a tale that journalists like to tell, but it is only half of the story. Sponsorship of individual news media by individual patrons was certainly moribund by the end of the nineteenth century, but such a relationship does not constitute the whole of government-media relations, let alone the most central part of it. Instead, what had already begun with the postal subsidies for newspapers ensconced in the Postal Act of 1792 and what developed much further from the middle of the nineteenth century and took definitive precedence in the twentieth century was a relationship characterized by institutional rather than individual networks of mutual support. The news media, instead of depending on the day-to-day sufferance of political patronage, access, and potential prosecution, entered a more stable era of political subsidies, indeed entitlements from government.

3

THE SUBSIDIZED NEWS MEDIA

Individual sponsorship was crucial for newspapers prior to the Civil War, but governmental support for newspapers as a whole was far from unheard of during the same epoch. The earliest federal bureaucracy within the United States was the post office, which was geared more for the prompt, widespread delivery of news than for individual correspondence. The colonial post had allowed printers to mail their newspapers for free to other printers; then, the Postal Act of 1792 passed rates whereby expensive postage for letters would make up the deficits incurred in mailing the news at cheap rates. New communication technologies were also supported by government. Take the telegraph, which became of crucial help to newspapers. Congress appropriated $20,000 for Samuel Morse's early experiments; the government absorbed some of the start-up costs but, despite Morse's suggestion that the Post Office control his invention, the government allowed private enterprise to take over thereafter, albeit with the boost of allowing telegraph companies to erect their wires gratis on railroad rights-of-way.[1]

As early as the Civil War—and certainly thereafter as newspapers became big businesses with greater production, circulation, and profit margins—the sponsorship of individual American news outlets by individual politicians was largely relegated to frontier newspapers and marginal outlets. In its place, subsidies worked to defray costs and to limit uncertainties of operating a news organization, thereby assuring profits. The process was one of gradual accretion. By the beginning of the twentieth century, added to postal subsidies were government public relations offices and operations. This public relations capacity, and a more proactive governmental role in making the news, helped to shape a system of newsbeats that both routinized and organized reporters' work and further strengthened the emerging social and professional networks of journalists. With the rise of governmental regulation that followed (starting particularly with radio in the 1920s and 1930s), other policies worked to stabilize and protect both old and new communication industries. The results of such policies and practices may well be akin to the benefits reaped by the sponsored press, but with a key difference: *any* news outlet that could provide evidence that it was indeed a news outlet was (and is) entitled to governmental benefits.

Equally important, these developments constituted crucial steps in the institutional development of the news media. Postal subsidies encouraged standardization of format and, even for a time, the development of particular publications that would be favored by them on account of their political contents. The rise of government's public relations apparatus toward the end of the nineteenth century next encouraged reporters to concentrate at particular locations to receive particular news. As the news-beat system thereby became cemented, it provided a basis for reporters to interact, identify with each other, and establish similar approaches to similar subjects, as well as a basis for news outlets themselves to shape routine ways of making news that transcend their organizational boundaries. When new media (radio and television) arose in the 1920s and on, the institutional structures were not merely encouraged by policies, they were, in no small part, a product of government regulation, albeit regulation in terms that the embryonic industry welcomed and was to find beneficial indeed.

Moreover, by examining these subsidies chronologically, we can juxtapose the gradual disappearance of the sponsored press (sketched in the previous chapter) with the equally inexorable rise of subsidies for the news media. And such subsidies are of great help to newsmaking. With an enormous public relations infrastructure that caters to journalists' needs at public expense, beneficial postal rates, policies that exempt news organizations from regulations that other private industries must follow, and regulation that stabilizes the industry and restricts entry of new enterprises, it is safe to say that these subsidies have contributed substantially to the ability of the news media to crank out their products.

These policies are not a matter of constitutional obligation. I will not discuss here any policies—for instance, the gradual liberalization of libel law—that may have been mandated by the First Amendment guarantee of freedom of the press but that end up subsidizing the news. Instead, a hallmark of the subsidies considered here is that they were not imposed by judicial interpretation of abridgments on a free press but instead by legislative and bureaucratic discretion. One cannot say that there is a coherent and logical public policy toward the news media. Instead—and not surprisingly given our understanding of American politics—such policies and practices emerged in incremental, particularistic, and inchoate manners, often by a process of explicit and implicit negotiation between political actors as a group and the news media as a group that ended up with mutual benefit far from philosophical questions of what kind of information is required for and in a democracy. In short, there is, whether we realize it or not, a public policy about the news—meaning that if we do not care for the kind of news we receive, we can change the policy to remedy that situation.

THE FIRST SUBSIDIES: THE POST OFFICE AND THE PAPERS

By 1765, a nascent political communication system extended across the British colonies in North America. The number of newspapers, and the number of cities with them, had grown. The percentage of news about British North America also increased, as news items from other colonies from 1728 to 1765 were taken less from London than from other colonial newspapers.[2] Interconnection resulted from improved intercolonial transportation, canny printers sending former partners and apprentices to distant cities to establish new enterprises,[3] and public policy. In 1754, the deputy postmasters general for America (ex-printers Benjamin Franklin and William Hunter) set forth the first policy on carrying newspapers in the mail. Their instructions restricted the delivery of newspapers to paying subscribers. Although they thereby prevented postmaster-printers from mailing their product without charge, Franklin and Hunter gave something back: they allowed free mail delivery for "the single Papers exchang'd between Printer and Printer."[4]

Printers' exchanges were essential for newspapers in inland outposts otherwise lacking access to the news in the seaports that were the center of colonial journalism. In fact, after the royal government dismissed Franklin in 1774, patriot printers became concerned about the security of the mail and, disinclined to pay the British for such service, they started up a volunteer "Constitutional Post" with printers serving as postmasters.[5] Colonial newspapers continued to pick up content from one another and republished news (with acknowledgment) far from the original locale. Public policy, subsidizing printers' exchanges, thus was placed behind the growth of the news media as well as communication between (and consensus across) the colonies during the revolutionary crises.

After the Revolution, postal policy toward newspapers expanded beyond the support of printers' exchanges. Indeed, postal subsidies of the press became one of the few substantial expenditures of the new and small federal government. All parties supported these services but for different reasons: Federalists envisioned a top-down communication from elite political and economic centers, downward and outward, whereas Jeffersonians hoped the proliferation of newspapers would maximize two-way interaction of core and periphery.[6] The initial proposals giving precedence to certain presumably official organs were defeated. The policies Congress enacted in 1792 extended to any and all newspapers; the only debate was over whether they should have to pay anything at all for the service.[7] In short, the law operated as an entitlement to any publication that could qualify as a newspaper; the press was recognized as something more than a collection of individual news outlets but a collective entity in its own right, a crucial step toward its development as an institution.

Those favoring free mail delivery did not prevail, but the 1792 act gave newspapers a huge subsidy: newspapers mailed up to a distance of 100 miles paid 1 cent postage, while those sent farther paid 1.5 cents. (This differential charge would be the first of many legislative attempts to protect small local papers from competition by metropolitan publications, which the congressional debate reveals was the key sticking point.)[8] The postage paid by newspapers did not cover the cost of delivery. The act also preserved free printers' exchanges and enlisted local postmasters to assist in collecting subscriptions, to be subscription agents, to use their franking privilege to allow subscribers to pay up, and to notify publishers when subscribers were in arrears.[9]

Such perks would be assiduously defended by printers, who had already shown they could organize collectively in pursuit of common goals toward government action when they opposed the reintroduction of newspaper taxes after the war.[10] For decades postmasters general complained that the Post Office would generate more income except that newspapers made up the bulk of the mailbags and brought in just a fraction of the income.[11] Besides losses from low newspaper rates and free printers' exchanges, postmasters had difficulty getting subscribers to pay—providing an additional "unintended subsidy."[12] Postmasters general frequently pleaded with Congress to raise rates, to require prepayment of subscriptions, and to abolish or restrict printers' exchanges. But Congress was resolute; the only changes seriously considered would have allowed all newspapers to be sent through the mail without charge.[13] Such unwillingness to tighten the subsidy is no surprise, given that well-connected publishers and publications were found in every state and district. One writer grumbled in 1843, "There does not appear to have been a man in Congress who suspected that newspapers had not a divine right to some exclusive privilege at the post-office."[14]

Postmasters general, presumably responding to stalwart congressional support of subsidies, thus ran the Post Office more for newspaper printers than for everyday letter writers. Thus, in 1792, the postmaster general decreed that printers could hire private post riders to use post roads, a privilege unavailable to all letters save through the U.S. mail. The Post Office sought to alleviate the burden of newspapers on stage-coaches by new methods of delivery, such as sending them by sea in 1798 or by versions of the Pony Express from 1825, which (contrary to popular legend) carried mostly newspapers and briefer "slips" sent for free by one editor to another.[15]

Implementation did not defer entirely to congressional sentiment. Despite their failure to alter the law, postal officials exerted leeway over *which* publications qualified for the cheap rates.[16] Their decisions would have a lasting influence on what was most readily admitted into the public arena, not to mention conceptions of "news." At first, magazines, deemed bulky and apolitical, did not qualify for cheap rates and could be left out of the mail if it inconvenienced postmasters; in 1815, pamphlets were barred altogether from the mail.[17] Books were totally excluded until 1851. To qualify for cheap rates, magazines and books tried to disguise themselves as newspapers, magazines by being printed on sheets not sewn together and books by being serialized.

With format no guide, executive officers through the first half of the nineteenth century routinely attempted to give precedence to political periodicals. For example, the U.S. attorney general ruled in 1847 that to qualify for the cheap rates, a newspaper "must be a publication communicating to the public intelligence of passing events. And it is to the contents, rather than to the form, that you must refer to determine the question."[18] Distinctions would become impossible to make; in 1852, the postmaster general said he could not tell the difference between magazines and newspapers and passed the buck to the attorney general, who demurred, saying that "lexicographers and publishers" were better suited to figure that out than lawyers.[19] Officials thus threw in the towel on distinguishing news by its content, further reducing political discretion over access to the subsidies. But by that time newspapers had already gained a more central place in the political information environment than either magazines or books, both of which would have to await later reforms that would accord them, too, some preferential treatment in the mail. The dominance of newspapers in the American public arena, memorably noted by Tocqueville in the 1820s, was, in part, a product of public policy.

Among newspapers, the small, country press received special treatment.[20] Jacksonians instituted nationwide pony expresses, in part, so editors in the distant west and south would gain a business advantage by printing the news before the metropolitan papers could be delivered by the mail.[21] In 1851, Congress enacted a law permitting weekly newspapers to be delivered in the mail, free of charge, to subscribers in the county where the paper was published—a perk exploited so quickly that within the next year about one out of five periodicals mailed used the new privilege.[22] When the policy was repealed in 1873, press associations and trade journals pressured Congress to reconsider; the following year, in-county free delivery was not only reinstated for weeklies but extended to dailies.[23] (This benefit was finally repealed only in 1962, but the new law continued below-cost delivery of in-county periodicals, a rare exception to the principle that the Post Office should be able to cover its costs when it became a public corporation in 1970.[24] In fact, it was only in 1993 that Congress finally stopped appropriating funds to the U.S. Postal Service to make up for "revenue foregone" from second-class mail and from the lower rates for in-county delivery.)[25]

Postal rates were simplified and rationalized by the 1863 act establishing first-class mail for letters and the second-class category for "all mailable matter exclusively in print, and regularly issued at stated periods."[26] Preferential treatments for news publications in general (and localized news in particular) have continued in one shape or another to this day. The subsidies are nowhere near as generous, nor as necessary, to print outlets as they were in the early Republic, but they have been rarely restricted. Privileges disappear only after outliving their utility; thus free printers' exchanges were not abolished until 1873, well after the ascendancy of telegraphic news and of the Associated Press.[27] New impositions on publishers might be sweetened by long-requested changes; in 1874, Congress mandated publishers to prepay postage but reduced their cost by charging per pound rather than per issue.[28] Finally, policy making on eligibility for second-class privileges passed increasingly from Congress to negotiated deals between postal administrators and prominent publishers, who cut costs while protecting themselves by seeking to remove advertising circulars and free samples from the second-class category reserved for periodicals with "a legitimate list of subscribers."[29]

Congress rarely attempted to attach conditions to the second-class privilege for newspapers and magazines, even after the Supreme Court clarified that doing so did not violate the First Amendment as long as the periodical was not banned from the mail altogether. The one exception— the case that provoked that Court decision[30]—was the Newspaper Publicity Act of 1912, which restricted the second-class subsidy only to periodicals that identified their owners, labeled advertisements that resembled news stories, and disclosed their circulation. As Linda Lawson demonstrates, the bill became law because both publishers and journalists were split over its wisdom; and it was never seriously challenged after the Court decision because the news media realized that the law boosted the credibility of the news and forced most outlets to do little differently.[31] Indeed, as Lawson has shown elsewhere, publishers of weekly newspapers, faced with economic difficulties after the Second World War, actually initiated legislation that extended these requirements to themselves.[32] In testifying before Congress, publishers and press association officials all pointed to the legitimacy such regulation would give to weekly newspapers and, thereby, to their ability to gain advertising revenue.[33]

Far from adopting a "hands-off" pose, public policy from the outset of the American Republic focused explicitly on getting the news to a wide readership, and chose to support news outlets by taking on costs of delivery and, through printers' exchanges, of production. The congressional debates culminating in the Postal Act of 1792 and the solicitude of the Post Office to the needs of the press also suggest that overtly political tasks were delegated by officialdom to news organizations. Not only has there been a public policy toward the news media as a whole for the entire history of the Republic, but it was justified by references to political and governmental functions specifically accorded to the media by the law.

THE PUBLIC RELATIONS INFRASTRUCTURE: ACCOMMODATION WITH STRINGS ATTACHED

Not just governmental policies but governmental practices as well subsidize the operations of the news media.[34] The shift over history has been toward an infrastructure made available to any and all reporters who have a virtual right of access on a routine basis.[35] As with the postal subsidies, the move has been away from political discretion toward making resources available to anyone who can claim the prerogatives of journalism, although this shift occurred at a later point in history.

In effect, government workers are paid by public funds to help generate the news. The compilation of raw material alone assists reporters' work. Sociologist Mark Fishman notes how city agencies have their own internal "reporting systems" of documents, records, and reports, upon which journalists can rely instead of trying to view unpredictable and wide-ranging phenomena directly.[36] "In routine newswork the detection, interpretation, investigation, and a good deal of the formulation of the written story have already been done by police, city clerks, insurance adjusters, morticians, and the like. And, of course, the work of these outsiders costs the news organization nothing other than the reporter's time to collect what is available."[37]

It is a truism that news production in the United States involves (and always has involved) collaboration and cooperation between officials and newspersons. John Campbell, the publisher of the first regularly produced newspaper in the North American colonies, once listed "Charges and trouble that arises" in assembling an issue, including "Waiting on His Excellency or Secretary for approbation of what is Collected." The historian Charles Clark has elaborated, "Next to the waterfront, the most important stop on Campbell's weekly 'beat' was to talk either with the governor or the province secretary. This call was not merely to receive 'approbation' for what he proposed to print; it was to collect a substantial part of the local news of the week."[38]

The newsbeat is of venerable lineage, but it has been transformed in the centuries since then. In the late nineteenth century, newsmaking shifted from interactions initiated, negotiated, and maintained by individuals in the press and in government, to an ongoing institutional relationship carried out by stable sets of public relations officers within government and newsbeat reporters in the media. This governmental evolution is far from a disinterested accommodation of the needs of journalists. Several developments operated to push government in that direction. One was simply the presence and availability of the increasingly large and stable Washington press corps in officials' work. Another was the evolution, starting in the 1870s, of politics away from popular spectacle toward a more ostensibly "educational" form.[39] And a third was the increasing reach of governmental policies and programs that made discussion thereof in the news important not only for normative reasons of democracy but also for the interests of officials.

The history shows how officials saw the news media as a whole as able to help pursue governmental interests and assist them in governance, and designed policies and practices of publicity to assist journalists in the latter's job of disseminating the news. Using the news media to govern went hand in hand with helping reporters in their work.

This simultaneous assistance and regulation of the press began with the decision in 1841 (noted in the previous chapter) when the U.S. Senate set aside a press gallery and opened it to any and all "bona fide reporters" who were certified by their editors. This decision gave privileges to reporters as a class, but it also restricted them from the floor and separated their work from that of the officeholders. The next step would be for officials to offer versions of their work that anticipated the news needs of reporters; next, they would stage events for the sole purpose of making news. These activities both assisted reporters in their work and enabled officials to direct attention and put their own interpretation on the ultimate product of the news.

Public relations in government followed the growth of the newspaper industry and the concomitant rise of Washington journalism. Already, when Civil War reports were channeled centrally through the capital, Washington news had taken on a new importance.[40] After the war, as newspapers and the demand for news swelled, the number and longevity of Washington reporters increased. Political scientist Samuel Kernell has outlined the growth of the Washington press corps and a decline in its turnover (from 75 percent in one two-year period at the end of the Civil War to just over half in the 1870s and then around a third by the early 1890s).[41] One historian notes reporters' greater willingness during this era to help each other in spite of inevitable rivalries; in his words, "Washington reporters held social receptions, sat by each other in the press galleries, drank at the same hotels, complained of the same snubs by public officials, shared the same miserable pay, and read each other's work. Quite naturally many of them struck up strong intimacies."[42]

With the growth of the news media came hierarchy and specialization. Reporters increasingly concentrated on a given subject matter or institution—the newsbeat—as a way to divide up the job of producing the news. One study has estimated that, by the end of the nineteenth century, over 70 percent of the content of the newspaper came from the beat system.[43] Today's pattern, where most news comes from "routine channels" rather than from the reporters' own "enterprise," was already locked in place.[44]

The commercialization of and growing market for news, the beginnings of a stable Washington press corps, and a newsbeat system all could be (and were) exploited by astute officials. During the Civil War, reporters gravitated to a section of Fourteenth Street between F Street and Pennsylvania Avenue. Close to the telegraph offices where stories were filed, to the executive agencies and to the trolley to Capitol Hill, newspapers established so many offices there that it came to be known as "Newspaper Row." Wartime reporters' standard "rounds" apparently consisted of gathering rumors at Willard's Hotel nearby and then visiting executive officials to confirm or disconfirm these stories.[45] Proactive politicians themselves began to search out reporters at Newspaper Row and at Willard's.[46] Consequently, during this time period, the interview first became a central form of newsgathering; some enterprising politicians went so far as to "interview themselves" and distribute the questions and answers to reporters—an early precursor of the press release.[47]

Government's response to the shift in the news was scattered and inconsistent until the beginning of the twentieth century. Only late in the century did officials start to realize that, if reporters were going to be interested in particular developments anyhow, the sources of the news could favorably influence the final product less by stonewalling or intimidating than by cooperating and providing them with help.

The Progressive Era provided a rationale: airing facts would serve to keep both private and public power accountable. The invention of corporate public relations is usually credited to a onetime reporter named Ivy Lee. Lee persuaded the Pennsylvania Railroad in 1906 to abandon its previous stance of secrecy toward the press and instead to be open and solicitously provide facts to reporters, even when accidents occurred. As one historian sums up Lee's philosophy: "The core of his message was that corporate relations with labor, press, and public were by nature harmonious. Most criticism of management resulted from misunderstanding. Thus, if businessmen managed news carefully, they would be appreciated by a public which might otherwise be misled."[48]

Lee's lesson of openness and assistance had already been learned in government during the presidencies of William McKinley and Theodore Roosevelt.[49] Their predecessor, Grover Cleveland, had followed nineteenth-century precedent, avoiding both policy statements and newsmaking. But his well-known hostility to reporters did not prevent the human-interest angle of his marriage and honeymoon in 1886 from attracting extraordinary news attention. He occasionally met with reporters to issue statements, but "these occurred at such infrequent intervals that Cleveland's occasional policy could not be called a practice."[50] Nevertheless, the press, by relying on the presidents' private secretaries (who were themselves increasingly experienced in the news business) for routine information and by interacting closely with presidents during their lengthier "swings around the circle" trips, was able to lay the groundwork for a full-fledged newsbeat system at the White House.[51] The standard practice, however, was still to gather at the White House gates to quiz entering or exiting officials of what was going on in the executive branch. In 1897, McKinley invited them inside the mansion, beginning with receptions after his inauguration, and proclaimed his general availability for inquiries. Later in his term, he instructed his secretary to brief reporters every evening at 10 P.M. on the developments of the day, and allowed them to wait in a reception room to intercept Cabinet officers—

though, by custom, the president was exempt from questions.[52] A contemporary account by journalist Ida Tarbell depicted how McKinley "has the newspaper man always with him. [The reporter] is . . . a part of the White House personnel . . . Accommodations are furnished him there and his privileges are well-defined and generally recognized."[53]

Succeeding to the presidency after McKinley's assassination in 1901, Theodore Roosevelt went one step further. He reserved a separate room for the White House press corps and then added permanent quarters adjacent to his secretary's office when the building was renovated the following year. Roosevelt, in his autobiography, would later expound a model of the president as "steward of the people . . . bound actively and affirmatively to do all he could for the people."[54] Not only did he see the office as energetic and closely involved in the legislative process, but as highly visible, using the press in governing. He contended in a 1910 speech, "Almost, if not quite, the most important profession is that of the newspaper man . . . The newspaper men—publishers, editors, reporters—are just as much public servants as are the men in the government service themselves."[55]

To be sure, access to the White House was not yet an entitlement to which reporters could claim a right. Roosevelt met only with a select group whose coverage he approved; not until Wilson would presidents defer to the press in deciding the membership of press conferences.[56] But by inviting reporters to base themselves in quarters of their own in the White House rather than at their own bureaus, by pursuing daily discussions with reporters, by issuing daily announcements of presidential activities, and by staging events such as tours and conferences that could become "pegs" for the news, Roosevelt not only instilled the presidency with the style and methods upon which it now relies; he also cemented a place of reporters within government as "public servants." Roosevelt could easily lay claim to the title "inventor of the White House press corps."[57]

The rapid dependence of Washington journalists on such official help became clear when Roosevelt's successor, William Howard Taft, advanced a concept of the presidency more in line with aloof nineteenth-century dignity. The interest of newspapers in the regular and predictable production of important stories with the president as protagonist continued to be high, as did their expectation of presidential assistance and their new reliance on presidential resources. But as an aide bemoaned shortly after the inauguration, "President Taft has no conception of the press as an adjunct to his office . . . Neither the President nor his secretary gives out anything of any real interest, nor do they understand the art of giving out news. In consequence the papers seek their information from whatever source they can find."[58] After his defeat for reelection, Taft mused that a president "should devote close attention to the proper methods of getting to as wide a circle of readers as possible the facts and reasons sustaining his policies and official acts." Taft tellingly added, "I was lacking in attention to matters of this kind"; reporters "properly complained that I did not help them to help me."[59]

But Theodore Roosevelt did not single-handedly initiate the public relations infrastructure that, by today, infiltrates all of government. Instead, a second logic was at work: public relations grew as the federal government shouldered increasing responsibilities in coordinating and directing economic and social life while it lacked the resources that would enable it to carry them out directly.

Attempts to seek policy through publicity were not unique to the Progressive Era. Notably, federal agricultural policy throughout the nineteenth century consisted largely of improving farming by getting useful information to the farmers. As early as 1828, the House of Representatives charged the treasury secretary with gathering and publishing up-to-date information on silk production. The 1862 act establishing a separate Department of Agriculture specified its major task "to acquire and diffuse among the people of the United States information on subjects connected with agriculture in the most general and comprehensive sense of that word."[60] When the department gained Cabinet status in 1889, Agriculture Secretary Jeremiah Rusk wrote in his first annual report, "The very essence of the duties devolving on this Department . . . is that its results shall be promptly made available to the public by a comprehensive scheme of publication." Faced with an overburdened Government Printing Office, Rusk turned his attention to getting the word out through newspapers by summarizing their advisories, pamphlets, and bulletins in terse press releases that could easily be reprinted as news stories.[61]

This use of publicity could be easily expanded upon when policy required cultivating public opinion, not merely informing it, or when it was deemed either improper or impractical to accomplish policy goals directly, by legislation. Not coincidentally, the pioneer here was based in the Agriculture Department: Gifford Pinchot, who became chief of the Forestry Division in 1898.[62] But the advantages that Pinchot perceived for publicity diverged from those the Agriculture Department had long used. When Pinchot took over, the division managed no public lands and existed only to gather and distribute information toward the goal of restraining the exploitation of forests for timber. Pinchot wished not only to push his doctrine of forest conservation but also to prepare public opinion for future presidential declaration of forest reserves which, he hoped, would then come under the supervision of his bureaucracy.

Pinchot became more aggressive in pursuing press attention—expanding the mailing list of editors, increasing the amount of material sent, and monitoring the results through clipping services. More important, through ex-journalists assembled into a separate "press bureau" in 1905, he began to anticipate reporters' needs when crafting his own communication. The Forestry Service began routinely sending out what Pinchot termed "press bulletins," summaries in the form of news stories of speeches and reports; by his own count, the number of these bulletins went from three in 1902 to 418 in 1908.[63] Newspapers were only too happy to reprint the bulletins, but such practice became the object of congressional scrutiny. Pinchot defended himself:

> To get information into the newspapers it is necessary to put it into newspaper form. The newspaper does not want essays, treatises, and reports, but news . . . By employing men familiar with the peculiar requirements of newspaper work and familiar also with the work of this Service it becomes possible to carry on the work of popular education on a far more extensive scale and at a far lower cost than in any other way.[64]

These efforts (well-publicized, after all) were soon imitated in other federal agencies. By 1912, one reporter noted, the Bureau of Education, the Bureau of Soils, the Biological Survey, the State Department, the Bureau of Public Roads, and the Post Office Department had all hired publicists under a variety of job descriptions.[65]

Such developments did not go unchallenged. In particular, legislators from western constituencies had most to lose from Pinchot's conservationist philosophy and bristled to see themselves as the target of lobbying via the news. But the congressional response only ended up embedding executive publicity in a deeper, more widespread way than had been the case theretofore. For instance, the House passed an amendment offered by Representative Frank Mondell to the appropriations for fiscal year 1909 barring the use of funds for "paying for in whole or in part the preparation of any newspaper or magazine articles." The Senate eviscerated the amendment by changing "preparation" to "publication" and adding the important proviso, "This shall not prevent giving out to all persons without discrimination, including newspaper and magazine writers and publishers, of any facts or official information of value to the public."[66] This law—made permanent several years later—turned an attempt to root out publicity agents into an authorization for government to provide information and prepare it for reporters. Indeed, it ensconced a journalist's entitlement to it on an equal basis. One senator prophetically warned: "If the right be accorded this Bureau, you must accord every bureau that right; and the first thing you know, every official will have his own special correspondent, whose duty it is to exploit and glorify the particular work."[67]

Later attempts to slow the growth of the public relations infrastructure foundered on the impossibility of distinguishing between legitimate and illegitimate forms of publicity. Mondell himself told the House, "I believe in the bureaus advertising their work widely," but distinguished this from agencies placing an "exaggerated value on its work" and impugning their critics in Congress.[68] In 1913, Representative Frederick Gillett, angered at reports of publicity agents in the Agriculture Department, introduced an amendment prohibiting the use of federal funds "for the compensation of any publicity expert." Gillett's amendment was adopted, but it has merely forced agencies to camouflage their presence, thus making it more difficult to figure out just how many government workers are employed to work with the media.[69] Last, in 1919, Congress prohibited appropriations from being spent to influence legislators, something reinforced by the still-typical tendency of appropriations bills to prevent executive officials from "propagandizing," that is, lobbying Congress on their behalf.[70] Government agencies will and do work to defend their budget, yet if they are thereby blocked from trying to persuade Congress and the people directly, it is within their power to do so indirectly via the news.

In short, it is hard to distinguish useful information from propaganda. Such persuasion through the news is even more attractive when, either out of principle or out of practicality, government cannot legislate behavior. Such efforts reached a new peak during the First World War, when President Wilson established a Committee on Public Information (CPI) to mobilize domestic public opinion to support nationalism and a conception of the war as a democratic crusade.[71] George Creel, the director of the CPI, saw public relations as an integral part of, rather than in opposition to, censorship, as he wrote the secretary of the navy before the CPI's establishment that "censorship policy must be based on publicity, not suppression."[72] In effect, Ivy Lee's public relations approach would work, since Creel believed "that the press is eager and willing to do the handsome thing, and its [the CPI's] attitude must be one of frankness, friendship and entire openness."[73] A similar government project, under Herbert Hoover, wartime head of the Food Administration, relied upon the news to persuade Americans to conserve food. Hoover noted in a 1917 interview, "We are good advertisers. A few phrases, too, would

turn the trick—and the world lives by phrases, and we most of all perhaps
. . . We need some phrase that puts the stamp of shame on wasteful eating,
dressing, and display of jewelry . . . We could not bring the law to bear
on this, only educate and direct public opinion."[74]

By the end of the First World War, then, publicity had emerged as
a crucial way for government to pursue public policy goals. An infrastructure had emerged, and would only grow, that sought to achieve political
ends by meeting the needs of all journalists on an equal basis. In turn,
Washington journalism became heavily subsidized. At the same time that
news has become an important avenue of governmental activity, journalism has received invaluable assistance, as the newsbeat system and the
public relations assistance helps to reduce the costs of news production.

REGULATION ON THE MEDIA'S OWN TERMS

The regulation of radio and television might not seem to be a governmental subsidy for the news. But such regulation has assisted more than constrained the communications industry. As economist Richard Du Boff
has outlined, the federal government has handled new communication
technologies in similar ways across history. Initial government assistance
enables the technology to emerge. A period of anarchistic development
precedes recognition of the economic possibilities of technologies. Then,
"As new technologies generate their own marketing needs and as business
dependence on telecommunications grows, joint demands are pressed
upon government to ensure a steady flow of revenues for the expanding
young industry and to absorb the social costs of its operations."[75] Such
technology is thereby regulated, but on terms amenable to, if not set by,
the communications industry itself.

But in fact, not just new technologies are regulated. Regulation of
print media occurs, and in a way that resembles in one key respect the
regulation of television and radio—it tends to buttress current arrangements, to discourage the entry of new competitors, and to maximize the
profitability of the overall enterprise. In other words, despite tut-tutting
of First Amendment absolutists who question the constitutionality of
broadcast and cable regulation, any of these industries have generally not
been the victims so much as the beneficiaries of regulation on their own
terms.[76] In fact, the communication industry has organized into lobbies
to advance and protect such beneficial policies. (State press associations
were organized as early as the 1850s to defend the lucrative practice of
legal printing; in 1887, the American Newspaper Publishers Association
was founded to further the economic interests of newspapers, which ne-

cessitated a common front on postal subsidies, newsprint tariffs, copyright, and libel law;[77] and, as I will note below, the National Association of Broadcasters was launched with the explicit intent of obtaining a regulatory commission toward radio.) The sum total of these policies provides strong evidence against a "hands-off" approach by government toward the news media; it also reveals a consistent proindustry bias.

To be sure, the law handles television and radio differently from print. Since their infancy, the broadcast media have been overseen, first by a variety of government agencies, then by the Federal Radio Commission (FRC) in 1927 and the Federal Communications Commission (FCC) in 1934. Years of Supreme Court precedent have distinguished between a more libertarian approach accorded to print from the regulation of television and radio, on the grounds that the finiteness of the broadcast band limited the number of communications that could be sent and therefore necessitated regulation. Given the shift away from a limited broadcast band to cable, satellite dishes, and soon to the internet, the "scarcity" argument no longer holds, yet television and radio are still—even in this period of deregulation—considerably more regulated than newspapers and magazines.[78]

But, after government had already underwritten the costs of the early technological development, regulation nurtured the industry by stabilizing its membership and winning concessions for private profit-oriented firms rather than promoting nonprofit or publicly owned operations. Once the industry was established and profitable, regulation worked against the entry of potential rivals; in the case of television, for instance, the FCC's policies probably ended up preventing a challenge for many years of a fourth alternative to the broadcast networks of ABC, CBS, and NBC.

Regulation undoubtedly has had its public-minded side; by establishing a standard of "public interest" in deciding when stations should be licensed, and by putting the concerns for the audience ahead of the rights of broadcasters, the FCC encouraged the broadcast media to develop news and other public affairs programming. Similarly, regulation has not always worked uniformly toward profitability, as when Congress required broadcasters to sell political candidates advertising time before elections at the lowest rate charged to any user in that time slot.[79] But not only by possible sanctions but by genuine rewards did regulation work; by assuring a stable, consistent, and high profit margin for these stations, the government made possible the rise of (initially unprofitable) radio and television news.

This tale is not unique. Previous telecommunications, such as the telegraph and the telephone, had also received similar governmental treatment, which proved influential given that the ultimate social consequences of the new invention had been far from certain at the outset.[80] With radio, politics had to decide a number of questions: Would it be turned over to programmers who would broadcast to passive listeners or instead to interactive communicators? Would stations produce their own programming over their frequency or rent it out to others just as the telephone company let its wires be used for private conversations? And would the medium be commercially exploited at all? The history is too complicated (and fascinating) to summarize adequately here. Suffice it to say that the ultimate outcome—whereby radio (and later, television) would be made up largely of powerful commercial broadcasters, each controlling a particular frequency to send out programs they themselves produced—would be the result only of years of political battles from the navy's first attempts to use the new medium to communicate with ships at sea at the turn of the twentieth century all the way to the Communications Act of 1934, which established the FCC.

Radio was initially understood in terms of the technologies preceding it. As Susan Douglas's splendid history of the early development of radio makes clear,[81] what was then known as "ether" was first used for "wireless telegraphy," in the style of Guglielmo Marconi's broadcasting dots and dashes from one point to another. When Reginald Fessenden and Lee De Forest demonstrated how speech and music could be broadcast, people then began to talk about "wireless telephony," where conversations could be carried on through the airwaves. Indeed, it is surprising to see that one strength of radio—its being broadcast from one point to many others—was thought of as a weakness by the chief governmental developer, the navy, which kept on trying to find ways to use the wireless communication without others eavesdropping or interfering.

Amateurs, not government or commercial interests, were the first to explore radio's possibilities of broadcasting. The anarchic use of the medium eventually pushed government toward the first regulation. The Radio Act of 1912 required the licensing of radio operators on a given frequency after stories circulated that amateurs interfered with the Titanic's broadcast pleas for help.[82] This act established a lasting precedent: the "ether" would be meted out by the government to individuals who hold their frequencies as property. World War I would occasion further development of radio under the navy's monopolistic direction. But when the war ended, the navy's proposal to continue their power in peacetime faced congressional opposition. Fearful of foreign control of the airwaves by the London-based American Marconi, the navy arranged instead the establishment of a private monopoly to receive its many patents. Thus was created the Radio Corporation of America (RCA).

Radio was still thought of primarily for wireless telegraphy until the radio station, KDKA in Pittsburgh (which Westinghouse had built from the amateur license of one of its employees), broadcast the election returns of the 1920 presidential race and provoked an upsurge in the sale of radio receivers (made, conveniently, by Westinghouse). As would happen with television in the 1950s, the first commercial exploitation of radio was to sell equipment to pick up the broadcasts, and programming was designed with that in mind. Only gradually did the new medium attract commercial advertisers, a development that some powers-that-be in Washington—most notably Commerce Secretary Herbert Hoover, who had taken a keen interest in the development of radio—looked at with disdain, and that nonprofit broadcasters (amateurs, educational institutions, churches) openly contested. Amidst this battle over the spectrum, and given the divergent visions that people had for the future of radio,[83] a group of independent commercial broadcasters moved into high gear. They formed a trade association in 1923—the National Association of Broadcasters (NAB)—to pursue common interests and lobby for legal protection.[84] Indeed, the NAB, under its first president, Eugene McDonald, was the first to propose an independent commission to regulate the industry, an idea initially opposed by small broadcasters and nonprofit operators who feared the possible domination of the commission by what they called "the radio trust."[85] Little wonder that Secretary Hoover could happily note, "I think this is probably the only industry in the United States that is unanimously in favor of having itself regulated."[86]

The NAB finally got its commission after McDonald successfully sued to block Hoover's attempts under the 1912 Radio Act to supervise the licensing of radio.[87] After the Justice Department endorsed the ruling in mid-1926, Hoover abandoned all efforts at regulation beyond awarding licenses to whoever asked for one. The ensuing chaos provoked the passage of the Radio Act of 1927, which established, on a year-by-year basis, the FRC. One scholarly team has noted the dynamic of such regulation: "The 'temporary' decision . . . spawned its own vested interests, and the preservation of the system these interests dictated became the determinant of Commission policy."[88] The NAB, noting the FRC's favorable treatment of commercial broadcasters, would eventually move to favor a permanent commission in 1933, launching what they called a "war plan" to "speed up the movement toward a thoroughly stabilized broadcasting industry."[89]

Broadcast networks began when the collaboration of RCA, General

Electric, and Westinghouse formed the National Broadcasting Company (NBC) in 1926. But it was not until the establishment of the FRC that broadcasting finally became highly profitable, following decisions the FRC made early on. The FRC concluded that the vague congressional charge to protect "the public interest, convenience, or necessity" would be best implemented in two ways. One was to favor applicants for licenses who would be most likely to do well; those who were well-financed, had sophisticated technical equipment and trained personnel were presumed best qualified to provide continuous service. In addition, the FRC decided that the listeners' well-being had priority over the rights of the broadcasters. Thus, they would prefer applicants who would appeal to "the entire listening public within the listening area of the station" over what they termed "propaganda stations" run by labor unions, educational institutions, churches, and local governments. They announced, "There is not room in the broadcast band for every school of thought, religious, political, social, and economic, each to have its separate broadcasting station, its mouthpiece in the ether."[90]

The FRC's decision rules implicitly favored large commercial broadcasters. Others were moved to less favorable frequencies, or approved only for part-time broadcasting at odd hours, or had their power reduced, or ultimately failed to have their licenses renewed. The FRC (and, after 1934, the FCC), would become the archetype of a commission that regulates an industry in ways that the latter finds beneficial and profitable—even while that industry might be able to fend off other governmental restrictions by pointing to that regulation.[91]

This proindustry bias was not necessarily deliberate. For instance, the FCC ended up paradoxically favoring an oligopoly of three large television networks by its policy of wishing to encourage local (rather than regional or national) stations. By reserving only so many slots on the twelve-channel VHF television dial per media market (some for out-of-the-way locales that could not possibly support any at all), and by not anticipating the temptation that "economies of scale" would pose for local stations to affiliate with a network, the policy of localism made it impossible to allow a competitor to emerge for ABC, CBS, and NBC.[92] What's more, the FCC's concern about interrupting service, along with the preference given to a proven record, meant that the benefit of the doubt, at renewal time for licenses, was given, both procedurally and in principle, to the existing licensee. As one commissioner tartly declared in 1958, "A fellow being denied an application before the FCC gets more due process than a murderer."[93]

If there were any successful reforms, they were in terms the industry could find acceptable. For instance, attempts to expand the spectrum and thereby increase diversity have always included protection for existing stations. The classic example is the FCC's difficulty in expanding the television band, by boosting UHF, which was economically far less viable than the twelve channels of the VHF band. Ultimately, the FCC abandoned its attempts to force media markets to be all-VHF or all-UHF, and instead threw its support to legislation in Congress mandating all television sets to be equipped to receive both UHF and VHF stations. This decision left established licensees with favorable frequencies and put off competition for VHF for a generation of television sets.[94] In general, regulation has served, sometimes explicitly, to defend the already existing stations from new competition, from the long debate over FM in the 1940s, or the limits placed on subscription and cable television in the 1960s, or the "must-carry" requirements in the Cable Television Consumer Protection and Competition Act of 1992 that requires cable systems to set aside several channels for local television stations.[95]

Thus, federal policy worked explicitly to subsidize the operation of for-profit radio and television broadcasters rather than encourage nonprofit broadcasting, let alone governmental control of the airwaves. FRC and FCC regulation added to this by reinforcing the existing arrangement and discouraging new competition to radio and television networks. Scholars have produced a few different explanations to explain this bias on the part of the FCC. One is the "capture" theory, whereby the greater interaction with the more politically organized interest co-opts the regulators, which need not respond except with symbolism to the fuzzier and more distantly understood public.[96] Yet the capture theory does not explain well the emergence of—and the failure of—commissioners ideologically committed not to support the industry.[97]

A more satisfying explanation is the commission's weakness vis-à-vis a Congress reluctant to disturb entrenched local interests. The FCC's limited resources already make it willing to punt on controversial points. If it does cross a line, its policies can be reversed by Congress, as happened in the mid-1960s when Congress overwhelmingly passed an amendment preventing the FCC from considering limitations on the amounts of advertising time.[98] And the FCC's long-standing bias toward localism in communications policy matches well the often noted parochialism of Congress.[99] Private broadcasters, usually affiliated with a network, were thereafter widely dispersed across constituencies; every legislator could then be warned that any threat to local stations might diminish the local news and its ability to send the legislators' messages home.[100] In the absence of widespread public salience, David Price found, in his study of the House Commerce Committee in the 1970s, any attempts to rethink broadcast regulation were classic examples of issues with low salience and high conflict with interest groups; under such circumstances, reformist members of Congress would only make enemies, and, not surprisingly, they soon turned to other issues.[101]

The federal regulation of radio and television thus worked to enable the industry to reap consistent high profits. By so doing, such regulation did make it easy for radio and television to accede to the expectations that the stations operate in "the public interest," most notably by adequate amounts of public affairs programming and by adhering to the Fairness Doctrine mandating balance. It is worth noting that, prior to the establishment of the FCC, news programming on the radio was sporadic and usually directly lifted the news printed elsewhere.[102] News programs may have, at the time, lost money, but such a loss was tolerable given the stable market and impressive overall profit margins that regulation enabled.

The treatment of newspapers and magazines in federal law has a similar outcome: they benefit from policies that help to protect profitability and to restrict new competition. In addition to the postal subsidy, for instance, news organizations have sought and received exemptions from regulations required of other industries. Such exemptions are particularly interesting since the Supreme Court has consistently resisted the temptation to rule that the First Amendment necessitates positive rights for the press that set it apart from other industries. On the contrary, the consistent judicial interpretation, starting with the antitrust suit against the Associated Press in the 1940s, has been that news organizations are not exempt from economic regulation that pertains to it as a business.[103]

Newspapers benefit from specific governmental assistance.[104] For example:

1. Starting in 1939, Congress specifically exempted news deliverers from minimum wage, overtime, social security, and child labor laws. In part, they were viewed as independent contractors, but legislators also spoke nostalgically about the supposedly educational role of the newsboy.[105] If one recent estimate is right that three-quarters of newspaper deliverers are minors exempt from the minimum wage, this enables significant cost cutting in the distribution of newspapers.[106]

2. Congress has provided tax exemptions for certain kinds of activities, including "establishing, maintaining or increasing circulation," which covers much activity. Several authors argue that this allows chains to deduct the costs of acquiring new newspapers.[107]

3. Congress removed newspapers with a circulation under 4,000,

most of which is within the county and surrounding counties, from the minimum wage and unemployment rules of the Fair Labor Standards Act. Since even small newspapers might, by being sent across state lines, participate in interstate commerce, a special exemption needed to be drafted. In the words of the House sponsor, "Under this bill, because one or two percent of a paper's circulation goes outside to people who want to get the hometown paper to see whether or not Lucy got married, or whether Sally's baby has been born yet, because that infinitesimal bit of their business is with people outside the county, these publishers fall outside the provisions of this bill, when on each side of this little printshop are the butcher and the baker, who are exempt and who are financially better fixed than he is."[108] (This law is especially intriguing insofar as it established that Congress may constitutionally treat newspapers of varying size differently from one another; subsidies need not be extended to all newspapers as a whole.)[109]

4. The Newspaper Preservation Act was passed in 1970 after a Supreme Court decision that decided that a joint operating agreement between two competing newspapers in Tucson engaged in restraint of trade and was therefore in violation of antitrust laws. The act exempts news organizations from antitrust prosecutions when an "economically distressed" newspaper, otherwise not "likely to remain or become a financially sound publication," with advance agreement from the U.S. attorney general, shares a physical plant with but has separate editorial functions from another newspaper.[110]

These laws all share two key characteristics. First of all, none was mandated by the First Amendment. In comparison with policies that have come from Supreme Court interpretations of the First Amendment—as when libel laws or taxes aimed at a narrow swath of newspapers were struck down—each emanated from legislative choice. Second, both the legislative intent *and* the policy outcome are to protect the ability of news organizations to make a profit, by removing regulation that they would otherwise have to undergo if they were just any other business.

Conclusion

Throughout the existence of the American Republic, then, there has been some kind of public policy toward the news media. These policies have grown in importance as the one-on-one arrangements I sketched in the previous chapter—those accomplished by patronage, threats of suits, and granting or denying of access to governmental proceedings—have waned. Moreover, these policies have worked to subsidize the operations of news organizations, rendering them more profitable and more likely to survive. Finally, these policies were designed with a presumption on the part of policymakers that the news media performed governmental and political functions and roles and needed to be assisted in doing so properly.

It may be that the United States, over the past two decades, has entered a "deregulatory moment" whereby media organizations no longer reap the same level of benefits they once did. To cite a couple of noteworthy examples, radio and television are much more deregulated nowadays, and the principle of a subsidy for second-class mail is slowly being abandoned by Congress, having been preceded by the demise of the in-county break for local newspapers. In addition, proposed regulations may be less beneficial for news organizations; for instance, newspapers are facing laws that would lessen profits, such as mandating the recycling of newsprint or limiting newsracks.

Yet it would be wrong to make too much of recent developments. Even with deregulation, this merely means that the public relations infrastructure has become the most important federal subsidy provided to the news—as one might have gathered from seeing its rise not only within the executive branch but within Congress and the judiciary as well.[111] The more important lesson is that a news media policy has been pursued consistently by the federal government throughout American history and with political goals in mind. The courts have generally approved these initiatives, which have had an impressive effect on the development and ultimate shape of the American news media.

We can speak then of the news media as a prominent example of American political development, being shaped by and in turn shaping the federal government. But does this mean that the news media indeed do act as a political institution in their own right? Certainly, we can think of many institutions that arose due to policies, and even from delegation of power, that we might not think of, at base, as political institutions— corporations and labor unions to name a few. To answer the question of whether the news media do now operate as an intermediary institution in American politics, we cannot stop merely with the historical political development of the news media; we must turn (as we do now) to the question of the media's contemporary institutional and political places.

PART TWO

THE MEDIA

AS A

POLITICAL INSTITUTION

If we are to take the role and power of the news media seriously, we must pay greater attention to their being a political
institution. Far too many observers end up succumbing to the
temptation to assess the ongoing negotiation of newsworthiness between the news media and of political actors via studies
of individual journalists interacting with individual politicians. Indeed, a central drawback of Cater's original consideration of the "fourth branch" was his use of it more as a metaphor for the news media's power than for its existence as an
intermediary institution.[1] Instead, the actions of political
actors and of journalists in the United States are contingent
upon the roles they occupy within their respective political
and social systems, and the resultant rewards and sanctions
to particular behaviors. In particular, when reporters make
choices on who and what to cover and how to cover it, these
choices are governed less by personal values prior to becoming
a journalist or by their placement within the social structure
as a whole than by "a logic of appropriateness"[2] based on
their professional and craft-related roles as journalist.

Yet referring to the media as *a* political institution, rather
than a set of institutions, or perhaps just a batch of different
organizations, still may rub the reader the wrong way. Indeed,
most of those who have substantially and successfully criticized the notion of individual journalists as the lone authors

of the news have gone only as far as an organizational, not an institutional, account. An organizational, rather than an institutional, account implicitly raises doubts about the political power of the news media. If each organization addresses different conceptions of news and adopts different methods to pursue them to present to different audiences, the power of the media is presumably much less than if there is considerable consensus and overlap that privilege particular political actors and political interpretation. But even if we find that the media do constitute an institution, such an institution may be social without being political.

If we are to take the possibility seriously that the news media now form an intermediary political institution, we must closely examine whether the media are institutional and whether they are political. Chapter 4 begins by establishing a current definition of institutions from recent empirical and theoretical work in political science and closely related fields, and then applying that definition to our knowledge about what the media do and how they do it. Chapter 5 then turns to the question of the independent political influence of such an institution. If the media largely distribute the voices of political actors, without shaping what those voices say, it cannot be a "fourth branch." As it turns out, the news media do have a powerful bias, but paradoxically it is embedded deeply into their operations (and institutionally across organizations) largely because of the ways in which politics is explicitly excluded, while being implicitly included in the production values of the news. In part, then, the very commitment of the news media to objectivity and disinterest gives the news its independent and far-reaching perspective, and its influence.

4

THE INSTITUTIONAL NEWS MEDIA

U nderstanding the news as an organizational product is nothing new. In the twenty-five years since the political scientist Edward Jay Epstein observed the inside workings of NBC News, we have had many opportunities to read about the organizational logics necessary to crank out the daily perishable commodity of the newspaper or the news broadcast.[1] To these scholars, a news organization is akin to other organizations: it needs to find the most efficient ways to come up with a satisfactory product on a regular basis at the lowest cost. One must anticipate where a story is likely to happen, figure out who to interview about what, share a common understanding about the news values and production values behind a "good story," and craft stories that can be quickly fit into the news. All of this enables the organization to produce news on a regular, consistent, and predictable basis. Such efficiency necessitates a division of labor both vertically (e.g., publisher, editor, beat reporter, general assignment reporter) and horizontally (across "desks" and newsbeats). The organizational impact is all the more central given that nobody quite knows what the news is, including journalists, who must rely on a vague "nose for news" rather than hard-and-fast guidelines of newsworthiness. The news in short is organizationally defined and constituted. Little wonder that most scholars would agree with Leo Rosten's statement from sixty years ago: "News in the last analysis is what newspapers choose to print."[2]

This organizational approach to the news remains highly insightful. Yet it only goes so far in our understanding of the news. For one thing, despite these authors' claims, an organizational approach may tell us of the necessity of routines but tells us little about what those routines are, or about the *content* of the news. Being a California native, I remember one example from Epstein. NBC News in the late 1960s sought to present its broadcast as coast-to-coast in order to win audiences west of the eastern seaboard. But time zone changes and the cumbersome requirements of transporting film made it more difficult to include breaking stories outside their two hubs of Washington and New York. Epstein claims that this organizational necessity pushed the news broadcast to routinely include feature stories from California that were sent well in advance and that could be aired on any given day; these stories generally focused on the Golden State as the site of new, quirky social developments.[3] While the organizational perspective can explain the predominance of features over breaking news from California, it cannot tell us why they typically followed this particular formula—let alone why that formula has persisted in the age of satellite uplinks and downlinks.

More important, an organizational approach would witness many diverse responses to different audiences, different environments, different technologies, different resources, etc., as each organization establishes its own niche and puts forth the most efficient means to achieve its particular goals. In fact, if there were as many different styles of organization as there are news media, we would have little cause to worry about the news media's power, given that they would be diverse and diffuse. There is, to be sure, a range of diversity between television, radio, newspaper, and newsmagazine news, between tabloid papers and papers of record, between dailies and weeklies, between small-town and big-city outlets. But what is striking is that, as we shall see below, this range is constricted. The news media, despite different technologies, deadlines, and audiences, are structured similarly in their internal organizations, the way they interact with sources, the formats they use, and in the content they provide.

The efficient pursuit of an individual organization's goals, in short, is not the only or even foremost thing for the personnel of news outlets. Indeed, given reporters' well-documented search for ways to maximize their autonomy, dislike of audience surveys and preference for such broad and flexible procedures that they become guardians of an undefinable "news sense" rather than codifiers of bureaucratic rules of newsgathering, efficiency may not even be the most important thing for most reporters most of the time, as long as they can meet their superiors' demands for a regular stream of stories.

This transorganizational agreement on news processes and content suggests that we should think of the news media not as a set of diverse organizations, or even a batch of individual institutions, but collectively as a single social institution. To explain the content of the news (and thereby its systematic biases) and to understand the activities and processes of journalism beyond the pursuit of organizational efficiency, we must go farther. This chapter explores the possibility that the news media may and should be conceived of as an institution; in the next chapter, I will turn to the question of whether and how this institution is political.

WHAT IS AN INSTITUTION?

The past several years have seen an upsurge in what has been grandly called the "new institutionalism" in political science as well as in sibling disciplines such as economics and sociology. In political science, this resurgence draws from the disillusionment with behavioralism—the central paradigm of political science in the 1950s and 1960s, which had displaced the "old" institutionalism, oriented around formal rules and procedures. Behavioralism, it appeared, could answer only so much. In particular, it could not account very well for political change, especially as evidence mounted of the crucial role of the historical context in shaping political outcomes.

But while it was easy to critique behavioralism for oversights, it was less simple to say what should take its place. One landmark, for instance (March and Olsen's 1989 *Rediscovering Institutions*), indicted behavioralism's failings quite effectively but then never defined the term "institution" clearly enough that we would know what was and what was not an institution; indeed, they seemed to conflate institutions with organizations.[4] Overall, a hallmark of much of the literature in new institutionalism has been to skirt—gracefully or not—the definition of "institution."[5] This may or may not be a problem when we are dealing with something like Congress that all political scientists would quickly consider an institution. But if this analysis is to be persuasive about the news media—which political scientists have not generally recognized as institutional—I need to address carefully the notion of just what an institution is.

In so doing, I will not try to choose one particular brand of institutionalism but will try to identify where the multitudinous competitors agree in a way that political scientists could easily recognize. After all, my point here is not to add to theories of institutions, but to throw light on our understanding of the news media. Happily, over the last few years, the practitioners of the various approaches have begun to address what they have in common rather than what they dispute.[6]

Bert Rockman has identified the three principal schools in political science: a "historical-comparative approach" examining the evolution over time of policy making, a "bounded rationality" school derived from organizational theory, and a rational-choice focus seeking evidence of a stable equilibrium maintained by institutional arrangements that otherwise is lacking in political bodies.[7] (I would add, under the "bounded rationality" variety, the recent work in sociology that is useful for our purposes here since it pays especial attention to social practices that transcend particular organizations.)[8]

The core of all institutionalisms is a denial that all social phenomena can be reduced to individual psychologism.[9] But the institutional dimension should be more than an organizational component. In traditional sociological usage, institutions are the site of systematized principles of action enduring across time and governing a central area of social life. This definition is akin to that used in mainstream political science, although it diverges from its more functionalist implications. Thus, if we were to look up "institution" in the index of the *Handbook of Political Science*, we would encounter Samuel Huntington and Jorge Dominguez's definition: "Politics—that is, deciding who gets what, when and how for a society—often, but not always, takes place through formal organizations and procedures. To the extent that these organizations and procedures become stable, recurring, and valued patterns of behavior, they become political institutions."[10]

The understanding of institutions that I set forth here adopts these criteria but views their dynamics in a more expansive way. In particular, I start from the presumption that institutions are the current result of long-standing and ongoing conflict and domination. However, limits on human information and knowledge prevent anyone—whether in the elites or in the masses—from being able to understand cause and effect well enough to be purely instrumental and purely effective.[11] Instrumentality becomes difficult as various competing social strategies accrete, all and any of which might be seen as ways to get something done in society and that are not, and cannot be, tested—particularly since some strategies are more legitimated than others by their connections to abiding cultural values, themselves the product of slow evolution and accretion, as they are applied in shifting political and social contexts. The political philosopher Robert Goodin thus has suggested three essential ways for institutions to arise and develop: accident, evolutionary accommodation to the environment, and intentional intervention—and that all three are "almost certain" to be implicated in institutional change.[12]

Let's note three implications in particular of the Huntington-Dominguez definition as most variants of institutionalism would see them.

First, the mainstream definition points not merely to formal structures that serve to constrain individual choice but to social patterns of behavior valued in and of themselves. Such social patterns encompass not only explicit rules and expectations but unspoken procedures, rou-

tines, and assumptions of ways to act socially and politically. These include rituals and other behaviors that have no empirically verifiable effect on the goal ostensibly being sought, yet become valued in and of themselves in the absence of any evidence of their actually discouraging the attainment of institutional goals.[13]

Institutions may be instituted, to be sure, but much of their development is by accretion. Particular isolated decisions can serve as precedents for later choices, which may quickly become ensconced as "the" way to get things done within and across organizations. While political actors may proceed according to established practices and gain beneficial outcomes, it is often tough to figure out just which rules and procedures actually advance the goals and which do not. All institutionalists concur that information costs and bounded rationality operate.[14] Even if rules *were* consciously adopted at an earlier time to maximize utilities, they may continue to exist and be valued, while the problems that occasioned their creation are no longer around. If political actors can't ascertain which approaches lead to preferred outcomes, the net result may be to value all existing rules and procedures that are not demonstrably harmful. The institutional structure, in other words, becomes invested with value in and of itself, and the routines become ends in and of themselves.[15] Thus, even those who adopt a rational-actor model of institutions refer not only to formal rules but also to "enduring regularities of human action in situations structured by rules, norms, and shared strategies . . . constituted and reconstituted by human interaction in frequently occurring or repetitive situations."[16]

There is also increasing consensus that institutions enable as well as restrict. The sociologist Anthony Giddens has provided the most defined rethinking of the role of institutions through his idea of the "duality of structure," whereby "the structural properties of social systems are both the medium and the outcome of the practices that constitute those systems."[17] Giddens takes a cue from the study of language, which both constrains *and* permits communication. To speak uses a variety of linguistic rules to shape communication, but perpetuates the language as a whole if one does so successfully. In the case of society as a whole, "[r]ules and resources are drawn upon by actors in the production of interaction, but are thereby also reconstituted through such interaction . . . Structure thus is not to be conceptualised as a barrier to action, but as essentially involved in its production."[18] To Giddens, the structures with the longest history and most widespread across interactions are "deeply-layered," and "the most deeply-layered practices constitutive of social systems in each of these senses are *institutions.*"[19]

Giddens's suggestions have been most broadly picked up within sociology, where the institutions studied are often of another sort from those in political science (e.g., the museum, the handshake, the family). But political scientists and economists, too, now use similar conceptions of institutions—first, both enabling as well as constraining decisions, and second, operating according to unspoken, often culturally agreed-upon, understandings beyond the formal explicit rules. Most notably, faced with the economist Kenneth Arrow's famous impossibility theorem (which demonstrated that, with multiple decision makers and multiple options, there is no naturally occurring single majority result), rational-choice scholars began looking to the institutional contexts for ways to enable public choice. Political scientists such as William Riker and Kenneth Shepsle have argued that even if equilibrium and stability cannot arise out of individual preferences, each might be "structure-induced."[20] Although, because of the prominent role of the skill of individual actors, the experimental and empirical evidence is thin at best for such structure-induced equilibria,[21] this does not deny that while a particular choice may not be foreordained by structural arrangements, the possibility that *some* choice can be made at all may depend on them.[22]

Institutional practices, then, are often valued whether or not they productively pursue the organization's particular goals in specific instances. Instead, such practices become valued as the quasi-natural way to do something. The evocative image of the anthropologist Mary Douglas tells us how to identify an institution: "When, in reply to the question, 'Why do you do it like this?' although the first answer may be framed in terms of mutual convenience . . . the final answer refers to the way the planets are fixed in the sky or the way that plants or humans or animals naturally behave."[23]

Second, given this taken-for-granted quality, *institutions extend over space and endure over time.* Historical duration is an obvious theme of institutions for political scientists; it also fits the sociological contrast against dependence on a single unique actor, as opposed to acts performed by anyone in a particular position.[24] To be sure, such endurance need not be equated with stasis. Scholars, critiquing this assumption, argue that institutions may be sources of change; using different approaches derived from different political contexts, they may not interact with one another smoothly, and such tension is a source of change.[25] There may also be change and resistance within lone institutions as well. After all, individuals and groups can and do pursue their own interests by trying to appropriate particular institutional orders and approaches;[26] and the application of old approaches in new contexts may come up with unexpected outcomes that can serve as future precedents.[27]

The extension across space is not as familiar, particularly given the ways in which classic political science definitions of institutionalization tend to emphasize differentiation from the environment and complexity.[28] Yet these two approaches to institutions are not mutually exclusive. For example, Steven Haeberle's nice study of the institutionalization of subcommittees in the House of Representatives points to their greater activity, permanency and distinctiveness (similar units with independent functions); but he could easily have illustrated institutionalization by showing how all House committees began operating in similar ways, designating subcommittees with substantive specialties to which legislation would be sent for consideration.[29] In other words, the process by which organizations become more differentiated from their environment as a whole and more internally complex can and does easily occur at the same time as they become more alike to others within what has come to be called an "organizational field," a set of different organizations that see themselves and are seen by others to cover a given area of social life.

Douglas's insight, that institutions may be viewed not as the result of human choice but as "the" natural way to do something, helps also to explain extension across space. Sociologists Paul DiMaggio and Walter Powell have found, "In the initial stages of their life cycle, organizational fields display considerable diversity in approach and form. Once a field becomes well established, however, there is an inexorable push toward homogenization."[30] DiMaggio and Powell propose three organization-level processes that contribute to homogenization. One, an organization responds to the political force of other institutions in order to buttress its own legitimacy and power; two, it models itself on other organizations as a means to deal with uncertainty about the links of means and ends; and three, it responds to normative pressures to professionalize.[31]

This concept of "organizational field" might, at first glance, seem to have little to do with politics. True, if one limits oneself to institutions that are single organizations, such as the U.S. Senate or the Supreme Court, it does not help us much. However, the study of politics, and of political institutions, often extends beyond organizational boundaries.

Much of the sociological work is akin to the literature in political science on diffusion of innovations; in this view, a practice is institutionalized when it becomes understood as "the" way to design a policy, after an earlier period when policies are more closely and individually crafted to the particular locale.[32] Moreover, if one suggests that institutions may well be transorganizational, we can move from, say, the level of "Congress" to the more general level of "legislature." State legislatures are organizationally and procedurally very similar to each other despite the huge variation by state in political cultures, social contexts, and resources. Though the theoretical rationale for bicameralism that holds at the federal level (i.e., one chamber elected on the basis of geographical jurisdictions, and the other by equally sized districts) was overturned by the Supreme Court, forty-nine of the fifty state legislatures continue to be bicameral as "the" way to pass laws, without much empirical evidence that bicameralism makes for better legislating than unicameralism. Given that many of the institutions that political scientists study *are*, in fact, transorganizational (e.g., the legislature, the bureaucracy, the political party, the interest group), attention to the organizational field seems to be in order.

Third, *institutions are expected to preside over a societal and/or political sector.* To Huntington and Dominguez, political institutions supervise the process of "who gets what." This point is tricky insofar as it flirts with functionalism, a once-popular approach in political science that sought to identify beneficial social and political functions for a range of observed practices. Not only does functionalism have a political bias of favoring the status quo, but it also stacks the deck by making it almost impossible to disprove, as clever political scientists could (and did) find novel functions for established practices. Nevertheless, this criterion is crucial, given the contrast between the expansive definition of "institution" adopted by many sociologists and economists and the more restricted understanding to which political scientists have usually adhered.[33] Again, the notion of "organizational field" can help us out, by asking us to identify the extent that organizations are generally recognized by themselves and outsiders to take on similar tasks in the polity and society. In other words, instead of theorizing from afar, we can pose empirical questions: whether or not organizations regard each other, and are recognized by outsiders, as performing similar jobs, and then what those jobs are understood to be. In other words, the process of deciding who and what will preside over political sectors is, itself, a result of politics, with the same processes of explicit decisions and implicit accretion outlined above.

To sum up this definitional foray: institutions are social patterns of behavior identifiable across the organizations that are generally seen within a society to preside over a particular social sphere. Although they make choice possible, the inherent cognitive difficulty of linking given practices to particular outcomes means that particular practices cannot be identified as the most beneficial, and all rules are valued in and of themselves unless and until they demonstrably harm the achievement of important goals. The rules and procedures that constitute institutions are understood as the quasi-natural way to get things done. As such, they endure over time and extend over space, and are widely recognized both within the organizations that constitute the institutions as well as from outside as all performing similar jobs that occupy a central place in the society and polity.

Let us begin our investigation of the news media by taking these one at a time. First, can we conclude that the news media create the news based on distinctive roles, routines, rules, and procedures? Second, have these practices evolved and endured over time and do they extend across news organizations? And finally, are the news media viewed by newspersons themselves, as well as those who are not, as together presiding over a given part of social and political life?

THE MEDIA AS INSTITUTIONAL I: UNSPOKEN PROCEDURES, ROUTINES, AND ASSUMPTIONS

Common sense usually tells us that reporters are the "authors" of their pieces. After all, we see bylines in newspapers and newsmagazines, and radio and television reports typically end as reporters identify themselves by name, affiliation, and location. But, as scholarship has generally concluded, newsmaking is a collective process more influenced by the uncritically accepted routine workings of journalism as an institution than by attitudes of journalists.[34]

This is not to say that the individual journalists are mere cogs in a huge news-producing machine. Journalists do exercise discretion, in part because the definition of news and the norms of journalism are so flexible. Yet we cannot directly extrapolate from surveys of individual newspersons to their daily work, let alone to the content of the news. To take some examples: one team found their sample of elite journalists in the late 1970s to express opinions characteristic of what they termed a "new elite"—liberal-to-left, particularly on social issues—and to respond to vague stimuli with stories that showed an anti-authority bias.[35] But, as critics have wondered, do such individual attitudes bear on the newsmaking process if they are not reinforced by the goals and procedures of the news organization as a whole?[36] In particular, do individual opinions enter much into newsmaking, given that journalists are conscientious about excluding their own personal values in pursuit of news that is demonstrably objective, impartial, and balanced? Likewise, surveys of both Washington reporters in the late 1970s and a national sample of journalists in the mid-1980s revealed that most reporters felt a strong sense of autonomy in their work.[37] But might this perception of autonomy simply mean that journalists have internalized the demands on them from superiors, sources, and audiences, and obtain satisfaction by creatively crafting a commissioned product—deciding what is the lead, whom to quote, the arrangement of the prose, etc.?[38]

It is especially problematic to move from individual journalists to journalism as a whole, because all of the studies of news organizations stress how the day-in–day-out process of putting together the news is a group process conducted within a hierarchical newsroom. This is, of course, most true for television, where individual reporters have to collaborate with producers, camera crews, tape editors, and the like to come up with a single isolated report. Television, requiring more personnel for a given story, thus cannot cover the waterfront in the same way as print reporters. Consequently, television news uses more general assignment reporters who are sent out on assignments by producers than newsbeat reporters who have the satisfaction of being able to suggest their own storylines—to the point that local television news, in particular, has been called a "news factory."[39] Television is then especially marked by a process of self-fulfilling prophecies: insofar as producers expect news to happen, and reporters are sent out to gather it, they will come back with something that will become news for the show.[40]

But while there is a difference between television and newspapers, it is a matter of degree. Newspapers, too, are assembled as a collective endeavor. Newsbeat reporters must often rely on others to "feed" them information that may then be "woven" into their own account if they cannot gather that information themselves. More fully, shared albeit implicit understandings of news are crucial to make the product of the news on a recurring basis. If editors and reporters on newspapers were not to share basic common conceptions of the news and of where it is likely to happen, the ensuing conflict and confusion would make it difficult to generate the news on a daily basis. (It is worth noting that this agreement on the news between superiors and subordinates in the news organization is not, as some have hypothesized, because a given political line is either explicitly or implicitly laid down from above and followed by those below. In particular, there is little evidence that editorial stances are much correlated with slants in the content of news.)[41]

Nobody knows what news is—beyond that it should be accurate, fresh, timely, and unexpected, and both interesting and important. Reporters, asked what news or newsworthiness is, usually cannot answer the question. Bernard Roshco, a reporter turned sociologist, noted, "Efforts to define news tend to dissolve into lists of newsmaking events."[42] Journalists are equally flummoxed by inquiries into how they decide what to cover, or where they get their ideas for stories.[43] It is perhaps no surprise that newspersons are not a reflective bunch; after all, the daily grind (or, in the case of periodicals, the weekly grind) necessitates that they crank out a regular stream of stories.[44] It is simply part of the job description to come up with a story every workday, even if it does not make it into the final news product, because their superiors are nervous (unjustifiably so, of course) about the prospect of running out of things to say or show. Indeed, reporters often cite one hallmark of professionalism—"the line dividing greenhorns from veterans"—as the ability to produce a story in a short time under poor conditions.[45]

So rather than ponder paralyzing questions of what is and isn't news (let alone what is and isn't the truth), journalists follow established rules and routines for coming up with the news. In Gaye Tuchman's unforgettable phrase, reporters must "routinize the unexpected."[46] Rather than recognize news by preexisting characteristics of events, newspersons then define what is news by the processes they used to come up with it. In that sense, as Rosten's comment above reveals, news is nothing more or less than whatever news organizations produce.

But does this entail choice? Do newspersons in fact make decisions about the news? Yes and no. Newspersons do make important choices, but they are generally implicit in the routines they follow rather than explicit, particularly because reporters rarely compare the news they assemble with any alternative visions of what they could have covered beyond looking to their competitors. Such adherence to routines does not occur only with general assignment reporters instructed to cover a particular event by their superiors. It also occurs with newsbeat reporters—those assigned to cover a particular locale, institution, or subject matter—who are expected not only to be "story producers," in Herbert Gans's terminology, but also "story suggesters."[47] Newsbeat reporters follow routines as well, because, to begin with, the very fact of a newsbeat is an organizational acknowledgment of not only its importance but also its productivity. Both general assignment and newsbeat reporters go where news is expected to happen; they rely on sources in a position to know; and they assemble the resultant bits and bites of information into a coherent and satisfying account. That description holds for television and radio as well as for newspapers and newsmagazines.

As I mentioned in Chapter 1, these choices are generally hidden not only from audiences but from reporters themselves. After all, in assembling the final story, journalists scrupulously adhere to what Tuchman termed the "strategic ritual" of objectivity: deferring to expertise, presenting both sides of the story, providing intuitively persuasive supporting evidence, and generally obscuring the reporter's own hand.[48] With the resultant story being defensibly objective and factual, news takes on a life of its own, and one more story is added to Roshco's "lists of newsmaking events" for future reference.

But we should be careful before concluding that this dependence upon routines predetermines the news. Kurt Lang, in a response to an early draft of this argument,[49] disputed the idea that routine processes need make for routine news, and suggested that newsmaking might be more akin to improvisatory social processes. Sociologists who have studied rumor, such as Tamotsu Shibutani, have noted this group improvisation, how individuals "caught together in an ambiguous situation attempt to construct a meaningful interpretation of it by pooling their intellectual resources."[50]

And indeed, neither routine nor ritual closely shapes the final product. Tuchman doubted whether the "strategic ritual" actually got her subjects any closer to objectivity. Likewise, Elizabeth Bird has shown how the personnel of overtly sensational supermarket tabloids consider themselves to be journalists, adhere to many of the same rituals of objectivity as mainstream news media (such as relying on experts for quotes), and defend the similarities of their methods.[51] Most fully, Nina Eliasoph has incisively demonstrated the flexibility of journalistic routines from her participant observation at an oppositional daily news outlet, the Berkeley radio station KPFA. She notes that routines that lead to what she terms "politically complacent news" in mainstream media—for example, the focus on events rather than conditions, reliance on experts for stories and quotes, the daily production of a predictable amount of news, attempts for balance and away from editorializing—also characterize KPFA's operations. KPFA's divergence arises from a closer and more ideological awareness of the audience, which leads to different understandings of what is news and who can make it, even though the routines are the same.[52]

In other words, despite the omnipresence of routines, journalists exercise considerable discretion; in Lang's terms, they improvise. And indeed, such wiggle room may give reporters the autonomy they crave and perceive for job satisfaction.[53] As political scientist Lee Sigelman suggested from his study of two Nashville daily newspapers with differing ideological stances, reporters may gain satisfaction—while working within the bounds established by editors' assignments—by acting as artisans commissioned to carry out a project.[54] Even cub reporters can and do make conscious choices over the lead paragraph, whom to quote about what, the arrangement of the paragraphs, etc. Such autonomy from editorial purview increases when one moves from general assignment tasks to being stationed at a newsbeat. Although being a beat reporter means additional deference to the sources at that beat, this may be more than an even trade for journalists who thereby have access to information in ways their superiors cannot rival and who can thus begin to suggest storylines. Even at a newsbeat such as the White House—usually portrayed as the epitome of a reactive pack trapped in the briefing room waiting for handouts—reporters have many ways of crafting news that stamp the final product as theirs rather than the president's.[55]

But improvisation does not let a thousand journalistic flowers bloom. Think of one of the most improvisatory of arts: jazz. One may be amazed by the capacity of jazz musicians, sometimes barely knowing each other, to sit down and come up with an extraordinary and unique collective performance. But jazz is not a free-flow process. The very uniqueness of jazz is based on much that is shared—a well-known, fairly constrained repertoire of tunes; standard chord progressions; a standard number of bars for each instrumentalist's contribution; and preset understandings of who plays when—and reinforced over years of work and experience.[56] Likewise for reporters, there are a limited range of quality storylines, shared and set understandings of who can make news and how that enables them to both routinize their work and come up with news that is indeed unique and fresh.

Routines are crucial for individual newsworkers *and* the news organization as a whole to report the news. But another organizational factor prevents news from being merely the products of individual journalists: in even the most prestigious news organizations, reporters must "sell" their stories to their superiors.[57] Given that they wish to advance their careers, reporters aim for prominence in the publication or broadcast; that means they must anticipate the preferences of their superiors (producers in television, editors in print) and "pitch" their story ideas accordingly. In the process of so doing, reporters end up internalizing the expectations of their editors in coming up with news ideas. Yet reporters rarely see their superiors as expecting news of a particular slant and instead perceive them as sharing similar conceptions of newsworthiness.[58]

Now what does all of this have to do with the news media as an institution? Stated simply, rather than think of journalists as free-wheeling individuals writing their stories, it reminds us that they work according to unspoken and uncritically accepted routines, procedures, and rules of who and what make news. News, in short, is an organizational accomplishment first and foremost. Such decisions of newsworthiness are embodied in and inseparable from the daily work routines, which are understood to be the "natural" way to gather news. And, to remember Giddens's analogy, just as speaking is both constrained by and adds to language, so newsmaking is both constrained by and adds to the rules and routines of journalism and contributes to their utility and perpetuation.

THE MEDIA AS INSTITUTIONAL II: ENDURANCE OVER TIME AND EXTENSION ACROSS ORGANIZATIONS

Now, skeptics may ask, all of this is well and good, but this only indicates the centrality of the organizational component of newsmaking. Surely, such doubters would continue, one cannot talk about the news media as a single institution, given the range and variety of news organizations.

It is true that news organizations vary widely in terms of audience (national vs. local, upper-class vs. working-class), technology (electronic vs. print), periodicity (daily vs. weekly), and so forth. Yet in spite of all of these cross-cutting differences, both the process of newsmaking and the content of the news are so similar across organizations that we can begin to talk of the news media as a single institution. Recall the three pressures DiMaggio and Powell identified that push organizations within a given field to resemble each other: outside politics, uncertainty, professionalization. In each case, these pressures push different news outlets closer together.

As we have already seen in Chapter 3, the news media operate within similar political environments. Most notably, they converge on official sources to benefit from information subsidies, which gives them all a similar reliance on political power. To the extent that reporters turn to the same persons-in-a-position-to-know, the news content is bound to look alike. Moreover, we have also noted how public policy, whether through subsidies or through governmental accommodation of the news media, refers to newspapers or other news outlets as a class subject to regulation and/or to subsidies, as well as to reporters as a group that may gain access to governmental proceedings.

Professionalization, similarly, exerts its power on almost all reporters, given how the preoccupations with objectivity and interpretive diffusion of information are shared across the board.[59] Journalism, to be sure, is something of a curious profession, if we were to compare it to learned professions, such as lawyers and doctors. The latter demand specialized education and official certification by the state. These professions also have developed a highly technical language that both serves to make sense of their work and exclude possible competitors to their prestige. In addition, professional organizations (e.g., the American Medical Association and the American Bar Association) serve to protect the self-interest of the profession and police its ethics. By such standards, journalism is not much of a profession; according to recent surveys, most journalists still do not graduate from a journalism school, and most do not belong to a professional organization,[60] and as we have seen in the previous section newsgathering does not consist of the application of technical principles to specific cases.

Perhaps these indicators of professionalism are not crucial, though, if we remember Eliot Freidson's point that we may be confusing means and ends. Freidson persuasively argues that standard indicators such as specialized training and collective orientations do not distinguish well between professional and other occupations. Instead, "Once we define the profession primarily as a special status in the division of labor supported by official and sometimes public belief that it is worthy of such status, we are liberated from the confusion and special pleading which permeates most discussions of professions."[61] Or as another sociologist, Steven Brint, phrases it, a profession is both "a type of organization occupation and a type of status category."[62] A profession then relies less on formal characteristics than the belief that members of an occupation have a special status that enables them to exercise control over their own work.

In that sense, journalistic professionalism is not inherent in formal structures or in particular individual attitudes but is instead *performed* as part of their daily work.[63] Indeed, such performances may become ever more central, precisely because the journalistic profession is necessarily so poorly demarcated. Just as nobody knows what news is, nobody can say, with any degree of certainty, just who is a journalist and why.[64] Journalists' quite natural desire for autonomy then leads to particular performances—consisting of a series of rituals that protect objectivity, factuality, and other indicators of so-called journalistic ethics. To be sure, some of these attributes of professionalism allow individual news organizations to control journalistic work for the organization's own interest.[65] The typical example here is objectivity, which some have claimed to be an internalization of the economic need to appeal to a large, undifferentiated audience.[66] But professionalism also furthers similarity between news organizations, reinforced by codes of professional ethics, think tanks monitoring media performance, professional journals—most notably the *Columbia Journalism Review,* which, in each issue, issues "darts and laurels" to news organizations that have, respectively, violated or valued professional norms—and media critics and ombudsmen to keep tabs on each other and their own organizations. And the claims to professionalism also facilitate movement across organizations, as journalistic careers are frequently built not by rising within a single news organization but by moving from one to another.[67]

But neither politics nor professionalism fully explains the isomorphism of the news. Political pressures are no more prominent than the assistance that subsidies provide. Likewise, professionalization is incomplete and sometimes inchoate. Probably as crucial is the nagging uncertainty over what news is, who makes news, and how to produce it. Such uncertainty leads to convergence of news content and newsmaking processes among individual journalists and across news organizations.

Consider the following dilemma: if you are an editor supervising a given reporter's work, how do you know if that reporter has come up with the best, most factual, most accurate story? Editors may be a long way from the newsbeat, but they can and do readily check other available news outlets—newspapers of record, the wires, or, nowadays, CNN. Reporters are aware of this and may, consciously or not, craft their stories to fit the emerging reportorial consensus. Journalistic competition, in other words, does not push reporters toward the exclusive "scoop" but instead toward risk-averse consensus, on the presumption that the glory they get from the former is less than the trouble they might face if the scoop came into question or if they missed out on the big news story everyone else covered.

Here's how ABC's Ted Koppel phrased it in introducing a *Nightline* show on the very topic:

> We are a discouragingly timid lot. By "we," I mean most television anchors and reporters, and most of our colleagues of the establishment press, the big metropolitan dailies and news weeklies. Never mind the self-confident bluster of our headlines; we tremble between daydreams of scooping all of our competitors and the nightmare of standing vulnerable and alone with our scoop for too long. We enjoy being ahead of our rivals, but not too far ahead. An old friend and rival, Bernard Kalb, coined a rule to that effect: "Get it first, but first, get it second." Never, in other words, be too far in front of the pack.[68]

Timothy Crouse, in his marvelous classic on the news media during the 1972 presidential campaign, not only coined the term for this ("pack journalism") but provided telling examples. For instance, reporters who all witnessed the same event in its entirety (a debate between Democratic hopefuls Hubert Humphrey and George McGovern) harangued Walter

Mears, the AP reporter, into revealing his lead paragraph, which was then widely copied; the fate for those who did not do so was to get time-consuming "call-backs" from their editors.[69] Even more pointedly, the competence of the reporters may be called into question (even by themselves) if their account is not reinforced by others. Crouse describes how reporter Curtis Wilkie wrote an eyewitness version of a Humphrey rally where the candidate was nearly reduced to tears by student protestors.

> The next day, when Wilkie went into the office, the managing editor was laughing about the story. "We've kind of started wondering," he teased Wilkie. "Several people have called and said that they didn't see anything about Humphrey on Channel Six, and they seem to think you made it up. And we're beginning to wonder ourselves, because none of the wire services mentioned it." Wilkie began to sweat; he nearly convinced himself that he had grossly exaggerated the incident. Late that afternoon, Wilkie came across a piece . . . [that] agreed with Wilkie's. With great relief, Curt clipped the article and showed it to the managing editor.[70]

Notably, this willingness to consult across news outlets links together national and local, television and print media despite their clear differences in perceived audience, format, and technology. Such dependence becomes clearest in news organizations with limited resources, as weekly papers rely on the wires and local television stations turn to the metropolitan newspaper for story ideas. As one of McManus's subjects in local TV news in the late 1980s warned him, "Welcome to plagiarism news. We rely a lot on the newspaper . . . And we don't check the stories, just incorporate them into video."[71] But even more financially flush organizations imitate others. For example, Gans documented in the 1970s how broadcast news and newsmagazines alike turned to the *New York Times* "because they need to believe that someone is certain about news judgments."[72] Reporters, too, frequently attend to other news media for story ideas. For instance, when I asked Capitol Hill reporters how they decided what to cover, one broadcast network correspondent told me, "You start out with an idea of the story of the day . . . by looking at the *Washington Post,* the *New York Times,* the *Wall Street Journal,* the *Washington Times, USA Today.* I guess I read five papers every day. I get the *Post* at home and it's the first thing I see, so it shapes my impressions of what might be the flow of news today. I look at how we might move the story farther down the road, beyond where it's already been."[73] At its most basic, reporters rely on the daybooks of the wires to cull out events that are most important, providing a list from which they can then pick and choose.

Such attempts to reduce uncertainty do not befall only those stuck in the newsroom but also the more autonomous reporters stationed at newsbeats. After all, news organizations pay attention not just to each other's content but how they are equipped to gather the news, leading to similar assignments for reporters. Sometimes, this mutual reliance is explicit, as when a subset of beat reporters form a pool to cover what's happening and pass along the news to the rest. With reporters converging on only particular subjects and locales, newsbeats become social systems in and of themselves rivaling the newsroom.[74] Reporters nowadays may avoid the once-popular practice of "blacksheeting" (giving carbon copies of stories to one another), but they still cooperate with one another on a routine basis—providing information from a missed event, referring each other to someone who might help out, giving tips about upcoming media events, and gossiping.[75] Hearing other questions at a press conference or briefing will tip off reporters to stories that their counterparts are following. Cues for newsworthiness are often given in inadvertent ways, such as when reporters see when others pick up or put down pens, notice the TV cameras being turned off, or doodle on their steno pads and grouse to each other when news is not being made.[76]

News, then, is, in Leon Sigal's apt phrase, "consensible." Sigal goes on, "This group judgment . . . imparts a measure of certainty to the uncertain world of the newsman. If no newsman knows what an event means, whether or not it is news, or who the reliable sources are, then reaching some agreement with colleagues on what is news and how to write a story about it helps to authenticate the news."[77] Add to this the many occasions, such as the Washington breakfasts for reporters and officials hosted by Godfrey Sperling of the *Christian Science Monitor,* or the daily internet compendium of campaign coverage, the *Hotline,* that provide opportunities for a lot of journalists to find out instantly what a wide range of colleagues are thinking and saying—not to mention a chance for the reporters who get diffused to have their work validated and reinforced.[78]

Moreover, many studies have illustrated the similarity of news content as well as news processes.[79] To be sure, such likeness is at its height among those news organizations that partake of the same format and conceptions of an audience, such as the three broadcast networks; similarly, these resemblances extend less to the precise interpretation given to the news than to the shared understanding of what and who is newsworthy and why.[80] Thomas Patterson said it best: "Although the press is not monolithic in how events are reported, it is in which events are covered."[81]

In short, in contrast to an organizational thesis that would suggest different organizations attempting to reach their diverse goals most efficiently, news content is more institutional, varying primarily as a result of the resources the media could bring to bear on reporting, and by the news sources that could be found in different locales. Thus, in the mid-1970s, David Altheide claimed that national and local television news shared a common "news perspective." He found that the main differences were that local news relied upon a narrower circle of local sources, focused on local angles, and used more modest resources. Likewise, Gans saw the much-vaunted visual dimension of television to be similarly overblown, given that the pictures were chosen to illustrate the spoken text to the point that he could term television to be a form of "visual radio"— a finding recently replicated in Ronald Jacobs's participant-observation in Los Angeles local television news. Finally, Matthew Kerbel compared the processes and contents of newsmaking at ABC and CNN during the 1992 campaign; though the profit motives of ABC, concerned with keeping audiences tuned in, clearly diverged from those of CNN, expecting viewers to dip in and dip out, the news was much the same.[82]

Uncertainty about news reinforces consistency over time as well as across space.[83] When reporters cover a subject, their first response is often to turn to past coverage—in former times going to the "morgue" where stories are kept, or nowadays through electronic searches such as Nexis. By sensitizing themselves with previous angles, reporters often end up repeating that angle in new stories. In other ways, too, reporters learn over time that only certain approaches to stories are guaranteed to gain prominence in the news. Consequently, most news is highly formulaic, with a limited set of implicit "enduring values" that make for repetition over time, producing "novelty without change."[84] Even—or especially— in the case of news that breaks the routines, reporters hearken back to whatever precedents they can find. Tuchman witnessed an example of this when President Johnson startled his audiences in early 1968 by declaring, at the end of a policy speech, that he would not run for reelection:

> Lifting their heads to answer telephones, bark orders, and then clarify them, the editors periodically announced, "*What* a story! . . . The story of the century . . . What a night, what a night! . . . Who would have believed it? There's been nothing like it since Coolidge said, 'I will not run.' "[85]

Indeed, one hallmark of journalism is the long historical pedigree of its routines, roles, rules, norms, values, and self-concepts, predating most of the technologies used to capture today's news. As we have seen above, the ideal of impartiality goes at least as far back as American newspapers themselves. It began to adopt its modern guise of neutral journalists developing fact-centered narratives around the time of the beginnings of the penny press in the 1830s, when the search for a large audience necessitated playing down partisanship.[86] The contemporary focus of news on events and individual actors within continuing stories rather than analyses of social and political conditions might seem to be a natural result of the demands of the medium of television, but in fact it predates the broadcast media. It dates back to the Progressive Era's emphasis on cleaning up the system by placing well-qualified individuals in positions of power where they would administer in a nonpartisan manner. The Progressive Era would witness the profession of journalism developed and ensconced, and the terms of journalism and roles of journalists devised then have not significantly shifted, even with the rise of radio and television.[87] As with the evolution of other political institutions,[88] the news media's current practices embody many of the same political presumptions and concerns that were extant at the time of its institutionalization.

THE MEDIA AS INSTITUTIONAL III: THE POLITICS OF COMMUNICATION

Finally, in the United States, the privately owned news media are relied upon to provide communication from the elite to the public, as well as within the public as a whole. The latter point is straightforward enough: as the population grew and face-to-face communication became less viable, newspapers changed from their early task during the American colonial era as historical repositories of what was already known to revealers of otherwise unknown information.[89] And the public seems to see the role of the news media in similar ways. Ever since the sociologist Bernard Berelson's pathbreaking study of what people "missed" when their newspapers were on strike, we have known that citizens use the news, at base, to reassure themselves that nothing has happened that would have an impact on their lives since the last time they encountered the news.[90]

As for the political elites, we need only remind ourselves that, since the demise of the official newspaper in 1860, there has been (with only one brief exception, an official journal during the First World War) no official mass publication or government news program. Public officials do occasionally communicate directly with the public, but such attempts are clearly adjuncts to the version mediated through the news and often end up being interpreted through the frames that the media provide.

Part of this reliance is sheer practicality. Congressional press secretaries, for instance, find that the greater reach and credibility of newspapers makes them more useful than self-generated communications such as tar-geted mail or newsletters.[91] Even presidents can no longer garner large national audiences by asking the broadcast networks to air their speeches or press conferences; part of this results from the erosion of network audiences, but it also reflects the increased reluctance of profit-minded television to give up valuable broadcast time for a presidential request.[92] Indeed, President Clinton recently abandoned a forum that had been John Kennedy's key innovation with the news media—the evening press con-ference, televised live—and begrudgingly backtracked on his initial plan to anchor his presidency in going direct to the American people via talk shows and interviews.[93] And even in direct (albeit mediated) communica-tion such as presidential addresses and campaign debates, television view-ers often rely upon reporters to sift out the core meanings of those com-munications.[94]

But practicality is not the only issue here. There is also a philosophi-cal agreement, it seems, that government does and should rely upon the news media to disseminate the news, apparent not merely in the subsidies I outlined in the previous chapter but also in the congressional delibera-tions over such policies. Likewise, the evolving judicial interpretation of "freedom of the press" gives the news media not only greater protection from governmental interference but also a greater responsibility in politi-cal life. Indeed, one might go so far as to say that in the absence of linking institutions such as strong political parties or mass movements, the Amer-ican news media have been delegated the job of organizing the public sphere.[95]

Journalists have embraced the part of disseminating governmental information to the public. Most strikingly, David Weaver and Cleveland Wilhoit, in their excellent national survey of journalists in the mid-1980s, asked about several "things that the media do or try to do today." They found only a small minority (less than 20 percent) advocating a stance as adversary of government or of business; instead, a majority of their respondents endorsed one or both of two overlapping approaches—being a neutral disseminator of information to a wide audience, and interpret-ing policy processes and problems and government claims.[96] Notably, these roles seem to be endorsed across modalities, although there is a significant difference between large and small organizations.[97]

The extent to which journalists claim control over the task of dissemi-nating and interpreting government information emerges most clearly when it is under attack. A good example occurred at the beginning of the Clinton presidency in January 1993, when a hall near the press secretary's office was cordoned off to reporters, who seethed that Clinton, already under suspicion for suggesting that he would continue to reach the American people through talk shows, was trying to take away their political function. The dean of White House correspondents, UPI's Helen Thomas, complained, "They feel we are expendable, and if they make an end run, they will get a better press, if you will, with the people. Eventually, they should realize the president has to be interrogated, and has to be accountable, and we're the ones to do it."[98] Thomas was, consciously or not, echoing a public service announcement by the American Society of Journalists that ended with a similar question: "If the press won't do it, who will?"

CONCLUSION

I would then argue that the news media in the United States are more than a series of organizations devoted to efficiently servicing a wide range of diverse audiences. Indeed, the news media are something more than a series of institutions as well, and the strong similarities of news processes and news content across modalities (television, radio, newspapers, and newsmagazines), size of organization, national or local audiences, etc., point to the news media as a single institution.

Recall our three criteria for an institution: taken-for-granted social patterns of behavior valued in and of themselves encompass procedures, routines, and assumptions, which extend over space and endure over time, in order to preside over a societal sector. Given how newsworthiness is inextricable from the journalistic methods that created the news, given the wide consensus on news processes and content across a wide range of media and modalities, and given the way in which both officials and the public turn to the news media to provide the societal function of communication, it is clear that the news media are a *social* institution. But do the news media serve to help organize politics as much as society? That is the subject of the next chapter.

5

THE POLITICAL NEWS MEDIA

The news media should be thought of not only as an institution but as political; in other words, journalists are political actors. This does not mean that reporters have political axes to grind or are consciously pursuing particular partisan or ideological agendas. On the contrary, what is so complicated about assessing the political role of newspersons is that their political influence may emerge not in spite of, but because of, their principled adherence to norms of objectivity, deference to factuality and authority, and a let-the-chips-fall-where-they-may distance from the political and social consequences of their coverage.

Just as in Chapter 4, where so much depended upon one's definition of "institution," here we have to figure out just what is "politics." After all, if one defines politics broadly enough--as many now do—it becomes difficult to draw any useful line, or even to establish what is not political at some level, and the term loses its practical utility. This task is particularly difficult because, as William Connolly has nicely outlined, "politics" is the epitome of an "essentially contested concept." Its multidimensional complexity both prevents an easy clarification and ensures that an attempt to define "politics" is itself a political act.[1]

To avoid undermining my case with an understanding of "politics" that will not be understood as such by some readers, I will instead concentrate on a core definition on which all would agree, even if some would add further areas and actions that they consider political.[2] I start with David Easton's venerable definition: "What distinguishes political interactions from all other kinds of social interactions is that they are predominantly oriented toward the authoritative allocation of values in a society."[3] Although Easton's systems theory has been rightly neglected for not being much of an empirical theory at all, his definition of "politics" is highly useful. It captures three different processes. Politics is about choice for a society. Politics is also about which choices are considered to be "authoritative," that is, binding on individuals who do not indepen-

dently contest the bases of that choice. And if we use the dictionary definition of "allocation" to encompass both designation and distribution,
it is clear that politics both establishes what is valuable in society and
seeks to distribute such values. Unlike Easton's overall theory, moreover,
which stresses continuity if not stasis, his definition of politics need not
favor consensus over conflict. Much of politics may go quite smoothly.
But if we drop the remainder of Easton's theory in favor of his insightful
definition, it encompasses conflicts over who or what is authoritative as
well as what should be considered to be central values in a society.

I confess some sympathy with more expansive understandings of politics and of the state, such as neo-Marxist arguments pointing out the
arbitrary distinction between public and private institutions, both of
which influence and embody societal decision-making processes. In such
a model, the news media would be part of the state-apparatus or would
assist in the process of political-cultural hegemony. Yet I would defeat
my purpose in the long run given that the media may and should be
productively understood as a political institution under a variety of theoretical foundations.

How do the news media enter into the authoritative allocation of
values? One way is by reinforcing political power or otherwise providing
resources to official actors to pursue their agendas. Thus, many studies
have suggested that the political role of the news media lies in augmenting
the reach of those who are already politically powerful. In that sense,
they would be primarily influential in buttressing official authority and
less in the allocation of values.

But matters are not as simple as that. The news media are at least
partially independent from their sources in producing the content of the
news. Consequently, they may be able to influence who is authoritative,
what the values of politics are, and which allocations are made. The news
media share a similar fate with the three constitutional branches being
partially independent from and partially dependent on other institutions
for themselves to accomplish their own task.

In that sense, we can and should go beyond Easton's definition to
contend that the news media are not just political; in the modern United
States, they have become part of government.[4] Terming something governmental is more restrictive than terming something political. For instance, social movements should certainly be thought of as political but
not governmental. Though some definitions of government concentrate
on the role of coercion,[5] the fuzzy line between coercion and consent
turns our attention to the key role of authoritative and ordered rule. Bert
Rockman's phrase, "In broadest form, government constitutes the insti-

tutions of governance,"[6] is not as tautological as it first appears, if we think of governance as the process whereby public institutions reach authoritative decisions about public life in order to allocate public resources.

What contribution do the news media then make to the governing process? To begin, we must return to those abiding questions of media bias and media impact. After all, if the news media are successful—as they often claim to be[7]—in simply mirroring an outside world, then their contribution would be limited. I will then turn to the question of the politics of news coverage, which pushes in two divergent directions at once. On one hand, the news does indeed work to emphasize official action and thereby to implicate the news media more deeply into government. On the other, the news presents and interprets such actions by means of agreed-upon production values, which contain an implicit politics therein that is not always so beneficial to those official actors. Consequently the news is the result of recurring negotiations between sources and newspersons, the daily results of which favor only certain authoritative allocations of values.

BIAS AND IMPACT

News is necessarily selective. Reporters can attend to only so many possible events. Once their ideas are sold and crafted, the sample shrinks further. In Gans's apt phrase, news is "the highlight of highlights": reporters highlight the potential newsworthy elements of a particular event when they sell them to their superiors, while the latter then choose among those in deciding whether to give the go-ahead to the story and how to play it in the context of the overall news product.[8] News may not then be a representative sample of occurrences, but journalists can and do credibly respond that they have come up with the most important occurrences and persons to include in the news. The problem, of course, is that such a spotlight confers status as much as the other way around. Journalists can create importance and certify authority as much as reflect it, in deciding who should speak on what subjects under what circumstances.

Selectivity, in and of itself, does not automatically lead to bias. After all, one would not get a biased view of the world if the news took a random sample of all possible events every day. Selectivity leads to bias when, day in and day out, certain kinds of political actors, political stories, and political issues become more covered and more favorably reported than others. Indeed, studies document great similarity of the news from day to day—similar stories with many of the same actors from established newsbeats producing a regular amount of news.[9] The journalistic reliance on routines discussed in Chapter 4 means that the majority of reporters are better positioned to encounter only some sources and gather only some news and are therefore more inclined to create certain kinds of stories.

As some of the earliest studies of bias noted,[10] merely showing that one political actor received consistently more favorable coverage than another does not mean that the news organization is biased—implicitly or explicitly—for or against one or the other. As the political scientist Richard Hofstetter argued, we must distinguish between several kinds of bias—political bias (derived from individual or collective political preferences of newspersons); situational bias (a political actor engages in particular behaviors that are better or worse suited for coverage); and structural bias (political actors receive better coverage by meeting the demands of the medium, including the search for timely, clear-cut, easily described, vivid, colorful and visualizable stories).[11] Hofstetter's careful study of the coverage of the 1972 election campaign by the three broadcast networks, two metropolitan daily newspapers, and a wire service showed some structural and situational bias but little political bias.

At a deeper level, the news media are drawn to particular kinds of stories, with particular values, more than to others. Herbert Gans's list of "enduring values" from the early 1970s—social order, national leadership, altruistic democracy, responsible capitalism, individualism, smalltown pastoralism, and the like—are easily recognizable in the news of the mid-1990s, and they reveal not merely journalists' understanding of how the world works but suggest a conception of how the world *should* work.[12] Gans speculated that the news reflects the reformist urges from the Progressive Era when journalism's modern approaches were to gel.[13] Consequently, the news favors nonpartisan and open politics, is suspicious of large bureaucracies and enterprises, and celebrates individual rather than collective approaches to public problems to the point that it may be rightly called "antipolitical."

However, such preferences are rarely explicitly enunciated by journalists, either in their newswork or in self-defense. Indeed, journalists' story preferences reflect a normative order more by their emphasis on threats or violations to that order. Gans concluded, for instance, that "the news defends democratic theory against an almost inevitably inferior democratic practice."[14] That means that journalists have the option to deliver negative assessments of the powerful, which have apparently accelerated since the 1970s when Gans conducted his research.[15] Although the normative order of altruistic democracy is then defended, such negative news does not comfort those who wish to believe that the system as a whole, let alone the incumbents, are doing a good job. The values thereby may be kept pure but at the expense of a critique of official power.

But the "enduring values," norms that scholars identify within the news, have little to do with the norms that journalists themselves would specify if we posed the question to them. The term "norm" thus has a different status for political scientists who study journalists than versus those who examine other political actors—at least to judge from the famous work on norms among members of Congress in the fifties and sixties that specified norms and folkways of Capitol Hill (e.g., reciprocity, institutional loyalty, apprenticeship, expertise) by observation, interviews, and surveys.[16] Journalists, when examining their work as well as that of others, are instead more likely to talk about stylistic questions (objectivity, specificity, drama, excitement, good visuals, etc.) rather than political notions of how the world works and how the world should work.[17] Production values, it appears, are at least as important to journalists—probably more so—as political values. After all, in the words of ABC's political director, Hal Bruno, "Politics is what I cover. Journalism is my life."

How can we connect, then, the work that journalists perform with the products they create? The usual response has been that work routines of journalists and journalism contain implicit biases. The search for newsworthy stories and newsworthy events does not equally favor all political actors and all issues. Given that news is commonsensically expected to be both important and interesting, journalists defer to official sources to cue them into important events and issues but are more inclined to reserve the power to decide whether something is interesting enough to run prominently in the news.

Thus, while politicians dictate conditions and rules of access and designate certain events and issues as important by providing an arena for them, reporters can and do take this material while deciding whether something is interesting enough to cover and then how to craft it into a coherent narrative. Journalists bring their own particular conceptions of newsworthiness to bear when they approach their work. In Gans's terms, sources may make themselves *available,* and reporters may be under considerable pressure to report on them in ways that the sources find congenial. But sources cannot make news unless and until journalists consider the initiatives to make for *suitable* news. Such considerations hearken to institutional criteria of what makes for a quality story rather than to the political and policy ends that the sources seek.[18]

Conflict is then built into the system of newsmaking. Above all, for any news medium, whatever the source does must be packaged into a narrative. Not only must the story have protagonists and antagonists in conflict, but the sources' actions must move the story along to a new episode. In the absence of such movement, journalists tend to conclude that "nothing happened" and there is therefore no news[19]—and if journalists do not consider something to be newsworthy by their own criteria for judgment, a source's power may not be enough to get it in print or on the air. At other times, sources may provide access to journalists for a particular purpose only to find that they have also unwittingly made themselves available to be questioned on other matters the journalists may find more newsworthy. Even when access is limited or controlled, their responses can be easily placed into another and often less favorable context.

Such a bias—and such a power—can be wielded by journalists, not in spite of but because of the power of objectivity. Reporters engage in explicit exclusion of values, by adhering to objectivity, disregarding the implications of their coverage, and by ignoring their own personal points of view. But they end up implicitly including other values, those that are inherent in work routines and the definitions of what makes for a "quality" story.[20] The taken-for-granted aspect of news, newsmaking, and newsworthiness that we considered in the previous chapter all contribute to journalists' nonconsciously biased accounts even (or especially) while they apply disinterested and apparently content-neutral criteria of objectivity and quality.

This built-in conflict leads to a process of newsmaking focused around what I have elsewhere termed the "negotiation of newsworthiness"[21]—the constant if implicit negotiations between political sources and journalists. With both sides controlling key resources, the negotiation is never one-sided. To be sure, we should adopt a fairly broad approach to "negotiation." Rather than restrict ourselves to overt bargaining over precise ways to solve agreed-upon problems, I follow the lead of others who define negotiation more broadly to encompass not just the whole range of interactions but also how the parties to a negotiation learn about each other and anticipate what the actual bargaining will be like.[22] As anthropologist P. H. Gulliver points out: "Throughout the process of interaction, the parties give each other information, directly and indirectly . . . Negotiation is a process of discovery. Discovery leads to some degree of reorganization and adjustment of understanding, expectations and behavior, leading (if successful) eventually to more specific discussion . . ."[23]

Now, sources and journalists have some interest in cooperation and collaboration, particularly in building a stable exchange relationship whereby journalists receive information in exchange for the publicity they offer sources. But such exchanges are fragile, because this interest is at least partially counterbalanced by the ongoing tensions between what sources want and what journalists want to get out of the news. A more expanded notion of negotiation would include stable exchange and the social system in which that relationship occurs, as well as the direct conflicts and bargaining over what information will be provided under what circumstances. But we should not neglect the ways in which journalists and political actors learn about and anticipate the other side, sometimes when they are isolated from each other. Thus, political actors can and do anticipate what is likely to attract journalists when planning their actions and words; likewise, journalists can and do anticipate what their sources' reactions will be to the story that they have crafted from the information that the sources have provided to them.

The result of all these negotiations, I will argue, is a political coloration to the news that consistently favors only certain approaches and outcomes. Whether or not problems and issues can rise to the American political agenda through the media depends on two things. First, the issues must be connected to powerful "authoritative sources." Second, they must be linked to journalistic criteria for quality news. The political power, and the political impact, of the news media are thus somewhat contradictory. The first serves to give greater access to the news—and by extension to the public sphere—to officials, who thereby have resources to direct attention to particular problems and issues (and away from others), to initiate (or close down) discussion and debate, and to frame responsibility and dodge blame. But the second implies that while officials have an easier time entering the public sphere, they cannot get their messages across in an unfiltered way. The production values of the news directs them—and us—toward particular political values and politics: not so much pushing politics either consistently left or right as toward officialdom and toward standards of good stories that do not make for equally good political outcomes.

OFFICIAL NEWS

Having established that the news media do not simply mirror the world, we can now ask the role that the news plays in the authoritative allocation of values. Let's begin with "authority." Journalists, of course, have to be concerned with who or what is authoritative enough to appear on the news, since the credibility of those sources will rub off on the overall report. Consequently, reporters constantly gravitate toward "persons in a position to know," whereby they may then defend themselves from potential criticism against giving airtime or print space to someone who did not deserve it. This preoccupation with who is authoritative enough to be quoted in the news is revealed by the ways in which sources are identified—such as in television, where the "supers" at the bottom of the screen tell us not only the name of the person speaking but also his or her official title or stereotypical role ("victim's stepfather," "concerned neighbor").

Yet, in this process, reporters do not only reflect authority; they reinforce if not confer it as well. And indeed, reporters do take care to note that anyone they quote—even a relatively powerless person—is qualified to discuss whatever it is they are speaking about. Presumably, parents of someone who has been murdered can speak with authority about the sadness of the death of a child, or someone whose house has been destroyed by a tornado can speak with authority about their resolve to rebuild their home. The key distinction is not whether powerful and powerless sources speak with authority so much as their relationship to the events that are in the news. The communication scholar Grace Ferrari Levine has documented how the more power the sources have, the more likely they are to be shown as making events happen, whereas for relatively powerless sources, they are portrayed as victims where events have happened to them.[24]

Thus, the first central bias of the American news media is the focus on official action, which permits the governmental role of the American news media. The contemporary interpenetration of the media and governmental institutions act, in Blumler and Gurevitch's thought-provoking phrase, as "a subtly composite unity."[25] Each increasingly relies upon the other to assist in the accomplishment of its own task.

Take the news media first—recall that modern journalism in the United States places a priority upon gathering information from sources who can provide raw (or more correctly, predigested) material for stories. For newsbeat reporters, we have already seen the ways in which the public relations infrastructure subsidizes and enables the regular production of news and places each day's development within the larger unfolding script of institutional action.

First, the newsbeat system as a whole tends to gravitate toward political institutions when defining reporters' responsibilities. Not only do newsbeats enable a reliable production of news on a variety of subjects, but it also gives some variety by means of quoted sources at the beat. In spite of such seeming variety, however, the newsbeat system may still overrepresent particular points of view. Thus, in my study of the first two months of broadcast news coverage after Iraq's invasion of Kuwait in 1990, the story of the invasion and the response thereto was divided among several newsbeats: White House, State Department, Pentagon, Capitol Hill, business, and what I called "the hinterlands"—that is, news filed from beyond the usual hubs of New York and Washington. Although different newsbeats concentrated on different characters (e.g., the White House dominated by President Bush, the Pentagon with a proportionately larger group of experts and analysts, the hinterlands being about the only place where average people could get into the news, etc.) and emphasized different processes (e.g., White House politics, State Department policy, Pentagon military operations), the newsbeat system overrepresented administration policy, producing across the beats a complementary understanding that suggested a military response to the invasion was inevitable.[26]

In that sense, we must look at the newsbeat system not only for the news it makes possible but for the news it discourages. For instance, the prominence of separate business sections in newspapers and business reporters on television presumably makes it easier for CEOs to gain access compared to union leaders who rarely have so much as a labor page to turn to these days. Take Tuchman's evocative image of a "news net": "The narrower the intersections between the mesh . . . the more can be captured. Of course, designing a more expensive narrow mesh presupposes a desire to catch small fish, not a wish to throw them back into the flow of amorphous everyday occurrences. Today's news net is intended for big fish."[27]

Officials are big fish. But beyond governmental processes being the subject matter, and official sources being quotably useful, government enables reporters to know when news happens, where they are in the development of the overall storyline, where it will go next, and who the principal characters are in that story—the sources who are either "in a position to know," preferably in a designated position of power within official hierarchies, or in a position to affect the final outcome, such as by providing a swing vote or acting as spokesperson for a recognized bloc. What is most productive for journalists is to turn to official actors who should be expected to disagree (e.g., Democrat vs. Republican, Congress vs. president, prosecutor vs. defense attorney, etc.). As Mark Fishman elegantly proposes, the sources' disagreements become the "two sides of the story"; any agreement constitutes "the facts of the case."[28]

Newsbeat reporters do interact with colleagues from other news organizations and sources, but usually on terms of access set down by political actors.[29] The temptation is then strong to "go native" and adopt the norms and values of the institution being covered. After all, reporters must try to figure out what makes the institutional actors tick, and selling the story to one's editors and producers means not only placing those individuals as their key protagonists but also adopting a vision of that institution as a crucial player. As a result, in Tuchman's words, newsbeat journalists "ask the questions appropriate to their sources' world."[30]

Moreover, dealing with sources alters the dynamics by which news stories are created, particularly if those sources are cooperative and forth-coming—or if they might later deny access if they suspect unfair reporting. In a 1989 symposium in *Columbia Journalism Review* on writer Janet Malcolm's self-criticism that sources' lives could be appropriated for journalists' stories, for instance, one reporter noted, "I think the journalist has a responsibility not to take advantage, for the sake of his own article, of the kind of human, weak, foolish things that we all do and say in the course of our lives . . . To me that is like breaching the sort of social contract you have entered into. It's a different matter if you are doing a story about a person who hasn't cooperated; the same sort of social contract doesn't exist."[31]

But newsbeat reporters are not alone in depending on official sources. The same is true of both those with less autonomy (general assignment reporters who are given a particular story by their superiors) and those with more (investigative reporters freed from the day-in–day-out grind). Gans has nicely outlined the pluses and minuses to relying on newsbeat reporters versus general assignment reporters; while the former are often socialized into a particular newsbeat culture and fret about their continuing contact with their official sources, the latter "do not have to worry about maintaining rapport with people they will never see again, and can more easily ask leading, loaded, or provocative questions."[32] This potential is counterbalanced, however, by the general assignment reporters' unfamiliarity with anyone beyond the most obvious sources—generally officials—and their reluctance to delve further for fear that it will complicate their ability to carry out their task on time.

Even investigative reporters rely heavily on official sources. The legendary investigative reporter, Bob Woodward of the *Washington Post*, may be unusually skillful in teasing out information, but it is well-known that he uses the stock-in-trade of mainstream journalists: interviewing people in a position to know rather than the tedious and potentially dead-end culling of documents. More fully, in the best study of investigative journalism, a team of scholars based at Northwestern University examined a series of cases where they had been tipped off in advance of the story, enabling them to chart both the development of the story and its impact on elite and mass opinion.[33] In particular, they tested what they called "the Mobilization Model" whereby the media publicize wrongdoing and then the public responds and puts pressure on politicians to enact reforms. Contrary to the impression that reporters start with an anonymous tip and move on from there, their information on wrongdoing often depends upon "the constant cooperation of official sources—more often politicians and bureaucrats than whistleblowers—to obtain government records and quotes for their stories."[34] What emerges is "coalition journalism," whereby enterprising policymakers and investigative reporters carve out a pact that pushes a policy problem in the news and raises its visibility and its place on the political agenda.[35]

The dominance of officialdom in American newsmaking can also be seen by the general difficulty that most persons outside of government have in serving as authoritative sources. Government officials tend to be the most often quoted sources for the news, particularly for Washington reporting.[36] In part, unofficial activists are not always organized to make news.[37] They often lack the resources to have a designated spokesperson sitting near a phone, even if their ideology did endorse such hierarchy and specialization. If groups do have such resources, they may simply elect to take their message directly to the people via advertisements rather than depend on the unpredictable news. And at other times, activists may be split about the importance and benefits of getting in the news.

Moreover, unofficial activists are usually not located at a standard newsbeat, given that the most prestigious newsbeats tend to be oriented around political institutions, or even social institutions (e.g., medicine, law) rather than issues. As a result, routine newsmaking gives most groups and movements little involvement with processes, and events that reporters will encounter and deem newsworthy are often scant. Without being able to routinize newsmaking on their end, some groups and movements never figure out how. As media scholar/activist Charlotte Ryan points out from one of her case studies, "This level of media work is the norm for many challenger organizations—their activities meet media notions of newsworthiness only occasionally, once or maybe twice a year, if that. This has intrinsic drawbacks; members can hardly learn sophisticated handling of news routines when contact with the media is so sporadic."[38]

In general, unofficial activists become newsworthy only under certain circumstances. First, they intersect with an already established newsbeat, where standard norms of newsworthiness favor expertise dictated by the commonsense understanding of how a continuing story on that beat unfolds. Social movements often receive remarkably different coverage, depending on how they are perceived to line up with official sources. One example of this divergence comes from amidst the civil disobedience at abortion clinics by the pro-life movement, Operation Rescue, in Wichita in the summer of 1991. Whereas the ABC reporter presented a cool and even-handed account that stressed (both in images and words) the orderliness of the demonstrations and a pep talk from Kansas's pro-life governor, the CBS account was much more dramatic, with close-ups of demonstrators being dragged off by police and soundbites from the local federal judge who was throwing the book at them.[39] Overall, the ability of activists to enter into a given discussion in the news relies fundamentally on official divisions that provoke reporters into generating debate, which is often, as the political scientist Lance Bennett calls it, "indexed" to the range of elite opinion.[40]

A second alternative is to risk disruptive news, which may gain coverage without control of the news, particularly if reporters turn to official sources to interpret the disruption. Think of it this way: demonstrators at the White House will almost always be balanced by a soundbite from a presidential spokesperson, whereas we all know there is plenty of White House news that is not automatically counterbalanced by reporters turning to demonstrators outside.

Third is to wait for an accident to occur that reveals the problem one had been pushing all along. Accidental news reminds us that authoritative sources are not always organized to make news. Officials gain access by being able to preschedule news; but when unscheduled accidents hit, the news may turn to individuals and groups that don't usually make news. Harvey Molotch and Marilyn Lester found in their pathbreaking study of the coverage of the 1969 Santa Barbara oil spill, that as the event receded over time the professionally honored reliance upon official sources reasserted itself, there was at least a brief window of opportunity for the opposition to be heard and to cast doubt on the willingness of officials to play down the accident.[41]

For an accidental story to have, in the journalistic parlance, "legs," it must be both empirically validated and elicit an official controversy or official response. The political scientist Regina Lawrence's study of how the beating of Rodney King by several Los Angeles police officers became big news is especially intriguing for showing the contrast with an earlier attempt by black activist Don Jackson to call attention to police brutality in the nearby city of Long Beach by provoking a beating with video cameras rolling. The Jackson story got a short burst of media coverage but fizzled out, as officials began questioning the authenticity of the incident; by comparison, King's beating persisted not only because it was filmed by an apparently objective stranger but because officials in Los Angeles used it as an indication of deep problems within the LAPD.[42]

A fourth possibility is to avoid the front-page hard news altogether and rely on the human interest story, which allows persons outside of authoritative positions to be in the news. Tuchman, for one, conceded that the "women's page" in the early years of the feminist movement may have ghettoized women's issues, but she concluded that, given its freedom from the standard routines of newsmaking, it offered a greater opportunity to air and discuss concerns than was the case when, as the feminist movement gained political power, stories were transferred to the front page.[43] Similarly, Gitlin documented how the journalistic "discovery" of the Students for a Democratic Society (SDS) in the mid-sixties occurred with respectful analytic stories outside of the standard news accounts in the *New York Times* and *CBS Evening News*.[44]

The dominance of official voices is not however simply because it is more efficient for newspersons to focus on them. Not only are officials well organized to help subsidize the news, but their presumed authority allows reporters to craft a defensible account. And at its most basic, journalists end up judging the utility of information at least as much by who says it than what it says. An "authoritative source" is an individual given a leading role in the narrative of that newsbeat. Someone in an official role within the governmental hierarchy tends to endow information with the credibility of his or her position in the hierarchy and/or with his or her involvement in the decision-making process; that same person outside that position saying the same thing would be more likely to be seen as providing speculation or hearsay.

But the greater access of official sources to the news does not mean, contrary to some scholars, that the news merely supports the status quo. To take one example, John Soloski damages an otherwise fine article by this incorrect syllogism: "News sources, then, are drawn from the existing power structure; therefore news tends to support the status quo."[45] Reporters' reliance on official sources for information and staged events does not determine what they do with the raw (or predigested) material they are given. For that, we must consider how reporters' production values influence the political tone and impact of their reports. The authoritative allocation of values may not occur by reporters overtly worrying about political values; instead, their production values may well push them toward favoring certain politics and certain political actors.

PRODUCTION VALUES AND POLITICAL VALUES

When most of the now-classic participant-observation studies of news organizations were written in the 1970s, production values seemed to be considerably less important than decisions about importance. To take one good example, Gans argued that production values entered in only as stories became less important.[46] But in the twenty-odd years since then, the news media have changed considerably, with greater concentration of ownership and more profit-oriented management. And the economic imperative to crank out a product on a regular basis that will attract an audience that advertisers will pay to reach may provide a greater and greater counterweight to the reliance on officialdom. Judgments of importance may or may not carry the day, especially since the balance that was hit in the 1970s has shifted by the 1990s. Standards of importance now pale next to the storytelling imperative for local television news; the diminishing corps of Washington network reporters is under increasing pressure to zip up their reports; and even the august *New York Times* under Max Frankel's leadership in the late 1980s began to promote reporters more on the basis of stylish prose than substantive scoops.[47] In addition, the news media as a whole are becoming more interpretive, with fewer stories "pegged" to the news of the day. Newspapers had already begun to carve out this niche, when it became clear to them that their readers would have gotten much of the breaking news from the previous evening's network news; now, the three broadcast networks are also becoming more analytic and interpretive, with segments like ABC's "Solutions" or CBS's "Eye on America" that focus on "news you can use" or more narrative-oriented pieces, given that all-news stations on radio and television may have beaten them, too, to the punch.

While governmental processes provide the stages, the actors and the lines for the accounts that journalists create, the latter cut and paste these elements together according to their own standards of quality and interest, which may well diverge from the optimal "spin" of the politicians. Recall again the answer that Lee Sigelman gave when observing how general assignment reporters at two Nashville newspapers with different political leanings could lay claim to both objectivity and autonomy: think of reporters as artisans commissioned to carry out a project.[48]

Sigelman's notion also directs our attention to an aspect of their work that, as the cultural historian Robert Darnton brilliantly reminded us over twenty years ago, remains curiously underexamined: journalists assemble *stories*. Darnton drew on his own experience as a cub reporter at the *Newark Star-Ledger* and the *New York Times*. Darnton, in one anecdote, had failed to get a by-line in his brief journalistic career at Newark. He decided to practice with a police report about a boy whose bicycle had been stolen in a park. He assembled a story and showed it to a veteran reporter, who told Darnton that he had written it "as if it were a press release" instead of a flesh-and-blood story. Without referring at all to the original, the veteran typed out a sample saga:

> Every week Billy put his twenty-five-cent allowance in his piggy bank. He wanted to buy a bike. Finally, the big day came. He chose a shiny red Schwinn, and took it out for a spin in the park. Every day for a week he rode proudly around the same route. But yesterday three toughs jumped him in the middle of the park. They knocked him from the bike and ran off with it. Battered and bleeding, Billy trudged home to his father, George F. Wagner of 43 Elm Street. "Never mind son," his dad said. "I'll buy you a new bike, and you can use it on a paper route to earn the money to pay me back." Billy hopes to begin work soon. But he'll never ride through the park again.

Darnton then phoned the father to ask a new set of questions drawn from this story, about the amount of the boy's allowance, whether he saved in a piggy bank, the color of the bicycle, and the like. "Soon, I had enough details to fit the new pattern of the story. I rewrote it in the new style, and it appeared the next day in a special box, above the fold, on the front page, and with a by-line."[49] Note that Darnton made nothing up. The story was not fiction; the formula directed his attention toward certain questions that could be used to elicit and retell a familiar but true story.

Of course, this narrative dimension of newswork is most apparent (and most studied) in television news. Political scientist Edward Jay Epstein's pioneering examination of NBC News reprinted a now-famous memo from Reuven Frank, then executive producer of the evening news broadcast:

> Every news story should, without any sacrifice of probity or responsibility, display the attributes of fiction, of drama. It should have structure and conflict, problem and denouement, rising action and falling action, a beginning, a middle, and an end. These are not only the essentials of drama; they are the essentials of narrative.[50]

And indeed, television news stories may look like the last province of structuralists, filled with strings of theses-antitheses-syntheses until the moral of the story (the tag line at the close) is intoned by the beat reporter, and the story is bridged by the anchor to the next narrative (or to a teaser to keep the viewer tuned in past the next spate of commercials).

The storytelling imperative on broadcast news is particularly prominent given the need to keep audiences tuned in. But the television news
format is, by now, so ensconced that it has been adopted by news outlets
that do not share that same economic motivation—most intriguingly,
CNN, which, given its round-the-clock format, would be more inclined
to expect viewers to sample the news rather than keep one station on.[51]

Newspaper stories, too, are stories, even though the "inverted pyra-
mid" form of newspaper accounts—which goes from most central to
most peripheral information—would seem not to have much to do with
narrative. First, any news story has the characteristics of narrative discussed by Frank—protagonists and antagonists, conflict, movement, and
(at least momentary) resolution. Moreover, to be able to crank out news
on a regular basis, reporters gravitate toward continuing sagas that can
give them an ongoing process to cover for more than a day. Not only
does this further routinize the news (not only generating stories for today
but helping to do so for tomorrow), it gives them a chance to try to fulfill
a venerable mission of the news—indicate where things are and where
they're going so that news audiences can react accordingly and intervene
if need be.

Most of all, if journalists can identify a continuing story, they are
able to ascertain newsworthy moments and give larger meaning to
passing events. Fishman, studying the habits of a city hall press corps,
concluded that reporters, faced with an ongoing institutional process,
construct an idealized "phase structure" (presidents ordering and
commanding, legislatures passing laws, courts deciding cases, etc.) that
can then be broken down into discrete units. News happens when the
process moves from one of these phases to the next. Similarly, Michael
Schudson has argued, "To ask 'Is this news?' is not to ask only 'Did it
just happen?' It is to ask 'Does this *mean* something?' " He provides this
example:

> Election stories are easy to report not so much because something newswor-
> thy happens each day in an election campaign . . . The reporter, the editor,
> and the reader all know *where they are* in the story—near the beginning,
> the middle, or the end. The election story has a cadence, a rhythm, and is
> easier to read and absorb because readers can tap out the beat.[52]

Such an emphasis on storytelling as a way of making sense of the
world should not be surprising, given the "scripted" nature of much of
human interaction and understanding.[53] But news is not merely made
up of daily narratives. The news stories each day are episodes of larger
continuing sagas that help the audience to construct "meta-messages."[54]

Simply put, for news to be produced routinely, journalists must be able to visualize each episode as merely one part of a larger, broader storyline and must figure out a way to move the plot seamlessly to the next chapter.

Consequently, the sine qua non of news is not conflict in and of itself but an endless series of conflicts and momentary resolutions. Conflict may be one of the few cross-cultural characteristics of news.[55] But without some resolution in sight, conflict is not newsworthy, because it does not move the narrative along to a new episode. A reporter whom I accompanied for a day on Capitol Hill in 1988 put it this way: "I made the judgment that the contras were going [today] to be a White House story, that there's nothing happening, that things muddled along, that there's no news . . . The House is taking up the budget resolution so we should have a story. With the contras, there's nothing on the level of a story because nothing's been decided."[56] A recent demonstration of the non-newsworthiness of conflict without movement would be the deadlock in late 1995 and early 1996 between President Clinton and congressional Republicans over the details of the seven-year balanced budget plan. After a while, once negotiations were not producing results, the news began referring to the conflicts as "bickering," "squabbling," or a just plain "mess."

If anything, this search for a storyline is even stronger in other forms of journalism which are not so "pegged" to breaking events as is usually the case with newsbeat reporters. And here, whether in the "back of the book" in newsmagazines or with timeless "evergreen" feature stories that can be used to fill out the news, that the storytelling imperative is even stronger. The criterion of importance wanes as one moves away from the front-page in newspapers or from lead stories in television news, further elevating "interest" as a criterion for quality, which focuses more on characteristics of good stories, such as drama, color, vividness, etc., or on formulaic stories that encapsulate the enduring values. At the other extreme, investigative journalism—where considerable resources are expended and journalistic independence is at its height—all but requires a clear plot with villains and victims for the story to become part of the news.[57]

The storytelling imperative, then, is strong throughout the news—the conflict/resolution pattern of the breaking news as it fits in as a single episode of a larger script, or the search for "good stories" to fill out the rest of the newspaper, magazine, or broadcast, or the investigative report with villains and victims. But, of course, not all narratives are created equal.

THE NEGOTIATION OF NEWSWORTHINESS

Each side then controls important resources. We now need to consider the ways that sources and reporters negotiate the news and thereby allocate values. Conflicts with officials arise when the latter do not give reporters material that meet production values. To be sure, the centrality of journalistic autonomy, as a hallmark of professionalism and a contributor to job satisfaction, has long provoked reporters to find ways to distance themselves from the sources, raise questions about what the sources are saying and doing, and generally assemble as independent an account as possible. But, in addition, if reporters are under increasing pressure to produce more news, they may have to figure out how to make journalistic silk purses out of the sow's ears that officials occasionally give them. (Indeed, legends adhere to reporters who were able to create a story out of something that otherwise would not be news.)[58] The flip side is that individuals out of power also can make news on their own terms, if (although perhaps only if) the material they provide is high in the production values that would make the news interesting. We see these dynamics below at either end of the spectrum of power—one in the White House, where presidents never get quite the coverage they want (and think they deserve); the other in social movements, where newsmaking is sporadic and almost always on reporters' terms but which can set the agenda and shift the terms of the debate.

The negotiation of newsworthiness occurs simultaneously on several different levels. One is the explicit battle over the forums in which interactions will occur, as officials and reporters seek to specify the conditions and circumstances under which they will meet. Another is the explicit interaction within those forums, perhaps exemplified by the give-and-take of press conferences. Finally, an indirect and implicit negotiation goes on when each party to the negotiation is out of sight of the other—as sources anticipate what will make news, and as reporters go back to their home organizations with the raw material and reshape it into a coherent news account.

First of all, sources and reporters negotiate the *process* of newsmaking. Take recognized authoritative sources, usually officials; journalists need them to create events and answer questions that they can then use in assembling their stories. Yet such sources are unlikely to keep their door open to any and all reporters. As officials' power, authority, and attractiveness to the news media grow, they are both more likely to and more able to dictate terms of access; indicate which modalities can be used to record their meeting; specify whether the questions are on the record, not for attribution, off the record, background or deep background; choose who will ask the questions or if questions will be permitted at all at a speech, statement, or photo opportunity; decide how to respond; and unilaterally opt when to stop.

Presidential press conferences are probably the most familiar format here. Presidents, not reporters, decide when press conferences will be held. They may open with a statement that more or less sets the agenda for their interaction, recognize questioners (sometimes doing so in order to change the subject or get a soft query), can decide whether to take a follow-up question, can run out the clock by evasive blathering, and can halt the proceedings after a certain number of questions.[59] Although the presidential press conference is established to the point of institutionalization, other officials are freer to improvise. Thus, during the opening weeks of his Speakership, Newt Gingrich held daily briefings with the news media, much as his predecessors had done but with the crucial difference that television was invited in, until the questions became increasingly distant from the agenda Gingrich wished to pursue, and then the briefings were summarily abolished. And if presidents are uncomfortable in the give-and-take of news conferences, they can substitute other forms of communication that permit even less participation on the part of journalists.

To be sure, there are limits on what official sources can do. For instance, presidents, despite occasional rhetoric to the contrary, rarely freeze out reporters or challenge their credentials. Attacks on individual journalists are likewise deemed unpresidential. And if reporters feel overtly pressured, they can always show the attempts to shut them up—as a CNN reporter did in early 1993 when President Clinton's then-director of communications, George Stephanopoulos, was televised hidden in back of a camera instructing CNN's White House correspondent, Wolf Blitzer, that the president never said what Blitzer was alleging.

But journalists do not have much power with officials in the negotiation of process. Only when they are deemed less crucial to news stories do reporters have much say over the ways in which they meet and interact with their sources. White House correspondents thus have been commonly identified as the exemplars of reactive journalism; some observers have seen the news media as virtual extensions of the White House, restricted by pack journalism, rarely questioning the president's agenda, and willingly participating in photo opportunities and other media events.[60] But by focusing exclusively on the negotiation of process, where officials have an advantage, such a view underestimates the capacities of journalists to prevail when it comes to another negotiation of newsworthiness: that of *content*—what the story will be all about, and whether it will be positive, negative, or neutral.

The negotiation of content is less dominated by authoritative sources, because they cannot control so neatly what other sources are saying, let alone what other stories are being reported from other newsbeats in Washington, across the country, and around the globe. Big stories may emerge that deflect attention away from carefully crafted events.

Even on stories that authoritative sources instigate, in forums they largely control, newsbeat reporters can and do "weave" comments and quotes gathered by themselves or their colleagues into their report. Thus, the many advantages that officials have in the negotiation of process do not carry over. For instance, the open access that Washington reporters have to a wide range of members of Congress means that, although Congress itself is less in the news, journalists can easily take a cue from congressional opinion about presidential actions.[61] Moreover, since journalists must find conflict to report, reliance on Congress can fit into two key Washington scripts: Democrat-versus-Republican and Congress-versus-president. Add the plethora of interest groups cranking out press releases, experts at think tanks whose job includes providing pithy (even glib) analysis and the ever-present possibility of taking a poll or going out to the hinterlands to see how the person-in-the-street responds, and even the president's power over the ultimate totality of the news may be quite limited.

All of this means that, in spite of the hermetically sealed White House press room, news from the White House newsbeat is not always news from the White House's chosen perspective. I reported elsewhere a study of seven different presidential media events, as recorded on C-SPAN, and the nightly broadcast network news coverage thereof from the first six months of the Bush presidency (chosen because of the diversity of forums Bush used, and reporters' perception of a more open, varied, and amiable relationship, compared to his immediate predecessor and successor). In all of the stories, presidential quotes consistently take up much less than half of the time of the White House reporter's account, and it is rare for more than half of the visuals to be of the president. In other words, most of the White House stories are taken up with audio and video from other sources—members of Congress, Washington experts, file footage, or the journalists themselves. And journalists can be highly selective, not only of who else to quote but of what to show from the presidential appearances themselves. In the Bush examples, the nightly news never included more than 10 percent of the total number of seconds of presidential statements or presidential visuals contained in the original media event.[62]

In other words, official sources may instigate the news and direct the attention of the reporters toward particular events and issues, without controlling the ultimate story. Each side relies on the other in the negotiation of newsworthiness, and neither fully dominates, because officials and reporters alike hail from at least partially independent institutions that command important and unique resources.

Journalists worry about maintaining access to powerful sources, but only if such access leads to a product that their superiors—who after all pay their salaries—favorably assess. They need to provide stories that maximize production values of vividness and clarity alongside journalistic norms of balance and neutrality. Given the satisfaction and self-esteem that reporters gain from their professional autonomy, any indication that they are mere "flacks" for the president would lead to a loss of prestige within a profession that lacks traditional markers for membership and accomplishment. Finally, even if sources can and do restrict access and focus news attention on particular topics, the news media still has final say over the ultimate product—by raising other issues, interjecting doubts, questioning motives, and seeking out critical sources for balance.

To be sure, sometimes such critical sources are not easily found; and it is clear that, following Bennett's indexing hypothesis, the widest range of opinions emerges in the news when there is disagreement among elites.[63] This pattern is most visible with wars and foreign policy crises. Thus, criticism of the Vietnam War emerged only when congressional sources began to raise doubts about presidential strategies. Likewise, critical voices emerged in the news during the build-up to the Gulf War only when Congress certified dissent, and as soon as Congress gave its support to the military option, the focus of the news shifted away from debate and toward operational considerations.[64]

Journalists taking the initiative to shape their stories with results unwanted by their sources are vulnerable to the question "Who elected *you?*" In general, they devise ways, in the words of Don Hewitt (executive producer of *60 Minutes*), to be "critical without being partisan," because their legitimacy rests on not being seen as autonomous political actors. Thus, they have to find how to provide critical coverage that cannot be taken as a politically based vendetta—whether by relying on already extant dissent, or by judging officials by the standards they themselves set up, or by critiquing style more than substance and methods more than goals. Even in foreign policy crises, the news media are thus far from uncritical. As the political scientist Jonathan Mermin has nicely documented in the coverage of the invasion of Panama in 1989 and the Gulf War, the lack of debate over the wisdom of the policy does not preclude reporters from criticizing the means to that end, thereby raising doubts about President Bush's ability to accomplish the goals he set forth.[65] Such an approach makes perfect sense, given that it enables journalists to include tension and conflict that would otherwise be absent from their stories, and it also provides a way for reporters to perform a political ritual that distances them from their sources. And as Mermin points out, such news helps to explain why government officials complain about news that outsiders (including most scholars) would find to be very positive; just about *any* news is not reported as sources would optimally prefer.

The journalistic contribution to the news is, not surprisingly, even greater in other circumstances: for instance, when reporters can pick and choose among a range of opinionated authoritative sources; when they can compare current performance to past promises; when they have another story to weave in; and so forth.

Most important, reporters may actually be compelled to challenge the official version of events, if that version fails to meet the standards set by the production values. Let's return to the seven media events from George Bush's first year in office.[66] In my study, I suggested that these events could be covered in four different ways: first, fitting all the president's interests; second, where the president may have ceded to the news media in the definition of the particular event but in such a way as to advance his larger interests; third, where presidential control of the most powerful visual imagery vied against journalistic control of the spoken text; and fourth, where the president has to cede to the news media on the definition of the event across the board. Of the seven media events, Bush was most able to control the news that fit the presidential script of action and a decisive order, when he sent 2,000 troops to Panama (prior to the invasion) to protect, he claimed, American lives.

Equally instructive are the events where Bush lost definitional control. In one, Bush visited the Pentagon to symbolize his continued support for his embattled nominee for secretary of defense, John Tower; this photo opportunity became a minor part of the continuing story in the Senate, where the nomination was on the brink of defeat. Not only was the continuing saga connected to congressional movement. Bush made no statement, except to chide one questioning reporter who, he said, "apparently doesn't know the ground rules." The video imagery of Bush's motorcade being greeted by Tower and of Bush and Tower seating themselves was bland and unexceptional. Not only was Bush relegated to only a few seconds of airtime alongside the debate on the Senate floor, but the reporters undercut even this gesture by again noting it to be a contrived and failed event.[67]

Another of the seven events was a formal visit by Japanese Prime Minister Takeshita to the White House, a good example of an official occasion with little overt news value. In its visuals and its spoken sections, it was formulaic and stilted, with "talking heads" rather than vivid action. The event provided no movement in the continuing story of the relationship between Japan and the United States. Presumably, if journalists were to cover any of this event, they had to find creative ways to rework it into a more newsworthy item.

The event in its totality unfolded as follows: Takeshita's vehicle arrived at the front of the White House and he entered the building; he reemerged on a balcony with Bush for a photo opportunity, where Bush, looking around for something to do, took one and only one question asking about his health, saying only, "Totally new man. All well. Totally recovered." Later, Bush and Takeshita reappeared and stiffly read statements of goodwill and friendship.

The three broadcast networks chose different strategies. ABC ignored the visit. NBC made it a brief peg for a commentary by John Chancellor on what the United States could learn from Japan's investment in research and development. Most enterprisingly, CBS zeroed in on Bush's off-the-cuff statement on his health and made it into both an example of a failed event and part of a separate, larger story on the apparent difficulties the Bush administration was having with some of its appointees:

DAN RATHER: President Bush planned to showcase his foreign policy credentials and experience today as he met with Japan's Prime Minister Takeshita. Instead, as CBS White House correspondent Lesley Stahl reports, Mr. Bush was dogged by questions about the ethics of some of his nominees for high office and by questions about his own health.
LESLEY STAHL: President Bush is having trouble getting his message across. Today's well-laid plans: highlight the importance of US-Japanese relations with his first foreign visitor, Prime Minister Takeshita, but what was the president asked? How's your health.
BUSH: Totally new man. All well. Totally recovered.
STAHL: More questions. What about John Tower's personal conduct? The White House spokesman said that the President had confidence in Tower and urges prompt consideration of his nomination. And more questions about other nominees—ethical questions that muddle the central message of President Bush's first thirteen days in office, the importance of ethics in government . . . [68]

Stahl's 1989 piece may be an unusually strong example of reportorial initiative in the face of unpromising material. But it reminds us of a point that was best made by Todd Gitlin in his famous study of the Students for a Democratic Society (SDS): news consists of "decontextualization."[69] Although clearly, the abilities of reporters to take an event out of its original context and put it into a context of their own is much greater with a relatively powerless group like SDS, powerful officials like presidents are far from immune from the same process.

In his outline of the dynamics of the cycle of coverage given to the New Left, Gitlin also reminds us that the newsmaking process is not impervious to less powerful political actors, including nonofficials such as social movements.[70] The SDS was initially ignored; it did not seek news, and reporters did not consider it important or newsworthy. The SDS gained publicity without seeking it through "discovery" stories. The reporters covering SDS may have been sympathetic to SDS, to be sure, but they were able to "sell" their stories to their superiors by charting something intriguingly new and appealing to news values of novelty, color, and drama.[71] These stories provoked angry criticism from authoritative sources, such as the conservative senator, John Stennis, or U.S. Attorney General Nicholas Katzenbach. The coverage moved into denigration (as government officials ended up using their greater access to the news) and simplified their complex social program into an anti-Vietnam War stance. The SDS became "old news" more quickly than did the officials. With activists newly attracted to the movement by the radical image disseminated in the news and craving increasingly costly publicity in order to "organize with mirrors," the SDS polarized with one wing becoming more extreme and theatrical in order to get coverage. Finally, partly as a response to this polarization and partly as (in the wake of the Tet offensive) elite opinion split on the Vietnam War, the media helped to elevate a moderate alternative, which was covered favorably and allowed to join the debate as an authoritative player.

In other words, the news media do not completely shut out unofficial activists, but their access is narrow in time and limited in scope. Officials have greater access on a regular basis to call attention to their issues, concerns, and events, and to obtain coverage that is closer to their own terms. But the official domination of the negotiation of process does not carry over to the content. In short, the bifurcated standard of news (important and interesting) provides a way to divide the labor of the news product. Official sources seem to have the greatest control in ascertaining importance, but the news media are more influential in designating interest. This division of labor was best captured by a plaque that appeared on the desk of Reagan's chief White House spokesperson, Larry Speakes: "You don't tell us how to stage the news, and we won't tell you how to cover it." Although jocular, Speakes's plaque reveals areas where each side is presumed to dominate—and suggests that the news is a constant if rarely conscious *coproduction* of officials and journalists.

WHAT KIND OF POLITICAL INSTITUTION?

If the news media then constitute a political institution, what *kind* of political institution are they? Although Cater's notion of the "fourth branch" is stimulating, here is where it begins to show its limits.[72] The three branches of legislature, executive, and judiciary were, after all, instituted by the Constitution with precise rules for how their members would be selected, the terms of office as well as their powers and responsibilities—thereby expecting them and enabling them to make authoritative decisions for the polity as a whole. The same simply cannot be said of the news media. True, as we have seen in previous chapters, the American news media's form may centrally depend on governmental decisions. And indeed the news media have a prominent place in the Constitution by dint of the protection of "freedom of the press" in the Bill of Rights. And true, the news media do have a powerful impact on political outcomes. But the fact that the media were instituted by and are largely controlled by private corporations makes them something other than another branch of government.

Instead, the news media share more with two other political institutions: the political parties, and the interest group system.[73] In each case, these political institutions are simultaneously inside and outside of government. Indeed, in the case of political parties, they emerged so early in the young Republic that it may be safe to say that, regardless of the anti-party rhetoric of the founders, the process may simply not have worked without essential intermediaries in a system marked by separation of powers.

At bottom, the news media are private associations and therefore at least partially independent of government. But, as we have seen, they are deeply shaped by official sponsorship, subsidies, protection, and legal recognition. Much the same is true for political parties and interest groups. In the case of political parties, not only are their rules essentially formulated by politicians to the point that they may be thought of as extensions of other political institutions.[74] As the political scientist Leon Epstein has argued, legal recognition and regulation of the role of parties in selecting and financing candidates for office meant that "Americans stopped treating their major parties as private associations and converted them into public utilities, if not actual government agencies."[75]

Even interest groups, which political science once saw as near-spontaneous expressions of social and political grievances, emerge in no small part because of governmental sponsors and patrons. The expansion of federal responsibility in the twentieth century created clienteles that sought to protect their programs, but more directly, the federal government often instigates advisory panels that help to mobilize an unorganized group, furnishes tax incentives to nonprofit groups, provides grants for projects, and (again) picks up part of the expense by beneficial postal subsidies.[76] Indeed, governmental officials and interest groups are so intertwined and interdependent that it is sometimes difficult to figure out just who is on what side.

Moreover, we can and should speak of the party system as *an* institution and the interest group system as *an* institution, each presenting only certain opportunities for—and biases against—mobilization and action.[77] As with the news media, the political party and the interest group are institutional by the definitions from the previous chapter. They proceed both by explicit rules and regulations on one hand but also by presumptions about what and how parties and interest groups should act, thus extending through space and across time. And they are also expected to perform central political and social roles in the articulation and aggregation of political interests and grievances.

Thus, the news media may be a political institution, but more like the intermediary institutions of party and interest group than the three constitutional branches of legislature, executive, and judiciary. Yet there is one key distinction between the news media on one hand and the party and interest group on the other: the latter are formed and maintained for the strategic collective pursuit of openly and specifically political aims. The news media (at least since the demise of the partisan press in the nineteenth century) are not. In comparison with the explicit politics of party and interest groups, the news media's politics, power, and impact may well be implicit and hidden, even (or especially) from its own practitioners.

CONCLUSION

What then is the politics of the American news media? What "authoritative allocation of values" flow out of the news media's involvement in political processes? It is clear that such political impact does not begin and end with the individual attitudes and worldviews of journalists. Indications of reporters' antiauthoritarian views, liberal stances, or support for Democratic candidates may not mean much for the news product, given their well-documented hard work not only to efface their own presence in a story but to come up with something approaching objectivity. But, as we have seen, in pursuing objectivity, reporters end up implicitly adding a particular bias to the news—a structural bias, in Hofstetter's terms, rather than an explicitly political bias—that favors only certain political actors, political events, political programs, and political issues.

The most abiding political bias of the news is, of course, its primary concentration on the events, ideas, preoccupations, strategies, and politics of powerful officials. This gravitation toward officialdom is what enables the news media to be not merely political but governmental. The availability and presence of the news media, both within their institutions and within government as a whole, provokes officials to think of them as a potential help to accomplish their goals and to assist the conversion of the news media into an "institution of governance."

But, as we have seen, that assistance rarely comes without a cost. Most important, the by-and-large private ownership of the news media and the increasing profit orientation of news organizations provides something of a counterweight to official power. Journalists apply standards of newsworthiness beyond importance in order to keep an audience interested, and therefore, to keep the viewership tuned in or the readership continuing to buy papers. The authority of officials, as represented in the news, depends, in no small part, on the ability and willingness of those political actors to fit their activities to the production values of the news. If they do not—as we have noted above—they run the risk of losing control of their agenda and/or being portrayed in negative terms. And indeed, American news—to a far greater extent than its European counterparts—tends not to maintain a consistent cool distance from the official sources it covers but instead vacillates more widely between news that deeply reinforces the officials' aims and news that undercuts them.[78]

The news media thereby enter into what political scientist Richard Neustadt described as "separated institutions sharing power." Although the news often acts to reinforce official power, it also provides incentives to act in only particular ways. This is not to say that reporters are thereby agents of the citizenry checking political authority: far from it. Journalists' professional autonomy means that they are often unwilling to pay much attention to readers' judgments, particularly since they can claim that while readers may know what information they like, they may not know what information they need.[79] Moreover, recall Baldasty's aforementioned contrast of the early nineteenth-century party press that saw citizens as potential voters, and the commercialized press of a hundred years ago as visualizing them as potential consumers. Advertisers can easily see news outlets as a way to deliver audiences to their messages, with news as the filler. It may be that political power is counterweighed by the logic of the market, with uncertain benefits for the citizenry.

In addition to the official leanings of the news, then, there are a number of other biases maintained by the commercial pressure to attract and keep audiences that affect the "authoritative allocation of values." Following Tuchman, the primary necessity is to convert occurrences first into events and then into news; and by so doing, one not only transforms happenings into stories but also takes the original occurrence out of its initial context and places it into another context of the journalists' choosing. In political terms, this means that issues and occurrences that do not easily become a narrative are likely to be neglected in favor of those that do. A good example comes from one of the six investigative reports studied by the Northwestern University team of scholars. A reform-minded interest group first captured reporters' attention by evidence of how nursing homes defrauded Medicare, but this angle ultimately was transformed into an NBC report focusing instead on how nursing homes abused patients—partly because of the need for clear villains and victims, partly because of the inability to visually present fraud as well as they could present abuse. As the executive producer of NBC News said when the producer unveiled a fraud piece, "It's just too complicated. Where are the victims?"[80]

Moreover, reporters' simultaneous needs to craft a story from the material provided to them while distancing themselves from the political responsibility of airing this information means that they find ways to show that they are not mere extensions of the government and that they, as argued above, must figure out how to turn unpromising material into a story that will be worth printing or airing. The fall-back stories seem to revolve around political manipulation, and political trouble, both of which are straightforward to report and an easy continuing focus to underlie, interpret, and explain the events of the day in relation to the stories produced on the day before and anticipating what's likely to come up the day after. Moreover, the story of political failure (e.g., Bush "having trouble getting his message across," *supra*) is an easy one to turn to in the event that officials do not live up to narrative expectations.

The consequence has been a greater negativity in the news across the board and in journalist-initiated stories in particular.[81] Even generally positive stories can and do call attention to the contrived nature of the staged events and/or raise doubts about the motives of the actors (usually laid at the feet of pure politics) and their effectiveness.

Add to the demands of the story the standard production values of the news: it should be timely, terse, easily described, dramatic, colorful, and visualizable. Again, those issues, concerns, and events that do not fit these criteria must either be transformed to fit production values lest they be jettisoned from the news. In particular, we can see the news media's allocation of political values by noting what stories and what elements of stories are not covered.

Timeliness is one of the oldest criteria for the news, but it works only in favor of certain issues, since long-standing conditions are considered simply to be old news. The attention to timeliness means that news is more likely to be episodic rather than analytical. The political scientist Shanto Iyengar has demonstrated in a series of experiments that episodic reporting leads to fragmentary understanding on the part of the people and less accountability placed on government.[82] In other words, this preoccupation with a constant present tense, and with what's new rather than what's constant, denies news attention to preexisting social problems and discourages solutions.

One way for political actors to get around this problem is for them to stage an event which will provide a momentary "peg," and therefore an opportunity to talk about an underlying condition. Thus, presidents make speeches, members of Congress hold hearings, activists hold rallies and demonstrations, and the like. The problem here is that the event must meet not only the standards of importance—whereby it will be more newsworthy as more authoritative sources are involved—but also production values.

If the event deals with a complex problem or, even worse, a series of problems, this runs into trouble with journalists who are looking for something easily described, and preferably an easy division between protagonists and antagonists. Likewise the speeches that have no pithy, lively, and very short "soundbites" (usually under ten seconds long) that can be extracted are disfavored over those that do; consequently, speakers concerned about getting into the news have to craft their communications so as to be littered with soundbites. And finally, given that many political problems are static, pallid, and abstract, they may be avoided by the news media's requirement for drama, color, and good visuals. Little wonder that so much attention is given not merely to the right kind of event but nowadays to the right kind of prop that will convey the message visually. The search for props reaches almost comic dimensions at times. In the summer of 1995, for instance, Attorney General Janet Reno was testifying before a House committee on the government's decision the previous year to storm the Branch Davidian compound near Waco, Texas, with tear gas, which preceded a fire that killed most of the inhabitants.

When one Republican House member (Mica of Florida) began quizzing Reno, one of his aides took a gas mask up to Reno's table and placed it front of her; Reno, glowering at the aide, then quickly put it on the floor, and the aide went back to place it on the table. This back-and-forth continued for some time, until Reno finally lifted the gas mask, at which point photographers snapped away. The irony of this is that while Mica may have achieved his goal in putting Reno on the spot and linking her to the teargassing, the photo, while widely reproduced the following day in many newspapers, seemed to have little to do with the accompanying stories.

These biases are doubly troubling. Not only do they affect the problems, issues, and worldviews that citizens are asked to contemplate; they may also push political actors, now concerned about making news as a way to achieve political power and accomplish policy goals, toward political phenomena that fit the agreed-upon standards of newsworthiness. Take the words of House Speaker Newt Gingrich in a 1995 *USA Today* interview. When the editorial staff asked him about his frequently colorful and extreme rhetoric, Gingrich shot back,

> Part of the reason I use strong language is because you all will pick it up . . . You convince your colleagues to cover me being calm, and I'll be calm. You guys want to cover nine seconds, I'll give you nine seconds, because that is the competitive requirement . . . *I've simply tried to learn my half of your business.*[83]

That last sentence captures the key theme of this chapter: that the news is a coproduction of sources (usually officials) and journalists, but that sources cannot simply snap their fingers and make news in their own terms. Instead, not only is the news a reworking of official actions, events, and statements with production values in mind. These production values favor particular kinds of news and information over others, and thereby end up endowing the news with a particular politics.

But beyond that, this coproduction pushes political actors to anticipate the needs of the news in designing what they will say and do. Not just journalism but politics in the process become obsessed with issues that can become timely, terse, easily described, dramatic, colorful, and visualizable.[84] Although these criteria—widely shared among journalists in a variety of modalities—seem content-neutral, they are not. Politics, it follows, should be simple and straightforward, with two sides to each story and differences thus being easily resolvable. Political actors are therefore expected to be direct and consistent. Likewise, action is a good in and of itself; inaction is taken as a sign of incompetence, bad faith, and/or pettiness. Evidence of problems is likewise presumed not to be difficult to master, given the presence of clear, often visually ascertainable indicators. Of course, given that politicians are often ambiguous and flexible, wish to deal with policies and issues rather than dramatic storylines, and given that their subject matter is complex and abstract, the production values can provide a roadblock to political actors and politics.

Insofar as political actors increasingly need publicity in order to set their issues on the political agenda and otherwise achieve their aims, they must shape their activities to accord with the production values of the news, and politics follows in turn. But why are political actors interested in "learning my half of your business"? It is to that question that we now turn.

PART THREE

GOVERNMENT
BY
PUBLICITY

The phenomenon whereby reporters became part of the political process was termed by Cater "government by publicity."[1] The term is apt: it reminds us that, rather than counterposing publicity-seeking and governing, they can be and often are complementary and mutually reinforcing. In the next two chapters, I develop three general areas where publicity can help out policymakers: where making news is, in and of itself, action; where it focuses the attention of other policymakers and thereby sets the agenda; and where it helps to persuade others into action.

The most commonly studied political institution in this regard is undoubtedly the presidency. And presidents clearly have several advantages in dealing with the news media that other political actors lack. The personalization of the office in one human being gives the news a recognizable protagonist, whose tribulations and triumphs can be a continuing saga in and of itself. Matched with the presumption that a U.S. president is the "leader of the free world," reporters gravitate toward presidents and their activities as natural news items, and presidents help them out by giving frequent speeches, staging news events to dramatize issues, and participating in colorful rituals as head of state.

But despite these advantages, presidents are by no means unique in being media-minded in today's Washington. Indeed, it is striking to note how all political actors, and all political institutions, spend more time on and are more concerned with making news than was the case a few decades ago. There is variation, to be sure, in the ways different political actors use media strategies as part of their governing strategies. But this variation is nowadays matched by a constant—there is no political institution that does not have some sort of link between publicity and governing (over and above whatever payoff that publicity might have for electoral benefit and self-aggrandizement).

In the next two chapters, I will suggest that the *extent* and *kind* of media strategy chosen depends on the size of the gap between the policy-making ambitions of the occupants of the institution and the resources available to them to accomplish those ambitions. In other words, media strategies become increasingly useful means for political actors to pursue governance—and become an increasing focus of their attention and their activities—as the disjuncture between the power of those actors and the expectations placed on them grows. To the extent that, in a separation-of-powers system, political actors lack the resources to accomplish policy directly, the news media become one way to help them do so indirectly.

A corollary of this thesis is then that incumbents of political institutions develop media strategies that are best suited to counter the central weakness of that institution bequeathed to it by the constitutional restrictions on its powers. Thus, we would expect the following:

1. Presidents, faced with high visibility and expectations to be "in charge" but with low ability to command, should find ways through their media strategies to persuade others to act in ways that fit their interests.

2. With bureaucracies, our expectations differ depending on, not surprisingly, the resources they have at hand to accomplish their policy goals within their jurisdictions. Bureaucracies with limited resources should use the news media to help accomplish those aims directly—in effect, using the performative functions of the news. By contrast, bureaucracies with greater resources, which are therefore more able to attain those ends directly, will work at making sure that their publicity is in line with protecting their budgets and their broad jurisdictions.

3. Members of Congress, both backbencher and leader alike, are faced with the inevitable difficulty of getting their 534 colleagues to concentrate on a particular agenda and come together to pass coherent legislation. Consequently, they will attempt to find mechanisms through the media to gain focus in a dispersed, coequal institution.

4. And the central problem that the Supreme Court faces is one of its legitimacy as an unelected group of lawyers, appointed for life, making policy in what otherwise is a democratic system. Consequently, they gear their media strategies toward buttressing their legitimacy, especially by discouraging perceptions of them as having political axes to grind.

In the contemporary United States, it has long been difficult to imagine the news media's job without the direct involvement of government officials in the newsmaking process. Nowadays, it is increasingly tough to envision government operating without the news media's communicative abilities or political actors whose functions do not include a sizable amount of mass-mediated communication.

6

THE USES OF NEWS:

THEORY AND (PRESIDENTIAL) PRACTICE

If there was a classic era in American political science, it undoubtedly would be located in the late 1950s and early 1960s, when many famous accounts of American politics were carried out and published. It was the heyday of the theory of pluralism, where officials amidst shifting coalitions were seen to be engaged in constant bargaining, usually directly and often behind closed doors, whether among themselves or with leaders of organized groups. With the status quo as the starting point, and through the constant give-and-take of negotiation among elite actors responsible to diverse constituencies, many authors were seemingly assured that viable democratic decision making was alive and well in the United States.

The news media were rarely seen in these "mid-century" accounts of American politics. Richard Neustadt's famous model of presidential influence saw the presidents' popularity (what he termed "public prestige") as merely conditioning the far more essential continuing assessments by Washingtonians of the incumbent's willingness and skill to use the powers of bargaining.[1] Scholars studying Congress saw a miniature political system, with cohesive folkways and norms that discouraged open conflict and dominated by effective leaders—Lyndon Johnson in the Senate or Sam Rayburn and Wilbur Mills in the House—who avoided the media that might force them to stake out public positions that would restrict their freedom to strike a deal.[2] Justices of the Supreme Court, presumably apprehensive about their legitimacy and wishing to be perceived as above politics, maintained a tradition of aloofness, speaking on record only on the most general matters of jurisprudence; but behind the august image thereby provided, they were bargainers as well, circulating and recirculating opinions in search of a winning coalition.[3]

To be sure, the normative theory of pluralism that undergirded the empirical theory of bargaining was always fragile. The political scientist E. E. Schattschneider revealed as much in 1960 when he demonstrated that the choice of a particular contest influences the outcome at least as much as the actual contest itself. Peter Bachrach and Morton Baratz expanded Schattschneider's insight to encompass nondecisions, the standing tacit agreements not to raise certain options or issues.[4] As the sixties wore on, the theoretical confidence that a system of bargaining elites would protect popular government became ever more contested.

But the *descriptive* model of pluralism from the studies of the 1950s and early 1960s is quite a contrast, too, with the politics of the 1990s. Nowadays, descriptions of American politics stress atomization, dispersion, unpredictability, and confusion as the natural state of things.[5] Instead of a small set of bargainers, there are many single-issue interest groups, often able to exert influence by the increasing role of their political action committees in financing elections. And the multiplication of interest groups is self-perpetuating: "[I]n the process of creating structures to control or adapt to uncertainty, they have contributed to the development of a more complex and rapidly changing policymaking environment. Interest representation has thus become a self-reproducing organizational field."[6]

The growth of government since the 1960s means more political actors within the three branches, too—as witnessed by the explosions in the number of congressional staffers and in the size of executive bureaucracies. Instead of slowly shifting games among a stable set of participants, more recent models show participation to be fluid and unpredictable, with the rise of political entrepreneurs selling particular issues and, along with them, their preferred solutions, which are, as often as not, in search of problems as much as the other way around. Instead of incrementally "muddling through," then, issues rise and fall with dizzying speed, and political fortunes along with them. While there have been centralizing tendencies in recent years as well—most prominently a resurgence in party organizations and congressional leadership—these can only partially counterbalance the complexities of contemporary governance. Indeed, in some ways, such centralization does not affect the problem at all; for instance, the resurgence of parties occurs by offering greater service to candidates who continue to be as autonomous as ever.[7] Add to this the growing uncertainties of the post–Cold War world and the globalization of the political economy, and the pluralist descriptions begin to sound like something from another era indeed.

The news media, too, have also become a more central and visible political player between the 1950s and the 1990s, as we have seen in the preceding chapters. Whether this development is a cause of the dispersion of American politics, an effect thereof, or a mere coincidence has been a subject of debates I will not enter into here.[8] What is more important for my purposes in this chapter is that American governmental officials, faced with an unpredictable and volatile political process, increasingly rely upon the news media in order to communicate strategically among and within its disparate parts—and without having to do so by being conveyed through public opinion. Indeed, the separation-of-powers political system in the United States may particularly encourage the news media to act in governmental terms as a political institution, given both the greater independence of journalists from political pressure as well as the greater need for intermediary institutions to bridge the gaps between the constitutional branches.[9]

When one compares the 1950s and the 1990s, not only do we find a more dispersed political system but *every* branch of government is more preoccupied with and spends more resources on the news media today than it did forty years ago. Presidents not only spend more and more time and energy in order to give speeches, but their activities and those of the executive branch as a whole are increasingly geared toward the "line of the day" charted out by the Office of Communications. Congress has opened up its floor deliberations to live cable television and its committee proceedings to the news media, while individual members' offices have, in the last twenty years, turned greater attention to the news media by the help of designated full-time press secretaries who often pursue not only local publicity for electoral purposes but national publicity for policy purposes. To the extent that congressional leadership has taken charge of an increasingly individualistic institution, it is in no small part due to those leaders going increasingly public themselves, with the apogee reached in the ascendancy of House Speaker Newt Gingrich. Even the Supreme Court has gotten into the act, with the justices giving speeches and interviews on a variety of subjects, including the decisions that they have reached, the philosophies they have used, and the implications for future politics; at the very least, justices now find they have to make public speeches in order to safeguard the private discretion they have long enjoyed.

In short, the work of the news media has been increasingly incorporated into the activities of the constitutional three branches, without becoming a mere extension of any one of them. After all, just because officials aim to get things done through the news media does not mean that they usually—or even often—succeed. This is, of course, exactly what we would have expected from seeing the news media as one among a number of semi-independent political institutions in Washington.

After all, a simplistic conception of separation of powers that neatly divides executive, lawmaking, and adjudicating powers into distinct presidential, congressional, and judicial spheres was specifically rejected by the founders in favor of what Madison (in *Federalist* 48) termed a "blended" political system.[10] Thus, to take one example, the president and the Justices of the Supreme Court are part of the legislative process itself: the former before and during deliberation as agenda setter and chief lobbyist and thereafter as arbiter through the veto, and the latter before and during deliberation as delineators of constitutionally available options and thereafter as arbiter through judicial review. In other words, the legislative process includes institutions other than just the legislature, and it includes institutional actors other than just legislators.[11] Much the same could be said of executing or of adjudicating.

As Neustadt famously put it in *Presidential Power*, "The Constitutional Convention of 1787 is supposed to have created a government of 'separated powers.' It did nothing of the sort. Rather, it created a government of separated institutions *sharing* powers."[12] The work of each branch is implicated in the work of the others, and vice versa. None of the three branches can act unilaterally without the cooperation—or at the very least the passive consent—of the other two. The result is a system marked, in Justice Robert Jackson's words, by "separateness but interdependence, autonomy but reciprocity."[13]

We have seen in the previous chapter how governmental officials are key participants in the process of newsmaking. What about the other way around: Are journalists now key participants in the process of governing? If the news media now enter into the process of separated institutions of sharing power, then we need to investigate the question: What uses does newsmaking serve for policymaking?

NEWSMAKING AS POLICY MAKING

As we have seen, if government officials need to enlist the news media to help them accomplish their goals, this assistance cannot come without some cost. After all, the news media have their own concerns and priorities which are never identical with those of the official sources upon whom they rely to help them make the news. This disjuncture was deemed so great by scholars in the 1950s and 1960s that they saw an almost inevitable clash between officials' pursuit of secrecy, in order to preserve maximum leeway, and reporters' devotion to publicity, in order to have enough content to write a story.[14] To be sure, the media can probably do more to derail an initiative through their negative coverage than they can assure its success by favorable coverage.[15] And indeed, insofar as newspersons enter the ongoing negotiation of newsworthiness with important resources of their own and divergent understandings of importance and interest, any political actor who relies on the news media must feel their impact.

Yet for officials seeking strategies to govern, running this risk is often acceptable for several reasons.[16] *First,* making news can be making policy in and of itself, particularly when the deeds of government are directly accomplished by words. *Second,* making news can call attention to one's preferred issues and alternatives (and build one's reputation in the process) and focus the public debate on their importance. *Third,* making news can persuade others to adopt one's stance, whether explicitly (by broadcasting one's inflexibility or amplifying threats) or implicitly (by influencing the context of others' decisions—establishing seemingly indisputable facts or representing public moods that are favorable to one's interests and positions). In a political system where centrifugal forces pulling outward seem to outnumber centripetal forces reinforcing power, both within and across organizations and institutions, the news media's assistance to officials should not be underestimated. Thus, as Martin Linsky's survey of federal officials concluded, "When these policymakers talk about time with the press, they do not see the press as an intrusion into their lives, but as a resource for them in doing their job."[17]

Words as Actions
In the most direct use of the news media in governing, publicity is policy in and of itself. One could easily think of rhetoric as a substitute for or a spur to action, but many governmental pronouncements partake of what the philosopher J. L. Austin dubbed "performative" language, where "the issuing of the utterance is the performing of an action."[18] As contrasted with purely descriptive statements, performatives are actions in and of themselves that could not be accomplished without the words. Take the examples of naming a ship or congratulating a graduate.

The epitome of performative language in political news is the noon briefing of the State Department, where the United States is placed on record as condemning, congratulating, doubting, agreeing, warning, and (in perhaps the most virtuosic use of performative language) not commenting.[19] But elsewhere in government, officials engage in the performative: presidents order, legislators proclaim, judges rule. By making statements in public and encouraging their use in the news, officials both enact policy and alert larger audiences to these actions presumably so that the latter may take this new information into account in planning what they do next.

Performatives are handy for both official and reporter. Reporters habitually use politicians' performatives in their stories because it enables them to produce an account without laborious, time-consuming fact-checking. A defining characteristic of the performative is that it cannot be said to be either true or false; we can doubt whether people who say "I'm sorry" are genuinely sorry or not, for instance, but we cannot doubt that they have apologized.[20] Consequently, as sociologist Gaye Tuchman pointed out in her famous account of the uses of objectivity, quotations are indispensable to journalists, who may not be able to say whether a given statement is a fact but who can confidently point to another fact: that the statement was made, and by a person presumed, usually by their institutional position, to be "in a position to know."[21]

For their part, officials doing something with words have the satisfaction of accomplishing something quickly and directly in a way that otherwise often evades them.[22] Performatives are accessible to officials who are also structurally advantaged through their control over the correct setting and timing of such utterances. Though performatives cannot be true or false, they can be what Austin termed "infelicitous." To work right, performatives must be accomplished by the "uttering of certain words by certain persons in certain circumstances . . . appropriate for the invocation of the particular procedure."[23] Performatives can thus go awry if misapplied; after President Reagan was shot and wounded in 1981, Secretary of State Alexander Haig probably alarmed his audience and undermined his authority by rushing to the podium in the White House press room to peremptorily announce, "I am in charge in this White House."[24] But more often than not, officials are provided with the trappings of office—the White House Oval Office, the well of the Senate, the state department briefing room complete with world maps, the Supreme Court's high bench—which endow them with the authority to make words into authoritative policy actions.

Setting the Agenda

When policy requires the assent of others, media strategies are useful for persuading others to act. As face-to-face communication has become more difficult with the growing reach of government, the increasing number of participants and the dispersion and confusion of power and authority, media persuasion is a more attractive and efficient use of resources.[25] By appealing to the media, one can attempt to indicate one's preferences, respond to ongoing events, and attempt to persuade en masse an entire and disparate set of political actors across branches and levels to the correctness of one's stance.

Officials rely on the news for information, which they often receive more quickly than through the bureaucratic channels of their institution, particularly with the rise of all-news stations on cable television and radio which enables new information to be accessible around the clock.[26] Although we usually think of political actors resorting to publicity to communicate across institutional divides or to leak information from the bottom to the top of a political organization, even those in collegial institutions rely upon the news media to reach the colleagues they could easily buttonhole. As far back as 1960, the political scientist Donald Matthews noted how senators relied on the news for understanding their own institution, even though the potential of persuasion that this thereby offered was not much availed at that time:

> [I]t is not so well known that the senators often find out what is going on in the Senate by reading the papers. Senators are incredibly busy people. Most of them have specialized legislative interests. Most important legislative events take place in the myriad committee and subcommittee meetings occurring all over the Hill. Senators have neither the time nor energy to keep tab on this hundred-ring circus. The newspapers help immeasurably in the senators' neverending struggle to keep track of what is going on in the Senate. It is ironic but still true that the members of so small a legislative body should find it necessary to communicate with each other via public print, but often they do.[27]

If Matthews was right about the intimate, clubbish Senate of the 1950s, imagine the uses of the news for individuals seeking to grasp a far more complex political system. It is not far-fetched to suggest that the American news media construct a conception of what any political institution is and does, from which audiences construct their understanding of that institution, even for the individuals who are within it. In thereby saying what an institution should be and what it should do, the news media contribute to the process of institutional leadership.

To use the news, a political actor must initially call attention to one's issues and concerns and place them on the political agenda as problems that demand attention and that could be solved rather than conditions to be endured; issues that are not judged consequential or soluble tend to be bypassed more frequently than those that are.[28] The publicity provided by the news media can offer key assistance to officials here in two ways. First, public opinion tends to see those issues discussed in the news as more important, and citizens are more likely to judge politicians by their stances on those issues, whether or not the news is linked to those officials or not.[29] Second, even if public opinion is not activated, politicians respond differently to more salient issues. As the political scientist

David Price found in his superb 1978 study of the House Commerce Committee, legislators understandably gravitated toward issues with high public salience that had little conflict among organized groups and spurned issues which generated high group conflict and low salience; in the former case they could only make friends, and in the latter they could only make enemies. But less obviously and more interestingly, committee members felt compelled to deal with high-salience issues even when they engendered group conflict, for the simple reason that they might be blamed for inaction if they did nothing about it.[30] In other words, increasing the visibility of a particular issue also enhances the odds that political actors will do something about it in a way that is responsive to public attention.

Of course, political actors rarely call attention to an issue merely for the sake of doing so; instead, they stress issues that hold together their coalition and fragment the opposition.[31] Moreover, they also strategically define the incipient dispute through terms that, if accepted, would almost automatically guarantee their success. Thus, much of political debate is not merely over what issues should be on the agenda but also what those issues are "really all about" and what "the" two sides of the issue are. Such debate often occurs behind the scenes, but it emerges into the open when an accident breaks the standard routines of officials and reporters alike.[32]

To take an example, how should we have conceptualized the enormous oil spill in Prince William Sound in 1989 caused by the *Exxon Valdez,* and how should we respond with appropriate policy responses? Was it a case of bad navigation by a drunken captain (in which case the courts can take care of it by punishing the infractor, and legislatures can increase penalties for navigating while under the influence)? Or was it the consequence of the use of fragile single-hull vessels (in which case the flow of oil can proceed but with the introduction of double-hull ships)? Or was it simply the inevitable risk of overconsumption of petroleum in the lower forty-eight states (in which case stringent conservation would have to be imposed)? As you can see, even though all sides would presumably see an oil spill of this magnitude as something that must be avoided, the public is led to divergent policies depending on how we understand the spill and its causes. Little wonder that the sociologists Harvey Molotch and Marilyn Lester, studying the news coverage of the Santa Barbara oil spill of 1969, concluded, "One dimension of power can be construed as the ability to have one's account become the perceived reality of others. Put slightly differently, a crucial dimension of power is the ability to create public events. And since access to media is a crucial ingredient in creating and sustaining the realities of publics, a study of such access is simultaneously a study of power relationships."[33]

Thus, merely calling attention to an issue does not ensure that one's preferred alternative will be pursued, let alone enacted.[34] But again, the savvy use of publicity can elevate a particular policy response. As Phyllis Kaniss has noted in her case study of local news coverage of a proposed convention center in Philadelphia, proponents were able to link the new proposal as a solution to an old, recurring problem—the economic decline of the city—by announcing their plan in a press conference that ensured a single-source story. By packaging the story in such a way that its economic benefits were unchallenged and seemed undeniable (when, in fact, such benefits were quite unclear and problematic), proponents were able to diffuse potential opposition and divert attention away from other alternatives.[35] Even strategic politicians, such as backbench legislators, who cannot automatically command the spotlight can also craft policy proposals in anticipation of recurring news items, of impending deadlines, or of breaking stories that can be anticipated if not predicted (e.g., airline crashes), so that when the topic thereby becomes newsworthy, the alternative can obtain publicity as a readily available response.[36]

Not least consequentially for officials, calling attention to one's preferred issues and policy options also calls attention to oneself. The House press secretaries I interviewed and surveyed in 1984 made few distinctions between using the news media to build a national constituency for an issue and to become a nationally recognized spokesperson on that issue.[37] By being covered as "in a position to know," a reputation can grow that will enhance one's stature, which can be reinvested in further news opportunities, and so on.[38] Those who are more frequently in the news are no less vulnerable to mass-mediated reputation building. Neustadt may have been right in 1960 when he said that Washingtonians assessed a president's "professional reputation" by keeping mental tally sheets of examples of the will and skill with which he pursued power, but he neglected to add that these examples were, by and large, filtered through the news media which apply their own standards of power and weakness, of success and failure.[39]

Persuasion

Having set the agenda and established oneself as a key participant may well be just the beginning. Bargaining is itself far from dead and gone. But even when political actors can specify particular individuals to be bargained with or otherwise persuaded (sometimes by means of mass-mediated reputations), the news media do not become irrelevant, because news influences the context in which governmental officials bargain and decide.

Coverage can influence or even create a public mood that may or may not be favorable to a certain issue or policy proposal, giving a sense of favorability, even inevitability, to some sort of resolution of the newly publicized problem. This may happen by mobilizing public opinion on a newsworthy issue, given that pollsters often do not ask questions on a topic (the responses to which then become the subject of yet further stories) until it has reached a critical mass of news attention.[40] At other times, the public mood represented in the news may override the more accurate soundings through polls. In 1989, for instance, the media focused on angry elderly citizens confronting their representatives on the catastrophic health care act. The public mood reported in the news pushed members of Congress to quickly repeal the act which had been passed by huge margins the year before—even though polls showed the public at large (including the elderly) favoring its retention.[41]

The news can also publicize particular facts that must be taken into account in the bargaining. The most famous instance is the leak. Information made public may make its way to high officials quicker within an agency or a department and force a decision.[42] But, more generally, success in sending forth a factual definition of a situation, whether by leaks or not, may enhance one's chances of policy success. A recent example has been the continuing political controversy over a particular late-term method of abortion, known technically as "intact dilation and extraction," but better known under the moniker used by the pro-life movement of "partial-birth abortion." Although the 104th Congress passed a bill in 1996 outlawing this method, President Clinton's veto was sustained, in part because of assurances from physicians and pro-choice activists that this was an uncommon procedure used primarily to protect the health of the mother. In early 1997, however, not only did one prominent abortion provider indicate that he had underestimated the number of such abortions, but physicians increasingly noted that there were a number of alternatives to that procedure—both giving renewed momentum to the legislation.[43] At the very least, political officials must make sure that the facts the news proffers are congruent with the information and policy recommendations they are privately providing.[44]

In a classic case of what organizational theorists call the "absorption of uncertainty," what starts out in the news as tentative hunches and extemporaneous phrases can become seemingly unquestionable fact upon being repeated from one news story to the next. An intriguing example occurred during the preparation for the 1990 International Conference on AIDS in San Francisco, which was facing a boycott over the federal policy restricting entry into the country of those infected with HIV, the virus associated with AIDS. One of the conference organizers, responding to journalistic questions about the impact of the boycott, was quoted as saying, "We expected twelve thousand registrants, but we may lose three thousand unless the travel policy is changed." This number gained the status of a taken-for-granted fact as it became published and aired many times over—and thereby put pressure on the Bush administration's commitment to the policy.

The conference's program director, Robert Wachter, wrote in his memoir of the conference that he found this both "amusing, and a bit disconcerting." He recalled that

> we had absolutely no idea how many people might participate in the boycott, but guessed it would be more than a thousand and less than five thousand. We settled on the number three thousand as a compromise: high enough (we hoped) to scare the Administration and Congress into fearing that the boycott would capture world attention, while not so high as to panic University of California administrators (whose continued support and funding were critical) into thinking that the meeting was in grave danger of collapsing. Despite the number's genesis from thin air, the press embraced it without challenge. And after enough repetition in print, everyone forgot where they first heard it—fabrication transformed into fact.[45]

Thus, as Linsky has noted, how the news initially frames an issue tends to be long-lived and to constrain later choices.[46] But although it is difficult to change that frame, it is far from impossible, and the advantages thereby gained may well make it worth the effort. Such frames may gain their force by sheer repetition, which may make previously unthinkable possibilities quite imaginable indeed.[47] Insofar as officials can influence the news media's framing so as to favor their preferences, they can boost their likely success in this particular contest and enhance their reputation for future battles.

THE PRESIDENTIAL PROTOTYPE

To see the uses of news in practice, I begin with sketching the benefits that newsmaking presents for modern presidents. This is, of course, the best-known story of governing with the news, so much so that it is almost a prototype for how to do it. Given the gap between the expectations placed on the office and the actual resources that presidents are able to control, it is no surprise that many scholars have begun to see the presidency as a largely rhetorical office, exercising influence by means of speaking. Given that their abilities to reach people directly seems to be on the wane, presidents must devote ever more time to finding ways to get to an audience indirectly, through the resources of the news media.

This is a familiar story, and I hope not to belabor it. It sets up nicely, however, a series of expectations that we may use to judge other parts of the federal government that are commonly seen to be less preoccupied with publicity. In the next chapter, I will present the less familiar evidence: how federal officials in any branch are media-minded as part of doing their job of governance.

For presidents, certainly, such preoccupation with the media is a daily task. Here is a description of one White House:

> All [the assistants to the president] interviewed agree the national media play a very significant role in the White House decision-making process. A few respondents reported that in White House meetings, on the whole, more time is spent discussing the media than any other institution, including Congress, and that all policies are developed and presented with the media reaction in mind. One respondent reported the media have "incredible power, far beyond what professors teach in college" . . . According to another respondent, "Those in the press are participants, not witnesses . . . A lot of every day is spent on anticipating how the press will cover [an event or policy], how they are going to evaluate it, and what kind of analysis they are going to give it" . . . According to another, "I have been amazed at how such a considerable amount of energy [in the White House] is spent on press relations . . ."[48]

The readers would be excused if they were to assume that this description pertained to the epitome of stage-managed presidencies, that of Ronald Reagan, or perhaps of Bill Clinton at the ascendancy of his spinmeister of the day. But on the contrary, these interviews come from a sizable sample of assistants to President George Bush, commonly portrayed as having a more relaxed and open approach to the news media.[49] More important for our purposes, these interviews reveal a continuing preoccupation with the news media, not merely for how to sell initiatives previously agreed upon behind closed doors but also in the very process of identifying problems, setting agendas, and formulating policy responses. Indeed, if we were to examine the four central tasks of leadership identified by the sociologist Philip Selznick in his classic *Leadership in Administration*—in his words, defining the mission and role of the institution, building those into the institutional structure, defending the distinctive

values and identity of the institution, and ordering internal conflict[50]—
we can also see that newsmaking helps presidents in every sphere.

It was not always so. The history of the presidency has been an ever-
growing trend toward a public office, as presidential activities have
become increasingly geared toward communication and rhetoric.[51] In the
nineteenth century, presidents remained largely aloof from public attention and received little press coverage except in election years.[52] This inattention to the occupant of the White House was due to several reinforcing
tendencies. Presidents conceived of their office as executing the will of the
legislature; the press understood congressional debate to be the principal
newsworthy continuing story in Washington; and the White House failed
to accommodate reporters with space of their own or to have regularly
scheduled opportunities for presidents to meet journalists. In the late
nineteenth century, all that began to change. The Progressive Era's shift
in values from debate to disinterested decision making both weakened
party government in Congress and strengthened the role of the president,
at the same time that the rise of large-circulation newspapers and the
concomitant pursuit of dramatic and colorful spectacle found the president to be an ideal protagonist for their stories.[53]

Nowadays, the typical stories at the White House focus on the indi-
viduality of the president, usually seen in Hamiltonian terms of deciding,
commanding, and ordering. The irony, of course, of this mass-mediated
vision has been that expectations of the president far outstrip the direct
powers of the office. As Richard Neustadt brilliantly posited over thirty
years ago, every presidential power is less an opportunity for the president to exert his influence than a chance for other actors to get the president to do what *they* want—what Neustadt termed the president's role
as clerk.[54] Maintaining presidential power is a Sisyphean task; each president's innovation finds political actors who benefit thereby, and the next
president may not be able to gain as much by its use as did his predecessor. Moreover, each presidential term is characterized by similar dynamics of declining influence. As the next election approaches, actors willing
to wait before they push their agendas grow restless; conflict grows within
the executive; the news media pick up on these disputes as well as any
disjunctures between policy promises and policy performances; and the
president's popularity declines.[55]

Activist presidents must grasp at whatever powers they can, and this
includes the considerable interest of the news media in the person of the
president. So, starting with William McKinley and especially Theodore
Roosevelt, presidents finding themselves in the news spotlight have taken
full advantage of it, not merely to boost their image but to accomplish

policy goals.[56] Lyndon Johnson's press secretary, Bill Moyers, invited Robert Kintner of NBC News to help coordinate the president's communication apparatus by noting, "The President is going to want your creative and sustained thinking about the overall problem of communicating with the American people. Some call it the problem of 'the President's image.' It goes beyond that to the ultimate question of how does the President shape the issues and interpret them to people—how, in fact, does he lead."[57] The central role of the news media in presidential leadership was clear to its aspirants even before Ronald Reagan, as Walter Mondale, then the vice president, revealed in 1980 when he proclaimed that if he had to choose between the power to get on the nightly news and the veto, he would keep the former and jettison the latter.

To be sure, given the potential dispersion and fragmentation within the executive branch, one reason that presidents gravitate toward public speeches and ceremonies is because these are among the few activities that can be entirely accomplished by their own efforts. Yet, while presidents since Truman have increased the number of person-hours devoted to speechmaking,[58] they are most interested in having their speeches reach a larger audience than those assembled to hear them in person. But this is difficult for presidents to manage. Their ability to speak directly to a large audience is limited in several ways—and may be shrinking further yet. Although presidents can ask for time from the major television networks during prime time, the networks can and increasingly do turn them down, as in mid-1992, when President Bush's request to televise his evening press conference was rejected by the three major broadcast networks. With the increased availability of other channels, a presidential prime-time address, even when it is carried on all the networks, reaches a smaller potential audience even before one takes into account the high drop-off endured by presidential addresses from the usual programming.[59] And presidents cannot go to the well too frequently, lest they diminish the impact of a nationally broadcast speech; instead, they are strategic speakers.[60] Finally, their ability to go directly to a national audience is limited by the increased tendency of the networks to give the opposition party equal time and journalists' "instant analysis" immediately after the speech—interpretations that help to shape the public response to its content.[61]

In short, to go public, presidents must go through the news media. To be sure, they often attempt an end run around the news outlets they consider more hostile: President Kennedy's decision to hold press conferences that were broadcast live was prompted, at least in part, by his perception of a Republican-controlled press; President Nixon's distrust of the national news media pushed his press operations to reach out to local and presumably more easily impressed journalists; and, most recently, President Clinton's early preference for televised interview programs and electronic town meetings represented the distrust of what he deemed scandal-preoccupied reporters. But just as often presidents find themselves frustrated by this mediation. For instance, in late 1994, President Clinton mused, "Sometimes I think the president, when I look at it, is least able to communicate with the American people because of the fog that I have to go through to reach them."[62]

Still, presidents face the news media with several advantages. What makes the White House attractive to journalists—its near guarantee of regular exposure in the news—also restricts their creativity. News from the White House is salable to editors and producers by the individual protagonist of the president. Not only do presidents carry particular political significance and particular political accountability, they are presumably the classic authoritative sources in a position to know. Given the tendency for the news media to craft stories around individuals rather than social forces, the president is the most familiar protagonist around. Whenever presidents act, that is a story; and when other stories occur without their agency, whether a bombing or a blizzard, a president's statement, even when it is banal, is an integral part of the news. Indeed, the problem for contemporary presidents may be the ability to absent themselves from the news in order to be distanced from public problems that might otherwise be laid at their doorstep.

Such forces direct the media toward the chief executive. Instead of having to seek out news opportunities, presidents have the news come to them. While this interest impels presidents to create newsworthy events, they, more than other sources, can dictate the terms of access, given their near-automatic news value. Consequently, reporters, dependent on presidents' cooperation, end up prisoners in the all but hermetically sealed press room, reluctant to roam far from their connection to fame and fortune in the news business. Instead of encouraging innovation and enterprise, the White House breeds concern among reporters about missing out on the story everyone else is chasing.

All of this makes news management easier, so the ultimate sanction of "freezing out" individual reporters is rarely used. Instead, presidents gear their media operations toward serving reporters in ways that will prove beneficial: anticipating reporters' questions in news conferences and preparing accordingly; designing prescheduled events that meet news values of drama, color, and terseness; and providing frequent access to the president albeit in constrained and directed ways. The monopoly over good information and the ability to regulate access to the key newsmaker means that news opportunities can be meted out on a basis decided by the newsmaker himself—*if* that newsmaker is aware of the habits and routines of the press.

As Chapter 5 suggests, that may be a big "if." The demands of the news media must be taken into account in order to get the kind of boost that presidents seek from publicity. After all, presidents may launch a news item that will go in unpredictable directions thereafter, depending on whether other sources fall in line or offer criticism. With the press corps working in close contact, the ensuing pack mentality of the press, too, can work for or against the president; if something slips, reporters may move against the president with critical questioning, each risk aversely following the next toward the big story. Third, press secretaries and communication directors must spend much of their time building bridges and minimizing antagonism between the president and the press. Insofar as press secretaries are ambassadors from the president to the press *and* from the press to the president, this reduces the possibility of one-way manipulation. Finally, presidents must anticipate the news values of journalism to get in on their own terms. Not just anything presidents do is automatically newsworthy, and even the savviest public relations campaign to project certain qualities or certain programs can't be used for just anything. To take one example, the line of the day in the Reagan White House meant controlling the message, keeping it simple, and constantly repeating it; under such conditions, there's a limited amount that can be accomplished.

Nonetheless, these risks are apparently acceptable, given that the power to go public becomes particularly valuable when other avenues are foreclosed. Rhetoric scholar Roderick Hart has shown that presidents tend to give speeches on exactly those topics that are not the subject of legislative initiatives, and when they are in strategic trouble: when the opposition controls Congress, in the second half of the term, when legislative success and/or popularity is low, when economic conditions are bad, and so forth.[63] Presidential communication is thus strategic, but unlike presidents such as Woodrow Wilson or Franklin Roosevelt who went public only when behind-the-scenes maneuvers failed, contemporary presidents often *begin* their initiatives with public appeals.[64]

In order to gain public attention on their own terms, presidents have consequently increased the size of the operations directly connected with the media—beginning with the White House Press Office headed by the press secretary and the White House Office of Communications instituted by President Nixon and resurrected in one form or another by all of his successors—and enhanced the importance of newsmaking in decision making in the White House.

Although White House records are too vague to indicate who is and who is not working on media-related matters, the best evidence suggests an impressive increase in recent decades.[65] The legendary presidential press secretaries, FDR's Stephen Early and Eisenhower's James Hagerty, ran virtual one-person shops. White House press operations ballooned in the Nixon White House and have stayed at roughly the same level since. In a 1990 panel of former press secretaries, Pierre Salinger, Kennedy's press secretary, said that his staff numbered ten, two of whom were exclusively handling foreign reporters, while moderator John Chancellor noted a "sevenfold increase" between Salinger and Gerald Ford's press secretary, Ron Nessen, a little over fifteen years later.[66] After adding on speechwriters, directors of White House projects, schedulers, and the Office of Communications, it is clear that a sizable percentage—perhaps even a majority—of the White House staff is primarily involved with public relations activities.[67]

Presidential press officers, of course, spend much of their day responding to the needs of reporters and acting as emissary from the president to the media and vice versa. Although presidents, of course, employ the press secretary, they may soon learn that it is in their interest not to be adversarial or unresponsive to the White House press corps. One reason, for instance, that President Clinton's news coverage improved in late 1994 was the shift from the apparent unwillingness (or ability) of Clinton's press secretary, Dee Dee Myers, to keep appointments, preschedule events, or otherwise anticipate the pressures on the news; by comparison, Myers's successor, Michael McCurry, worked diligently to coordinate both the schedules and the messages from the White House, to provide advance texts of speeches, and otherwise give off a sense of what McCurry called "a sense of customer service" to reporters.[68] Moreover, as the press office has grown, press secretaries must spend more of their time supervising a specialized bureaucracy rather than be ministers without portfolio, as press secretaries until the Nixon presidency often were.[69]

It would be a mistake, however, to see the press secretary as either a cog in the hierarchy on one hand or a simple go-between or an official who reacts more than acts. Although the influence of the press secretary within the White House has varied greatly from one to the next, much of their credibility depends upon being perceived as a well-connected source, and presidents have an incentive to include them in decision making. Again, Clinton's first press secretary, Dee Dee Myers, was hampered by her initial exclusion from decision-making circles; as part of the White

House effort to focus their news efforts in mid-1994, Myers finally won the rank of assistant to the president and was included as part of the small group that had access to senior staff and foreign policy meetings. After Myers's resignation at the end of the year, Michael McCurry built on what she had won and also gained access to whatever meetings he wished to attend and had frequent interaction with the president. Indeed, McCurry practices what he calls "jetstreaming," assuming that, until he is told otherwise, he can sit in on any meeting.[70]

It is true that few press secretaries play a role as an advisor on substantive policy, beyond its implications for communication, as part of their job. For instance, Nixon's press secretary, Ron Ziegler, commented in a 1990 forum that "the primary role of the press secretary is to be a spokesman and to reflect the president as accurately and as clearly as he can. Even though we do during the course of our work advise the president on the number of press conferences and his communications approach, that takes place in the course of our daily activities."[71]

But, even in such a limited role, by helping presidents to prepare for press conferences (anticipating questions and suggesting answers); by gathering intelligence for the president and the White House staff about reporters' perspectives, opinions, and responses; by searching for initiatives to present proactively to the press; and by advising on when, where, and how to go public, the press secretary helps to set the policy agenda, delineates available options and likely responses among a key constituency (the media), and participates in policy decisions.

Still, for press secretaries, short-term care and feeding tends to overwhelm long-term planning. Even Hagerty, that most powerful of press secretaries, wrote in his diary that Eisenhower "hoped I could get freer so that I could start fires rather than have to put them out all the time."[72] Proactive media strategies have instead become lodged in the White House Office of Communications, and its activities have further cemented the bond between governing strategies and media strategies.[73] The Office of Communications was launched in the Nixon presidency and was soon institutionalized. Ford and Carter, the two presidents after Nixon, initially sought to avoid such an office so as to exude an image of openness rather than manipulation, only to find late in the term the benefits of an organization that could attempt end runs around the Washington media, such as to local and regional reporters who might be more easily impressed, as well as develop, coordinate, and standardize the policy agenda throughout the executive branch. In particular, by means of the "line of the day" pioneered by Charles Colson under Nixon, and perfected by Michael Deaver in Reagan's first term, newsmaking and public relations have become an integral and crucial part of daily decision making in the White House.

The "line of the day" originated in Nixon's 1970 campaigns for Republican senatorial candidates. As part of the new public relations orientation that the president demanded, surrogate speakers on the campaign trail would all stress a particular point that, it was hoped, would be picked up by the news—particularly television, which was reluctant to present more than one White House story per day anyhow. As the 1972 presidential campaign neared, the line of the day was the subject of a daily meeting at 8:00 A.M. with the president's chief policy advisors, who examined new polls to assess appropriate potential actions. In communicating what White House chief of staff H. R. Haldeman termed in a memo "the necessity for [Cabinet members] to recognize that their job is to sell the Administration, not themselves or their departments,"[74] the Office of Communications thereby not only maintained a united front for the purposes of the news but helped maintain internal control of the executive branch. By the time that Gerald Rafshoon reinstituted that office under Carter, the tasks included "help formulate themes, formulate speeches . . . and try to sell [the president's] programs, not only to the public but to the Congress."[75]

But it was only under Ronald Reagan that the Office of Communications became a key part of a presidential governing strategy from the start. Journalist Mark Hertsgaard describes a typical start of the White House staff's day in Reagan's first term. The day began with a 7:30 meeting of the "troika" which supervised the White House (James Baker, Michael Deaver, Edwin Meese) where overnight developments, often in the news, were assessed, to be followed by an 8:00 meeting of the senior staff. An 8:15 meeting to determine the line of the day was chaired by Baker, with Communications Director David Gergen and chief spokesperson Larry Speakes in attendance. At an 8:30 communications meeting, Deaver presided to set forth the day's planned events. Reporters became involved in the 9:15 briefing, when Speakes would announce these events, indicate which ones they could cover, and the conditions thereof.[76] In other words, the distinction between policy making and publicity seeking in White House deliberations of what to do, if it ever existed, was blurred if not erased. The "line of the day," which originated as a means largely to control the mass-mediated image of the president for electoral purposes, has become a way to specify what the presidency is to *be* and to *do*, setting out goals and missions, and coordinating the pursuit thereof throughout the executive branch.[77]

This is not to say that these efforts are always successful. On the contrary, as the political scientist Samuel Kernell has shown in his nice contrast of Reagan's first three budgets, similar media tactics have different successes, depending upon contextual factors such as the state of the economy, the president's popularity, and the place in the term.[78] And if circumstances seem to overwhelm presidents, they may be left with the distasteful task which Neustadt in the Carter presidency termed "the sheer incongruity of playing the clerk on national television."[79]

Nonetheless, mass-mediated strategies of governing may now be central to chief executives. Take state governors, who are favorite subjects of local news.[80] Although the evidence is spotty, there are tantalizing indications that state governors' public relations are their most time-consuming activity; indeed, one survey of governors in the 1970s showed a small but statistically significant relationship: the weaker the governors' formal powers in their state, the more aggressive were their press operations.[81] Thus, like presidents, governors have found publicity in the news as a potential way to combat entrenched actors, such as in the state legislatures.[82] Little wonder that one governor in the 1970s advised his successor as follows: "Decide early what two or three things you want to accomplish; develop a sound public information program to let people know; and devise and constantly revise methods for evaluating your own performance, using outside sources."[83]

In short, the work of the news media is of particular interest to chief executives, whether at state or national levels, who are not only the usual beneficiaries of media attention but may be willing to use their place in the spotlight to counterbalance their weakening authority. Public relations are geared toward the news media, and newsmaking becomes of central importance, not merely in calculating how chief executives spend their time but in assessing how they make decisions and seek to make policy.

CONCLUSION: NEWSMAKERS IN GOVERNMENT

In the presidency, then, officials not only acknowledge the role of the media in governing but perpetuate its importance when professionals—usually ex-journalists—are brought in to serve as directors of communication and press secretaries; their presence and activity end up reinforcing the priority of making news within an organization.[84] Now, just as I do not argue that a media strategy is inevitably a key component of decision making, neither do I argue that the presence of press secretaries and public information officers invariably reveals a key role in policymaking.

Presidential press officers are largely concerned with facilitating the flow of information without worrying about its impact on policy.

Yet even if we understand the presidential press secretaries' role to be limited, they do not merely react to reporters but keep themselves up-to-date about what reporters want to know about the activities within their beat, and they advise political officials on short-term possible responses and long-term information policy. In short, such an awareness of newsworthiness influences decisions of others on what to push and what to do; and though many press officers are mere spokespersons and "flacks," they may have to be involved in policy decisions if they can provide reporters with useful information. These press officers may be in but not of the political institution, given that they exhibit different recruitment patterns and fill a "boundary role"[85] that builds bridges to another occupant of a boundary role, the reporter at the newsbeat. So, not only do the news media act as political institutions. Official roles for dealing with the media and consequently the news media's interactions with government have become institutionalized in their own right.

This pattern has, as we shall see in Chapter 7, held for other agencies within the executive and the two other branches of the federal government. All political institutions have personnel to deal with and often to guide news media coverage in an optimal direction. The trick here is that the very desire to exploit the news media in pursuit of one's own policy goals may only implicate the needs of news deeper into the process of governing. When we talk about "governing with the news," then, it may be that newsmaking helps political actors in the short run but pushes them toward particular issues, concerns, and events and away from others, to the point that news values become political values, not only within the news media but within government as well.

7

BEYOND THE WHITE HOUSE

The presidential prototype is more important for other federal officials in its portrayal of the benefits for governing of media-mindedness than in its presentation of a precise model to be imitated elsewhere in Washington. Good news for one institution, and sometimes for different players within one institution, may differ widely. Political institutions organize their newsbeats differently; government officials have varying needs for publicity; and understandings of typical continuing stories diverge between institutions. In other words, the negotiation of newsworthiness proceeds in different ways in different newsbeats, and the negotiated procedures shape and constrain the potential for political actors therein to exercise a media strategy as part of a governing strategy.

In short, the American news media enter into the governmental process of separated institutions sharing power. The American news media need government officials to help them accomplish their job, and American politicians are now apparently finding the media more central to getting done what they want to get done. At federal, state, and local levels, the news media are now an integral part of the work of the executive and legislative branches, and increasingly important to the job of the judiciary. Let us now turn to the perception of newsmaking from beyond the White House.

BUREAUCRACIES

Presidents are not the only ones, of course, in the executive branch who graft media strategies onto governing strategies, even if they are the most visible and the most frequently examined. Political appointees and civil servants in the executive bureaucracies practice media strategies, too. Most famous is the leak, but the executive branch is also permeated with assistant secretaries for public affairs in every department and public information officers in every agency, enabling each subunit to explicitly use the news as a way to govern.[1] As with the president, these press officers find that, to get their messages out, they cannot rely solely on the means of communication that they directly control but must turn to the news media for help.[2]

As any student of the American executive branch could tell us, the interests of even presidential appointees to serve as Cabinet secretaries or heads of agencies, let alone the interests of civil servants, often diverge from those of the president—tempting them as well to turn to the news media to help them accomplish their particular goals. These similar bureaucratic imperatives, and their similar tasks of serving and servicing the media, push press offices throughout the executive branch to resemble each other. Political scientist Stephen Hess concluded in his superb study of press offices in the State Department, Pentagon, Department of Transportation (DOT), and the Food and Drug Administration (FDA): "Regardless of how they were organized or how different their sizes, each performed the same duties in a similar manner. Indeed, it becomes possible to generalize in this study because the Pentagon's press operation appears much like the FDA's writ large."[3]

To be sure, bureaucratic independence has been limited by the rise of the White House Office of Communications and the invention of the line of the day, which allows presidents to coordinate the media strategies of the various departments and agencies. But such coordination is necessarily incomplete. For one, the news media's interest in the vast majority of departments and agencies—particularly the outer circle beyond State, Defense, and Justice—is highly sporadic, and, when reporters turn elsewhere in the executive branch, they are most interested in news that differs from that peddled by the president. For individual beat reporters, this divergence increases their ability to "sell" their story ideas to otherwise doubtful editors; for the news organization as a whole, it provides a greater range of storylines.

At the very least, presidents must accept or even embrace some diversity among the news from Cabinet secretaries. When a subject crosses across beats, the news media will seek complementarity among stories from different beats. Thus, in the first month after Iraq's invasion of Kuwait, stories from the White House beat stressed the president's individual (and remarkably clear-cut and unwavering) decision making, those from the State Department focused on official policy pronouncements, and those from the Pentagon provided operational expertise to explain the American response, but all three were squarely behind the military option.[4] Even apparent splits between the White House and a department can be strategically used, if the news can thereby reinforce a perception

of a Cabinet secretary as an immovable "true believer" who may pull
the recalcitrant bureaucracy in his or her direction and who can be the
object of criticism that would otherwise hurt the president—and who·
can be jettisoned if that criticism becomes too intense.[5]

The trick for Cabinet members is to find an issue that can raise their
profile and prestige—and their reputation as a player along with it—
without taking away the spotlight from the White House on a presidential
issue.[6] A good example is Bush's Health and Human Services Secretary,
Louis Sullivan, whose reputation was languishing until he found an issue
on which he could take center stage in the news: cigarette companies
targeting black consumers. With Sullivan's authoritative role as the government's leading health officer and as a black physician in his own
right, the coverage he received ended up significantly improving his
stock among Washingtonians.[7] Similarly, Clinton's Energy Secretary,
Hazel O'Leary, responded to Republican attempts to abolish her department by a proactive media strategy that involved series of revelations of
past governmental radiation testing on human subjects—a strategy that
proved controversial when it was revealed, late in 1995, that O'Leary
had used public funds to hire consultants to recommend approaches to
the news and to monitor reports and reporters.[8] Although the accolades
in the news do not always match the perception of the Cabinet secretary's
performance within Washington, such positive coverage may give them
greater power than they would otherwise have and, indeed, allow them
to keep their jobs.[9]

Most Cabinet departments and agencies, however, labor in comparative obscurity, with little attention from journalists and even less in the
ultimate attention that the media pay. Below the "Golden Triangle" of
the White House, the State Department, and the Pentagon, news coverage
of the executive branch is little or less, arising usually only during an
accident or other unexpected crisis or when the appointee has made himself or herself newsworthy by disagreeing with the president in public or
in private.[10] This leads Hess to imply that the press officers are
"spokesmen without influence"—since management and decision making are often distinguished from the dissemination of information, and
given that much if not most of what press officers must do is react to
reporters' sometimes infrequent queries.[11]

Now, it may be that press officers in the bureaucracies do not deal
often with much of the news media. Yet anticipation of media attention
is a continuous effort within agencies. When that agency becomes newsworthy, it is not purely reactive and impartial; instead, it has a particular
agenda ready.

Two published case studies are instructive: Lewis Helm's recounting of his 1972 experience as chief public information officer of the Interior Department during the Pennsylvania relief effort after the devastation left by Hurricane Agnes; and Hess's own participant-observer account of DOT's media strategies, after an Air Florida plane crashed into the Potomac River in Washington in 1982.[12] Both cases show vividly how press officials work on one hand to coordinate information, correct misinformation, and get the word out about agency efforts, at the same time that they steer criticism away from their operations and otherwise ensure favorable news for their performance and legitimacy for their agency during an unexpected crisis.

In the case of Hurricane Agnes, Helm noted, the federal flood relief effort was "not falling into place quickly enough" in an election year: "My job was to help the White House 'neutralize' the situation, to make it a nonissue. I was to see what was happening, report back shortcomings in personnel and programs, and focus public attention on the positive steps being taken by the administration."[13] What is instructive about Helm's case study is how blended his tasks were, including both policy and politics: informing the public about relief measures, pressuring other federal workers and state officials with the threat (sometimes carried through) of adverse publicity if they did not cooperate, and presenting both the practice and the image of hands-on responsiveness by a special presidential representative "to help give the victims a recognizable government leader with whom they could identify."[14]

Likewise, Hess noted that Linda Gosden, director of public affairs for DOT, sought to filter out unsubstantiated information, which served on one hand the goals of accuracy and calm, but also served the political goal of keeping the department free from any criticism that this crash might have been due to the less experienced air traffic controllers hired after the PATCO strike the previous year. "Gosden . . . began a series of quick calls to the networks, whose prime-time news programs were about to go on the air. She did not rule out an error on the part of an air controller; only the National Transportation Safety Board—not an arm of DOT—can determine the cause of an accident. Rather, Gosden gave reporters information that she hoped would allow them to draw a conclusion that the crash could not be blamed on the people in the control tower."[15]

Hess's view of "spokesmen without influence" must be modified in several other ways. Agencies vary not only by the newsworthiness of the bureaucracy but also by the agency's interest in the uses that can be obtained from publicity. Moreover, agencies by their emphases cue reporters in on what's newsworthy. Press officers thus react to stories they helped to instigate. The classic example is the State Department, which has long served to cue reporters into foreign happenings of interest to domestic audiences; as one State Department desk officer noted as far back as the 1960s, "I'm doing the same kind of analysis as the newsmen—we can talk their language."[16]

Finally, for reporters, a reactive bureaucrat or one who is merely a conduit may not be good enough. In most agencies, policy personnel have no objection to the active involvement of press officers in policy making or even expect it.[17] Again, for reporters to be satisfied with the information provided them by the press officers, the press officers have at least to be perceived as being "in the loop," close to the decision makers and involved in policy discussion.[18] And again, certainly press officers are less concerned with the substantive details of the policy than they are in the impact that it may have upon the continuing operation of the agency. Their involvement, however, changes the tone and content of the evaluation of problems and alternatives.[19] But as political scientist David Morgan has phrased it, "By being the expert on managing appearances, senior PIOs [public information officers] evolved slowly into being general policy advisers."[20]

As one goes deeper into the bureaucracy, the inexperience and short duration of most presidential appointees below Cabinet rank—and the limited attention of the news media—causes them to turn responsibility for dealing with the media over to public information officers who are often career civil servants.[21] These civil servants, as part of the bureaucracy, are undoubtedly like most bureaucrats in being vitally interested in self-preservation—not merely for self-interest or because of inertia but because the pursuit of worthwhile policy goals and the maintenance of the organization cannot be easily distinguished. In the incremental development of organizations, standard operating procedures evolve that encapsulate particular values, which in turn arise as these procedures are applied to real-world problems. The way things have always been done is inseparable from the worthy goals they pursue, and it becomes the job of the press officer to help maintain the legitimacy of both.

Self-preservation becomes particularly important for new enterprises and for departments and agencies with huge programs and large budgets. If an agency is just getting established or if its mission is otherwise threatened, a savvy media operation can be a way to emphasize the importance of their issue domain and the effectiveness of their responses—and not coincidentally satisfy public expectations and protect their budget in the process. As far back as the 1930s, political scientist James McCamy's pioneering study noted how FDR's recently founded New Deal agencies had more aggressive media operations than older, more established bureaus.[22]

Other departments and agencies rely heavily upon the news media as a key way to accomplish policy goals when they lack resources otherwise to do so. In particular, if the agency cannot enforce its decisions on its own, the news media become an important avenue of policy making, getting the word out to a larger audience who will then respond in a way that, it is hoped, will accord with the aims that it seeks. Much of what is disseminated is performative language, such as praising, cautioning, condemning, or warning. That story is directed outward through the news and through press releases, but it also reaches audiences inside the bureaucracy who thereby are constantly reminded of the missions of their agencies.

These two approaches have been exemplified, respectively, by the Pentagon and by the State Department. State, by focusing its attention on the daily noon briefing, satisfies both the needs of reporters for the facts on American responses to events abroad and of bureaucrats who are attempting to assemble that policy. The noon briefing began during the 1944 Dumbarton Oaks conference on the establishment of the United Nations. Undersecretary Edward Stettinius was backed into a corner at a lengthy press conference and sheepishly told Secretary of State Cordell Hull that he had given them more substance than he had intended. As Stettinius's diary recorded it, Hull "did not seem concerned with the fact that I had to give out some substance, saying 'the world is not going to come to an end if you give the press a little information to keep them happy.'"[23] Given the performative nature of these speeches, Stettinius's risk averseness has continued on with his successors, who read carefully constructed statements that often leave reporters seeking to pin down a story, painstakingly comparing the words from today with those from yesterday in a form of "nuance journalism."[24]

But although the State Department's approach to the news media could well be characterized as damage control, the primacy of the briefing is no longer just to keep reporters happy. Press officers, from reading the morning prestige press and from meeting with political appointees, derive a sense of what is likely to be asked, send questions to the various bureaus for written statements that may then require clearances from other bureaus, from other departments and agencies, and from the White House, and gather these "guidances" for the spokesperson and file them away as an official policy reaction to the events of the day. Thus, as Hess incisively notes, "[T]he State Department now sees . . . the purpose of the meeting [to be] a clearance mechanism for official reactions to world events. The briefings have been co-opted by government officials and are only secondarily related to the reporters' needs."[25] Yet, partly because it is as definitive as one can get in the world of government, partly because it is on the record, and partly because it parallels the reporters' task of analyzing a confusing outside world, the daily briefing and the statements by the official spokesperson become the crucial ingredients of State Department correspondents' reports. In effect, the policy making of the State Department is coterminous with the newsmaking of State Department reporters.

The formal processes of newsmaking are less visible at the Pentagon. For one, the newsbeat is remarkably intimate. Estimates of the number of "regulars" outside of specialist publications have ranged between ten and twenty,[26] and reporters and press officers with adjacent large, unpartitioned spaces interact informally. On-the-record briefings occur only about twice a week, a far less frequent ritual than the daily counterparts at the White House or State. The Pentagon's strategy is less inclined toward the minutiae of policy than toward educating the public on the need for a big defense, sophisticated (and expensive) weapons systems, and a large bureaucracy. Their attitude is perfectly captured by security reviewers who sought to quash Pentagon whistle-blower Ernest Fitzgerald: "Unfavorable comment on established practices might cause the public to lose confidence in the management of the Department of Defense, and this in turn would undermine security."[27]

This comment—and our recollections of the many restrictions placed upon the news media during the 1991 war against Iraq[28]—makes it sound as if the Pentagon is primarily concerned with restricting information. But it would be more accurate to say that the Pentagon's media strategy is influenced by whatever will allow it to fulfill its perceived mission and protect its programs and its budget. Robert Sims recounted a telling story about George Wilson of the *Washington Post* in his in-house profile of Pentagon beat reporters:

> The fleet oiler *Canesteo* had to remain tied at the dock in Norfolk because it did not have enough experienced petty officers below decks. Wilson heard about this problem, flew to Norfolk [and] interviewed the skipper and crew members . . . The ship's skipper resisted the interview, but his superiors felt the story—admittedly embarrassing—would dramatize the need to raise pay to attract and keep specialists. And refusing to address the subject with the *Post*'s reporter might spawn a worse story than the true one. So the *Canesteo*'s skipper was urged to go ahead with the interview, and he

did. The story was embarrassing; it was front page, but it spotlighted personnel problems confronting the fleet, and was the impetus for a spate of news reports and congressional hearings that ultimately resulted in a military pay raise.[29]

We might set forth State and the Pentagon as two alternative models for executive agencies. The State Department's budget is comparatively small, reflecting its inability to influence directly the unfolding events abroad. The Pentagon, by comparison, supervises an enormous budget and bureaucracy that it seeks to protect. For State, the power of the news is more to specify and broadcast American foreign policy inside and outside the United States. For the Pentagon, the power of the news is less to make policy than to provide coverage that will safeguard, if not expand, the programs and budgets under its purview.

Thus, where an agency is small or otherwise lacks the resources to make enforceable decisions, the State Department model will be an attractive use of the news. Agencies seeking to manage the free market, such as the Federal Trade Commission or the Consumer Product Safety Commission, may find their procedures too complex and cumbersome or their resources stretched to the limit to pursue infractors through court cases or other legalistic procedures.[30] Instead, they can accomplish as much by drawing the news media's attention to unsafe products or unsavory practices, and, by doing so in a public manner, may provoke, at low cost, the corporations into reforms in order to avoid similarly damaging publicity in the future.[31] Indeed, it is cost-effective for agencies to use a media strategy to induce adherence to the law. The best example I have encountered on this was in April of 1995, when the state of Connecticut was preparing to host the Special Olympic games. Faced with a lawsuit from a mentally retarded citizen who claimed discrimination by a travel agent who refused to issue a ticket and concerned about the prospect of further discrimination toward athletes coming to Connecticut for the Special Olympics, the state decided to make a public example of the travel agent, pointedly adding, "We are doing this so that citizens will police themselves, rather than be policed by the state."[32]

By comparison, the Pentagon's model of aggressively selling itself and its policies comes into play when an agency needs to defend its turf and justify itself and its practices. By raising the salience of the issue area with which it deals and thereby increasing the prominence of their responses thereto, agencies can influence the public mood whereby they will continue to reap appropriations. Such a strategy was apparently put into play at the Immigration and Naturalization Services (INS) within the Justice

Department in the early years of Ronald Reagan's presidency. Facing across-the-board budget cuts, the INS went into a full-court press to raise the salience of immigration as a public problem. Once those stories were written, it consequently became much more difficult to cut the INS.[33] More recently, too, the director of the Agency for International Development went public to defend his agency, faced with potential abolition, with what one newspaper account termed "a passionate round of lobbying, speech making, letter-writing, log-rolling, string-pulling and plain old pleading."[34]

Thus, even an agency with a small budget that has predominantly relied upon news to accomplish policy can add on a more aggressive public relations stance should their budget—and thereby their central mission—be threatened. That seems to be one of the lessons that the State Department has recently learned, at least to judge from the changes after Madeleine Albright succeeded Warren Christopher as President Clinton's second Secretary of State in early 1997. Faced with a Republican Congress hostile to foreign aid, Albright began her tenure with high-profile trips—first to Texas where, in a gesture worthy of the Pope, she put in a stint at a local passport office, and then on an around-the-world voyage filled with Reaganesque photo opportunities such as when she solemnly stared through her binoculars across the demilitarized zone separating South and North Korea. The logic of her media events was, as one sympathetic journalist put it, to convey "that foreign policy is as relevant today to jobs at home as it is to threats from abroad and that the United States needs diplomatic representation—and an international budget—worthy of what she calls 'the indispensable country.' "[35]

But whichever model is followed, it seems clear that for personnel throughout federal bureaucracies, policy making and newsmaking are increasingly intertwined. Our popular impression of bureaucrats is as individuals pushing papers and avoiding any outside attention, which might threaten their beloved routines. But, far from shunning the spotlight, bureaucrats and bureaucracies are all concerned with making news, not merely because they are willing to react to reporters' queries but because it serves their political and policy interests at the same time inside and outside of their agencies.

CONGRESS

The other end of Pennsylvania Avenue has not been immune to the increasing lure of using the news as a way to govern. Indeed, just as the numbers of White House staffers devoted to working with the news media ballooned in the late 1960s, and just as the executive branch oriented itself more and more to media-related activities, so too Congress has shifted in the last fifty years from an institution where its members dealt almost exclusively with the press back home in their constituencies for electoral purposes (with a few high-profile exceptions of investigations or mavericks) to one where both backbenchers and leaders routinely seek national publicity to influence national policy.[36]

This transformation can best be seen by two trends. The first is institutional: the incursion of television into Congress, so that, by now, virtually every stage of the legislative process can be—and often is—broadcast. The second is individual: the rise of the press secretary as an integral part of the personal staffs of virtually all senators and most House offices.

The saga of congressional television has been a gradual opening of its procedures to being broadcast.[37] Although Senate committees had allowed television from the medium's infancy—with dramatic results in the investigations led by Estes Kefauver and Joseph McCarthy in the early 1950s—the House did not do so until 1970. Following the almost uniformly positive response of the public to the televised hearings of the House Judiciary Committee on the impeachment of President Nixon, the House leadership moved in 1977 to install a closed-circuit system of televising the proceedings on the House floor, which could eventually be used to broadcast the floor to the outside world, as occurred in 1979. The Senate, sensing—not without reason[38]—that their public prominence was being eroded by House television, eventually followed suit in 1986. With floor proceedings from both chambers being sent over the two channels of the Cable-Satellite Public Affairs Network (C-SPAN) as well as fed to the networks, and with committee hearings being televisable, too, Congress has opened its process up to public view, either directly through C-SPAN or indirectly through the television news.

At an individual level, too, we readily find indicators of greater concern with the news media. With the reforms of the 1970s, and the growth in congressional staff to counter the rise of the seemingly imperial presidency, members of Congress were able to appoint staffers who would deal full-time with working with the news media. As in the executive branch, press secretaries often have come to Congress by different routes from other staffers, with less Capitol Hill experience and, instead, significant journalistic background, including previous professional training and employment in news or public relations.[39]

To be sure, these developments cannot be taken to mean that every member of Congress now covets and obtains national media attention. For one thing, given that Congress's institutional workings are usually more newsworthy than individual actions, members of Congress are not equal in the eyes of the national news media, which tend to gravitate toward leaders, committee chairs, and others who are understood to be pivotal players in the continuing script of how-a-bill-becomes-a-law.[40] Reporters most interested in the members, and most inclined to have regular contact with them and their press secretaries, are instead from the home-town media, particularly local newspapers, which are, in turn, evaluated as the most reliable and valuable news outlets in their job.[41] This greater interest from the local media in most legislators, combined with the bottom-line concern in all congressional enterprises to work toward reelection, gives most members' media operations a decidedly local tilt.

But national media attention is not beside the point for most members of Congress most of the time; it is simply more important for those who are interested in making national policy, setting an issue on the national agenda and (not coincidentally) raising their profile as a player to be reckoned with. Moreover, measures of the coverage that members of Congress actually receive simply cannot be equated with the effort they put into pursuing publicity or with the value they place on being in the news. A single appearance on the nightly news is presumably more valuable to a junior legislator than to the Speaker of the House or the Senate Majority Leader, but it is also less predictable; consequently, backbenchers, denied the forums to translate effort into news, may devote a great deal of attention to the news in the hopes that it will eventually pay off.

We might think of the relationship of internal power with effort spent wooing the national media to be parabolic. With newly elected members still working on perfecting their constituency relations and figuring out how the institution works, their concern is almost exclusively the local news. Party leaders and powerful committee chairs, on the other hand, have reporters gravitate toward them with little resistance. But at what political scientist Burdett Loomis has nicely called the "middle management" of Congress, medium-seniority members who are chairs or ranking minority members of subcommittees or caucuses, the pursuit of national media takes on some urgency, especially among those on policy-oriented committees who would like to bring an issue to national attention—and themselves along with it.[42]

To understand this point more fully, we must recognize that members of Congress have multiple and not always completely reconcilable goals. While David Mayhew, in a classic essay, suggested that congressional activity could be best understood by the "single-minded pursuit of reelection," a more complete explanation follows a model from Richard Fenno positing that all members are interested in multiple goals (albeit to differing degrees across individuals and over time): not just getting reelected but also making good public policy and wielding influence within the institution.[43] It is certainly true that much of congressional legislation is parochial, particularistic, and aimed at reelection; but what remains to be explained is why so much is not.

One answer is that reelection is, for many if not most members, a means to other ends. As Fenno's famous study on representatives' "home style" in their districts concludes, House members have distinct careers in what another scholar has termed "the two arenas of Congress," one in the constituency, and the other in Washington. Members seek to establish an image among their constituents that will increase the credibility of their explanation of their Washington activity, giving them more leeway to do what they want to do within the institution.[44] Congressional action is influenced, then, by members' concerns about avoiding blame and by what actions they can explain back home.

This process has been complicated by the relaxation in the last few decades of the norms and folkways, such as apprenticeship and deference to committees, that constrained individual action. With the help of congressional reforms of the 1970s, that gave more power to an increased number of subcommittee chairs and enhanced individuals' personal staffs to the point that we can think of members' offices as miniature enterprises, members in both chambers can call on significant individually controlled resources.[45] Party leaders who faced increasing difficulty after the reforms at meeting their dual goals of getting legislation passed and keeping peace in the family had little choice but to craft increasingly elaborate rules in the House and unanimous consent agreements in the Senate—which has only partly counterbalanced the centrifugal shifts in Congress.[46]

While the growing homogeneity of the two parties and the "fiscalization" of policy through the dominance of budgetary concerns in congressional decision making has produced a recentralization of Congress since the mid-1980s,[47] this trend has paradoxically produced a number of middle-management members who may have to appeal to the media in order to have their issue appear on the leaders' agendas. Indeed, members in recent years have been resorting to stunts borrowed from the repertoire of social movements, with a fair amount of success. In the mid-80s, for instance, the question of U.S. policy toward South Africa gained particular force when the arrests of protestors at the South African embassy began to include members of Congress; the homelessness issue was propelled along by a batch of House members keeping an overnight vigil on a Washington heating grate.

Or take one example of this ability to resort to outside strategies when inside power has been abridged: the case of Tony Hall, an Ohio Democrat who was chair of the House Select Committee on Hunger in early 1993.[48] After newly elected members convinced the party leadership not to allow a vote on reauthorizing any select committee, Hall held a press conference outside the Capitol and began a fast where he consumed only water. Hall said he hoped to raise the national salience of the issue and to put pressure on the House leadership to establish a permanent committee on hunger. Within two weeks, Hall reaped the benefits of publicity, with favorable feature stories in national newspapers such as the *Washington Post* and the *Christian Science Monitor*. The announcement that a group of some forty actors and celebrities would join in for twenty-four hours gave new momentum to the story. After fasting for twenty-two days and losing some twenty-two pounds, Hall stopped his fast only after obtaining promises from the World Bank and Agriculture Secretary Mike Espy to hold international and national summit conferences on hunger, and from the Democratic Caucus to consider creating a party task force on hunger.

Hall's case may not be typical, but it beautifully illustrates what can happen to officials once news becomes a central focus of policy-making activity. Hall's approach was perfectly geared to the habits of the American media: his issue was straightforward and easily understood by the American public with an easily described solution; the approach of a fast was a dramatic continuing story with increasing urgency. Thus, even after the abolition of his inside forum, Hall still controlled resources through the media to pressure other political actors—and to try to regain an arena for his issue and himself, even at the cost of alienating colleagues and party leaders.

Thus far, media strategies would seem to be better geared toward winning publicity and power for individuals rather than for the institution and its leaders. Even in the traditionally less newsworthy House, however, every Speaker since Rayburn has devoted successively more time to dealing with the media and has become increasingly proactive in his attempt to win publicity.[49] Moreover, the textbook conventional wisdom stresses Congress's inability to act, which raises the question: When can Congress pay collective attention to the general national interest? There are two problems here: getting Congress to act, and to do so in a way that is not restricted to servicing the organized. The answer may be that even if we agree with Mayhew that members are fundamentally risk averse, we must remember that there are times when the costs of inaction are higher than the costs of action.

Media attention comes in handy for members of Congress seeking to gain collective action for three reasons: increasing the costs of collective inaction, concentrating the attention of distractable colleagues on their preferred issues and alternatives, and protecting them from the potentially negative consequences of their votes. I have already mentioned David Price's analysis of the issues considered by the House Commerce Committee in the 1970s, which found that members were less inclined to avoid issues that provoked high group conflict as the public salience of that issue grew. Political scientist Douglas Arnold has expanded this insight with the important concept of "traceability." Arnold notes that members will be more inclined to anticipate public reaction when a particular policy or political result can be "traced" back to a member's action or vote; in such a situation, members either can be forced to respond to public opinion or can be protected therefrom by rules, parliamentary maneuvers, or the range of options.[50] Although Arnold does not mention the media, it is clear that the chances of traceability are greater when actions and issues are in the news.

The classic case where the costs of collective inaction overrode group conflict was the 1986 tax reform legislation.[51] Tax reform emerged, almost accidentally, as an important issue in the 99th Congress. President Reagan, expecting that his Democratic opponents in the 1984 election would endorse the Bradley-Gephardt tax reform proposal, had asked Treasury Secretary Donald Regan to study the problem and report back after the election. But with entrepreneurial staffers at Treasury keeping it alive past the election, it soon became clear that no one wanted to be fingered as being responsible for killing tax reform. With the president passing the buck to the House, which then did the same to the Senate, all with the media watching the progress closely, the strong interest group opposition to changes in the tax code was overridden—even though public opinion was split and far from confident that tax reform would personally benefit them.

But surely the poster child for media-mindedness on Capitol Hill is the current House Speaker, Newt Gingrich, who not only gained power by a heavy reliance upon a media strategy but continued to exercise power through the news. In the first hundred days of the 104th Congress, Gingrich rode herd over his newly elected Republican majority to pass most of the bills featured in the "Contract with America" that he and his party promulgated the previous fall. By setting forth an agenda of bills supposedly bottled-up by earlier (Democratic) Congresses, giving them catchy titles based in part on focus group and polling research and a deadline for their passage, and by continuing to push the agenda with zippy speeches in a variety of public settings that had been bypassed by his predecessors as Speaker, Gingrich was able to focus attention on the House, maximize traceability, and raise the stakes for inaction or postponement. With the news media counting down the clock, Gingrich was able to maintain extraordinary Republican unity and pass all but one of the bills. Although, at the time, what was most noteworthy about Gingrich's approach was deemed to be his break with the past (especially by televised press conferences and his almost presidential request for prime-time television time for a speech), in some ways, Gingrich took the congressional media strategy to its logical culmination.[52]

Increasing the costs of collective inaction can be accomplished by a variety of legislators, even by backbenchers in Congress, willing to push an issue before the media. But it is considerably harder for those members to ensure that their preferred alternative is linked to that issue, in particular because party and committee leaders can use their media prominence (linked to their control over legislative processes) to hijack a now-prominent issue and link it up to a different piece of legislation that they can credibly claim addresses the designated problem. To use the example that I develop in more detail elsewhere, when Rep. Don Pease, seeking to focus attention in 1985 on the continuing problem of unemployment, successfully called attention to the upcoming expiration of a federal unemployment program and the dramatic possibilities of hundreds of thousands of unemployed workers being suddenly cut off from unemployment compensation, he lost control of the issue to more powerful and prominent individuals—President Reagan and Dan Rostenkowski, chair of House Ways and Means—who could credibly say that the solution to this particular problem need not be to renew the expiring program but to make sure that everyone then on unemployment received their full six-weeks' benefits. In that process, members were protected from any negative reaction that might be incurred by their opposition to renewing the entire program and were able to proclaim that they got "something done."[53]

It is thus only when a given bill is viewed in the news as *the* only response to a particular problem, sometimes by its title (e.g., *the* Clean Air Act), that members can concentrate attention on their preferred alternative. Little wonder, then, that members spend so much time arguing about what a piece of legislation is really all about. Take President Clinton's spending package, which he sent to Congress in the spring of 1993. Clinton and the Democrats termed this "a stimulus plan," but the Republicans responded by noting, in often derisive detail, the hodge-podge of pork-barrel projects contained therein. The ultimate showdown in the

Senate thus became a dispute as much about the appropriate meaning of the legislation, and we should not be surprised if the media's attentiveness to the various elements of the plan alongside the ostensible macro-economic benefits stopped the momentum of Clinton's plan.

In short, both houses of Congress now engage in newsmaking as an integral part of the legislative process. To be sure, the Senate, because of its size, both contains more opportunity for individual action and for senators to be noticed in the news than the larger, more structured House, and for that reason the Senate and senators are more centrally engaged with the media and with tasks accomplished via the media such as agenda setting. Yet despite the moves toward recentralizing the House in the last ten years, despite the relative lack of the national news media's interest in House members, and despite the comparatively limited forums for making news, House members do not and cannot find the news media to be irrelevant to their policy-making tasks. It is true that much of the pursuit of news is done without the direct involvement of the members themselves, but far from pointing out the lesser importance of newsmaking, it suggests that it is integrated into the very structure and daily routine of congressional enterprises.

THE SUPREME COURT

Of the three branches established in the Constitution, the judiciary would, at first glance, seem to be unlikely to link media strategies and governing strategies.[54] In particular, once Supreme Court justices are confirmed for lifetime appointments, their public life almost disappears. Unlike the case with their congressional neighbors across the street, tape recorders, microphones, and television cameras are barred from the Supreme Court when arguments are held and decisions handed down. Instead, reporters gathering information at the Court for any medium are restricted to the venerable tools of pen and pad. When decisions are reached, the Public Information Office gives out the text, with a synopsis thereof as a headnote, but, almost uniquely in Washington, issues no press releases, holds no briefings, and does not investigate reporters' queries. Important decisions are often clumped together on the last days of a session with no attention to the difficulties this may pose for reporters. Justices hold no press conferences to explain their votes but instead exit out a rear door where no reporters can waylay them. Some justices refuse to give any interviews or speeches. Among those that do, they hold back from commentary on ongoing cases or issues and prefer to dwell on larger topics of philosophy or constitutionalism, and may decline answering more pointed questions afterward. Leaks are even rarer. The law clerks that work for them are sworn to secrecy, and even they are not fully apprised or aware of the discussions and disputes that go on among the nine justices assembled to vote and decide. As Richard Davis puts it, "The result is an absence of continual overt guidance from the institution about what constitutes news."[55] Or in the words of *New York Times* Court correspondent Linda Greenhouse, "The journalist's job is almost entirely paper-dependent . . . While most politicians will cheerfully or angrily critique any story in which their name has appeared, Justices rarely respond to public comment, or even to rank error."[56]

Moreover, justices would seem to be less reliant on the news media in their jobs. They inform themselves through formal channels more often than other officials in Washington. Unlike those in the executive or in the legislature who find out about issues and problems, in part, through news attention, the justices are presented with controversies that have arisen through the judicial system, and they attempt to limit themselves, whenever possible, to the facts of the case generated at lower levels and to deciding on the narrowest constitutional or statutory grounds possible. Moreover, the intimacy of the Court, with its constant circulation of opinions and conferences among its nine members, decreases the necessity of using the media as a way to communicate with one's colleagues that one finds in the executive and the legislature.

Finally, the costs of communicating through the news media are higher for technical experts such as the justices, whose finely shaded conclusions are often exaggerated and misunderstood in the news. The news media, for instance, are often criticized for missing the distinction between deciding a case and affirming a decision versus declining to grant certiorari and thereby allowing the lower court decision to stand. Relatively few cases are deemed newsworthy enough to be reported in depth, and journalistic rather than judicial criteria dominate that decision. Moreover, particularly in television, coverage has tended to personalize the disputes, focusing on the stories of the individual litigants, and adopting a who won/who lost mentality about the outcome that obscures the jurisprudential implications of the decision.[57]

So the Court's behavior toward reporters would seem to substantiate an observation made in 1959 by Anthony Lewis of the *New York Times* when he worked there as a law correspondent: "All of official Washington except the Supreme Court is acutely conscious of public relations. The Supreme Court is about as oblivious as it is conceivable to be."[58] Greenhouse, Lewis's most recent successor, echoes, "I see a Court that is quite blithely oblivious to the needs of those who convey its work to the outside world."[59] But Lewis was not altogether correct even for the less media-conscious 1950s. The Supreme Court is, to be sure, far more aloof than its executive and legislative counterparts. But much of the image of aloofness from publicity and the news is itself a product of publicity and the news. In other words, as with the other branches, justices are conscious of maintaining the mass-mediated image that buttresses their authority; in their case, that image is that they are above politics.

Moreover, in recent years, as the Court has taken on more (and more highly politicized) issues and has increasingly moved into the spotlight of the news, some justices have begun cautious individual media strategies of their own, to influence the public mood, shape public opinion, lobby for bills, and to pressure other actors in Washington, including their fellow justices. They do so by giving speeches, granting interviews, and, above all, providing off-the-record information to reporters.[60] Media strategies at the Supreme Court thus reflect the ambiguous position of the institution: though authorized to preside over the court system in a disinterested and principled fashion and to build a coherent jurisprudence, their decisions have political impacts of which the justices are well aware, and some of them end up embracing a policy-oriented stance.[61] Since the Supreme Court is simultaneously an institution that is jurisprudential and disinterested on one hand, and political and highly interested on the other, the media strategies practiced therein reflect this split role.

Justices cannot be "oblivious" to news coverage for a number of reasons. As with all Washingtonians, justices are news consumers and pay attention to the news. Chief Justice William Rehnquist has written that he and his colleagues "read newspapers and magazines, we watch news on television, we talk to our friends about current events."[62] In so doing, they end up (whether intentionally or not) gauging the importance and public salience of issues and the likelihood of particular public responses to particular decisions. Thus, the Court, in certain cases, is well aware that it is operating in the spotlight; in the Bakke case, the first test of the constitutionality of affirmative action, Justice Lewis Powell, who crafted the solomonic compromise, noted as the decision was announced, "Perhaps no case in my memory has had so much media coverage."[63]

The news, of course, may poorly estimate the eventual public response. Abortion had not been much of an issue in the public eye until after the decision establishing a women's right to an abortion, Roe v. Wade, was handed down in 1973; the amicus briefs from outside interest groups disproportionately favored the prochoice side, and the topic had not been an important controversy in the news. Ironically, then, Roe ended up mobilizing a prolife constituency, the visible absence of which had been one reason that the decision was reached in the first place.[64]

More important, of course, is the fact of life first expressed in *Federalist* 78: that the Court, lacking the enforcement power of the executive or the appropriation power of the legislature, would necessarily be the "least dangerous" branch. The Court's authority derives from public support and its moral force as guardian of the law, which requires, in turn, a carefully defined image as above politics. Communications must be designed in such a way as to reinforce that view: hence, the image of aloofness from image making.[65] Not only must the Court as an institution safeguard its prestige to ensure compliance. So too, policy-oriented justices must cultivate what Walter Murphy termed "reputations . . . both for skill in their craftsmanship and for determination in seeing that their judgments are followed"[66]—reputations which could rise or fall on the basis of news coverage for justices as much as for presidents and members of Congress. And of course, their decisions must be communicated to those that will carry it out—state and lower courts, to law enforcement officers, to other officials, and the like. Given that few people actually read the opinions themselves, the Court must rely upon the news to do so, and in terms that will persuade otherwise recalcitrant individuals amidst the well-known tendency of Court reporting to rely upon the reactions of other sources in day-after stories.[67] In short, in the words of retired Justice William J. Brennan, "[T]hrough the press the Court receives the tacit and accumulated experience of the nation, and . . . the judgments of the Court ought also to instruct and to inspire—the Court needs the medium of the press to fulfill this task."[68]

The most dramatic example of this use of the news actually hails from the days of ostensible obliviousness: the school prayer decisions, *Engel* v. *Vitale* (1962), which overturned a prayer composed by the New York Regents, and *School District of Abington Township* v. *Schempp* (1963), which prohibited Bible reading and the Lord's Prayer in public school.[69] The earlier decision was actually more limited, based as it was on the "establishment clause" of the First Amendment, but press coverage was much more critical, apparently because the reassurances of the limits of the decision that Justice Hugo Black placed in his majority opinion were placed in a footnote and were overshadowed by concerns raised by Justice William O. Douglas in his concurring opinion. A month later, Justice Tom Clark, part of the majority, responded to the coverage of *Engel* with an unusually open criticism of the media in a speech in San Francisco. Clark blamed in particular the wire services and "pressures on reporters to communicate the ruling rapidly." [70] When *Schempp*, a farther-reaching decision, was reached the following year, Clark himself was assigned to write the majority opinion and did so in a far more straightforward way, indicating in simple language just what was and was not decided as well as acknowledging the continuing role of religion in American society. Largely because of this attention to the clarity of the message, the press reaction was balanced and dispassionate, contributing in part to the less unfavorable public response to *Schempp*. But most important for our purposes was Clark's reaction: a realization that how one communicates the decision, both directly and indirectly, matters for the impact of the Court.

The Court institutionally, as well as justices individually, can use the news in this way for a couple of reasons. First, the unfolding process of receiving appeals, accepting cases for review, hearing oral arguments, and issuing decisions is a perfect way to organize journalists' routines. [71] By sorting out stories that might be worth following, and then dividing those into stories that are best reported at the argument stage versus those that are more suited to being covered when a decision is handed down, journalists build continuing stories that can be well anticipated—enabling them to fill in the blanks whether by legal research or by going to the locale where the case originated and personalizing it by interviewing the parties involved.

In this process, there is an extraordinary number of documents at every stage. Even in the Minnesota trial courts that journalism professor Robert Drechsel studied, where judges welcomed (though rarely initiated) contact with journalists to explain their decisions, reporters continued to rely primarily upon documentary evidence rather than observation of ongoing processes or quotes by participants to use as the bases for their stories. [72] And the quantity of documentation is much greater at the Supreme Court. In the words of Fred Barbash, a former *Washington Post* law reporter, "No other institution explains itself at such length, such frightening length." [73]

Thus, unlike the executive and legislative branches, the judiciary is covered largely through its own documents and at times that it as an institution determines—in part, of course, because the Court presents the formal proceedings and the Public Information Office makes the documents available far more readily than the other tried-and-true journalistic methods at other newsbeats. But these processes and documents also offer opportunities for individual justices to advance their own agendas. Oral argument can provide a forum for a justice who asks pointed, dramatic, or clear-cut questions—so that it is no surprise that one study found the conservative activist Antonin Scalia to be the most often mentioned in network news oral argument stories of the 1990–1991 term.[74] At the decision, observers of the Court have noted the explosion of opinions, not only individually written dissents but concurring opinions that allow each of the justices, if they so choose, to explain their vote.[75] Such opinions, not hamstrung by the necessity of marshaling five votes behind them, often speak in remarkably individual voices aimed not at their fellow justices or lower courts but at the public. Most dramatically, when Justice Harry Blackmun, the architect of the *Roe v. Wade* decision, saw *Roe* survive by one vote in the 1992 *Casey* case, he warned not only of the possible future overruling of *Roe,* but added, "I am 83 years old. I cannot remain on this court forever, and when I do step down the confirmation process for my successor well may focus on the issue before us today"[76]—a barely veiled reference to the then-upcoming 1992 presidential election. Given journalists' reliance upon the opinions as the most heavily relied-upon evidence in their stories, decisions often reflect both institutional and individual agendas—as does the coverage thereof.

But as in many other areas of their collective endeavors, the Supreme Court operates by self-restraint, holding back from more aggressive media strategies since that could begin to chip away at the beneficial image provided in the news. The irony of the Supreme Court's institutional media strategy is that, even to those who participate in it, it is not a media strategy.[77]

To be sure, justices do act in ways designed to gain publicity. For one, political scientist Richard Davis found that even justices that abjure on-the-record interviews often engage in off-the-record "backgrounders" with reporters and do so to a much greater extent than they did twenty years ago. In Davis's words, "It is not that the Court does not participate in the creation of its own image, but that it seeks to do so without the risk of public exposure."[78] And even when the justices communicate in public on philosophy or try to turn the publicity toward noncontroversial topics, such a strategy is delicate. By doing so, they can find themselves—inadvertently or not—in the center of a political storm. Thus, Chief Justice Rehnquist made front-page news when he gave a 1996 speech defending the independence of the judiciary. This discourse might well have gone unnoticed if it had not followed quickly on the heels of a controversy between the two presidential front-runners: President Clinton, who criticized one of his own appointees' rulings (subsequently retracted), and Senator Robert Dole, who denounced the liberalism of Clinton's judicial appointees. The *New York Times* headline suggested, nonetheless, that "Rehnquist Joins Fray on Rulings," although the initial paragraph did point out that the chief justice was "as oblique as some other Federal judges have been direct in response to the recent tide of political criticism of sitting judges."[79] Likewise, while justices may be willing to talk to journalists, even on television, and are presumably gratified to hear it called (as they are) a "conversation" or a "chat" rather than an "interview," these sessions provide potential opportunities for reporters to ask more probing (and more political) questions than justices might otherwise like to answer.[80]

The Supreme Court is then not as oblivious as it seems to publicity; indeed, that very stance of obliviousness is, in part, a product of a carefully crafted media strategy. But beyond that, it seems that the justices are now increasingly aware of the possibilities of the news, not merely in informing the public but in making sure that, in ways large and small, their decisions are honored and enforced.

CONCLUSION

The presidential prototype reviewed in the Chapter 6 cannot be extended to the uses of the news for other actors and in other branches. Indeed, the uniqueness of the presidents' position vis-à-vis the news media—the focus on a single protagonist, the hermetically sealed press room, the resources placed into going public and into staging visually compelling events—ensures that media strategies elsewhere in Washington are studies in contrasts. Yet these apparent contrasts only obscure a deeper constant: all political actors in Washington are now using publicity as part of their strategies for governing and to a greater extent than they were twenty or thirty years ago. Another constant is perhaps the most intriguing: that the media strategies of governmental actors are carefully designed to help counter the main deficiencies they encounter in accomplishing their tasks, including those bequeathed that institution by the Constitution. The consistency with which we have seen this last theme reminds us anew that working with the news is not simply for ego gratification, self-aggrandizement, or public popularity; it is now part of the job of governing. This point gets frequently lost when attention is called to apparently thin-skinned political actors who are envious of others who try to horn in on their spotlight, justifiably or not; but, in fact, such individuals are merely trying to protect one key political resource: the ability to attract media attention to build a reputation that can then be used to reinvest that attention into getting something done.

But as I have intimated throughout, such assistance does not come without a price. Political actors seeing the news as crucial to governing increasingly anticipate the needs of journalists attempting to craft news-worthy stories. As press secretaries and press officers multiply within government, the irony is that they are better able to manipulate the content of the news as they become more deeply involved in the day-to-day operations of their home institution. In other words, politicians may then win the daily battles with the news media, by getting into the news as they wish, but end up losing the war, as standards of newsworthiness begin to become prime criteria to evaluate issues, policies, and politics.

Is the future of American politics then to be dominated by the search—by journalists and political actors alike—for narratives that are timely, clear-cut, terse, easily described, dramatic, colorful, and visualizable? Are political actors to be increasingly judged by their successes as performers, judged by journalists with their own particular set of criteria rather than by policies that work? Can journalists break out of this? Can politicians? Can citizens?

8

CONCLUSION: THE FIRST AMENDMENT AND THE

FOURTH BRANCH—TOWARD REDESIGNING

A NEWS MEDIA POLICY

This book has investigated the possibility that the news media in the United States nowadays constitute a political institution in their own right. Drawing initial inspiration from Douglass Cater's 1959 book, *The Fourth Branch of Government*, I have argued that the news media are an intermediary institution in Washington, D.C., and a crucial one in a separation-of-powers system where action does not come easily. We have seen how the development of the current news media has always been closely fostered by practices and public policy, how the news media perform governmental tasks, how reporters themselves (like it or not) are political actors, and how government officials attempt to use the news as part of their daily jobs of governing. So the American news media do not only constitute a political institution; they are part of government.

To review the argument: the historical evidence assembled in Chapters 2 and 3 demonstrates that the development of the American news media was never free from politics. The history that is most often told concerns the demise of governmental control in the form of licensing, seditious libel, and censorship, and the decline of the individually sponsored partisan press. This story of the widening "progress" of freedom of the press must be joined by a less frequently recounted tale, whereby the news media have long been (and continue to be) subsidized by a variety of governmental policies and practices. The shapes, formats, and contents of the news, in other words, were never "free" from governmental intervention. On the contrary, a good case can be made that the news might not be possible if it weren't for what government does for and to the media.

To be sure, such governmental involvement is true of other institutions that would not readily be termed "political" by most observers (such as the corporation). As I argue in Chapter 4, the news media constitute a political institution, not merely in the sense that individual news outlets reinforce each other's coverage, not simply in the way that processes of newsmaking are similar from one organization to the next, but most centrally, in having been bequeathed a central role in a political and social process, that of communication. Yet the irony and the paradox of journalistic power is how it is hidden even (or especially) from its practitioners. By applying standards of objectivity, importance, and interest, and judging stories by how well they fit the "production values" of the news, journalists may believe they are contributing no political bias. The content suggests otherwise. And, as I developed in Chapter 5, the news media are political because the choices they end up making do not equally favor all political actors, processes, and messages. Far from holding up a mirror to external political actions, the news media are directly involved in instigating them.

The most impressive evidence, however, on the news media as a political institution comes not from what journalists and their organizations do, but instead from the increasing attention that political actors in other institutions give to newsmaking as a central part of their own job. Newsmaking is now a central way for governmental actors to accomplish political and policy goals. In that sense, the news media may well be an "unwitting adjunct" to power. And incumbents in every institution devote more time and energy to newsmaking than did their predecessors a few decades before. Making news, in other words, is not merely a way to get elected or reelected, to boost one's own ego or to be a show horse instead of a work horse; instead, it is a way to govern. The constitutional framework specified that when the executive, the legislature, or the judiciary acts, it needs the assistance, or at least the passive consent, of the other two for their decision to stand. Nowadays, the same may be said of the news media, which require aid and assistance from other political institutions to accomplish their task, but which in turn themselves participate directly in the Washington politics of "separated institutions sharing power."

WHAT IS THE PROBLEM?

All this is not necessarily such a problem. The mere facts that the news media or that journalists embed bias in the news or that the news media exercise political power might disconcert some. So would the idea that the practice of American politics is increasingly centered on getting into the news. Yet these possibilities do not bother me in the abstract.

I do not share the apparent conviction on the part of journalists that they can approximate or even approach an objective, unfiltered account of what is going on in the world. Instead, my view of social science—let alone a more intuitive enterprise such as journalism—would lead me to indicate that our ability to understand social and political processes hinge on making arguments and marshaling evidence behind those arguments, and that lone facts cannot be judged in the absence of the framework of understanding that generated them. Individual journalists' biases and omissions seem less of a concern than the very real possibility that journalism, as a collective enterprise across individuals and indeed across organizations, implicitly contains an entire series of assumptions about how the world works, and how the world should work, that bring with it a limited set of political interpretations. This homogeneity across news outlets and repetition over time makes for the political force of the news. As the assumptions and routines produce predictable news over time and homogenized news across news outlets, their worth is reinforced. The tools of journalism are rarely the object of direct scrutiny when journalists, by applying them conscientiously, often inadvertently disguise their presence, let alone their impact; and when something goes awry, it is usually easier to blame the individual infractor, not the sacrosanct rules and routines that enable newsmaking.

This is not to suggest that the main problem of the news nowadays, as jeremiads have claimed,[1] is that television now provides an oversimplified, overdramatized version of the news. One theme in the above chapters is that technology itself is rarely as much of a problem compared to how it is used. Even in its current state, television's capabilities for presenting compelling and vivid evidence and breaking barriers of inattention are often greater than newspapers, which require previous interest and, often, previous knowledge.[2] And the problem is the news as a whole, not just television news. Any biases attributable to individual modalities become less central when one recognizes there is no single "main source" from which Americans receive their news.[3] The news habits of citizens are usually haphazard; important information is often derived from hearing the top-of-the-hour news summary on radio, scanning the headlines of the newsstand in front of the post office, or channel surfing on television. Thus, ABC News's proclamation, "More people get their news from ABC than from any other source," may be less a tribute to ABC than a commentary on the fragmentary news habits of American citizens.

Rather than bemoan this fragmentary approach, we should instead be impressed, not only at the capacities of citizens for creatively assembling political impressions of their own, but also at the way in which this reliance on a variety of news sources can alleviate the problems of relying on a single biased outlet. But this apparent willingness on the part of the public to consult multiple news outlets is vitiated by the considerable homogeneity in the news, a direct effect of the difficulties that news organizations have in figuring out just what is and isn't news. In particular, profit-oriented news organizations (and even to a lesser extent, their non-profit counterparts)[4] seek advertisers to whom they will sell access to their audiences. This economic imperative nurtures "production values" shared by almost all news outlets. The corresponding consensus on routines of newsmaking that exist across news organizations in order to crank out a predictable regular product pushes only toward certain political possibilities and away from others that are foreclosed.

Nor should we quickly decry the increasing media-mindedness of American political actors. Publicizing one's activities can be, and occasionally is, a powerful way to maintain official accountability, to ensure that the issues being addressed within political institutions correspond to the concerns of the public, and to bring the public into the democratic debates and deliberations in Washington. The problem is not that political actors have to "go public." Instead, the dilemma stems from the costs imposed on going public: namely that they must incorporate notions of newsworthiness and thereby particular politics not only into their communication strategies but into the very criteria for decisions and actions.

The governmental news media in the United States present a twofold problem. One is the *capacity* of the news media to perform the role that has devolved on it.[5] Journalists are not well trained, nor are news organizations well equipped, to help weigh problems, set political agendas, examine alternatives, and study implementation. Journalistic criteria of importance and interest simply may or may not have much to do with societal concerns of politics and policy making. I have argued that the work of journalists favors news that is easily and regularly gathered, that is timely, terse, simply described, concrete, dramatic, colorful, and visualizable. So, to the extent that journalism organizes politics and wields power in the American political system, it directs attention: toward episodic outcroppings rather than continuing conditions; toward issues that fade quickly in public consciousness as newspersons begin to assume that the audience is getting as bored as they are with the same old concerns; and away from abstract complexity toward simple if not simplistic renderings of problems, policies, and alternatives.

Another problem, at least equally important, is that of *accountability*. If, as this book contends, journalists end up wielding political influence, one can only wonder: Who elected them? And to whom are journalists responsible? Newspersons will rightly contend that they are answerable to their audiences. But on what grounds? As in other areas of capitalism, one can easily doubt that consumers gravitate toward the better mousetrap. Instead, the public makes such choices shaped by how a product is marketed, whether oligopolies provide openings for innovation, and how investors react to new or old products.

Although journalists claim that they are acting as the "surrogate" for their audience,[6] research has consistently found that they know little about their audiences and are even less interested. Avoiding this information may be rational for reporters, given how they already feel considerable direct pressure from superiors, colleagues, and sources. By paying less attention to the public, they can devote their energies to satisfying (or at least working on not upsetting) those immediate actors. Beyond opting out of the news, ways for citizens to hold the news media accountable are few. Newspapers may reprint corrections, but these far more often refer to errors of fact (e.g., the wrong middle initial) rather than of judgment. Even when news organizations do admit to the latter, such admissions tend to leave the routines and rules of newsworthiness intact and shift blame to individual lapses in conscientiously applying the rules, or, even more conveniently, to sources or the audience. Letters to the editor may be routinely solicited and reprinted, but similar rules of newsworthiness by which the news was selected seem to apply in culling out which letters to reprint.[7] Even the recent rise of the "ombudsman" in news organizations does not accomplish much, given that most ombudsmen see their position as a form of public relations for newspapers, explaining journalistic work to audiences, not an office to remind their colleagues of the demands and needs of the citizenry.[8]

Contemporary news organizations are primarily oriented toward their audiences, not as citizens but as consumers. The most prominent audiences for the news are advertisers. Advertisers, not readers, after all, provide the bulk of the income and profit to news organizations. In an increasingly consolidating and profit-minded media industry, such profits become ever more central. How powerful the readers and viewers of the news can be under such circumstances is open to question. Mass circulation may simply be too expensive for news organizations, as compared to targeting a smaller, more affluent audience. The classic examples remain the mass circulation photo-weeklies such as *Life* and *Look* that continued to attract large readerships in the 1960s, but whose advertisers had increasingly gravitated toward television as the best way to sell their products, leading to the weeklies' paradoxical demise at the height of their popularity. Similar processes may be at work with metropolitan newspapers, who are often all too happy to see their circulation decline, if it trims costs of distribution without limiting the advertisers' interest in reaching readers with greater disposable income.

If the American political system has become increasingly dependent on the news media, not merely to communicate with the American people but to communicate among elites and activists and to help in the very process of government, it has empowered an institution that is neither well-designed to do so nor effectively politically accountable. Political actors have become ever more conscious of the need to make news, and they have become skilled at it as well, but, as sketched above, the demands of the news do not match the needs of a polity.

In the pages that remain, I will explore some possible ways to make American politics less beholden to the current biases of the news media. One is technological: that the explosion of communication networks, such as 500-channel television and the Internet, will make the mass media, as we know them today, obsolete, and will dilute the single-minded biases and power of the news, succeeded as it will be by a greater variety of information. Another possibility is to turn to journalists and charge them with greater vigilance and greater attention to ethical standards in choosing the news.

Finally, I turn to politics. Two complementary possibilities present themselves. One, suggested by distinguished media scholars such as Thomas Patterson and Daniel Hallin, is to point to the empty "public sphere" or the dearth of other political institutions that connect together political actors with each other and with the populace.[9] In other words, a key way to counter the downside of media power is to build other political institutions that could remove political actors from their dependence on the news to get something done. Second is to begin discussing not merely the kind of news that we want in the United States but the ways we can reach it, with particular attention to revitalizing a public policy toward the news media. Ironically, as Chapter 3 has shown, the federal government has always had specific policies toward the news. But the more recent preoccupation with the First Amendment's prohibition on abridging freedom of the press has been so paralyzing that almost nobody discusses in much detail a public policy that would facilitate, indeed maximize, freedom of the press. It is time to start doing so.

But before we do that, perhaps I should also address a possible objection. We may not *need* to grapple with a national policy toward the news if the technology of mass communications is changing rapidly in the direction of greater democratization and diversity, or if journalists themselves are and should be capable of changing their methods and enterprises with no need for government intervention.

TECHNOLOGICAL SOLUTIONS

The end of the century has produced much speculation about the "information superhighway" and how both information and communication will be revolutionized by the so-called new media. The new technologies as a whole contrast with the old. All enable increased volume of information at a greater speed, more individual control over information by citizens as well as greater "narrowcasting" of messages through decentralized and interactive media.[10] There is no doubt that the days of the domination of the mass media are now behind us. Most notably, the old saw about the "two-party political system being replaced by the three-network political system" seems anachronistic given that the audience for the three networks has dropped precipitously since the seventies when they were watched by over 90 percent of the audience. The increasing availability and use of video cassette recorders (VCRs) for entertainment, and the expansion of cable television to approximately two-thirds of the American populace, has simply chipped away at the previous oligopoly. As satellite dishes shrink in size and price, and as the 500-channel cable looms in the future, additional possibilities for communication open up. And then, of course, there is the Internet and the World Wide Web, with its virtually unlimited capacity for near-instant intercommunication, the near-impossibility of centralized control and its multiplication of sites (Web and otherwise) of political debate and discussion.

History, however, teaches us that technology is no panacea. And we would be clearly exaggerating to announce the demise of the mass media, or, for that matter, of the mass audience. As I have repeatedly noted, a technology offers a range of possible uses, but it is initially understood in terms of previous forms of communication; its ultimate shape owes as much to politics and society as anything else. The utopian-sounding predictions of the impact of the Internet are, sadly, quite reminiscent of similar prophecies of how new communication technologies—the telegraph, the telephone, the radio—would transform politics. Indeed, the development of the Internet shows remarkable similarity to earlier technologies, in its early reliance on government subsidies and support of the technology, the exploration by amateurs that established new possibilities, and eventually the entry of large-scale for-profit businesses that effectively took over the technology and shaped its possibilities.[11] Nor are the predictions uniformly in one direction; instead, some warn that the result of new technologies will be to fragment and undermine information, knowledge, and deliberation.[12]

Also, access to new technology is far from equal. Even with now-venerable cable television, around one-third of American households are not wired for it even if they could afford the increasingly expensive monthly costs. Likewise, those individuals connected to the Internet are a small minority, and disproportionately affluent and well-educated. The irony of the communication revolution, as the sociologist Todd Gitlin has acutely noted, is that we may be facing a political communication system increasingly fractured along economic lines, with the well-to-do having ever more opportunities for elite interaction, and the poor and working class having access only, at best, to a constricted system concentrating on the increasingly sparse products of broadcast radio and broadcast television.[13]

Even if the technology itself might push toward democratization, it does not act alone. The political scientist W. Russell Neuman has concluded in his excellent study, *The Future of the Mass Audience*,[14] that the democratizing impulses of the technology are counterbalanced by two phenomena. First, the public is only "selective and semiattentive." Whether most people would take the time and effort to surf the Net on a daily basis is doubtful; indeed, even sophisticated Net surfers have standard routines of getting information, such as by "bookmarking" the site or otherwise constructing programs to gather it for them.

Second, as Neuman has noted, the political economy of the media provokes a small number of economies of scale to gravitate toward lowest-common-denominator programming. Thus far, the information superhighway is not carrying substantively different kinds of communication. The expansion of cable has been accomplished largely by taking old formats and inflating them to twenty-four-hours-a-day programming; thus, segments of the nightly television news shows were the model for such cable spin-offs as CNN (all-news), the Weather Channel (all-weather), ESPN (all-sports), and CNBC (all-business).[15] And while news is now available through the Net—such as an on-line version of the *Wall Street Journal* that is individually personalized for one's own concerns, whether for a particular subject, stock, or sports team—it, too, relies heavily on preexisting formats and versions of the news. The old wine of the news is simply being poured into the new bottles of technology.

This process should only accelerate as established news media move into the Internet and establish Web sites.[16] The short history of the Internet as of mid-1996 has witnessed three phases already following its establishment by government-sponsored researchers: the initial exploration by amateur hackers; the emergence of on-line Internet service providers, such as America Online which organized access on a "closed-gate proprietary model"[17] to the Net; and the partial displacement of those firms by those such as Netscape which developed software to run the Internet's bandwidth and provide quick access to the totality of the Web. Next, apparently, companies will derive income from content on the Internet to be produced by already established media industries such as Disney, News Corporation (media baron Rupert Murdoch's business), and NBC (which in 1996 launched an alliance with Microsoft called MSNBC with both an all-news cable channel and an interactive Web site).[18] Scarcity is not the same concern as it was for radio,[19] so these enterprises will not physically force out the amateurs (as the initial licensing of radio did). But the greater quality and verve of the commercial sites will attract larger audiences, much as community cable access was overshadowed by commercial cable offerings. Such commercial sites will be funded either by fees and subscriptions, or, perhaps more likely, by advertising, with all the attendant influences upon content, format, and style.

And as has been the case with previous technologies, the government is getting out of the business of subsidizing the Internet now that private enterprise will take over. The little-noticed privatization of the Internet is proceeding, as the federal government sells off its portion of what began as an invention of the Defense Department. As one journalistic observer has written of this trend, the previous "communal system was possible because the costs of maintaining electronic links were largely absorbed by research institutions and the U.S. government, leaving cyberspace gurus free to work on their pet projects. But now, as the Internet is sponsored by corporations and other for-profit groups, the gift economy is being supplanted by the dollar economy."[20]

Certainly, there is much that is positive to say for recent technological shifts. For one, it increases the possibility of interactivity, if only at the level of selecting among lead stories on a television broadcast, or at preediting a newspaper to highlight one's preferred subjects. Once video is routinely sent over the Net, the new media can then begin to combine the advantages of television (speed, vividness, personal connections) with the pluses of newspapers (as much depth as one wants when one wants, selectivity over material, and taking it at one's own pace). As presidents put their speeches on the Net and politicians and members of Congress establish Web sites, new beneficial opportunities for direct communication with the public emerge. Add to that the ability of activists to build narrowcast networks through the Internet, and the new media that provide ways of mobilizing a constituency in a way never possible through the existing mass media before.

But these advantages are at least equally counterbalanced by the probability that the most readily accessible—and most user-friendly—information on the Internet and in the World-Wide Web will simply be an extension of familiar forms of journalism. The technology cannot be counted on to single-handedly counteract the negative side of governing with the news.

JOURNALISTIC SOLUTIONS

This discussion returns us, then, to journalism. Most critiques of journalism, whether outside or inside the enterprise, operate from a tacit assumption that if we could only get journalists to change how they go about doing their job, the news would be much improved. Yet such critiques, whether they decry the inaccuracy of reporting (as often occurs, say, in studies of scientific reporting or coverage of the Supreme Court), or the failures to report a particular topic (such as foreign countries) or to cover all the angles (like too much political strategy and not enough substance), may miss the point in many ways. Not least, they underestimate the pressures on journalists to do their job and overestimates the resources they have (most notably, time) to do it right. Criticism of journalists must be able to figure out how their goals can be accomplished under the real-world pressures to crank out a daily product called the news.

The problem of the news is much larger than what individual journalists do. Indeed, the problem is bigger than journalism, given that what scholars traditionally have termed the "news organization" has now become a "news department" in a much larger corporation, itself within a rapidly consolidating industry. In effect, much of the story of the news over the past twenty-five years or so—since the apogee of journalistic influence and prestige in the wake of Vietnam, the Pentagon Papers, and Watergate, and since the still classic studies of news organizations cited above—has been the decreasing autonomy and resources of individual journalists working within ever more profit-oriented enterprises.[21]

The "newshole" for politics and government, in particular, has diminished considerably. Television news both locally and nationally gravitates toward "news you can use" and scrutinizes the ratings to see which stories provoke the quickest channel surfing; newspapers gather focus groups to pinpoint what readers would like to see in the news. Note what vanished when the *Miami Herald* initiated cost-cutting moves in 1995: it not only began to "attrit" its staff but also reoriented its newsbeats. A memo circulated by its publisher said the *Herald* would "focus its news-room resources on nine subject areas that readers have told us are especially important and useful: local government; education; sports; environment; consumer news; Florida news; Latin America; health/medicine and crime."[22] Format changes have also shrunk the news, as some newspapers imitate the emphasis of *USA Today* on "context" rather than "content" while others try to find ways to make their product "easier to read," entailing enlarging the typeface or increasing the white space around stories—either of which makes for less news. Finally, the technological shifts that have sped up the news cycle means that news is increasingly broken by round-the-clock radio and television shows and then analyzed by one news outlet after another: first by the evening network news, then by the daily morning papers, and finally by the weekly newsmagazines, all of which only exacerbates the homogenization of the news.

So the dilemma for political actors today is that the news is ever more useful to them in their jobs exactly when it has become less accessible on their own terms. This creates a new quandary when they try to reach larger audiences in ways not channeled by the news. Much of President Clinton's difficulty with the White House press corps at the beginning of his first term stemmed from his well-stated intention to rely on talk shows and the other forums that had worked well for him in his successful election campaign. Not only did this raise the hackles of reporters, who considered it "our job" to disseminate news from the White House, but it also resulted in an unusually negative bounce in the news from his appearances on various programs, which were often derided as trivial and thin when in fact they were strongly substantive occasions.[23]

There are, in fact, some changes that journalists could make that would at least partially alleviate the problems of accountability and capacity. As a starter, they should acknowledge more fully their position within the American systems of communications and politics. Journalists would serve the public and politics more completely if they stopped seeking the same kind of professional monopoly traditionally enjoyed by lawyers and doctors. Instead, journalists need to realize that they are but one set of contributors to the news; beyond that, they should realize the philosophical benefit if political actors can communicate directly to the public. Reporters need not muzzle themselves or refrain from tough questioning. Instead, I would stress that the news is more than just what journalists produce and involves a variety of communications, some from politicians alone, some from reporters alone, and some by both sides whether collaboratively or not.

Similarly, journalists need to deal more constructively with their own involvement and power in American politics. At the very least, they need to avoid the disingenuous notion that they are mere private citizens. This self-concept/self-defense emerged quite clearly in late 1995 after stories accumulated of reporters' high-flying honoraria for speaking engagements—even as they skewered politicians for doing the same. When Howard Kurtz of the *Washington Post* began calling some of what he called "buckrakers" to find out about their compensations, they all demurred with statements such as "We are private citizens" (David Brinkley), "I of course do not make the laws" (Sam Donaldson), "I'm not an elected official" (Gloria Borger), or "I don't exercise the power of the state" (George Will).[24] Once again, the unwillingness to face the consequences of their reporting may be rational for individual reporters, if only because it gives them the freedom from what Gans calls the "paralyzing" consideration of the many possible effects of their coverage choices. If short-term second-guessing would undermine the ability to produce the news, long-term examination is worth pursuing, not according to the usual journalistic ethics of objectivity but instead by careful examination of which interests were consistently assisted and which were submerged by the way that news was made. In particular, journalists need to conduct more careful assessments of whether their readers, viewers, and listeners were both satisfied and well-served by coverage, preferably by consulting them.

In other words, journalists, to be accountable representatives of the public, must find ways of being responsive. As Hanna Pitkin developed the theme of "responsiveness" in her classic account, representation involves not only independently acting on behalf of the represented and their interests, but also engaging in dialogue that would hopefully lead to some kind of accord on the best course of action.[25] In that sense, some recent developments are laudable, notably the various activities loosely assembled under the rubric "public journalism."[26] In the first book devoted to public journalism, Arthur Charity defined its philosophy as what would "make it as easy as possible for citizens to make intelligent decisions about public affairs, and to get them carried out."[27] Instead of envisioning journalists as distant, impartial observers of politics and dispassionate revealers of wrongdoing and scandal, public journalism emphasizes their role as citizens fully involved in their communities and engaged in ongoing dialogue not only with their sources and peers but with their audiences as well. Public journalism involves consulting with the public as to their concerns; grounding the news proactively to address those issues and working to hold other political actors accountable thereto; paying primary attention to the needs of citizenship in crafting a story, not the stage of the individual episode; and providing forums for discussion and deliberation among citizens and between citizens and officials.

Public journalism is a clear step in the right direction. It recognizes the institutional role of the news media among other institutions; it reorients the attention of the reporters away from sources and colleagues back to audiences; it supplements the chase for the glitzy narrative with a focus on information that can become useful in public deliberation and decision; and it pushes journalists away from the let-the-chips-fall-where-they-may style of objectivity toward grappling with the social and political consequences of their reporting.

Yet it is far from clear whether public journalism can address the needs of the news media as a whole and over a longer period of time. First of all, it is labor-intensive and requires supplementing previous journalistic commitments with new ones. Whether news outlets can make the expensive commitment to this style of journalism—that is, if it loses money even while it provides greater legitimacy for the news outlet and satisfaction for readers—is an open question. As of yet, the core financial support provided by foundations[28] raises doubts about the long-term financial feasibility of public journalism. Second, we do not know if public journalism can work in large metropolitan areas where there are few news items that draw together an entire community. Is it a coincidence that the vast majority of news outlets engaged in public journalism have been monopoly newspapers in fairly cohesive medium-sized cities (e.g., Akron, Charlotte, Dayton, Norfolk, Tallahassee, Wichita)?[29] Also, public journalists are still in line with earlier modes of journalism, examining a large and undifferentiated citizenry rather than addressing smaller audiences with shared situations, backgrounds, or points of view, and often relying on the same tried-and-true methods for what is a "big issue." In that light, the main choice for public journalism has been to conduct polls to decide what issues to cover—which may not substantially expand the public debate if one is restricted to what the public as a whole thinks and what government officials are pushing. Finally, how public journalism can be routinized rather than devoted to special projects is unclear, especially if, as Charity claims, it is to transform rather than supplement traditional forms of journalism. Public journalism, in other words, is another important piece to the puzzle, but it cannot solve the whole problem on its own.

CONSTITUTIONAL SOLUTIONS

Whenever I get to the end of a semester of teaching a class on mass media and politics in the United States, students want to know: What are we to do about this? And when I have gently proposed that the time may be ripe to begin a more thorough consideration of public policy toward the news media, the protest is inevitably: What about the First Amendment? Because any discussion of media policy ends up invoking the central constitutional concept of freedom of the press, it is worth taking some time to discuss what the First Amendment does and does not mandate, permit, or proscribe when it comes to the news.[30]

The language of the First Amendment is direct: "Congress shall make no law . . . abridging the freedom of speech, or of the press." The brevity of the phrase obscures great confusion over its meaning. For one, the apparent clarity of "make no law" is countered by the ambiguity of what it means to "abridge" freedom. And then there is the problem of just what "freedom of the press" means. The deliberation in the Congress that adopted the amendment was not recorded; the original legislative intent is forever lost. Nor have investigations of understandings of freedom of the press at the time of the founding produced consensus either.[31]

We would be better off to note an essential duality to "freedom of the press." Law professor David Anderson has explored the most common meanings of that phrase up through the American revolution.[32] Recall the evidence I reviewed in Chapter 2 that shows a contradictory legacy of newspaper history from the colonial period between crusading against corrupt authority and acting as a impartial conduit for other persons' opinions. Similarly, Anderson has shown that "freedom of the press" was split. Some used the phrase to imply that crusading printers were free to publish whatsoever they chose; others looked to the right of ordinary individuals to have access to a printing press and publicize their views. This duality was hidden because, of the early state constitutions, only one went beyond vague references to the wonders of freedom of the press as a "bulwark of liberty." The exception was the Pennsylvania Constitution of 1776. It contained two clear clauses: "[T]he people have a right to freedom of speech, and of writing, and publishing their sentiments; therefore the freedom of the press ought not to be restrained," and, "The printing presses shall be free to every person who undertakes to examine the proceedings of the legislature, or any part of government."[33] Note how this language—the apparent basis of James Madison's first draft of the Bill of Rights—emphasized the people's right to "publish their

sentiments" and valued the press as a public forum open to all. Freedom
of the press, in other words, was aimed at and for the benefit of the citizenry, before the printers.

True, the Supreme Court has tended to treat freedom of the press in
almost exactly the same way as freedom of speech, rather than devise a
different approach. Surprisingly few cases have been decided on a logic
unique to the freedom of the press. Although the news media have
claimed particular rights and privileges derived from freedom of the press,
the Supreme Court has refused to agree.[34]

The Court's failure to recognize a distinct constitutional mission for
the press has not gone unchallenged, even from within the Court. The
late Justice Potter Stewart argued, in a 1974 speech, that freedom of the
press is "a *structural* provision of the Constitution."[35] As Stewart saw it,
the distinct phrase "or of the press" means that (unless the founders were
redundant), freedom of the press was accorded not to individuals but to
an institution, "the only organized private business that is given explicit
constitutional protection."[36] Stewart went so far as to conclude that the
First Amendment was designed "to create a fourth institution outside the
Government as an additional check on the three official branches."[37]

It is intriguing to find the "fourth branch" thesis in the musings of
one Supreme Court justice. And although Stewart's logic never became
embraced by the Court during or after his time on the bench, he himself
contended that "this constitutional understanding . . . provides the unify-
ing principle underlying the Supreme Court's . . . decisions dealing with
the organized press."[38] That point is debatable.[39] Nevertheless, given the
ways in which the evidence reviewed in this book points toward the news
media as a political institution and as a part of government, it is worth
considering more fully the implications of recognizing the news media as
a "fourth institution" authorized and legitimized by the Constitution.

To Stewart, the implication was quite clear: in order to provide
"organized, expert scrutiny of government," the First Amendment sought
"the institutional autonomy of the press."[40] But such a contention is
problematic, given the radical difference between the press of the 1790s
(open, ephemeral, small operations with low start-up costs) and the news
media of the 1990s (institutional, long-lasting, large operations with ex-
tremely high start-up costs). The press of the 1790s was neither "organized" nor "expert." Institutional autonomy is no precondition to the
people's right to "publish their sentiments." And the interpretation of
freedom of the press throughout the case law of the nineteenth century
gave no greater credence to institutions than to individuals.[41]

Above all, Stewart's *theory* of "checks and balances" is at odds with the *practice* in American government (reviewed above in Chapter 6) of "separated institutions sharing power." His presumption that the news media work to check government is simply empirically wrong. As the evidence compiled above copiously demonstrates, the news media can be and are used as an extension of government and officials at least as much as a check. But if we see the news media entering into the institutionally shared power, this makes greater sense: each institution has a modicum of autonomy from the rest, but such autonomy is not absolute, especially given the involvement of other institutions in the process of each.

The law professor William Van Alstyne, provoked by Stewart, posed a fascinating fable, suggesting that if freedom of the press were to be interpreted as providing a special institutional role, such a preferred position could easily lead to equally special obligations.[42] In fact, the Supreme Court, in a number of decisions, has come close to establishing that the First Amendment imposes particular obligations on news organizations if the rights of citizens are to be maximized, rather than merely provide rights for those in control of the media. The duality of the First Amendment at its creation, in other words, continues into constitutional interpretation today.[43]

Many of these cases concerned broadcasting. Here, government action was traditionally justified by the scarcity of frequencies that necessitated greater regulation.[44] But consider the *Red Lion* case in 1969. The Supreme Court unanimously upheld the constitutionality of the Fairness Doctrine (later abolished by the Reagan-era FCC) that required broadcasters to give reply time to political candidates or to those who had been personally attacked. Justice Byron White's opinion for the Court specifically rejected broadcasters' First Amendment claim of a right to broadcast whatever they wanted: "Where there are substantially more individuals who want to broadcast than there are frequencies to allocate, it is idle to posit an unabridgeable First Amendment right to broadcast comparable to the right of every individual to speak, write, or publish."[45]

But White went further. He provided a reading of the First Amendment that was considerably broader than the scarcity rationale, to the point that it provides a new perspective for government policy toward the news media:

[T]he people as a whole retain their interest in free speech by radio and their collective right to have the medium function consistently with the ends and purposes of the First Amendment. It is the right of the viewers and listeners, not the right of the broadcasters, which is paramount . . . It is the right of the public to receive suitable access to social, political, esthetic, moral, and other ideas and experiences which is crucial here. That right may not be constitutionally abridged either by Congress or by the FCC.[46]

This striking reading of the First Amendment focuses on the rights of citizens to information, not on the rights of those in the media industry to disseminate what they want. To White, the central benefit of the Fairness Doctrine was how it opened up the debate rather than "abridged" it, making it both laudable and constitutional.[47] In so doing, White not only hearkened back to the concerns with the people's rights exhibited in the Pennsylvania Constitution of 1776, but he suggested that the very institutional role of the press, as embodied in the First Amendment, requires greater governmental attention to preserve and expand the range of voices represented in the news.

To be sure, *Red Lion* does represent roads not taken more than doctrines developed. In particular, the Court, only a few years later in *Miami Herald* v. *Tornillo*, unanimously invalidated a Florida law requiring newspapers to allow candidates who were attacked in the news to reply.[48] *Tornillo* did not overturn *Red Lion*, because the Court continued to argue that broadcasting regulation was conditioned on the scarcity of frequencies.[49] However, the tension between *Red Lion* and *Tornillo* has been puzzled over by lower courts, particularly as the presumption of scarcity seemed technologically more and more problematic. Thus, in 1987, the D.C. Court of Appeals suggested, "All economic goods are scarce, not least the newsprint, ink, delivery trucks, computers, and other resources that go into the production and dissemination of print journalism . . . Since scarcity is a universal fact, it can hardly explain regulation in one context and not another."[50] This logic equating broadcast and print media was picked up by the FCC when it revoked the Fairness Doctrine that same year.[51]

Yet we would be wrong to conclude that the ringing rhetoric of the *Red Lion* decision holds only—at most—for television and radio broadcasts. For one thing, if all news media operate under scarcity, that may signal a need to develop more policies toward print, not to adopt a more hands-off approach to broadcast media. In fact, the Supreme Court's pioneering considerations of freedom of the press also envisioned that the First Amendment places an affirmative obligation on newspapers as well as radio and television, to open up debate, versus the news organizations' claim that it foreclosed such regulation.

So, in 1936, the Court struck down a Louisiana tax on large-circulation newspapers, most of which just happened to have been critical of Senator Huey Long. Instead of taking the easy route of relying on a First

Amendment right of newspapers to be free of differential taxation, Justice George Sutherland's opinion for a unanimous Court emphasized the rights of the public to receive the information they need and a positive role to the government in protecting those rights:

> The . . . abridgment of the publicity afforded by a free press cannot be regarded otherwise than with grave concern. The tax here involved is bad not because it takes money from the pockets of the appellees . . . It is bad because . . . it is seen to be a deliberate and calculated device in the guise of a tax to limit *the circulation of information to which the public is entitled in virtue of the constitutional guarantee.*[52]

Likewise, the 1945 antitrust case against the Associated Press followed earlier precedent suggesting that the First Amendment gave newspapers no protection from regulation that applied to them as businesses.[53] But Justice Hugo Black's majority opinion went beyond that argument to point out:

> It would be strange . . . if the grave concern for freedom of the press which prompted adoption of the First Amendment should be read as a command that the government was without power to protect that freedom . . . That Amendment rests on the assumption that the widest possible dissemination of information from diverse and antagonistic sources is essential to the welfare of the public . . . Freedom of the press from governmental interference under the First Amendment does not sanction repression of that freedom by private interests.[54]

Many Court cases have noted a corollary to freedom of speech—the constitutional right to receive information and ideas. Too often these cases are summarized under the moniker "the right to know," a term coined not by judges but by a journalist (Kent Cooper of the Associated Press) and often used as a sweeping justification of reportorial claims to access.[55] Although the right to information was initially distant from the press,[56] it became more pertinent to the news media when the Court sided with a public interest group seeking to overturn a Virginia law barring pharmacists from advertising the prices of prescription drugs.[57] Justice Harry Blackmun's majority opinion concluded, "Freedom of speech presupposes a willing speaker. But where a speaker exists, . . . the protection afforded is to the communication, to its source and to its recipients both." In an intriguing aside, Blackmun noted that the Court had never "recognized any . . . limitation on the *independent* right of the listener to receive the information sought to be communicated."[58] To be sure, citizens have lost every court case seeking to block changes in format or ownership of even regulated media.[59] But the mere recognition of the right of citizens to information reinforces an understanding of the First Amendment around what citizens need in a democracy, not just what journalists and news organizations have the privilege to do.[60]

Finally, and most important, we must remember that Congress is only prevented from making a law that *abridges* freedom of the press. The Bill of Rights does not advocate a "hands-off" governmental position vis-à-vis the news media. Indeed, legislation that facilitates or enhances freedom of the press would presumably not only be permitted but warranted by the First Amendment. As law professor Cass Sunstein has recently argued, the notion of a laissez-faire marketplace of ideas is as fictitious as the supposedly laissez-faire economic system prior to the New Deal. Given that laws of "property, contract and tort had produced the entitlements that yielded market hours and wages," the New Deal laws of minimum wages and a forty-hour workweek "simply substituted one form of regulation for another."[61] Sunstein has extended this logic to news organizations, saying that the property rights created by the law enable them to exclude whatever views they want and contends that we may wish to think of a New Deal for speech as well.[62] Sunstein's point is a good one, but could be strengthened. It is not merely laws of property, contract, and tort that undergird the ability of the news media to do their jobs. As outlined in earlier chapters here, the subsidies provided to journalists in the form of beneficial postal rates, favorable regulatory rules, and, above all, the public relations infrastructure within government, point to an already existing public policy toward the news media, a form of regulation that could be substituted by another more in line with our conclusions about what kind of news a democracy needs to have.

So much of the history of the First Amendment has focused on whether government can regulate or restrict the press that we tend to forget that it is eminently constitutional for government to shape the news by providing subsidies or otherwise encouraging a diversity of points of view. Indeed, in an intriguing flip-side to their unwillingness to recognize affirmative rights for the news media, the Court has also been clear that the subsidies that government provides to the news media can have strings attached, or can be directed only to certain kinds of news outlets. The history is a bit convoluted, but the Supreme Court has generally authorized governmental subsidies (or exemptions from taxation, which essentially amount to the same thing) that distinguish between different large classifications of news outlets.[63]

Does the First Amendment's guarantee of freedom of the press thus block attempts at putting together a more coherent and full federal policy toward the news media? Not at all. An equally strong case can be made that the First Amendment may authorize proactive government action, to ensure that the rights of the citizenry to the information they desire and need to participate in politics and keep government accountable are not abridged. What we should do, however, is to turn our attention away from the more problematic government regulation and restriction of information toward the ways that government policies and practices can nurture a greater diversity and range of viewpoints.[64]

POLICY SOLUTIONS

The evidence that I have mobilized above shows not only how the news media now occupy a role as one political institution among and between other political institutions, but also how government officials have increasingly turned to newsmaking as a central part of their task of governance, and have incorporated the needs of the news in their priorities, options, and decisions. As important, this state of affairs is the result of a public policy toward the news media, captured not only in statutes but in governmental practice, that shaped the growth, formats, and direction of the news media and continue to subsidize the work of newsmaking today. Thus, if we as citizens are not pleased with the current state of governing with the news, there is something we can do about it.

To be sure, the United States does not have a *coherent* public policy toward the news media. The media scholar Leo Bogart has recently depicted "the crazy quilt of regulations that constitute our ad hoc national media policy, one that even its most dedicated interpreters find hard to make sense of, much less apply in any rational way."[65] Indeed, many of the policies that we have examined are not always primarily comprehended as examples of media policy.

Our task is threefold, then: we need to establish what policies make up the current federal policy toward the news; we need to indicate the principles that undergird them; and then we need to reexamine both in light of the problems and prospects already addressed in this book.

Almost all of the subsidies discussed in earlier chapters continue in some form today. It is true that we are in the midst of a deregulatory moment. Since the late seventies, the powers of the FCC over television and radio broadcasting have been gradually relaxed.[66] In particular, the FCC decided in 1981 that radio stations no longer were required to provide minimum levels of public service programming or limit commercial time; in 1984, it did much the same for television; and in 1987, it abolished the Fairness Doctrine. Cable television, meanwhile, was deregulated in 1984 by the removal of the FCC's authority, which was reinstated by an act of Congress enacted over President Bush's veto in 1992 that set new regulations of rates and services. The telecommunication law passed in early 1996 went further down this road, by again deregulating rates for cable television services beyond the basic channels, repealing the ban on telephone companies transmitting video, loosening up restrictions on the ownership of broadcast stations, and extending the term of broadcast licenses.[67]

Elsewhere, too, there have been recent impulses to cut back. The postal subsidy for periodicals was endangered in 1995, when the Postal Service proposed (to the Postal Rate Commission) a new pricing structure that would grant subsidies only for periodicals presorted for automated processing; the rates could not be used for bundles of less than twenty-four pieces going to an individual zip code.[68] The two-tier pricing system would have lowered postal rates around 14 percent for high-circulation periodicals and raised them around 17 percent for their low-circulation counterparts. The eventual compromise by the Postal Rate Commission (endorsed by lobbyists for the news organizations) kept this two-tier system but with much lower divergence in cost. It is no surprise that the Postal Service would come up with such a proposal, given over two centuries of Postmasters General going before Congress to complain about the postal subsidies, but the conflict shows how the Postal Service's goals of efficiency can overshadow the venerable government commitment to use the mails to support a wide variety of publications.[69]

Given these trends, some may think that now is not a propitious time to set forth a more complete, coherent, and proactive public policy toward the news media. Yet many subsidies are alive and well, most notably the help that government provides to reporters through the public relations infrastructure, which continues, apparently unabated. And even with the telecommunications reforms of 1996, the FCC's role is still strong in regulating on behalf of those already established in the system, much as earlier regulation had consolidated the power of private broadcasters and discouraged new competition. For instance, the 1996 law specifies that current license holders had a virtual right to renewal without competing applicants for that license, as long as their record showed service to the public interest and no serious violations of FCC rules or law. Likewise, the law has limited the initial eligibility for the part of the electromagnetic spectrum that will be consecrated to digital high-definition television; only existing license holders need apply (although it is unclear if the latter will have to pay for the new frequencies or not). Clearly, we are a long way from laissez-faire.

And at least one underlying principle of these news media policies is consistent—and laudable. In particular, the practice of American newspapers for the first century of the republic, the rhetoric of the Supreme Court decisions on the First Amendment, and the legislative intent behind public policy initiatives have all revolved around the benefits of a diverse and wide range of information for public debate and deliberation. Many of the policies still in place—whether the "in-county" break on postal rates for periodicals, the exemption of small weekly newspapers from labor laws, the Newspaper Preservation Act of 1970, the "must-carry" regulations of the 1992 cable act—have always noted the chief rationale of protecting existing, more vulnerable services from the competition of more powerful competitors.

Yet the pursuit of diversity in the news media is incomplete. In particular, the relentless focus on the ownership of the news media—whether by antitrust cases for newspapers and print media, or in the various, and still continuing, restrictions on the number of affiliates a network may own, the number of radio stations an individual company may own, and "cross-ownership" of television stations by cable operators and/or newspapers—has obscured the more important question, that of the diversity (or lack thereof) of the *content* of the news. This connection is by no means straightforward. Whether economic competition actually produces better news coverage is an open and contested question.[70] Nor is diversity of ownership necessarily a precondition for diversity of content. One could easily imagine a media empire aimed at different audiences that was controlled by one company. As I have documented above, even across competing outlets, news content is fairly homogenized, influenced by similar production values, journalistic commitments, and definitions of news. We should not allow the commendable crusade against concentration in any industry to preclude the more central task of increasing the diversity and range of politics to be found in the news media.

And pursuing diversity seems especially important given the problem of accountability. The media are largely unaccountable to the public. Journalists generally are unwilling to solicit the public's reactions and are more preoccupied with the immediate need to deal with powerful political sources and superiors. Moreover, the for-profit orientation of the media requires satisfying the needs of advertisers to reach a large audience with disposable income. In many ways, the accountability of the news media has declined because of their commercialization; accountability was much higher when newspapers were extensions of parties and factions in the first half of the nineteenth century. Above all, accountability is a problem because of the tendency across news outlets to favor only certain political subjects, processes, and outcomes. If the news media were not so homogenized, their independent power would not be as great vis-à-vis either the political actors or the public. Policies should be crafted to diversify and vary all political communications to the public, with a greater commitment to the notion that each outlet should aim at a different readership, viewership, and listenership, along demographic, partisan, and ideological lines. In other words, replacing the usual journalistic attempts to reach a large, undifferentiated audience with more targeted approaches by individual news organizations toward particular segments, and modeling the news on that basis, will not only enhance the ability of the citizenry to find the information that they need; it reduces the problem of the news media's unaccountable power.

The news media's limited capacity for the tasks they have inherited also may be dealt with, in the same way. But moreover, Thomas Patterson has incisively concluded that the news media have ended up being powerful actors in part because of an absence of other political institutions that could perform the same task. His argument was developed to explain how the news media inherited a central role in the presidential nominating process after reform in the early seventies weakened the traditional party structures. But Patterson more broadly suggests that we should work to build new political institutions to fill the vacuum currently filled by the news media. In part, then, dealing with the downside of governing with the news cannot occur without finding ways to address the reasons that impel political actors to do so in the first place: the dispersion and confusion of the American political system.

What follows is less a detailed consideration of particular policy options than a list of possibilities that can serve to provoke thought and engage discussion. In particular, I emphasize three chief avenues for policies, working to expand and enhance the amount and range of political communication rather than regulate what is there already.

Before that, however, I should underscore that *regulation still has a role to play*. The currently ongoing discussion about how to make the transition to high-definition television reminds us that the frequencies that government will license to broadcasters are still enormously lucrative for media organizations. As of this writing in early 1997, it is unclear whether these frequencies will be auctioned off or simply given away to existing licensees, who will gradually move their programming to the new frequencies. In addition, it is difficult to imagine anyone concluding that the deregulation of broadcast media has made for better-quality programming. Commercial radio in general, and radio news programming in particular, has declined in diversity and willingness to tackle controversial issues since the FCC relieved radio stations of quality checks and then discarded the Fairness Doctrine.[71] To be sure, the FCC's "regulation by raised eyebrow" may not have meant much to outside observers, but at the very least it may have enforced minimum standards on risk-averse broadcast owners who exaggerated the likelihood of not having their licenses renewed.[72]

Certainly, the evolution of cable and satellite transmission signals the beginning of the end of the "scarcity" rationale that undergirded the governmental regulation of radio and television. However, an equally established principle—that the American people, through their government, own the airwaves—suggests that the forthcoming distribution of frequencies for digital television should be at an auction, and unlike politicians' proposals who see this as a way to balance the budget or finance their own pet projects, this money from the media industry should go directly into financing more economically marginal news outlets. More broadly, given that broadcast licensees now have a virtual claim on what the law has long recognized as the public ownership of the airwaves, their "licenses to make money" should come at a fee. These funds, for instance, should go into a trust fund, or a genuine endowment for public television and public radio, that could then protect these enterprises from pressures from politics or from advertisers.[73]

But the discussion needs to get beyond regulation of broadcast and electronic media, and address policies that would extend to a wide range of news outlets. In fact, the decline of the mass media and the already fragmentary newsgathering habits of the American public both suggest that we can and should take advantage of the new potentials of multiplicity.

First, *subsidies to the news media should be continued, but increasingly expanded and targeted toward more economically vulnerable news outlets and news organizations.* As I noted above, subsidies to the news media arose as virtual entitlements to whole classes of individual organizations and individual reporters, in comparison to the political sponsorship of the news that lasted through the first part of the nineteenth century. I do not propose taking away the postal subsidies given to large periodicals, or restricting big media from the public relations infrastructure. But instead, public policy should recognize more clearly that not all news media have equally deep pockets that would allow a diverse range of news to survive. Without being directed toward the more vulnerable,

these subsidies do little to assure diversity. The dynamic that J. H. Freiberg noted for the French press holds more generally: "The smaller, independent enterprises need these extra funds to survive, while the larger
corporate press groups use the funds to expand their domination."[74]

Now, while the principle of maintaining diversity is quite familiar,
the current policies only sporadically advance this goal. For instance, the
notion that the Cable Act of 1992 included "must-carry" provisions for
endangered local broadcasts overlooked the rising audience and profitability of local television stations.[75] Likewise, scholars have generally
agreed that the Newspaper Preservation Act of 1970, designed to protect
competition among metropolitan newspapers by allowing them to merge
their physical productions, has failed to preserve threatened newspapers;
in fact, some publishers contend that this only results in metropolitan
dailies having a leg-up on competition with suburban and weekly
papers.[76]

Several vulnerable classes of news outlets should be granted special
advantages by public policy. We cannot, of course, step into the domain
where such assistance would be clearly unconstitutional—namely if the
benefit (or cost) is narrowly targeted at a small number of news outlets
or if governmental benefits are conditioned on the content of the communication. But endangered classes include: low-circulation newspapers and
magazines (including journals of opinion) that lack the economies of scale
of large media; high-circulation newspapers and magazines that are not
financially viable because advertisers either wish to reach more upscale
audiences or have shifted over to the dominant publication in the market;
other periodicals with a disproportionately low ratio of advertising to
editorial space; and nonprofit news media, including public television and
public radio.[77] Whether these subsidies would consist of direct grants,
low-interest loans, tax breaks, tax incentives, reduced prices for access
to services (such as mail delivery), and the like, would obviously be an
important subject for debate and discussion.[78] Moreover, we need not
raid the general budget to pay for these subsidies, given that there are
many sources of income that the government has not tapped. A tax on
newspaper advertising would probably be both more constitutionally
viable and laudatory than a tax on large newspapers.[79]

Accountability to the public has another aspect. While diversity
would assure greater responsiveness to a wider range of the citizenry, and
would work to dilute the power of the news media that comes from the
homogenization of news processes and news content, all of this means
little if the news media are not oriented toward influencing and informing
public debate. The standard dynamics of the American news media, in

fact, push journalists and journalism to be more responsive to elites, as they interact on a daily basis with powerful official sources, anticipate the needs of advertisers, and view their job as informing the public in a top-down way about what happened rather than crafting their stories to mobilize the citizens to discussion and action.

It may be hard to imagine a governmental policy that would further journalists' attentiveness to public needs and concerns beyond the proposals I've already outlined or beyond the initiatives of "public journalism." But *as new technologies evolve, policies must be crafted to allow maximum access by as many citizens as possible.* A media system bisected by class means, of necessity, that only certain citizens will be invited into the debate. Government could consider ways to extend cable television's programming to the minority of the country that is not yet wired, whether by cooperative agreements with broadcasters to carry programming, or by programs that would finance their extension, possibly by taxes on extended cable service. If cable continues to be regulated (as is currently uncertain), we may wish to require "must-carry" channels to include public service channels such as C-SPAN and a variety of all-news programs. Above all, public policy should be squarely behind all attempts—including federally funded research—to ensure that access to the Internet and the World Wide Web be as cheap and widespread as possible. The interactivity of the new media will help us here, with projects to produce VCR-like boxes at a cost of around $300 that, once plugged into telephone and television, allow people to gain access to the Web via their television remote control. Policies can also enhance access to the Internet in public institutions, such as libraries and city halls, and develop networks of publicly accessed terminals that would be the counterpart of pay phones. Perhaps few people will use the full range of possibilities of the Internet or the Web. But the same is true of the VCR, which most people cannot even program to tape a show, although its ubiquity has indeed transformed America's media habits.

Finally, Patterson is on the money when he argues that dealing with the incapacity of the news media to organize public debate is not so much a problem that we can solve by changing the news media, but by changing the political context, particularly the political institutions in which and with which the news media operate. This study has concurred that one of the greatest pitfalls of governing with the news is that it provides an incentive for political actors to anticipate the needs of the news in deciding what to do, needs that often detract from extrinsic standards of governance.

Consequently, *in crafting public policy and practice, we should find ways for political actors to have more opportunities to reach each other and the public directly, without having to be channeled by the news.* This may well be my most controversial proposal, because it smacks of encouraging direct "propaganda." Yet there is much to be said for having a mix including news and analysis, but also including less aggressively mediated forms of political communication. In elections, already, scholars have addressed the benefits of encountering candidates through advertisements or long interview programs.[80] There is also no doubt that the rise of C-SPAN has made not only for an increased opportunity for constituents to watch the Congress close-up, but also—and less expectedly—a better chance for the members themselves to communicate to one another.[81]

Would it be too much to expect that the 500-channel cable television system could have counterparts to C-SPAN (for the House) and C-SPAN2 (for the Senate) elsewhere in Washington? If so, we need to rethink the current policies which, starting with the Mondell and Gillett amendments early in the century, discourage the work of the executive branch in dealing with the press and otherwise engaging in what Congress deems "propaganda." Annual appropriations bills routinely include a clause, "No part of any appropriation contained in this Act shall be used for publicity or propaganda purposes not authorized by the Congress." This clause seems as simple to evade as the Gillett amendment which sought to preclude the employment of press agents; the intent is again the same, and unfortunate, because it seeks to restrict the ability of the executive branch to communicate about its activities, an important component of governance. As pernicious are attempts such as those in the 104th Congress, led by Representative Ernest Istook, to remove tax-exempt status from any nonprofit organization that engages not only in lobbying but in any form of "political advocacy"[82]—pernicious because it limits communication and has a means of enforcement.

We should be thinking the other way, looking to policies that would encourage rather than limit the ability of officials and activists to get their messages out directly. In particular, we may need to rethink the usual condemnation of the partisan press of the nineteenth century and encourage political parties to develop whole channels of communication devoted to their news and their points of view, which could then act, as the nineteenth century's partisan press did, to mobilize the electorate. And efforts have already begun, most notably with the launch in 1994 of a weekly hour-long Republican party news program, "Rising Tide," produced by "G.O.P.-TV," and broadcast by satellite.[83] Ironically, we cannot solve this quandary of the news media's problematic capacity to aid in governance if everyone thinks that the key question is the *quality* of the information that is passed along to the public. Instead, making sure that the public sphere is as full of information from a variety and *quantity* of viewpoints and sources may be every bit as important for the political engagement of the public and for democracy.[84]

CONCLUSION

There is still much to be done to refine, clarify, and emend the thesis of the news media as a political institution. Students of American political development would help enormously if they addressed the evolution of such institutional manifestations as the Washington press corps or particular newsbeats, with close attention to the parts played by the initiatives of both officials and reporters. The conclusion that the news media do indeed constitute an institution relies heavily on the continued validity of what has been called the "homogeneity hypothesis," namely the convergence of newsmaking processes and news content across outlets; with the myriad changes in the technology and the political economy of the news media since the classic studies of the 1970s, this hypothesis needs to be revisited frequently. But above all, the argument hinges on the ways in which political actors have become deeply implicated in the very process of newsmaking and rely upon publicity as a crucial tool of governance. The involvement of political actors in the creation of American news, and the effect of that news upon political decisions and outcomes, are not well understood, particularly since most studies of news sources have been based in the newsroom with less awareness of the separate, sometimes countervailing social world of the newsbeat. Similarly, the motivations of officials in approaching the news have not been well examined. One thesis to test would follow from my suggestions in Chapters 6 and 7 that the amount of time and energy that officials spend on getting into the news rises with the gap between resources directly at their disposal and expectations of their task (many of which stem from their constitutional mandate).

Clearly, we are only beginning to understand the ways in which the news media act as a political institution, in which politicians help to create the news, and in which journalists operate as political actors. The news media are commonly recognized as wielding political power. Instead of arguing over whether the media do so, we should turn our attention to the more important question of what kind of power is wielded and to what effect. We also must remember that the American news media rarely work in isolation. The journalist Tom Rosenstiel has acutely noted, "The press, contrary to common mythology, is rarely if ever a lone gunman. More often, it is society's accomplice."[85] Even there, we might wish to amend this insight by asking: To which part of society are the news media an accomplice? Or, to put it slightly differently, when Dan Rather signs off by saying "That's part of our world," which part is he talking about? And whose world is it anyway?

Most crucially, we need to be able to gauge who wins and who loses as a result of the routine production of American news, and to figure out how to respond. Such an effort seems well overdue. After all, in 1815, John Adams wrote:

> If there is ever to be an amelioration of the conditions of mankind, philosophers, theologians, legislators, politicians and moralists will find that the regulation of the press is the most difficult, dangerous, and important problem they have to resolve. Mankind cannot now be governed without it, nor at present with it.[86]

As Adams reminds us, perhaps it is chimerical to imagine a government that can operate without the aid and assistance of news to one extent or another. Particularly today, when not only face-to-face communities but face-to-face political organizations and policy-making networks are endangered, institutions must emerge that serve to bring diverse actors and activists together, to focus attention on given problems, to suggest possible avenues of response, and to monitor how well such solutions work. For better or worse, the news media have now evolved to fit that role. And for better or worse, political actors use the news to help them accomplish their own jobs as well. It is now time to work toward getting the kind of news, and the kind of politics, that we want and that we deserve.

NOTES

CHAPTER ONE

1. Douglass Cater, *The Fourth Branch of Government* (Boston: Houghton Mifflin, 1959), p. 7.

2. The "fourth branch" metaphor is ironic, in part because it derives from the "fourth estate" metaphor credited by Thomas Carlyle in the nineteenth century to Edmund Burke. Boyce points out the role played by nineteenth-century British journalists in constructing a "fourth estate" mythology, allowing the press to take on a legitimate political role. Although the ideas of independently checking governmental power are similar, American journalists have been leerier than their British counterparts of accepting the "fourth branch" designation, placing them as it does squarely *within* the government. Whereas Boyce shows the "fourth estate" concept to have slowly lost its empirical validity in twentieth-century Britain, the reverse may be true of the "fourth branch" in the United States. See George Boyce, "The Fourth Estate: The Reappraisal of a Concept," in George Boyce, James Curran, and Pauline Wingate, eds., *Newspaper History from the Seventeenth Century to the Present Day* (Beverly Hills, CA: Sage, 1978), pp. 19–40.

Moreover, as I shall note below, it may be that the three branches established by the Constitution are so different from other political institutions, because of the authority and powers they thereby take on, that referring to other branches does not add much in the way of explanation. And given that authors sometimes refer to other institutions, such as the bureaucracy, as the "fourth branch," it may simply confuse rather than clarify. Although at times I will return to Cater's notion below for rhetorical flourishes, I will refer to the news media more as an intermediary institution—most comparable to the political party system or the interest group system—than as the fourth branch.

3. David R. Mayhew, *Congress: The Electoral Connection* (New Haven: Yale University Press, 1974), p. 9.

4. E. Barbara Phillips, "What Is News? Novelty without Change," *Journal of Communication* 26, no. 4 (1976): 87–92. On enduring values, see Herbert J. Gans, *Deciding What's News: a Study of CBS Evening News, NBC Nightly News, Time and Newsweek* (New York: Vintage, 1979), chap. 2.

5. Gaye Tuchman, "Objectivity as Strategic Ritual: An Examination of Newsmen's Notions of Objectivity," *American Journal of Sociology* 77 (1972): 660–679.

6. This account comes from "A Call for New Trial Rejected," *Boston Globe*, August 20, 1995, p. 21.

7. Ibid. Quotes are of Ken Cooper, Les Payne, and Gerald Boyd, respectively.

8. Such is one of the themes of Paul Weaver's important article, "Newspaper News and Television News," in Douglass Cater and Richard Adler, eds., *Television as a Social Force* (New York: Praeger, 1975), pp. 81–94.

9. See Gaye Tuchman, *Making News: A Study in the Construction of Reality* (New York: Free Press, 1978), chap. 6; Richard Campbell, *60 Minutes and the News: A Mythology for Middle America* (Urbana: University of Illinois Press, 1991), provides shot-by-shot analyses of *60 Minutes*.

10. Barbie Zelizer, *Covering the Body: The Kennedy Assassination, the Media, and the Shaping of Collective Memory* (Chicago: University of Chicago Press, 1992), esp. part 2.

11. See esp. W. Lance Bennett, Lynne A. Gressett, and William Haltom, "Repairing the News: A Case Study of the News Paradigm," *Journal of Communication* 35 (Spring 1985): 50–68; and David L. Eason, "On Journalistic Authority: The Janet Cooke Scandal," *Critical Studies in Mass Communication* 3 (1986): 429–447. Consider a sample of these occasions in recent years: the revelation that Janet Cooke had fabricated her Pulitzer prize-winning story in the *Washington Post;* a television camera crew in Alabama that stood by and filmed while a man protesting unemployment set himself afire; the libel suits of General William Westmoreland against CBS News that revealed numerous rejected "outtakes" that undercut the CBS angle; the Boston media being duped by the racist hoax of Charles Stuart who apparently shot and killed his pregnant wife and blamed it on an unknown (and fictional) black gunman; the attempt by General Motors to blame a loss in court over the safety of their pickup trucks on NBC News's rigged crash tests; and, of course, the many examples of scandals in campaign coverage, starting in particular with the *Miami Herald* staking out Democratic presidential front-runner Gary Hart's Washington townhouse in 1987 to document his weekend tryst with model Donna Rice.

12. This quote is from Stephen Hess, *News and Newsmaking* (Washington, DC: Brookings Institution, 1996), p. xi, but it is found elsewhere in his books.

13. Thomas E. Patterson, *Out of Order* (New York: Knopf, 1993), p. 28. This echoes his earlier quote: "If the press is neither so trivial nor so self-interested as critics suggest, it is much less adequate as a linking mechanism as is commonly assumed. The problem is that the press is not a political institution and has no stake in organizing public opinion." Patterson, *The Mass Media Election: How Americans Choose Their President* (New York: Praeger, 1980), p. 173.

14. Daniel C. Hallin, "The American News Media: A Critical Theory Perspective," in John Forester, ed., *Critical Theory and Public Life* (Cambridge, MA: MIT Press, 1985), pp. 121–146 at 141. To be sure, since then Hallin has modified his view to refer to the media as "a hybrid institution, at once economic, political and cultural-professional." Hallin, *We Keep America on Top of the World: Television Journalism and the Public Sphere* (New York: Routledge, 1994), p. 5.

15. A number of otherwise very fine books run into trouble on this problem of "power." See, e.g., David L. Paletz and Robert M. Entman, *Media Power Politics* (New York: Free Press, 1982); Shanto Iyengar and Donald R. Kinder, *News*

That Matters: Television and American Opinion (Chicago: University of Chicago Press, 1987), esp. chap. 12; W. Lance Bennett, *News: The Politics of Illusion*, 2d ed. (New York: Longmans, 1988). For instance, Iyengar and Kinder conclude from their outstanding experimental results showing clear influence from television reports on priorities and assessments of politicians: "Television has become a mature and powerful force in American politics. In commanding attention and shaping opinion, television is now an authority virtually without peer" (p. 133). But Iyengar and Kinder do not show, or even note, where the political content of television comes from, raising questions about who or what is exactly exerting power. More complexly, Bennett says, "By regulating the flow of 'who' and 'what' passes through the public information gate, the media hold enormous power in the system" (p. 15). He then, however, goes on to note the news media's deference to official voices, leaving us wondering exactly whether or how the media do hold such power.

16. This literature is vast. A good introduction, while focusing perhaps a bit much on the centrality of labor, is Dan Schiller, *Theorizing Communication: A History* (New York: Oxford University Press, 1996).

17. C. Wright Mills, *The Power Elite* (New York: Oxford University Press, 1956), esp. chap. 13; Mills, "Mass Media and Public Opinion," in Irving Louis Horowitz, ed., *Power, Politics and People: The Collected Essays of C. Wright Mills* (New York: Oxford University Press, 1963), pp. 577–598; Max Horkheimer and Theodor W. Adorno, *Dialectic of Enlightenment* (New York: Continuum, 1972); Herbert Marcuse, *One-Dimensional Man* (Boston: Beacon Press, 1964).

18. This phrase comes from Stuart Hall, "The Rediscovery of 'Ideology': Return of the Repressed in Media Studies," in Michael Gurevitch, Tony Bennett, James Curran, and Janet Woollacott, eds., *Culture, Society, and the Media* (New York: Methuen, 1982), pp. 56–90 at 86. See also Hall, "Culture, the Media and the 'Ideological Effect,' " in James Curran, Michael Gurevitch, and Janet Woollacott, eds., *Mass Communication and Society* (Beverly Hills, CA: Sage, 1977), pp. 315–348. The finest empirical account of this process remains Todd Gitlin, *The Whole World Is Watching: The Mass Media in the Making and Unmaking of the New Left* (Berkeley: University of California Press, 1980). Other representative works include Stanley Cohen and Jock Young, eds., *The Manufacture of News: Social Problems, Deviance and the Mass Media* (London: Constable, 1973); Stuart Hall, Chas Critcher, Tony Jefferson, John Clark, and Brian Roberts, *Policing the Crisis: Mugging, the State, and Law and Order* (London: Macmillan, 1978); Edward S. Herman and Noam Chomsky, *Manufacturing Consent: The Political Economy of the Mass Media* (New York: Pantheon, 1988); Philip Schlesinger, *Media, State and Nation: Political Violence and Collective Identities* (Newbury Park, CA: Sage, 1991).

19. Hallin, *We Keep America on Top of the World*, p. 13, critiquing Herman and Chomsky, *Manufacturing Consent*.

I should add that, at times, scholars studying the news media's political power have talked past each other, not only because of their disciplinary or ideological presumptions but the ways in which those have interacted with and shaped their empirical accounts. Take two particularly notable examples: the neoconservative study by S. Robert Lichter, Stanley Rothman, and Linda S. Lichter, *The Media Elite* (Bethesda, MD: Adler and Adler, 1986); and the neo-Marxist examination by Herman and Chomsky, *Manufacturing Consent.*

The Media Elite concludes that the news media have become dominated by a "new class" of Northeastern journalists, "politically liberal and alienated from traditional norms and institutions," and inclined to come up with stories with antiauthority themes. *Manufacturing Consent,* on the other hand, points out that the news media serve to disseminate propaganda on behalf of government and dominant private interests. It is impossible to join a debate between these two works, however, because they examined wholly inconsistent bodies of data. *The Media Elite* based its argument on surveys and thematic apperception tests of journalists for top national news organizations (compared to another elite, namely businessmen), along with case studies of news coverage of nuclear safety, busing, and the oil industry amidst the 1970s energy crisis. *Manufacturing Consent* derived its conclusions from evidence about the increasing concentration of ownership of news media, the importance of advertising and advertisers, the dependence on authoritative sources and conservative pressure groups, followed by case studies of news coverage from the 1980s' wars in Central America, the attempted assassination of the pope, and the wars in Vietnam, Laos, and Cambodia. Could both books be right? There is no way to know, due to a classic "levels-of-analysis" problem. In each case, the error these scholars make is not within the bounds of the study they establish but in failing to recognize their studies' limits, as they examine one distinct part of the news media's involvement in politics and then make (unwarranted) generalizations about mass-mediated politics as a whole.

20. Dan Nimmo and David L. Swanson, "The Field of Political Communication: Beyond the Voter Persuasion Paradigm," in Swanson and Nimmo, eds., *New Directions in Political Communication: A Resource Book* (Newbury Park, CA: Sage, 1990), pp. 7–47.

21. This section draws in particular on Steven H. Chaffee and John L. Hochheimer, "The Beginnings of Political Communication Research in the United States: Origins of the 'Limited Effects' Model," in Everett M. Rogers and Francis Balle, eds., *The Media Revolution in America and Western Europe* (Norwood, NJ: Ablex, 1982), pp. 263–283.

22. Paul F. Lazarsfeld, Bernard Berelson, and Hazel Gaudet, *The People's Choice* (New York: Duell, Sloan and Pearce, 1944).

23. Angus Campbell, Gerald Gurin, and Warren E. Miller, *The Voter Decides* (Evanston, IL: Row, Peterson and Company, 1954), p. 30.

24. E.g., see Kurt Lang and Gladys Engel Lang, "Mass Media and Voting," in Eugene Burdick and Arthur J. Brodbeck, eds., *American Voting Behavior* (Glencoe, IL: Free Press, 1959), pp. 217–235.

25. In this light, recall Harold Lasswell's influential model of the communication process: Who says what through what channel to whom with what effect?

26. Stephen Hess, *The Ultimate Insiders: U.S. Senators in the National Media* (Washington, DC: Brookings Institution, 1986), p. 103.

27. My response to Hess is contained in Timothy E. Cook, *Making Laws and Making News: Media Strategies in the U.S. House of Representatives* (Washington, DC: Brookings Institution, 1989).

28. This is, of course, the 1981 tax cut; see Samuel Kernell, *Going Public: New Strategies of Presidential Leadership*, 2d ed. (Washington, DC: CQ Press, 1993), esp. chap. 5 ; and Darrell M. West, "Activists and Economic Policymaking in Congress," *American Journal of Political Science* 32 (1988): 662–680.

29. John W. Kingdon, *Agendas, Alternatives, and Public Policies* (Boston: Little Brown, 1984), p. 99.

30. Ibid., p. 103.

31. This example, of course, may remind us that reactivity does not limit discretion when there are many cases to choose from. An excellent recent investigation of the Supreme Court's agenda-setting power in deciding whether or not to grant certiorari is H. W. Perry, *Deciding to Decide: Agenda Setting in the United States Supreme Court* (Cambridge, MA: Harvard University Press, 1991).

32. Scholars noting this asymmetry include Herbert J. Gans, "News Media, News Policy and Democracy: Research for the Future," *Journal of Communication* 33, no. 3 (Summer 1983): 174–184; Richard V. Ericson, Patricia M. Baranek, and Janet B. L. Chan, *Negotiating Control: A Study of News Sources* (Toronto: University of Toronto Press, 1989), chap. 1; and Philip Schlesinger, "Rethinking the Sociology of Journalism: Source Strategies and the Limits of Media-Centrism," in Marjorie Ferguson, ed., *Public Communication: The New Imperatives* (Newbury Park, CA: Sage, 1990), pp. 61–83.

33. Leon V. Sigal, "Who? Sources Make the News," in Robert Karl Manoff and Michael Schudson, eds., *Reading the News* (New York: Pantheon, 1986), pp. 9–37.

34. Kingdon is wise enough not to suggest, as would the most die-hard defenders of the news media, that the news merely holds up a mirror to reality, given the way in which that "reality" is created expressly for their use.

35. Robert Darnton, "Writing News and Telling Stories," *Daedalus* 104, 2 (1975), pp. 175–194; and Gans, *Deciding What's News.*

36. The phrase "negotiation of newsworthiness" is from my *Making Laws and Making News,* p. 169. A fuller discussion of this position is in ibid., chap. 1; and in Jay G. Blumler and Michael Gurevitch, "Politicians and the Press: An Essay on Role Relationships," in Dan D. Nimmo and Keith R. Sanders, eds., *Handbook of Political Communication* (Beverly Hills, CA: Sage, 1981), pp. 467–493. For a good study of this process at work in campaigns, see F. Christopher Arterton, *Media Politics: The News Strategies of Presidential Campaigns* (Lexington, MA: Lexington Books, 1984).

37. Cook, *Making Laws and Making News,* chap. 6.

Part One

1. The best statement of this conclusion is Donald L. Shaw, "News Bias and the Telegraph: A Study of Historical Change," *Journalism Quarterly* 44 (1967): 3–12, 31.

2. Thoughtful assessments of the political differences between television and print include, above all, Weaver, "Newspaper News and Television News"; and Kathleen Hall Jamieson, *Eloquence in an Electronic Age: The Transformation of Political Speechmaking* (New York: Oxford University Press, 1988).

3. Richard B. Kielbowicz, *News in the Mail: The Press, Post Office, and Pub-*

lic Information, 1700–1860s (Westport, CT: Greenwood Press, 1989). See also Richard R. John, *Spreading the News* (Cambridge, MA: Harvard University Press, 1995), pp. 109–110, who notes the impressive way in which the postal system emphasized greater speed and reliability from 1792 to 1828 with no commensurate technological breakthrough to help: "In 1828, as in 1792, American postal officers had at their disposal few mechanical contrivances that would have been unfamiliar to the ancients."

4. At the very least, as Carolyn Marvin insightfully notes, "New practices do not so much flow directly from technologies that inspire them as they are improvised out of old practices that no longer work in new settings." See Marvin, *When Old Technologies Were New: Thinking about Electric Communication in the Late Nineteenth Century* (New York: Oxford University Press, 1988), pp. 3–8 (quote is on p. 5). Furthermore, the case can be made that new technologies are not allowed to develop into large-scale modes of communication until their disruptive influences have been identified and controlled. See, for instance, "the 'law' of the suppression of radical potential" discussed in Brian Winston, *Misunderstanding Media* (Cambridge, MA: Harvard University Press, 1986).

5. For variants of this interpretation, see John C. Nerone, "The Mythology of the Penny Press," *Critical Studies in Mass Communication* 4 (1987): 376–404.

6. Michael Schudson, *Discovering the News: A Social History of American Newspapers* (New York: Basic Books, 1978), chap. 1.

7. This formulation draws upon Karen Orren and Stephen Skowronek's preface to vol. 1 of the annual, *Studies in American Political Development* (New Haven: Yale University Press, 1986), pp. vii–viii.

Chapter Two

1. The most thorough scholarship of the *Boston News-Letter* and its "undertaker," John Campbell, has been provided by Charles E. Clark. See, in particular his *The Public Prints: The Newspaper in Anglo-American Culture, 1665–1740* (New York: Oxford University Press, 1994), chap. 4.

2. Quoted in Victor Hugo Paltsits, "New Light on 'Publick Occurrences': America's First Newspaper," *Proceedings of the American Antiquarian Society* 59 (1949): 75–88 at 84, which also includes a helpful synopsis of the newspaper's content. Nice accounts of the political and social context of the *Publick Occurrences* and its demise include William David Sloan and Julie Hedgepeth Williams, *The Early American Press, 1690–1783* (Westport, CT: Greenwood Press, 1994), pp. 1–10; and Charles E. Clark, "The Newspapers of Provincial America," *Proceedings of the American Antiquarian Society* 100 (1990): 367–389.

3. Royal instructions to the colonial governors up until 1730 continued to stress that printing could be permitted only by prior consent, but attempts to impose licensing responded to disputes already reported in print and were thus usually stymied. Examples are recounted in Clyde Augustus Duniway, *Development of the Freedom of the Press in Massachusetts* (Cambridge, MA: Harvard University Press, 1906), pp. 86–89; Mary Patterson Clarke, *Parliamentary Privilege in the American Colonies* (New Haven: Yale University Press, 1943), p. 126; Jeffery A. Smith, "A Reappraisal of Legislative Privilege and American Colonial Journalism," *Journalism Quarterly* 61 (1984): 97–103, 141 at 98–100; and id.,

Printers and Press Freedom: The Ideology of Early American Journalism (New York: Oxford University Press, 1988), p. 98.

4. This, of course, is the cornerstone of Leonard W. Levy's famous revisionist interpretation of the constitutional guarantee of "freedom of the press," first set forth in his *Legacy of Suppression: Freedom of Speech and Press in Early American History* (Cambridge, MA: Harvard University Press, 1960), revised as *Emergence of a Free Press* (New York: Oxford University Press, 1985).

5. The jury thereby defied the judicial practice of being limited to deciding whether or not the printer had in fact produced the document in question, while the judge would rule on its libelous intent and effect. Harold L. Nelson, "Seditious Libel in Colonial America," *American Journal of Legal History* 3 (1959): 160–172, provides a convincing argument about the ineffectiveness of seditious libel prosecutions after the Zenger case. For one thing, the publication of the defense of Zenger's lawyer made it accessible for those who would later be accused of seditious libel.

6. Nelson, "Seditious Libel in Colonial America," p. 163. Smith, in *Printers and Press Freedom,* p. 83, counts around twenty instances between the Zenger trial and the Sedition Act of 1798 where persons were summoned before a legislative body to account for publications critical of the legislature. See also Clarke, *Parliamentary Privilege in the American Colonies,* pp. 122–128; and Levy, *Emergence of a Free Press,* pp. 17–19 and passim.

7. See Smith, "Reappraisal of Legislative Privilege."

8. Other printers had to apologize to the authorities in order to be released— a seeming slap on the wrist but an important concession in a society relying on reputation as a way to maintain community and consensus. E.g., see Andrew Bradford's apology in 1722 to the Governor's Council, cited in ibid. On other libel and slander trials, Norman L. Rosenberg notes the centrality of apologies in colonial slander and libel trials as a means of underscoring the norm of social harmony and denouncing licentious expression. Rosenberg, *Protecting the Best Men: An Interpretive History of the Law of Libel* (Chapel Hill: University of North Carolina Press, 1986), p. 22. The negative impact of the Zenger trial on most printers is discussed in Thomas C. Leonard, *Power of the Press: The Birth of American Political Journalism* (New York: Oxford University Press, 1986), pp. 34–35.

9. Take the mission the *Boston News-Letter* established for itself and the purposes it served. Its reach was small. Boston, then the largest American city, had a population of around 6,000, but the *News-Letter's* weekly paid circulation probably never exceeded a few hundred. John Campbell, the *News-Letter's* publisher, apparently saw that his task was to provide short bits of intelligence to elites much as his work (and that of his father) as Boston postmaster encompassed sending handwritten newsletters to the governor of Connecticut and other VIPs. The intelligence that he passed along would not be so different from what any well-placed Bostonian would have found out independently; see Richard D. Brown, *Knowledge Is Power: The Diffusion of Information in Early America, 1700–1865* (New York: Oxford University Press, 1989), chap. 1. On newsletter writers in general and Campbell's task in particular, see Clark, *Public Prints,* pp. 16–23 and 77–78. Campbell's habit of listing events in chronological order regardless of their importance hearkened back to a more venerable form of pub-

lishing—the almanac—and suggests that his newspaper was a repository of what was known, not a revealer of previously unknown information. Compare Clark, *Public Prints*, pp. 95–101, with the innovative reading of almanacs as news in David Paul Nord, "Teleology and News: The Religious Roots of American Journalism, 1630–1730," *Journal of American History* 77 (1990): 9–38.

10. "Campbell was, after all, a pioneer, and he naturally approached his task of publishing from the point of view of royal officeholder, which he was, rather than from that of independent journalist, an occupation that had yet to be defined." Charles E. Clark, "Boston and the Nurturing of Newspapers: Dimensions of the Cradle," *New England Quarterly* 64 (1991): 243–271 at 255.

11. Peter J. Parker, "The Philadelphia Printer: A Study of an Eighteenth-Century Businessman," *Business History Review* 40 (1966): 25–46; Mary Ann Yodelis, "Who Paid the Piper? Publishing Economics in Boston, 1763–1775," *Journalism Monographs*, no. 38 (February 1975); id., "The Press in Wartime: Portable and Penurious," *Journalism History* 3 (1976): 2–6, 10; and Clark, *The Public Prints*, chap. 9.

12. Compare Parker, "Philadelphia Printer," Yodelis, "Who Paid the Piper?" and Dwight L. Teeter, "Press Freedom and the Public Printing: Philadelphia, 1775–83," *Journalism Quarterly* 45 (1968): 445–451, for two large cities, with the evidence compiled by Stephen Botein, " 'Meer Mechanics' and an Open Press: The Business and Political Strategies of Colonial American Printers," *Perspectives in American History* 9 (1975): 127–225, for smaller settlements and the conclusions reached by Robert M. Weir ("The Role of the Newspaper Press in the Southern Colonies on the Eve of the Revolution: An Interpretation," in Bernard Bailyn and John B. Hench, eds., *The Press and the American Revolution* [Worcester: American Antiquarian Society, 1980], pp. 99–150) for the colonial South. All would agree, however, with Botein, when he notes that "the amount of public work available in any one colony was generally inadequate by itself to guarantee a printer's complete devotion"; " 'Meer Mechanics,' " p. 171.

13. "Three quarters of the colonial printers in business between 1700 and 1765 undertook to produce newspapers at one time or another. It was apparent within the trade that this was what an ambitious man had to do." Botein, " 'Meer Mechanics,' " p. 147. The nature of such ambition need not have been political, even if newspaper publication was rarely very profitable, given that they "afforded their publishers the opportunity of keeping their names before the business community both within the city and beyond. With their reputations thus established, it was a simple matter . . . to attract customers from the hinterlands and develop satisfactory credit arrangements with other colonial cities and abroad." Parker, "The Philadelphia Printer," p. 29.

14. See, in particular, Botein, " 'Meer Mechanics,' " esp. pp. 158ff.; and Clark, *The Public Prints*, pp. 207–214.

15. For an exhaustive discussion of "licentiousness," consult Levy, *Emergence of a Free Press*, esp. chap. 5. In the most developed statement of the doctrine of neutrality, Benjamin Franklin wrote in his 1731 essay, "An Apology for Printers," that while printers "chearfully serve all contending Writers that pay them well," they must avoid what might "countenance Vice or promote Immorality," or what could "do real Injury to any Person" or "such Things as Usually give Offence either to Church or State." Benjamin Franklin, "An Apology to Printers,"

in Leonard Labaree et al., eds., *The Papers of Benjamin Franklin*, vol. 1 (New Haven: Yale University Press, 1959), pp. 194–199, at 195, 196, and 198–199.

16. From a close comparison of London and American printing offices, Botein concludes, "By English standards, then, colonial printers could not expect to prosper from their craft alone, and poverty was more than a remote contingency for some." " 'Meer Mechanics,' " p. 143.

17. Duniway, *Development of the Freedom of the Press in Massachusetts*, p. 78n. The leading study of the linkages of public policies on the mail and on the press notes that franking privileges had risen in England as a means to supplement the low postmaster's salary. Kielbowicz, *News in the Mail*, p. 17. In Campbell's case, such support was crucial; with its small paid circulation and the perennial difficulty of collecting on subscriptions, the *News-Letter* never became profitable under Campbell's tutelage, even during the fifteen years when he had an effective monopoly.

18. In his *Autobiography*, Benjamin Franklin recalled how becoming Clerk of the Pennsylvania Assembly in 1735 assisted his task as printer of the *Pennsylvania Gazette*: "Besides the Pay for immediate Service as Clerk, the Place gave me a better Opportunity of keeping up an Interest among the Members, which secur'd to me the Business of Printing the Votes, Laws, Paper Money, and other occasional Jobbs for the Public, that on the whole were very profitable." Benjamin Franklin, *Autobiography*, ed. Leonard W. Labaree (New Haven: Yale University Press, 1964), p. 171.

To be sure, Mary Ann Yodelis's close analysis of printing volume in Boston from 1763 to 1783 (in "Who Paid the Piper?" and "The Press in Wartime") suggests that the amount of religious printing far outweighed either governmental or political printing and, in most years, constituted a majority of pages printed. Yodelis, however, may underestimate the importance of patronage in general. First of all, Boston, with its high literacy and many religious disagreements, was unusual in its high printing output. Second, and as important, by categorizing all printing by ministers as "religious," she undercounts the political volume, given the many political and election sermons, commentaries on current events, and jeremiads that characterized the Massachusetts clergy.

19. Charles E. Clark and Charles Wetherell, "The Measure of Maturity: The *Pennsylvania Gazette*, 1728–1765," *William and Mary Quarterly* 46, 3d ser. (1989): 279–303, esp. tables 3–5.

20. Clark, *The Public Prints*, p. 180, describes here the first newspaper in New York, the *New-York Gazette*, but earlier in the same paragraph draws its similarities to the *Boston News-Letter* and Philadelphia's *American Weekly Mercury*.

21. For a good account of James Franklin as an early precursor of crusading journalism, see Leonard's *The Power of the Press*, pp. 24–32. For an interpretation that stresses the origins of Franklin's crusade in the split between Anglican and Puritan authorities, see William David Sloan and Thomas A. Schwartz, "Freedom of the Press, 1690–1801: Libertarian or Limited?" *American Journalism* 5 (1988): 159ff.

22. Stephen Botein (in "Printers and the American Revolution," in Bailyn and Hench, eds., *The Press and the American Revolution*, pp. 11–57) goes so far

as to suggest that such crusading journalism was necessary under these political situations. Moreover, both Franklin and Zenger faced doubtful economic benefits if they did not take up the jobs; see, e.g., Clark, "Boston and the Nurturing of Newspapers," on the surfeit of printers in Boston by the 1720s; and Clark, *Public Prints*, p. 181, on Zenger's meager output prior to allying with the Morris faction. Instead of the romantic notion best associated with the work of Arthur M. Schlesinger, Sr., in *Prelude to Independence: The Newspaper War on Britain, 1764–1776* (New York: Alfred A. Knopf, 1957), whereby printers took advantage of split elites, Botein argues that printers were often pushed into taking sides against their best intentions. "When attitudes polarized, a printer sometimes had to work for a single faction; otherwise he might antagonize everyone. That this solution might be at least briefly lucrative, as well as unavoidable, is evident from the experience of such printers as John Peter Zenger and [Benjamin] Franklin's brother James." Botein, "Printers and the American Revolution," p. 21. See also Botein, " 'Meer Mechanics,' " pp. 172–177.

In addition, while continuing newspapers might be more cautious, printers easily accepted riskier rhetoric when publishing pamphlets, often written anonymously. Gary B. Nash (in "The Transformation of Urban Politics," *Journal of American History* 60 [1974]: 605–632) has documented the exponential growth in pamphleteering in Boston, New York, and Philadelphia, especially between 1715 and 1734 as electoral campaigns became aimed beyond the upper class (ibid., p. 617 n.43). Nash concludes that this development "made the use of the press a particularly important part of the new politics," but he notes that this was directed by "the professional pamphleteer[,] . . . a new figure in politics" who was generally not a printer but often a schoolteacher (ibid., pp. 619, 618). The comparison would be similar to today's contrasts between the more measured news broadcasts on television vs. the "attack ads" paid for by candidates—which, in either case, satisfies the economic imperatives of the news media.

23. This point is well made in Botein, " 'Meer Mechanics,' " pp. 205–206.

24. Take, for instance, the two printers identified by Smith (*Printers and Press Freedom*, p. 9) as having spent the most time in jail for contempt: James Franklin and James Parker. Both portrayed themselves as impartial printers of other people's opinions. Franklin, in the only piece he signed in the *New-England Courant*, claimed, "What my own Sentiments of things are, is of no Consequence, or any matter to any Body." Quoted in Leonard, *Power of the Press*, p. 30. Parker, in 1752, claimed that he was not competent to decide what should or should not be printed and added, "If a Man wrongs the community, every Member of that Community has a right to complain." Quoted in Smith, *Printers and Press Freedom*, p. 128.

25. David Ramsay, quoted in Philip Davidson, *Propaganda and the American Revolution, 1763–1783* (Chapel Hill: University of North Carolina Press, 1941), p. 226.

26. Botein, "Printers and the American Revolution," p. 35.

27. In the case of Samuel Loudon in New York in early 1776, vigilantes destroyed the plates of the pamphlet, burned the printed copies, and printed a broadside threatening anyone who printed such tracts with "death and destruction, ruin and perdition." Levy, *Emergence of a Free Press*, p. 175. Similar threats

had been exercised against patriot printers, particularly in Boston, by Tory sympathizers and even British troops. Schlesinger, *Prelude to Independence*, p. 219.

28. See, in general, John C. Nerone, *Violence against the Press: Policing the Public Sphere in U.S. History* (New York: Oxford University Press, 1994), chap. 2.

29. Schlesinger, *Prelude to Independence*, pp. 208–217.

30. Ibid., p. 189.

31. Quoted in ibid., p. 92.

32. Thus, Dwight Teeter ("Press Freedom and the Public Printing") notes that Philadelphia newspapers during the revolutionary war contained "vigorous, tough-minded, often scurrilous comments about government in the midst of a conflict that was both revolution and civil war," and that although official contracts may have been offered with loyal printing in mind, they rarely resulted in such docility because of the presence of large factions within both the Pennsylvania legislature and the Continental Congress (based in Philadelphia). Yodelis, "Press in Wartime," documents that, whether in Boston or in Philadelphia, the printing volume was only sporadically dominated by political or government publications.

33. See, for instance, Daniel N. Hoffman, *Governmental Secrecy and the Founding Fathers: A Study in Constitutional Controls* (Westport, CT: Greenwood Press, 1981), pp. 20–24.

34. Robert A. Rutland, "The First Great Newspaper Debate: The Constitutional Crisis of 1787–88," *Proceedings of the American Antiquarian Society* 97 (1987): 43–58.

35. Culver H. Smith, *The Press, Politics, and Patronage: The American Government's Use of Newspapers, 1789–1875* (Athens: University of Georgia Press, 1977), p. 13.

36. Quoted in Noble E. Cunningham, Jr., *The Jeffersonian Republicans: The Formation of Party Organization, 1789–1801* (Chapel Hill: University of North Carolina Press, 1957) p. 14.

37. Ibid., pp. 17–18. Madison urged one fellow Virginian to subscribe "not only from a persuasion that in bestowing it you will aid a very useful undertaking, but from a desire of testifying my esteem and friendship for the conductor of it by contributing to render the profits as proportionate as may be to the justice of his title to them." Ibid, p. 17. For examples of Jefferson's correspondence, where he wrote such things as "I take it for granted you receive Freneau's paper from hence regularly," see James Pollard, *The Presidents and the Press* (New York: Macmillan, 1947), pp. 58–59.

38. For good accounts of this episode, see Smith, *Press, Politics, and Patronage*, pp. 16–19; and Cunningham, *Jeffersonian Republicans*, pp. 24–28. The quote comes from Smith, *Press, Politics, and Patronage*, p. 16.

39. Quoted in Cunningham, *Jeffersonian Republicans*, p. 25.

40. Smith, *Press, Politics, and Patronage*, p. 19.

41. Ibid., p. 69. For further evidence, see two articles by Gerald J. Baldasty: "The Boston Press and Politics in Jacksonian America," *Journalism History* 7 (1980): 104–108; and "The Washington, D.C., Political Press in the Age of Jackson," *Journalism History* 10 (1983): 50–53, 68–69.

42. Gerald J. Baldasty, *The Commercialization of News in the Nineteenth Century* (Madison: University of Wisconsin Press, 1992), p. 5. Baldasty's first chapter is both an excellent synopsis of other studies and a fine content analysis of the party press in its own right. See also id., "The Press and Politics in the Age of Jackson," *Journalism Monographs*, no. 89 (August 1984).

43. The metaphor echoes John A. Nerone, *The Culture of the Press in the Early Republic: Cincinnati, 1793–1848* (New York: Garland Publishing, 1989), p. 175. Baldasty astutely notes (in "Washington, D.C., Political Press," p. 52) that "editors were forced to rely not just on partisan bluster but to develop reasoned and reasonable arguments for their ideas and party policies." His example is how the initial intraparty feud of the editors Duff Green and Francis P. Blair evolved first into a split between personal sects (Calhoun and Jackson) and then into a full-fledged debate over nullification, the Constitution, and the nature of the Union.

44. Compare Lawrence C. Wroth, *The Colonial Printer* (Portland, ME: Southworth-Anthoensen Press, 1938) with Milton Hamilton, *The Country Printer: New York State, 1785–1830* (New York: Columbia University Press, 1936); and Rollo Silver, *The American Printer, 1787–1825* (Charlottesville: University Press of Virginia, 1967). Silver (p. 40) does note that "in the first quarter of the nineteenth century . . . the equipment of the shop changed more than in all the past three and a half centuries put together," what with the introductions of iron presses, horsepower or steam power, stereotype and lithography, but one should point out that such improvements were rarely applied at that time to the more marginal production of most newspapers. A more recent investigation by William S. Pretzer points to the late 1820s as the turning point where technological development pushed away from printers and toward a more mechanized and specialized industry requiring unskilled labor; prior to that time, "the iron handpress looked very much a member of the same family as the sixteenth-century wooden common press. And the processes of typesetting, imposition, and presswork were carried out in a routine, traditional fashion." Pretzer, "The Quest for Autonomy and Discipline: Labor and Technology in the Book Trades," *Proceedings of the American Antiquarian Society* 96 (1986): 85–131 at 90–91.

45. Botein, "Printers and the American Revolution," esp. pp. 50–52, persuasively makes the point that printers would not long fulfill the central role they had won in the Revolution as printers became more specialized and withdrew from entrepreneurship once linked to their craft, while publishers and editors increasingly established newspapers first, hiring printers to produce them. The exact timing of this shift is in some dispute, given the uneven developments in politics, technology, and economics. Parker, "Philadelphia Printer," specifies the turn of the nineteenth century as the start of the shift from artisan to "fledgling capitalist"; Pretzer, "Quest for Autonomy and Discipline," points instead to the late 1820s.

46. Cunningham, *Jeffersonian Republicans,* p. 168. Note also that most of the first newspapers in each of the new territories were begun at an official invitation, usually with the promise of patronage or other support. Silver, *American Printer,* chap. 5.

47. The best indication comes from Carolyn Stewart Dyer's data from Wis-

consin from 1848 to 1860, apropos here simply since it covered the settlement of the state. She estimates that a typical Wisconsin weekly in 1860 should have brought in $1,050 per year in subscriptions and $900 in job printing (both commercial and governmental), more than covering the operating expenses: $600 for raw material, particularly paper, and $1,100 for a payroll. See Dyer, "Economic Dependence and Concentration of Ownership among Antebellum Wisconsin Newspapers," *Journalism History* 7 (1980): 42–46 at 42; and id., "Political Patronage of the Wisconsin Press, 1849–1860: New Perspectives on the Economics of Patronage," *Journalism Monographs*, no. 109 (February 1989), esp. p. 5.

48. This list is derived from William David Sloan, " 'Purse and Pen': Party-Press Relationships, 1789–1816," *American Journalism* 6 (1989): 103–127 at 108–113.

49. John Israel, quoted in Sloan, " 'Purse and Pen,' " at 108.

50. Carl E. Prince, "The Federalist Party and Creation of a Court Press, 1789–1801," *Journalism Quarterly* 53 (1976): 238–242 (quote is on p. 239).

51. This practice had already lost ground under the Federalists. See John, *Spreading the News,* pp. 120–121.

52. Smith, *Press, Politics, and Patronage,* pp. 41–46. Smith notes that this law, enacted in 1799, was designed to prop up a Federalist press, but there had not been enough time to put the scheme into practice. The law was further expanded by the Jeffersonians in 1804, however, to include one newspaper per territory as well. Ibid., p. 42.

53. Quoted in Cunningham, *Jeffersonian Republicans,* p. 248.

54. The most complete (though rather long) reference is William E. Ames, *A History of the National Intelligencer* (Chapel Hill: University of North Carolina Press, 1972). A useful definition of the "official press" is in Frederick B. Marbut, "Decline of the Official Press in Washington," *Journalism Quarterly* 33 (1956): 335–341.

55. Ames, *History of the National Intelligencer,* pp. 29–31; Cunningham, *Jeffersonian Republicans,* pp. 260–261. The *National Intelligencer* was to lose House sponsorship in 1804 when Congress gave printing contracts to the lowest bidder, a system that would last until 1819. See, in general, Smith, *Press, Politics, and Patronage,* pp. 34–36. Opting for the lowest bidder, however, did not remove political considerations; as one scholar of newspaper patronage notes, "Awarding contracts to low bidders is regarded as a means of avoiding partisanship and subjectivity, but the system works only if there are criteria by which to determine which bid is the lowest." Dyer, "Political Patronage of the Wisconsin Press," p. 9.

56. The latter point is best made in Jeffrey Tulis, *The Rhetorical Presidency* (Princeton: Princeton University Press, 1987). Mel Laracey (in a series of convention papers) has noted that one reason that presidents of this era did not "go public" is that the official organ relieved them of having to do so. This may be true, at least up until the 1850s, but it does point out that the public approaches of twentieth-century presidents are qualitatively different in terms of how they were carried out, the constitutional presumptions behind such presidential behavior, and so on.

57. Letter from Jefferson to Smith, October 23, 1802, reproduced in F. B. Marbut, *News from the Capital* (Carbondale: Southern Illinois University Press,

1971), plate following p. 144. For more information on Jefferson's attempts to get his point of view, albeit anonymously, into the *Intelligencer* and other newspapers, see Cunningham, *Jeffersonian Republicans,* pp. 255–264 and 271–272; for examples of Jefferson's frequent claim that he wished to minimize publicity, see Pollard, *Presidents and the Press,* p. 66.

58. Quoted in Cunningham, *Jeffersonian Republicans,* p. 259.

59. Donald H. Stewart, *The Opposition Press of the Federalist Period* (Albany: State University of New York Press, 1969), pp. 621–622.

60. As late as the period from 1820 to 1832, a majority of news stories were clipped from other newspapers. Donald Lewis Shaw, "At the Crossroads: Change and Continuity in American Press News, 1820–1860," *Journalism History* 8 (1981): 38–50 at table 1. See also Gerald J. Baldasty, "The Charleston, South Carolina, Press and National News, 1808–1847," *Journalism Quarterly* 55 (1978): 518–526. This is not to say that there was a stable political communication system; newspapers were short-lived, given unpredictable support of either advertisers or politicians or both. See, e.g., Sloan, " 'Purse and Pen,' " pp. 126–127.

61. See Robert V. Remini, *The Election of Andrew Jackson* (Philadelphia: J. B. Lippincott Company, 1963), esp. pp. 76–86. Remini concludes, "Perhaps the single most important accomplishment of the Democrats in Congress and in the states was the creation of a vast, nation-wide newspaper system. The initiative and drive for this enterprise came from congressmen, but the work was aided by governors, state legislators, county leaders, and politicians of every rank" (p. 76).

62. Baldasty, *Commercialization,* p. 16.

63. These figures are from Baldasty, "Press and Politics in the Age of Jackson," p. 14.

64. Smith, *Press, Politics, and Patronage,* chap. 7.

65. The Sedition Act is reprinted in the standard history of the Alien and Sedition Acts, James Morton Smith, *Freedom's Fetters: The Alien and Sedition Laws and American Civil Liberties* (Ithaca: Cornell University Press, 1956), pp. 441–442.

66. This estimate comes from Rosenberg, *Protecting the Best Men,* p. 87. More complete information on the individual trials is in Smith, *Freedom's Fetters,* parts 2 and 3.

67. After all, judges usually left little for juries to decide except for the facts of the case and adduced seditious intent from the "bad tendencies" of the expression. See Smith, *Freedom's Fetters,* esp. p. 424.

68. Quoted in Rosenberg, *Protecting the Best Men,* p. 105. In general, see Levy, *Emergence of a Free Press,* chap. 9, esp. pp. 307–308; and Rosenberg, *Protecting the Best Men,* pp. 101–107.

69. See Rosenberg, *Protecting the Best Men,* chap. 6. While some politicians continued to bring libel cases, they focused on damage to their individual reputations. "By the nineteenth century . . . , civil libel cases, ostensibly private cases, came to replace criminal prosecutions as the most prevalent restraint on political expression." Ibid., p. 121. As the century wore on and such civil cases proved not to pack much punch, even the threat of libel suits was bypassed.

70. On the greater newsworthiness of Congress compared to the White House during this time period, see Samuel Kernell and Gary C. Jacobson, "Congress

and the Presidency as News in the Nineteenth Century," *Journal of Politics* 49 (1987): 1016–1035; Tulis, *Rhetorical Presidency,* esp. chap. 3. The old chestnut of breach of privilege was still occasionally trotted out. In 1800, for instance, when the Jeffersonian editor William Duane disclosed a Federalist bill to change (to its advantage) the way of certifying the electoral college vote, the Federalist-controlled Senate declared that Duane was guilty of a "high breach of privileges." After a complicated series of legal maneuvers, Duane did not show up to hear the verdict but went into hiding where he continued to edit his paper. The whole story is told by Smith, *Freedom's Fetters,* pp. 288–300.

71. Elizabeth Gregory McPherson, "The Southern States and the Reporting of Senate Debates, 1789–1802," *Journal of Southern History* 12 (1946): 223–246.

72. Elizabeth Gregory McPherson, "Reporting the Debates of Congress," *Quarterly Journal of Speech* 28 (1942): 141–148 at 142; Hoffman, *Governmental Secrecy and the Founding Fathers,* pp. 49–50.

73. The whole story is told in Ames, *History of the National Intelligencer,* pp. 23–27.

74. Marbut, *News from the Capital,* p. 20.

75. For examples, see ibid., pp. 22–23, 49–51, 56–62, 68–69 and 71–73; and Donald A. Ritchie, *Press Gallery: Congress and the Washington Correspondents* (Cambridge, MA: Harvard University Press, 1991), pp. 21–22, 26 and 38–39.

76. This point is incisively made in Leonard, *Power of the Press,* chap. 3.

77. See Smith, *Press, Politics, and Patronage,* esp. chaps. 16 and 17.

78. Cf. Dyer, "Political Patronage of the Wisconsin Press"; and Barbara Cloud, "The Press and Profit: Newspaper Survival in Washington Territory," *Pacific Northwest Quarterly* 79 (1988): 147–156, for indications of the extent, respectively, of the newspaper patronage system in Wisconsin just prior to the Civil War and the role of politics in starting new publications in the Washington Territory in the late nineteenth century. See also Ritchie, *Press Gallery,* pp. 75–78; and Mark W. Summers, *The Press Gang: Newspaper and Politics, 1865–1878* (Chapel Hill: University of North Carolina Press, 1994) pp. 149–151 and 310; both discuss the ways congressional correspondents found part-time work in Congress after the Civil War, with especial reference to the dean of the Capitol Hill press corps, Benjamin Perley Poore.

79. Marbut, "Decline of the Official Press," pp. 339–341.

80. The whole curious story is best told by Ritchie, *Press Gallery,* chap. 6.

81. "Public officials and candidates found it very difficult to sustain a successful civil suit or initiate a criminal prosecution. During the decade from 1865 to 1876 there were fewer than twenty reported libel prosecutions in the entire country." Rosenberg, *Protecting the Best Men,* p. 156.

82. See, for instance, Marbut, "Decline of the Official Press"; Pollard, *Presidents and the Press,* pp. 201–225; and Smith, *Press, Politics, and Patronage,* pp. 160–162.

83. Smith, *Press, Politics, and Patronage,* pp. 219–230. Presidents in the 1850s tacitly accepted the limits of the official press, bypassing it to publicize their State of the Union messages; Fillmore, Pierce, and Buchanan all sent out special Post Office couriers to carry copies to postmasters in many cities, who would in turn give them to local editors once they had been informed, via tele-

graph, that the message had been received by Congress. Marbut, "Decline of the Official Press," p. 339.

84. See, e.g., Hazel Dicken-Garcia, *Journalistic Standards in Nineteenth-Century America* (Madison: University of Wisconsin Press, 1989); and Baldasty, *Commercialization*.

85. The classic statement of this is J. Cutler Andrews, *The North Reports the Civil War* (Pittsburgh: University of Pittsburgh Press, 1955). More recent arguments include Schudson, *Discovering the News*, pp. 66–68; and Dicken-Garcia, *Journalistic Standards in Nineteenth-Century America*, pp. 51–62.

86. See particularly Baldasty, *Commercialization*, passim; and Dicken-Garcia, *Journalistic Standards in Nineteenth-Century America*, chap. 3. It is worth noting that the depoliticization of the news did not occur until after the Civil War, to judge from the content analysis of Shaw, "At the Crossroads," for the period from 1820 to 1860. The 1870s are noted as the key turning point in Jeffrey B. Rutenbeck, "Newspaper Trends in the 1870s: Proliferation, Popularization, and Political Independence," *Journalism and Mass Communication Quarterly* 72 (1995): 361–375.

87. Michael McGerr, *The Decline of Popular Politics: The American North, 1865–1931* (New York: Oxford University Press, 1986); Gerald J. Baldasty and Jeffrey B. Rutenbeck, "Money, Politics, and Newspapers: The Business Environment of Press Partisanship in the Late 19th Century," *Journalism History* 15 (1988): 60–69; Summers, *The Press Gang*, chaps. 3–4.

88. See, for instance, the symposium around John C. Nerone, "The Mythology of the Penny Press," with responses by Michael Schudson, Dan Schiller, Donald L. Shaw, and John Pauly, and a reply by Nerone, all in *Critical Studies in Mass Communication* 4 (1987): 376–422. Shaw's own content analysis of newspapers from 1820 to 1860, in "At the Crossroads," shows more change in format than in subject matter.

89. David Paul Nord, "The Evangelical Origins of Mass Media in America, 1815–1835," *Journalism Monographs*, no. 88 (May 1984), p. 2.

90. This heritage is well laid-out in Dan Schiller, *Objectivity and the News: The Public and the Rise of Commercial Journalism* (Philadelphia: University of Pennsylvania Press, 1981), chaps. 2–3; and Alexander Saxton, "Problems of Class and Race in the Origins of the Mass Circulation Press," *American Quarterly* 36 (1984): 211–234.

91. This shift occurred across the board prior to the Civil War. Donald Shaw's content analysis of newspapers (both dailies and others) shows a shift of 54 percent of the news stories being clipped from other newspapers in the period 1820–32 to 30 percent in 1847–60, while stories by reporters and editors went from 25 percent to 45 percent in the same time period. Shaw, "At the Crossroads," table 1.

92. Quoted in Marbut, *News from the Capital*, p. 60. On the penny press's creation of the job of reporter, see Schudson, *Discovering the News*, esp. pp. 23–24.

93. The fullest description of this debate is in Marbut, *News from the Capital*, pp. 56–62. See also Ritchie, *Press Gallery*, p. 26.

94. This is Marbut's quote in *News from the Capital*, p. 62.

95. See Richard A. Schwarzlose, *The Nation's Newsbrokers*, vol. 1 (Evanston, IL: Northwestern University Press, 1989), chaps. 2–3.

96. This notion of profession draws on the influential work of Eliot Freidson, discussed more fully in Chap. 4. He argues that "a profession is distinct from other occupations in that it has been given the right to control its own work" by elites who give advantages to the occupation and facilitate its autonomy. See Freidson, *Profession of Medicine: A Study of the Sociology of Applied Knowledge* (New York: Dodd and Mead, 1970; reprint, Chicago: University of Chicago Press, 1986), p. 71.

97. Parenthetically, a thorough historical account of the beginnings of journalistic professionalism—with reference to the government decisions that encouraged it—is still badly needed. In particular, Freidson's approach would direct us to the elite decisions that facilitated journalism to become a profession. The closest we come to one would be Schudson's very fine *Discovering the News,* but the role of political and economic elites is less studied than the more general economic and especially societal factors that pushed it.

98. Marbut, *News from the Capital,* pp. 71–72, contains the most extensive account of this episode, but see also Schudson, *Discovering the News,* pp. 28–29; and Ritchie, *Press Gallery,* pp. 38–39. My earlier discussion of this incident is in Cook, *Making Laws and Making News,* pp. 18–19.

99. Marbut, *News from the Capital,* documents two incidents on pp. 69 and 139–140. In 1847, one senator introduced two resolutions—one that would deny access to the editors of the *Union* from the floor, the other doing the same for reporters in the gallery—after the newspaper had published articles questioning the patriotism of senators opposed to sending more troops into the Mexican war and mischaracterizing Senate debate on an army appropriation bill. When one of the *Union*'s stenographers claimed the imbalance to have been inadvertent, the resolutions were defeated. (See also Pollard, *Presidents and the Press,* pp. 246–247.) In 1870, one representative took offense at a story in the *New York Evening Post* that alleged how several House members had been approached with bribes, and he proposed a motion that the author, William Scott Smith, be "expelled from the reporters' gallery for libelous statements reflecting upon the integrity of members of this House." When the motion was adopted, Smith was arrested and questioned, but when an investigative committee decided that the leaked affidavits upon which Smith based his story were forged, the move to expel him was dropped.

100. See, in general, Thomas H. Kaminski, "Congress, Correspondents and Confidentiality in the 19th Century: A Preliminary Study," *Journalism History* 4 (1977): 83–87, 92. For instance, in 1848, 1857, and 1871, a reporter revealed either the confidential document of a treaty or alleged a corruption scandal. In each case, an investigative committee arrested and questioned the reporters, but the latter largely clammed up, and they were each released quietly with little new evidence and no confession of guilt. See Marbut, *News from the Capital,* pp. 85–92, 97–102 and 140–146; and Ritchie, *Press Gallery,* pp. 28–29, 51–52 and 90–91.

101. The language comes from press gallery credentials reproduced in Marbut, *News from the Capital* (see plate following p. 144). Marbut discusses the passage of the resolution in ibid., p. 97.

102. For many years, the best historical evidence on the evolution of the Standing Committee of Correspondents consisted of the bits and pieces reported in Marbut, *News from the Capital*, but this has been superseded by Ritchie's painstaking archival research reported in *Press Gallery*, esp. pp. 120–126.

CHAPTER THREE

1. We can find similar examples of where government absorbed technological start-up costs across the twentieth century: from the Weather Bureau's support of Reginald Fessenden's experiments with radio broadcasting as a prospective way to inform people of storms, all the way to the government's development of the Internet as a national defense initiative that was then taken up by colleges and universities and, from there, private business. On the telegraph, see Robert Luther Thompson, *Wiring A Continent: The History of the Telegraph Industry in the United States, 1832–1866* (Princeton: Princeton University Press, 1947), chap. 1; on radio, see Susan J. Douglas, *Inventing American Broadcasting, 1899–1922* (Baltimore: Johns Hopkins University Press, 1987), esp. pp. 45ff.; on the Internet, see Katie Hafner and Matthew Lyon, *When Wizards Stay Up Late: The Origins of the Internet* (New York: Simon and Schuster, 1996).

2. Clark and Wetherell, "Measure of Maturity," p. 296. Their content analysis also reveals how the *Pennsylvania Gazette* had different methods of finding the news depending on the topic: consulting London newspapers for European and British news, relying upon other colonial newspapers for news from other colonies, and tapping the local grapevine for news of the city and Pennsylvania. Ibid., table 5, and pp. 294–297. What happened in Philadelphia was a continuation of a process occurring elsewhere as well; for instance, see Clark's comparison of "intercolonial" news in the *Boston Gazette* of the 1730s to the Boston *News-Letter*'s first issues thirty years before in *The Public Prints*, pp. 168–169.

3. Benjamin Franklin is the best example. See Ralph Frasca, "Benjamin Franklin's Printing Network," *American Journalism* 5 (1988): 145–158. For evidence that Franklin's virtual family tree of printers was no anomaly, see also Carol Sue Humphrey, "Producers of the 'Popular Engine': New England's Revolutionary Newspaper Printers," *American Journalism* 4 (1987): 97–117.

4. Quoted in Richard B. Kielbowicz, "Newsgathering by Printers' Exchanges before the Telegraph," *Journalism History* 9 (1982): 42–48 at 42. Kielbowicz notes that the exemption annually saved nine pence per fifty miles of delivery per issue.

5. In 1775, the system became adopted by the Continental Congress, and the British post collapsed. Overall, see Schlesinger, *Prelude to Independence*, pp. 190–195.

6. Kielbowicz, *News in the Mail*, chap. 3, esp. p. 38; John, *Spreading the News*, pp. 59–63.

7. John, *Spreading the News*, pp. 30–37.

8. Richard B. Kielbowicz, "The Press, Post Office, and Flow of News in the Early Republic," *Journal of the Early Republic* 3 (1983): 255–280 at 257–259.

9. Kielbowicz, "Newsgathering by Printers' Exchanges"; Smith, *Press, Politics, and Patronage*, p. 10.

10. See, for instance, John B. Hench, "Massachusetts Printers and the Com-

monwealth's Newspaper Advertisement Tax of 1785," *Proceedings of the American Antiquarian Society* 87 (1977): 199–211; and Carol Sue Humphrey, " 'That Bulwark of Our Liberties': Massachusetts Printers and the Issue of a Free Press," *Journalism History* 14 (1987): 34–38.

11. Thus, the Postmaster General said in 1794 that newspapers constituted 70 percent of the mail but only brought in 1/29 of the postage earned from letters. Some thirty years later, a Senate committee found that newspapers weighed fifteen times as much as letters but contributed 1/9 of postage. In 1850, the Postmaster General compared postage, with letter rates averaging around $3.16 a pound and newspaper rates around 16 cents a pound. Kielbowicz, *News in the Mails*, pp. 43, 108; Smith, *Press, Politics, and Patronage*, p. 7. This is not to say that the Post Office consistently ran a deficit; on the contrary, up until the late 1820s, Postmasters General usually returned an annual surplus to make up for the national debt, an extension of the colonial expectation that postage could be a source of revenue for governments. See John, *Spreading the News*, pp. 26 and 107.

12. The term is that of Kielbowicz, *News in the Mail*, p. 39. See also Wayne E. Fuller, *The American Mail: Enlarger of the Common Life* (Chicago: University of Chicago Press, 1972), pp. 131–132.

13. Such a proposal came within a vote of passing the Senate in 1832, defeated only by Jacksonians who feared that such a law would allow large-city periodicals to overwhelm their country counterparts. Kielbowicz, *News in the Mail*, p. 60.

14. The Congregationalist minister Leonard Bacon, quoted in John, *Spreading the News*, p. 40.

15. These examples come from Kielbowicz, "Press, Post Office, and Flow of the News in the Early Republic," pp. 266–267 and 276–277; and from Richard B. Kielbowicz, "Speeding the News by Postal Express, 1825–1861: The Public Policy of Privileges for the Press," *Social Science Journal* 22, no. 1 (1985): 49–64.

16. See in particular, Kielbowicz, "The Press, Post Office, and Flow of News in the Early Republic," esp. pp. 265–270; and Richard B. Kielbowicz, "Mere Merchandise or Vessels of Culture? Books in the Mail, 1792–1942," *Papers of the Bibliographic Society of America* 82 (1988): 169–177.

17. Postmaster General Return Meigs did quickly amend this to exempt religious publications, but even these magazines had to pay at a higher rate, and Meigs did reaffirm earlier practice by telling his employees not to accept magazines if it proved burdensome. Kielbowicz, "Press, Post Office, and the Flow of News in the Early Republic," p. 269.

18. Kielbowicz, *News in the Mail*, p. 130.

19. Ibid., p. 131.

20. "The little newspapers in rural America . . . were the special darlings of Congress, whose policies were deliberately designed to foster them and make them competitive with city newspapers." Fuller, *The American Mail*, p. 113.

21. Postmaster General Amos Kendall urged Congress to establish expresses thusly: "The editors will have the advantage of being the original dispensers of the news to their subscribers; and the people will obtain it through their own papers, without postage five or six days sooner than it can reach them in the New York papers with postage." Quoted in Kielbowicz, "Speeding the News by Postal Express," p. 54.

22. Richard B. Kielbowicz and Linda Lawson, "Protecting the Small-Town Press: Community, Social Policy and Postal Privileges, 1845–1970," *Canadian Review of American Studies* 19 (1988): 23–45 at 26.

23. Ibid., pp. 26–27.

24. Ibid., pp. 37–38.

25. See Stephen Lacy and Todd Simon, *The Economics and Regulation of United States Newspapers* (Norwood, NJ: Ablex, 1993), p. 254; and "Newspapers and Capitol Hill," *Editor and Publisher* (1994).

26. Quoted in Richard B. Kielbowicz, "Origins of the Second-Class Mail Category and the Business of Policymaking, 1863–1879," *Journalism Monographs*, no. 96 (April 1986), p. 6.

27. Richard B. Kielbowicz, "News Gathering by Mail in the Age of the Telegraph: Adapting to a New Technology," *Technology and Culture* 28, no. 1 (1987): 26–41 at 38–40. Kielbowicz does note, however, that the impact of the telegraph on the content of the news was not immediate because of the continued use of printers' exchanges; editors routinely relied upon the telegraph for bulletins while the mail was still the transportation medium of choice for correspondence or other prolonged stories.

28. Kielbowicz, "Origins of the Second-Class Mail Category," pp. 6–12.

29. Ibid., esp. pp. 14–22; Richard B. Kielbowicz, "The Growing Interaction of the Federal Bureaucracy and the Press: The Case of a Postal Rule, 1879–1917," *American Journalism* 4 (1987): 5–18. It is worth noting here that the ANPA's activism on postal subsidies has not only been to keep second-class mail cheap but to raise the cost of third-class mail, used by advertising circulars that cut into newspaper profitability by competing with them for advertisers.

30. *Lewis Publishing Co. v. Morgan*, 229 U.S. 288. See also *Houghton v. Payne*, 194 U.S. 88 (1904).

31. Linda Lawson, *Truth in Publishing: Federal Regulation of the Press's Business Practices, 1880–1920* (Carbondale: Southern Illinois University Press, 1993). Lawson concludes that the act was "a victim . . . of reformers' naive faith in the power of publicity, industry's success in using the regulatory process, and the government bureaucracy's reluctance to assume new responsibilities." Ibid., p. 142.

32. Linda Lawson, "When Publishers Invited Federal Regulation to Curb Circulation Abuses," *Journalism Quarterly* 71 (1994): 110–120. The House sponsor of the bill, a newly elected representative, was quick to note he did not instigate the legislation, telling the committee, "I introduced the bill at the request of various newspaper associations throughout the United States. I have not heard from any administration official about this bill. I have been in contact only with the weekly newspapermen." Quoted in ibid., p. 114.

33. Far from bridling under government regulation, publishers defended it and asked that it "be a little tougher" when postal officials, in 1962, asked Congress to repeal the public disclosure requirements for second-class mail. Ibid., p. 116.

34. See, in particular, Mark Fishman, *Manufacturing the News* (Austin: University of Texas Press, 1980); Oscar H. Gandy, Jr., *Beyond Agenda Setting: Information Subsidies and Public Policy* (Norwood, NJ: Ablex, 1982); and Judy Van-

Slyke Turk, "Information Subsidies and Media Content: A Study of Public Relations Influence on the News," *Journalism Monographs*, no. 100 (December 1986). This approach is best captured by Gandy's term, "information subsidies," whereby "the price of information may be reduced selectively by interested parties in order to increase the consumption of preferred information." Gandy, *Beyond Agenda Setting*, p. 30.

35. Moreover, the development of the governmental public relations infrastructure has, at times, directly subsidized the media when it produces programs that can be wholly reprinted or rebroadcast for free. Take the remarkable story told by Nancy Bernhard how the nascent television networks aired regular series produced by the Departments of Defense and State in the early 1950s, in part to fill up their schedule. In one case, over 200 episodes of a series called *Strength for a Free World* about the Marshall Plan, produced by the Economic Cooperation Administration within the State Department, ran on ABC. After two years, it was moved to the same time slot as the top-rated *Texaco Star Theater,* starring Milton Berle. One official fumed, "I am frankly of the opinion that we are being used by ABC to fill a half-hour of their time when it would be impossible for them to put anything else on the air that could stand up to the competition at that time. Since they are getting our show free of charge, it is rather obvious what they are doing." Nancy E. Bernhard, "Ready, Willing, Able: Network Television News and the Federal Government, 1948–1953," in William S. Solomon and Robert W. McChesney, eds., *Ruthless Criticism: New Perspectives in U.S. Communication History* (Minneapolis: University of Minnesota Press, 1993), pp. 291–312 (quote is on p. 301).

36. Fishman, *Manufacturing the News,* p. 45, and more generally, pp. 141–145.

37. Ibid., p. 151.

38. Clark, *Public Prints,* pp. 92–93. Clark notes elsewhere that although Campbell sought "more practical expressions of official approval," these were not successful, suggesting that approbation was not the same as official endorsement. See Clark, "Boston and the Nurturing of Newspapers," 243–271 at 254.

39. See McGerr, *Decline of Popular Politics.*

40. The standard history of Civil War reporting, for example, notes that just prior to the war, Baltimore papers were awaited for general news, not to mention the Philadelphia and New York newspapers that the trains would bring later in the day; they were so anticipated that reporters organized pony expresses to bring the papers from the depot over to Newspaper Row. See Andrews, *The North Reports the Civil War,* p. 27.

41. Kernell, *Going Public,* table 3-1. Working conditions continued to be difficult, however, and outside of Washington, careers continued to be short; see Ted Curtis Smythe, "The Reporter, 1880–1900: Working Conditions and Their Influence on the News," *Journalism History* 7 (1980): 1–10; and Baldasty, *Commercialization,* pp. 88–94.

42. Summers, *The Press Gang,* p. 99.

43. Baldasty, *Commercialization,* table 4-1, and pp. 96–97. On the increasingly hierarchical organization of newspapers in the later nineteenth century, see William S. Solomon, "The Site of Newsroom Labor: The Division of Editorial

Practices," in Hanno Hardt and Bonnie Brennen, eds., *Newsworkers: Toward a History of the Rank and File* (Minneapolis: University of Minnesota Press, 1995), pp. 110–134.

44. These terms and conclusions, of course, are derived from Leon V. Sigal's *Reporters and Officials: The Organization and Politics of Newsmaking* (Lexington, MA: D. C. Heath, 1973).

45. A revealing description of the daily round was provided by James Barrett Swain in the *New York Times* in 1861, reprinted in Andrews, *The North Reports the Civil War*, pp. 51–53. See Ritchie, *Press Gallery*, pp. 77–79, for a particularly useful discussion of the genesis of Newspaper Row, as well as Summers, *The Press Gang*, pp. 97–98.

46. Ritchie, *Press Gallery*, p. 78.

47. Michael Schudson, "Question Authority: A History of the News Interview," in Schudson, *The Power of News* (Cambridge, MA: Harvard University Press, 1995), chap. 3, provides the best analysis of the rise of the interview. The transcribed questions and answers were not used as the basis of a news story, as is the case today, but constituted the news item itself. Interviews, to be sure, were not unknown prior to the Civil War; for instance, reporters routinely met with presidents, but instead of documenting the questions and answers, treated their meeting as an event comparable to a royal audience. See excerpts from James Gordon Bennett's and Anne Royall's accounts of their meetings with President Van Buren in 1837 in Pollard, *Presidents and the Press*, pp. 189–191.

48. Richard S. Tedlow, *Keeping the Corporate Image: Public Relations and Business, 1900–1950* (Greenwich, CT: JAI Press, 1980), pp. 36–37. Stanley Kelley, Jr., emphasizes how the development of public relations in business was, in no small part, a political move to avoid further regulation; see his *Professional Public Relations and Political Power* (Baltimore: Johns Hopkins University Press, 1956), chap. 1, esp. pp. 12–13.

49. Most students of the development of public relations point to the "parallel" evolution in government and in business; see, e.g., Kelley, *Professional Public Relations*, p. 13.

50. Pollard, *Presidents and the Press*, pp. 500–533 at 513.

51. See in particular the splendid archival work of Martha Joynt Kumar on the beginnings of the White House news beat, to be reported in her *Wired for Sound and Pictures: The President and White House Communications Policies* (Baltimore: Johns Hopkins University Press, forthcoming). This information comes from "The White House Beat at the Century Mark: Reporters Establish Position to Cover the 'Elective Kingship,' " her paper delivered at the 1996 annual meeting of the American Political Science Association, San Francisco.

52. Two revealing contemporary accounts by David S. Barry and Ida Tarbell are partially reproduced in Pollard, *Presidents and the Press*, pp. 556–558. See also George Juergens, *News from the White House: The Presidential-Press Relationship in the Progressive Era* (Chicago: University of Chicago Press, 1981), esp. pp. 15–16.

53. Quoted in Pollard, *Presidents and the Press*, p. 557.

54. Theodore Roosevelt, *Theodore Roosevelt: An Autobiography* (New York: Macmillan, 1913), p. 389.

55. In an address to the Milwaukee Press Club quoted in Pollard, *Presidents and the Press*, p. 594.

56. See Elmer E. Cornwell, *Presidential Leadership of Public Opinion* (Bloomington: Indiana University Press, 1965), chaps. 1–2. Cornwell credits the Coolidge presidency with being the first to admit all reporters on an equal basis. Ibid., chap. 3.

57. Historian George Juergens put it this way: "[Theodore] Roosevelt took a major step toward making journalists what they are today, part of the Washington establishment." Juergens, *News from the White House,* p. 66. In general, see ibid., chaps. 2–4; Tulis, *Rhetorical Presidency,* chap. 4; Cornwell, *Presidential Leadership of Public Opinion;* and Pollard, *Presidents and the Press,* pp. 551–600. To be sure, the routine release and embargoing of information predated Roosevelt's presidency, as Kumar ("White House Beat at the Century Mark") makes clear for Cleveland, Harrison, and McKinley. What was new was both the permanence of the relationship and the direct personal involvement of the president.

58. Archibald Butt, quoted in Juergens, *News from the White House,* pp. 98–99; and in Pollard, *Presidents and the Press,* p. 607.

59. Quoted in Juergens, *News from the White House,* p. 125.

60. T. Swann Harding, "Genesis of One 'Government Propaganda Mill,' " *Public Opinion Quarterly* 11 (1947): 227–235; J. A. R. Pimlott, *Public Relations and American Democracy* (Princeton: Princeton University Press, 1951), p. 79.

61. Leonard D. White with Jean Schneider, *The Republican Era, 1869–1901: A Study in Administrative History* (New York: Macmillan Company, 1958), pp. 240–242 (quote is on p. 241).

62. On Pinchot, I have relied on the writings of Stephen Ponder. See his two publications: "Federal News Management in the Progressive Era: Gifford Pinchot and the Conservation Crusade," *Journalism History* 13 (1986): 42–48; and "Executive Publicity and Congressional Resistance, 1905–1913: Congress and the Roosevelt Administration's PR Men," *Congress & the Presidency* 13 (1986): 177–186. I have also benefited from the information presented in his unpublished Ph.D. dissertation, "News Management in the Progressive Era, 1898–1909: Gifford Pinchot, Theodore Roosevelt, and the Conservation Crusade," University of Washington, 1985. Whenever possible, I have cited the articles.

63. Ponder, "Federal News Management in the Progressive Era," p. 44.

64. Quoted in Ponder, "News Management in the Progressive Era, 1898–1909," Ph.D. diss., p. 198.

65. Ponder, "Executive Publicity and Congressional Resistance," p. 184.

66. Ponder, "News Management in the Progressive Era, 1898–1909," Ph.D. diss., p. 202. See also Pimlott, *Public Relations and American Democracy,* p. 71.

67. Senator Charles Fulton of Oregon, *Congressional Record* 42 (May 11, 1908), p. 6072, quoted in Ponder, "Executive Publicity and Congressional Resistance," p. 182.

68. Quoted in Ponder, "News Management in the Progressive Era, 1898–1909," Ph.D. diss., p. 196.

69. Gillett had been prompted to act when he noticed an advertisement by

the Office of Public Roads in the Agriculture Department for a "publicity expert" with five years of newspaper experience. Ponder, "Executive Publicity and Congressional Resistance," p. 184. As for the effect of the Gillett amendment, see the exchange between Cedric Larson, "How Much Federal Publicity Is There?" *Public Opinion Quarterly* 2 (1938): 638–644 and James McCamy, "Discussion: Measuring Federal Publicity," *Public Opinion Quarterly* 3 (1939): 473–475; and Pimlott, *Public Relations and American Democracy*, chap. 5, who ends up concluding, "There is in fact no stopping short of the conclusion that every official who comes into contact with the public is an agent of government information." Ibid., p. 120.

70. Pimlott, *Public Relations and American Democracy*, p. 89.

71. Although much has been written on the CPI, a dispassionate and analytic treatment is still badly needed. A good start is Robert Jackall and Janice M. Hirota, "America's First Propaganda Ministry: The Committee on Public Information during the Great War," in Robert Jackall, ed., *Propaganda* (New York: New York University Press, 1995), pp. 137–173. The standard citations otherwise are James R. Mock and Cedric Larson, *Words That Won the War: The Story of the Committee on Public Information, 1917–1919* (Princeton: Princeton University Press, 1939); and Stephen Vaughn, *Holding Fast the Inner Lines: Democracy, Nationalism, and the Committee on Public Information* (Chapel Hill: University of North Carolina Press, 1980).

72. Quoted in Vaughn, *Holding Fast the Inner Lines*, p. 17.

73. Ibid., p. 18.

74. Quoted in Craig Lloyd, *Aggressive Introvert: A Study of Herbert Hoover and Public Relations Management, 1912–1932* (Columbus: Ohio State University Press, 1972), p. 45. See also Stephen Ponder, "Popular Propaganda: The Food Administration in World War I," *Journalism and Mass Communication Quarterly* 72 (1995): 539–550.

75. Richard B. Du Boff, "The Rise of Communications Regulation: The Telegraph Industry, 1844–1880," *Journal of Communication* 34, no. 2 (Summer 1984): 52–66 at 53. Similarly, McChesney has written—with especial application to the Internet, "The primary function of the nonprofit sector in U.S. communications has been to pioneer the new technologies when they were not yet seen as profitable—for example, AM radio in the 1920s and FM radio and UHF television in the 1950s—and then to be pushed aside once they have shown the commercial interests the potential of the new media." Robert W. McChesney, "The Internet and U.S. Communication Policy-Making in Historical and Critical Perspective," *Journal of Communication* 46, no. 1 (1996): 98–124 at 102–103.

76. Fortunately, the history of radio and television, with particular attention to the role of politics and policy, has been splendidly chronicled, most notably by Erik Barnouw's magisterial *History of Broadcasting in the United States*, 3 vols. (New York: Oxford University Press, 1966, 1968, and 1970). Although other books tend to overemphasize a particular time period as *the* turning point in the development of broadcasting, I have found the following histories of the time period up to the establishment of the FCC to be most useful: Susan J. Douglas, *Inventing American Broadcasting, 1899–1922* (Baltimore: Johns Hopkins University Press, 1987); Philip T. Rosen, *The Modern Stentors: Radio Broadcasters and the Federal Government, 1920–1934* (Westport, CT: Greenwood Press,

1980); Susan Smulyan, *Selling Radio: The Commercialization of American Broadcasting* (Washington, DC: Smithsonian Institution Press, 1994); Robert W. McChesney, *Telecommunications, Mass Media, and Democracy: The Battle for the Control of U.S. Broadcasting, 1928–1935* (New York: Oxford University Press, 1993); and Robert Britt Horwitz, *The Irony of Regulatory Reform: The Deregulation of American Telecommunications* (New York: Oxford University Press, 1989), chaps. 3–4. On the FCC from the Communications Act of 1934 up through the deregulatory moves that began in the late 1970s, I have relied, in particular, on Murray Edelman, *The Licensing of Radio Services in the United States, 1927 to 1947* (Urbana: University of Illinois Press, 1950); Roger G. Noll, Merton J. Peck, and John J. McGowan, *Economic Aspects of Television Regulation* (Washington, DC: Brookings Institution, 1973), esp. chap. 4; Erwin G. Krasnow, Lawrence D. Longley, and Herbert A. Terry, *The Politics of Broadcast Regulation*, 3d ed. (New York, St. Martin's Press, 1982); Stanley M. Besen, Thomas G. Krattenmaker, A. Richard Metzger, Jr., and John R. Woodbury, *Misregulating Television: Network Dominance and the FCC* (Chicago: University of Chicago Press, 1984); and James L. Baughman, *Television's Guardians: The FCC and the Politics of Programming, 1958–1967* (Knoxville: University of Tennessee Press, 1985).

77. Edwin Emery, *History of the American Newspaper Publishers Association* (Minneapolis: University of Minnesota Press, 1950); Baldasty, *Commercialization*, pp. 107–110.

78. In lieu of the scarcity rationale, the Supreme Court, in upholding the constitutionality of regulation of cable, now has found that "the physical connection between the television set and the cable network gives the cable operator bottleneck, or gatekeeper, control over most (if not all) of the television programming that is channeled into the subscriber's home . . . A cable operator, unlike speakers in other media, can thus silence the voice of competing speakers with a mere flick of the switch." *Turner Broadcasting System* v. *Federal Communications Commission* (1994), 512 U.S. 622 at 656. The majority opinion, written for a highly split Court, contrasts print: "A daily newspaper, no matter how secure its local monopoly, does not possess the power to obstruct readers' access to other competing publications." Ibid., p. 656.

79. This and other examples of Congress's "tinkering with" the Communications Act are listed in Krasnow, Longley, and Terry, *Politics of Broadcast Regulation*, chap. 3.

80. See Du Boff, "The Rise of Communications Regulation"; and Horwitz, *Irony of Regulatory Reform*, esp. chap. 4. See also Thompson, *Wiring a Continent*, esp. chap. 1; and Lester G. Lindley, *The Constitution Faces Technology: The Relationship of the National Government to the Telegraph, 1866–1884* (New York: Arno Press, 1975).

81. This section is indebted to Douglas, *Inventing American Broadcasting*.

82. Ibid., chap. 7.

83. For instance, Mary S. Mander has intriguingly documented, from an analysis of congressional debates in the early 1920s, three competing models for radio: one, a public utility model that was linked to the common carrier format of telephony; another, a newspaper model that would emulate the free press; and a third (ultimately the one that won out), that saw regulation much as with transporta-

tion, trying to get what Hoover called the "congested lanes of ether" to run smoothly. Mander, "The Public Debate about Broadcasting in the Twenties: An Interpretive History," *Journal of Broadcasting* 28 (1984): 167–185.

84. David R. Mackey, "The Development of the National Association of Broadcasters," *Journal of Broadcasting* 1 (1957): 305–325, is a serviceable history. As Mackey notes, the NAB emerged as a result of demands by the American Society of Composers, Authors and Publishers (ASCAP) for royalties for the music broadcast; their first legislative initiative was to have a bill introduced into the Senate that would indicate that musical copyright did not apply to radio performances. Though this effort failed, it presaged later political pressures applied by broadcasters as a whole.

85. Rosen, *Modern Stentors,* pp. 84–85, 103.

86. Different versions of this quote circulate. This one is from Krasnow et al., *Politics of Broadcast Regulation,* p. 11; but see also Rosen, *Modern Stentors,* p. 49; and McChesney, *Telecommunications, Mass Media, and Democracy,* p. 13.

87. See Rosen, *Modern Stentors,* chap. 7.

88. Besen et al., *Misregulating Television,* p. 174.

89. Quoted in McChesney, *Telecommunications, Mass Media, and Democracy,* p. 179. McChesney's exhaustive account of the debates leading from the Radio Act of 1927 to the Communications Act of 1934 is full of evidence—although he does not explicitly make the case—that one reason why the reformers, who wished to boost nonprofit radio, got nowhere was the unanimity of the commercial broadcasters on the course of the new commission versus the ambivalence and disagreement over policy and tactics among their opponents.

90. See McChesney, *Telecommunications, Mass Media, and Democracy,* chap. 2; and Rosen, *Modern Stentors,* chap. 8. Quote is from McChesney, p. 27.

91. McChesney, *Telecommunications, Mass Media, and Democracy,* chap. 9, is especially insightful on the broadcasters' shifting rhetoric toward regulation following the institution of the FCC in 1934.

92. This point is well developed in Noll et al., *Economic Aspects of Television Regulation;* and Besen et al., *Misregulating Television.*

93. Quoted in Baughman, *Television's Guardians,* p. 17.

94. See Krasnow et al., *Politics of Broadcast Regulation,* chap. 6.

95. Indeed, Justice Kennedy's majority opinion in the *Turner Broadcasting* case that tested the constitutionality of cable regulation points precisely to congressional intent to protect local broadcasters from loss of revenue: "The provisions are designed to guarantee the survival of a medium that has become a vital part of the Nation's communication system, and to ensure that every individual with a television set can obtain access to free television programming . . . It reflects nothing more than the recognition that the services provided by broadcast television have some intrinsic value and, thus, are worth preserving against the threats posed by cable," pp. 647, 648.

96. A good example of this is Edelman, *Licensing of Radio.*

97. Baughman, *Television's Guardians,* makes this point well in examining the career of the FCC chair Newton Minow, an appointee of President Kennedy.

98. Ibid., chap. 8.

99. This preference began with the Davis amendment, passed in 1928, which forced a reallocation of frequencies so that the previously underrepresented South

and West would be better served; this directive not only embedded localism but allowed the FRC to rearrange virtually all broadcasters, favoring the commercial broadcasters in the process. Rosen, *Modern Stentors,* pp. 127–130.

100. It is, of course, impossible to know if such threats worked. Perhaps more important is the presumption on the part of the NAB that it would. For instances of such campaigns, see the fight for the Rogers amendment that would deny the FCC from limiting the amount of advertising in Baughman, *Television's Guardians,* p. 129.

101. David E. Price, "Policy Making in Congressional Committees," *American Political Science Review* 72 (1978): 548–574; see also Krasnow et al., *Politics of Broadcast Regulation,* chap. 9.

102. Indeed, at one point, the "Press-Radio War" in the early 1930s, during which newspapers were refusing to publish radio schedules as long as radio was usurping the print media's job of disseminating the news, was resolved by negotiations and an accord (the "Biltmore agreement") whereby broadcasters would cut back on news and newspapers would again print radio schedules. In the process, the earlier concerns of the American Newspaper Publishers Association about the commercialization of broadcasting were shelved. Only after the FCC was established did radio networks launch news services pioneered by H. V. Kaltenborn and Edward R. Murrow. See, among others, McChesney, *Telecommunications, Mass Media, and Democracy,* pp. 163–177.

103. See, in particular, *Associated Press* v. *National Labor Relations Board,* 301 U.S. 103 (1937); and *Associated Press* v. *United States,* 326 U.S. 1 (1945). On the AP antitrust suit, and the attempts of publishers to overturn the decision in Congress, see Margaret A. Blanchard, "The Associated Press Antitrust Suit: A Philosophical Clash over Ownership of First Amendment Rights," *Business History Review* 61 (1987): 43–85.

104. On these laws, see, in general, Lacy and Simon, *Economics and Regulation of United States Newspapers.* Other highly useful treatments include David C. Coulson, "Antitrust Law and Newspapers," in Robert G. Picard, James P. Winter, Maxwell E. McCombs, and Stephen Lacy, eds., *Press Concentration and Monopoly* (Norwood, NJ: Ablex, 1988), pp. 179–195; Marc Linder, "From Street Urchins to Little Merchants: The Juridical Transvaluation of Child Newspaper Carriers," *Temple Law Review* 63 (1990): 829–864; John C. Busterna and Robert G. Picard, *Joint Operating Agreements* (Norwood, NJ: Ablex, 1993); and Todd F. Simon, "Newspaper Regulation, Policy and Taxation," *Newspaper Research Journal* 14 (1993): 40–54.

105. Linder, "From Street Urchins to Little Merchants," pp. 839–849.

106. Ibid., pp. 829–830.

107. See, e.g., Coulson, "Antitrust Law and Newspapers," p. 191; James N. Dertouzos and Kenneth E. Thorpe, *Newspaper Groups: Economies of Scale, Tax Laws, and Merger Incentives* (Santa Monica, CA: Rand, 1982); Ben Bagdikian, *The Media Monopoly,* 4th ed. (Boston: Beacon Press, 1992), pp. 9–10.

108. Quoted in *Mabee* v. *White Plains,* 327 U.S. 178.

109. The Supreme Court cases are ibid.; and *Oklahoma Press* v. *Walling,* 327 U.S. 186.

110. There is a lively debate over whether or not the Newspaper Preservation Act actually did accomplish its goal of preserving otherwise failing newspapers.

The general conclusion is that it did not, but that it may have prevented third competitors, or suburban challengers to metropolitan dailies, from arising. See Lacy, "Content of Joint Operation Newspapers"; and Busterna and Picard, *Joint Operating Agreements.*

111. See below, chap. 8.

PART TWO

1. Indeed, when Cater returned to the press in his later *Power in Washington,* he termed them "outsiders on the inside."

2. James G. March and Johan P. Olsen, *Rediscovering Institutions: The Organizational Basis of Politics* (New York: Free Press, 1989), p. 160.

CHAPTER FOUR

1. For a good overview of this literature, see Michael Schudson, "The Sociology of News Production," *Media, Culture and Society* 11 (1989): 263–282.

Edward Jay Epstein, *News from Nowhere: Television and the News* (Random House, 1973), remains the earliest and purest statement of the organizational approach, although Chris Argyris's study of the *New York Times* in his book, *Behind the Front Page: Organizational Self-Renewal in a Metropolitan Newspaper* (San Francisco: Jossey-Bass, 1974), is a close runner-up in both instances. Sigal's deservedly influential *Reporters and Officials* continues to be essential for understanding the bureaucratic politics behind newsmaking, both in the newsroom and with officialdom. Other classic participant-observation studies from the 1970s of the news media also call attention to the omnipresent need for newsmakers as individuals and the news organization as a whole to routinize their collective work. The two best examples here are Gans, *Deciding What's News;* and Gaye Tuchman, *Making News: A Study in the Construction of Reality* (New York: Free Press, 1978). Both also place the organizational approach into larger contexts.

While Epstein, Sigal, Gans, and Tuchman gave us the greatest contribution into how news organizations work, the 1970s saw a spate of other participant-observation books, mostly in sociology, that fill out their portraits. See, for instance, Bernard Roshco, *Newsmaking* (Chicago: University of Chicago Press, 1975); David L. Altheide, *Creating Reality: How TV News Distorts Events* (Beverly Hills, CA: Sage, 1976); and Fishman, *Manufacturing the News.* After this scholarship appeared—most of it overlapping in the authors' conclusions—it is as if a virtual moratorium were placed on further studies until recently. Most of the attention given to organizational studies of the news in the 1980s focused on growing economic pressures. For instance, see Doug Underwood, *When MBAs Rule the Newsroom* (New York: Columbia University Press, 1993); and Bagdikian, *The Media Monopoly.* The dramatically changed political, economic, and technological landscape from the time period of the classic participant-observation accounts has not provoked as many new studies as we need, but for one splendid signal exception, see John H. McManus, *Market-Driven Journalism* (Newbury Park, CA: Sage, 1994).

2. Leo C. Rosten, *The Washington Correspondents* (New York: Harcourt Brace, 1937), p. 261.

3. Epstein, *News from Nowhere,* pp. 244–246.

4. That conflation is easily seen in the full title of the book: *Rediscovering Institutions: The Organizational Basis of Politics.*

5. For instance, in an oft-cited theoretical article, Kenneth Shepsle says, "I have not, to this point, ventured to define what an institution is, nor shall I." Kenneth A. Shepsle, "Institutional Equilibrium and Equilibrium Institutions," in Herbert Weisberg, ed., *Political Science: The Science of Politics* (New York: Agathon Press, 1986), pp. 51–81 at 66. In fairness, this is not unique to the new institutionalist literature. In fact, political scientists have been more comfortable talking about the process of institutionalization rather than about institutions per se. The best example is Nelson W. Polsby's justly classic article, "The Institutionalization of the U.S. House of Representatives," *American Political Science Review* 62 (1968): 144–168, which adroitly indicates elements of institutionalization without clearly defining what those institutions are and what they are evolving toward.

6. For instance, in political science, see the essays collected in Lawrence C. Dodd and Calvin Jillson, eds., *The Dynamics of American Politics: Approaches and Interpretations* (Boulder, CO: Westview Press, 1994); James G. March and Johan P. Olsen, *Democratic Governance* (New York: Free Press, 1995), chap. 2; Sue E. S. Crawford and Elinor Ostrom, "A Grammar of Institutions," *American Political Science Review* 89 (1995): 582–600; "*Polity* Forum: Institutions and Institutionalism," *Polity* 28 (1996): 83–140; and Robert E. Goodin, "Institutions and Their Design," in Goodin, ed., *The Theory of Institutional Design* (New York: Cambridge University Press, 1996), pp. 1–53. Goodin's essay is especially useful in tracing commonalities among the new institutionalisms in history, economics, political science, sociology, and social theory.

This spirit is evident elsewhere, not only in looking for commonalities between new institutionalisms but also between the new and the old; in particular, the old institutionalisms in economics, best represented by Thorstein Veblen and John R. Commons, and in sociology, epitomized by Philip Selznick, still have much to offer to political science. Malcolm Rutherford has also written a nice overview of old and new institutionalist thought in economics to argue that there is much more overlap and sources for mutual assistance than the practitioners of each are willing to admit. His conclusion that each side would do well to see things in terms of an "institutional individualism" that emphasizes the interactions of institutions and individuals is most helpful; see his *Institutions in Economics: The Old and the New Institutionalism* (New York: Cambridge University Press, 1994), esp. p. 178.

7. Bert Rockman, "The New Institutionalism and the Old Institutions," in Lawrence C. Dodd and Calvin Jillson, eds., *New Perspectives on American Politics* (Washington, DC: CQ Press, 1994), pp. 143–161.

8. An indispensable introduction to this literature is Walter W. Powell and Paul J. DiMaggio, eds., *The New Institutionalism in Organizational Analysis* (Chicago: University of Chicago Press, 1991). See also W. Richard Scott, "The Adolescence of Institutional Theory," *Administrative Science Quarterly* 32

(1987): 493–511; and Lynne G. Zucker, ed., *Institutional Patterns and Organizations* (Cambridge, MA: Ballinger, 1988).

9. This, in fact, could be a definition of institutionalism. See, e.g., Joseph Agassi, "Institutional Individualism," *British Journal of Sociology* 26 (1975): 144–155 at 145. Goodin also notes that "new institutionalism might be seen as nothing more (and nothing less) than the recognition of the need to blend both agency and structure in any plausibly comprehensive explanation of social outcomes." Goodin, "Institutions and Their Design," p. 17.

10. Samuel P. Huntington and Jorge I. Dominguez, "Political Development," in Fred I. Greenstein and Nelson W. Polsby, eds., *Handbook of Political Science*, vol. 3 (Reading, MA: Addison-Wesley, 1975), pp. 1–114 at 47.

11. For instance, one problem of the presumption that elites can manipulate the masses by means of a "dominant ideology" is that dominant classes may have been more effectively socialized into that dominant ideology than subordinate classes. This argument is well made in Nicholas Abercrombie, Stephen Hill, and Bryan S. Turner, *The Dominant Ideology Thesis* (Boston: Allen and Unwin, 1980).

12. Goodin, "Institutions and Their Design," pp. 24–25. Goodin is quick to add, however, that his category of "intentional intervention" need not mean that institutions are deliberately created in instrumental ways, as he includes those actions that may have "gone wrong—unintended by-products, the products of various intentional actions cutting across one another, misdirected intentions, or just plain mistakes . . . An institution can thus be the product of intentional action, without its having been literally the intentional product of anyone's action." Ibid., p. 28.

13. Terry M. Moe, "Interests, Institutions, and Positive Theory: The Politics of the NLRB," *Studies in American Political Development* 2 (1987): 236–299, nicely argues that one should expand the public choice approach by moving beyond formal rules, noting, "Routines, norms, and other aspects of regularized or 'cooperative' behavior are . . . informal but highly consequential political institutions." Ibid., p. 293. However, I would make a slight but crucial shift in Moe's next point when he claims, "The structure as a whole works and becomes entrenched because it is consistent with the incentives of all the major participants" (p. 294). Given the difficulty of linking particular means to particular ends, we might be better off striking "because it is consistent" and replacing it with the words "as long as it is not inconsistent."

14. See, e.g., Rutherford, *Institutions in Economics*, sec. 4.3, on "rationality and rule following" in new institutionalism in economics. If this is true of economics, it is also true of the public choice literature in political science and clearly informs the other schools in political science and sociology.

15. Although these points are most developed in the sociological version of new institutionalism, rational-choice theorists in economics and political science also stress the disconnection between current activity and the institutional context in which that occurs. Take, for instance, William Riker's conception of institutions as "congealed tastes" from the past to which current incumbents must modify themselves, introduced in his "Implications from the Disequilibrium of Majority Rule for the Study of Institutions," *American Political Science Review* 74 (1980): 432–446 at 432. Even more strongly, Shepsle, in his "Institutional Equi-

librium and Equilibrium Institutions" (esp. pp. 68–70), discusses how legislative majorities might ideally prefer a different institutional arrangement but are more risk-averse than is the case when they might consider alternative policies.

Even those who defend the notion of institutions as rational adaptations recognize a lag between structure and action. For instance, Andrew Schotter begins discussing institutions, in *The Economic Theory of Social Institutions* (New York: Cambridge University Press, 1981), as follows: "The proper analogy to make is between the evolution of an economy and the evolution of a species. Biologists know that a particular animal reveals a variety of features that it has developed to solve specific evolutionary problems. If these problems cease to exist, the animal is left with vestigial features whose function is a mystery to us. But if the problems remain, the function of the feature may be obvious for all to see. The problem of the scientist is one of inferring from observed appearances the evolutionary problem that must have existed to produce what we observe today." Ibid., p. 1. Where I differ from Schotter is not only in pointing out that institutional elements may have evolved in a way that is neither conscious nor deliberate (much as biological evolution often occurs by accidental variation), but also in underscoring the problematic connection—at which Schotter only hints—between a given problem and a given response.

Perhaps the best statement here is Robert Goodin's puckish point that, indeed, institutional constraints are often "advantageous to individuals and groups in the pursuit of their own more particular projects" precisely *because* "the same contextual factors that constrain individual and group actions also shape the desires, preferences, and motives of those individual and group agents." Goodin, "Institutions and Their Design," p. 20.

16. Crawford and Ostrom, "Grammar of Institutions," p. 582. This definition of institutions shares much with Douglass North's "regularities in repetitive interactions among individuals." North, "The New Institutional Economics," *Journal of Institutional and Theoretical Economics* 142 (1986): 230–237 at 231.

17. Giddens's fullest development of this comes in the context of his "structuration theory." The terms are defined in Anthony Giddens, *Central Problems in Social Theory: Action, Structure and Contradiction in Social Analysis* (Berkeley: University of California Press, 1979); and the theory is most fully developed in his *The Constitution of Society: Outline of a Theory of Structuration* (Berkeley: University of California Press, 1984). Two useful crash courses into Giddens's social theory are Ian Craib, *Anthony Giddens* (New York: Routledge, 1992); and Philip Cassell, ed., *The Giddens Reader* (Stanford, CA: Stanford University Press, 1993). The quote here is from *Central Problems*, p. 69.

A similar way of understanding the duality of institutions is Claus Offe's point that institutions contain elements both of social norms and strategic action, "doing things 'the right way' and 'getting things done.' " Offe, "Designing Institutions in East European Transitions," in Goodin, ed., *Theory of Institutional Design*, pp. 199–226 at 201.

18. These quotes appear in Giddens, *Central Problems*, pp. 70–71. Italics that were in the original were removed.

19. Ibid., p. 65 (emphasis in original).

20. The term is that of Kenneth A. Shepsle. See his "Institutional Arrange-

ments and Equilibrium in Multidimensional Voting Models," *American Journal of Political Science* 23 (1979): 27–60, and, more generally, his "Institutional Equilibrium and Equilibrium Institutions." See also Riker, "Implications from the Disequilibrium." This deep skepticism about the natural appearance of equilibria, incidentally, seems to separate public choice scholars, especially in political science, from new economic institutionalists. For a trenchant analysis, see Moe, "Interests, Institutions, and Positive Theory," esp. pp. 274–281.

21. See, in particular, Donald P. Green and Ian Shapiro, *Pathologies of Rational Choice Theory: A Critique of Applications in Political Science* (New Haven: Yale University Press, 1994), chap. 6.

22. For instance, to be able to drive effectively requires some rules of the road, but whether people drive on the left or right is immaterial as long as everyone agrees, and it is not against their interests to maintain that rule. See, e.g., Rutherford, *Institutions in Economics*, pp. 74–75. This theme is especially strong in Riker, "Implications from the Disequilibrium," but Shepsle, "Institutional Equilibrium," p. 52, also notes, "A configuration of institutions . . . prescribes *and* constrains . . . the way in which business is conducted" (emphasis added).

23. Mary Douglas, *How Institutions Think* (Syracuse: Syracuse University Press, 1986), pp. 46–47.

24. See, e.g., Lynne G. Zucker, "The Role of Institutionalization in Cultural Persistence," *American Sociological Review* 42 (1977): 726–743, esp. at 728.

25. This argument is well made in Karen Orren and Stephen Skowronek, "Beyond the Iconography of Order: Notes for a 'New Institutionalism,'" in Dodd and Jillson, eds., *Dynamics of American Politics*, pp. 311–330. See also Zucker, "Organizations as Institutions," in Zucker, ed., *Institutional Patterns and Organizations*, p. 2, who argues that "transformations of institutional structure . . . generally involve the reallocation of individuals among existing institutional definitions, rather than the creation of new definitions."

26. This point is nicely made in Roger Friedland and Robert G. Alford, "Bringing Society Back In: Symbols, Practices, and Institutional Contradictions," in Powell and DiMaggio, eds., *The New Institutionalism in Organizational Analysis*, pp. 232–263, esp. at 254–256.

27. This point is inspired (like so much else) by Charles Lindblom's indispensable "The Science of 'Muddling Through,'" *Public Administration Review* 19 (1959): 79–88.

28. See esp. Polsby, "Institutionalization of the U.S. House of Representatives," p. 145. Polsby's classic definition has also been used effectively for institutions beyond Capitol Hill; see, for one good example, John P. Burke, *The Institutional Presidency* (Baltimore: Johns Hopkins University Press, 1992).

29. Steven H. Haeberle, "The Institutionalization of the Subcommittee in the U.S. House of Representatives," *Journal of Politics* 40 (1978): 1054–1065.

30. Paul J. DiMaggio and Walter W. Powell, "The Iron Cage Revisited: Institutional Isomorphism and Collective Rationality in Organizational Fields," *American Journal of Sociology* 48 (1983): 147–160, reprinted in Powell and DiMaggio, eds., *The New Institutionalism in Organizational Analysis*, pp. 63–82 at 64.

31. Ibid., esp. pp. 67–72.

32. See, most notably, Pamela S. Tolbert and Lynne G. Zucker, "Institutional

Sources of Change in the Formal Structure of Organizations: The Diffusion of Civil Service Reform, 1880–1935," *Administrative Science Quarterly* 28 (1983): 22–39.

33. This is not to say that new institutionalists in sociology reject this formulation out of hand; for instance, see Scott, "Adolescence of Institutional Theory," esp. pp. 499–501. It is also important for our consistency with the definition of "politics" essayed by David Easton and cited in chap. 5 which distinguishes between political and "parapolitical" actors on the basis of their action on behalf of a society.

34. The literature is remarkably consistent in its portrayal of what news is and how it gets produced. Differences are ones of degree rather than kind. This next section draws on the research cited in n.1. Instead of confronting the reader with a barrage of citations to literature that often ends up saying the same thing with different data, I will only put in additional citations for particularly insightful discussions, for strong differences in interpretations, and for additional research.

35. The stimuli were thematic apperception tests (TATs), with illustrations to which stories were elicited. See Stanley Rothman and S. Robert Lichter, "Personality, Ideology, and Worldview: A Comparison of Media and Business Elites," *British Journal of Political Science* 15 (1984): 29–49; and Lichter et al., *The Media Elite*.

36. A good statement of this is Herbert J. Gans, "Are U.S. Journalists Dangerously Liberal?" *Columbia Journalism Review* 23 (November/December 1985): 29–33. To be sure, Lichter-Rothman-Lichter have attempted to respond to one of Gans's criticisms—namely that they did not do a good job of connecting together these attitudes with their work. The authors of *The Media Elite* did include several policy areas for content analyses that largely confirmed their conclusions, but their selection of nuclear energy, busing, and desegregation, and policy toward large oil companies is quite incomplete. One wonders if they would have found such reinforcing results with a wider sample of issues (e.g., foreign policy, deregulation, tax cuts). It should also be pointed out that there are many methodological flaws in the Lichter-Rothman-Lichter study; in particular, their constant tendency to leave out neutral responses (e.g., note to table 4, pp. 64–66) may exaggerate the liberalism of journalists and bolster the statistical significance of their results.

37. Stephen Hess, *The Washington Reporters* (Washington, DC: Brookings Institution, 1981), chap. 1; David H. Weaver and G. Cleveland Wilhoit, *The American Journalist: A Portrait of U.S. News People and Their Work*, 2d ed. (Bloomington: Indiana University Press, 1991), pp. 71–77.

38. See, in particular, Lee Sigelman, "Reporting the News: An Organizational Analysis," *American Journal of Sociology* 79 (1973): 132–151.

39. The term is that of Charles R. Bantz, Suzanne McCorkle, and Roberta C. Baade, "The News Factory," *Communication Research* 7 (1980): 45–68. See also Epstein, *News from Nowhere;* Altheide, *Creating Reality;* and McManus, *Market-Driven Journalism.*

40. This dynamic is, not surprising, strongest with local television, where few of the reporters gather ideas for the news outside of the newsroom but instead react to other news (wire services, newspapers, networks) or to initiatives such

as press conferences and the like. See Altheide, *Creating Reality;* and, esp., McManus, *Market-Driven Journalism.*

41. For instance, a recent careful study of the content of a random sample of American newspapers during the fall of 1992 finds only weak correlations between the evaluative contents of news reports and of editorials about the three major candidates. See Russell J. Dalton, Paul A. Beck, and Robert Huckfeldt, "The Media and the Voters: Information Flows in the 1992 Presidential Election," paper delivered at the 1996 annual meeting of the American Political Science Association, San Francisco, pp. 16–17. It may be, as Benjamin I. Page has recently speculated on the basis of three case studies of mass-mediated deliberation, that editorial positions may have a greater impact on the "play" the story receives, but this idea has yet to receive more rigorous testing. See Page, *Who Deliberates? Mass Media in Modern Democracy* (Chicago: University of Chicago Press, 1996), pp. 112–116.

42. Roshco, *Newsmaking,* p. 9. See also Judee K. Burgoon, Michael Burgoon, and Charles K. Atkin, *The World of the Working Journalist* (New York: Newspaper Advertising Bureau, 1982), p. 7: "News people say they know what makes news but can't explain it to others."

43. See, e.g., Robert O. Blanchard, "Congressional Correspondents and Their World," in Blanchard, ed., *Congress and the News Media* (New York: Hastings House, 1974) pp. 183ff., for examples of the inability of Capitol Hill reporters to figure out their chief sources for story ideas.

44. The intuitive choice of news is best revealed by Burgoon et al.'s study of journalists whose perceptions, they argued, are that "newsworthiness must be judged within the context of events in the world at a given time . . . They and only they have access to the totality of the 'news day.' Therefore, the reader cannot decide what has consequence in this context. Neither can the academic researcher who searches for generalities about what is newsworthy." *World of the Working Journalist,* p. 9.

45. Darnton, "Writing News and Telling Stories." Other examples cited by cultural historian Darnton, reflecting on his cub reporter days at the *New York Times* in the late 1950s, led him to conclude, "Reporters gradually develop a sense of mastery over their craft—of being able to write a column in an hour on anything, no matter how difficult the conditions." Ibid., p. 187.

46. Gaye Tuchman, "Making News by Doing Work: Routinizing the Unexpected," *American Journal of Sociology* 78 (1973): 110–131.

47. Gans, *Deciding What's News,* pp. 87–89.

48. Gaye Tuchman, "Objectivity as Strategic Ritual: An Examination of Newsmen's Notions of Objectivity," *American Journal of Sociology* 77 (1972): 660–679.

49. At the annual meeting of the International Communication Association, Chicago, Illinois, May 1991.

50. Tamotsu Shibutani, *Improvised News* (New York: Bobbs-Merrill, 1966), p. 17. Indeed, the sociological study of rumor would seem to be most pertinent to newsmaking, given that the chief processes in one classic study are leveling (rumors, as they are passed along, become shorter and more concise and quickly understood), sharpening (selective attention causes only certain details to remain, which then become the dominant theme), and assimilation (new material fits into

the previous rumor to build a more coherent overall structure). Indeed, the division of news into breaking events and features would seem to parallel the social split into rumors and gossip. But that is for another day. For a serviceable overview, see Ralph L. Rosnow and Gary Alan Fine, *Rumor and Gossip: The Social Psychology of Hearsay* (New York: Elsevier, 1976).

51. S. Elizabeth Bird, *For Enquiring Minds: A Cultural Study of Supermarket Tabloids* (Knoxville: University of Tennessee Press, 1992).

52. Nina Eliasoph, "Routines and the Making of Oppositional News," *Critical Studies in Mass Communication* 5 (1988): 313–334.

53. On the link of perceived autonomy to job satisfaction, see Hess, *Washington Reporters,* pp. 2–9; Burgoon et al., *World of the Working Journalist,* table 3.8; Weaver and Wilhoit, *The American Journalist,* pp. 88–100.

54. Sigelman, "Reporting the News." Indeed, Burgoon et al., *World of the Working Journalist,* p. 61, suggests that job satisfaction is linked to both receiving clear directives from their supervisors and greater autonomy: "Journalists seem to be saying that they enjoy freedom to make decisions about their work but also want clear direction from their boss as to exactly what he or she wants done."

55. For further elaboration of this last point (including an exploratory empirical analysis of the first year of the Bush presidency), see Timothy E. Cook, "The Negotiation of Newsworthiness," in Ann N. Crigler, ed., *The Psychology of Political Communication* (Ann Arbor: University of Michigan Press, 1996), pp. 11–36.

56. See Paul F. Berliner, *Thinking in Jazz: The Infinite Art of Improvisation* (Chicago: University of Chicago Press, 1994).

57. See esp. Gans, *Deciding What's News,* pp. 90–92.

58. See, e.g., Burgoon et al., *World of the Working Journalist,* tables 1.6 (on perceived similarity of newsworthiness between reporters and editors) and 3.2 (on no "unified editorial approach").

59. Tuchman has superbly discussed the translation of the strategic ritual of objectivity into televisual language in *Making News,* chap. 6. Weaver and Wilhoit's surveys of American journalists also revealed considerable consensus: "While there are *slight* tendencies for the role conceptions to be stronger among certain types of journalists, the more significant fact is that these basic roles are almost universal perceptions among journalists. They are, in a sense, the primary colors of the profession: their pigment and hue may be grayer or darker in some, but they are present in virtually all journalists of all media . . ." *The American Journalist,* p. 144 (emphasis in original).

60. Weaver and Wilhoit, *The American Journalist,* pp. 105–112.

61. Freidson, *The Profession of Medicine,* p. 187. Chap. 4 presents the full argument.

62. Steven Brint, *In An Age of Experts: The Changing Roles of Professionals in Politics and Public Life* (Princeton: Princeton University Press, 1994), p. 23. Italics in original removed.

63. See, most notably, Philip Elliott, "Press Performance as Political Ritual," *Sociological Review Monograph,* no. 29 (1980): 141–177. Such a perspective is implicit in the justly famous work of Gaye Tuchman (e.g., *Making News*) and the scholars who have studied "repair work" cited above.

64. For instance, such anxiety seems to pop up when politicians and government officials exploit their new-won fame to move directly to high echelons

within journalism. Journalists may protest about the importance of keeping the distinctions clear and of, to use another metaphor, halting the "revolving door" between journalism and government. See Lewis W. Wolfson, "Through the Revolving Door: Blurring the Line between Press and Government," research paper R-4, Joan Shorenstein Barone Center, Kennedy School of Government, Harvard University, 1991. Yet without a clear pattern of recruitment, training, and licensing, it is impossible to prescribe any preparation as being more legitimate than any other. Moreover, there are any number of media personnel, especially but not exclusively in television, who have shifted back and forth between journalism and entertainment.

65. This point is made in John Soloski, "News Reporting and Professionalism: Some Constraints on the Reporting of the News," *Media, Culture and Society* 11 (1989): 207–228. For the best general statement on the ways in which professionalization and bureaucratization are complementary rather than at odds, see Magali Sarfatti Larson, *The Rise of Professionalism: A Sociological Analysis* (Berkeley: University of California Press, 1977).

66. See, e.g., Schiller, *Objectivity and the News*.

67. E.g., one journalist friend of mine, in the space of fifteen years, began at the *Berkshire Eagle* in Pittsfield, Massachusetts, and went from there to the *New Orleans Times-Picayune,* then the *Atlanta Constitution,* then the *Wall Street Journal,* then the *Washington Post,* and finally the *New York Times.* Journalistic careers spanning newspapers and/or newsmagazines and/or television and/or radio are common as well.

68. *Nightline,* September 27, 1989 (transcript).

69. Timothy Crouse, *The Boys on the Bus: Riding with the Campaign Press Corps* (New York: Ballantine, 1973), pp. 21–23.

70. Ibid., p. 13.

71. McManus, *Market-Driven Journalism,* p. 94. See also Phyllis Kaniss, *Making Local News* (Chicago: University of Chicago Press, 1991). Matthew C. Ehrlich, "The Competitive Ethos in Television Newswork," *Critical Studies in Mass Communication* 12 (1995): 196–212, documents a similar impact from local television news broadcasts monitoring each other's work.

72. Gans, *Deciding What's News,* p. 181.

73. Quoted in Cook, *Making Laws and Making News,* p. 48. More generally, see Burgoon et al., *World of the Working Journalist,* which concludes, "Information suppliers are information addicts" (p. 83), with heavy attention to news in other outlets besides their own.

74. This theme is best developed in Fishman, *Manufacturing the News.*

75. This list comes from ibid., pp. 21–22.

76. "One of the perennial sources of astonishment for the nonprofessional is to attend a congressional committee hearing and witness the row upon row of reporters seated at the press tables as they lift their pencils and lay them down with almost ballet corps precision while the flow of testimony moves along." Cater, *Fourth Branch,* p. 16. For elaboration, see Fishman, *Manufacturing the News,* pp. 76–84; and Cook, *Making Laws and Making News,* pp. 53–54.

77. Sigal, *Reporters and Officials,* pp. 37 and 39.

78. Two good recent journalistic accounts of these forums are Eleanor Ran-

dolph, "For Many in the Media, Hotline Is a Must-Read Daily Source," *Los Angeles Times,* November 28, 1995, p. A-5; and Francis X. Clines, "At Breakfast with Godfrey (Budge) Sperling Jr.: Politicians and the Press, Once Over," *New York Times,* January 10, 1996, p. C1. The Randolph article quotes the publisher of the *Hotline,* "In the minds of a lot of reporters, Hotline validates their work."

79. Most of these, to date, occur within the context of presidential campaigns, such as C. Richard Hofstetter, *Bias in the News: Network Television Coverage of the 1972 Election Campaign* (Columbus: Ohio State University Press, 1976); and Patterson, *Mass Media Election.* However, the results seem to hold for non-election coverage as well; e.g., see James Lemert, "Content Duplication by the Networks in Competing Evening Newscasts," *Journalism Quarterly* 51 (1974): 238–244.

These findings have been convincing enough to later scholars so that they don't investigate variations among news outlets, so long as the principal concern is what became news rather than the angle thereupon. For instance, Bartels's impor-tant and influential book on media momentum in presidential primaries refers to earlier work and notes, "Throughout this book I have treated media content as a single undifferentiated flow." Larry M. Bartels, *Presidential Primaries and the Dynamics of Public Choice* (Princeton: Princeton University Press, 1988), p. 315. Likewise, in my study of the visibility of members of the House of Representa-tives, I summed across networks, "given the evidence that they tend to overlap greatly in their choice of subjects, even if they do differ stylistically." Cook, *Making Laws and Making News,* p. 179.

80. For instance, Dan Nimmo and James E. Combs found three distinct narra-tive visions for the crisis coverage of the broadcast network news in the late sev-enties, even though the methods of gathering the news and the sources to whom they turned did not diverge much; see Nimmo and Combs, *Nightly Horrors: Crisis Coverage in Television Network News* (Knoxville: University of Tennessee Press, 1985).

Assessments across modalities for campaign coverage include C. Richard Hof-stetter, "News Bias in the 1972 Campaign: A Cross-Media Comparison," *Journalism Monographs,* no. 58 (November 1978); Holli A. Semetko, Jay G. Blumler, Michael Gurevitch, and David H. Weaver, *The Formation of Campaign Agendas: A Comparative Analysis of Party and Media Roles in Recent American and British Elections* (Hillsdale, NJ: Lawrence Erlbaum Associates, 1991), chap. 5; and Marion R. Just, Ann N. Crigler, Dean E. Alger, Timothy E. Cook, Montague Kern, and Darrell M. West, *Crosstalk: Citizens, Candidates, and the Media in a Presidential Campaign* (Chicago: University of Chicago Press, 1996), chap. 4. Semetko et al. noted virtual identity in the subjects being covered by two Mid-western newspapers and the three broadcast networks in 1984, but somewhat less accord on the "themes" of the election. Just et al. found for the 1992 cam-paign that there tended to be greater consensus within a particular modality (local TV news, network news, and newspapers) than within a given community, but overall "[t]here was a remarkably similar pattern of candidate coverage across media. Candidate coverage appears to be governed by shared understandings about what is a good focus for a story (candidates' activities or campaigning rather than issues), about what is newsworthy about candidates in general (namely their personal qualities and strategies) and in particular (Bush's presidential decisions, Clinton's and Perot's chances for beating the incumbent, or Perot's unusual campaign organization)." Ibid., pp. 103–104.

Finally, in my earlier work on the visibility of House members in the news, I found the rankings to be so similar between the *New York Times* and the three broadcast networks that they appear to measure the same phenomena. Cook, *Making Laws and Making News*, p. 63, and more fully, Timothy E. Cook, "House Members as Newsmakers: The Effects of Televising Congress," *Legislative Studies Quarterly* 11 (1986): 203–226.

81. Patterson, *Mass Media Election*, p. 100.

82. See Altheide, *Creating Reality;* Gans, *Deciding What's News;* Matthew Robert Kerbel, *Edited for Television: ABC, CNN, and the 1992 Presidential Election* (Boulder, CO: Westview Press, 1994); and Ronald N. Jacobs, "Producing the News, Producing the Crisis: Narrativity, Television, and News Work," *Media, Culture, and Society* 18 (1996): 373–397, esp. pp. 378–381.

83. See especially Darnton, "Writing News and Telling Stories."

84. On enduring values, see Gans, *Deciding What's News,* chap. 2. The definition of news as "novelty without change" comes from Phillips, "What Is News? Novelty without Change."

85. Tuchman, *Making News,* p. 61. Emphasis and ellipses in original. Harvey Molotch and Marilyn Lester's famous analysis of the 1969 Santa Barbara oil spill, "Accidental News: The Great Oil Spill as Local Occurrence and as National Event," *American Journal of Sociology* 81 (1975): 235–260, convincingly demonstrates that while certain dramatic, and empirically undeniable, accidents disrupt the standard storylines and dependence on official sources, routines reimpose themselves as the original event wanes over time. Some "normal accidents" (only predictable in that they will happen, but not when, where or how) may even have almost stereotypic storylines that develop from them over the course of several days; see, for instance, Richard C. Vincent, Bryan K. Crow, and Dennis K. Davis, "When Technology Fails: The Drama of Airline Crashes in Network Television News," *Journalism Monographs,* no. 117 (November 1989).

86. Schudson, *Discovering the News,* chap. 1; and Schiller, *Objectivity and the News.*

87. For scholarship that points to the Progressive Era as a crucial moment, see, for instance, Schudson, *Discovering the News;* Gans, *Deciding What's News;* Leonard, *The Power of the Press;* McGerr, *Decline of Popular Politics;* and Dicken-Garcia, *Journalistic Standards in Nineteenth-Century America.*

88. See Orren and Skowronek, "Beyond the Iconography of Order," for a good statement of this argument.

89. This theme is nicely delineated in Nord, "Teleology and News;" and Clark, *The Public Prints.*

90. Bernard Berelson, "What 'Missing the Newspaper' Means," in Paul F. Lazarsfeld and Frank N. Stanton, eds., *Communication Research 1948–49* (New York: Harper, 1949).

91. Cook, *Making Laws and Making News,* table 4-2.

92. This is a theme of Joe S. Foote, *Television Access and Political Power: The Networks, the Presidency, and the "Loyal Opposition"* (New York: Praeger, 1990).

93. Elizabeth Kolbert, "Prime Time Snubs Mr. Clinton for Reruns," *New York Times,* April 23, 1995, p. E3; Alison Mitchell, "Without TV, Clinton Lets Tradition Lag," *New York Times,* January 6, 1996, p. 7. The latter article quoted White House press secretary Michael McCurry as indicating that the networks' reluctance to air a nighttime press conference live meant that it had become "a kind of dinosaur."

94. David Paletz and Richard Vinegar, "Presidents on Television: The Effects of Instant Analysis," *Public Opinion Quarterly* 41 (1977): 488–497; Frederick T. Steeper, "Public Response to Gerald Ford's Statements on Eastern Europe in the Second Debate," in George F. Bishop, Robert G. Meadow, and Marilyn Jackson-Beeck, eds., *The Presidential Debates* (New York: Praeger, 1980), pp. 81–101; and James B. Lemert, William R. Elliott, James M. Bernstein, William L. Rosenberg, and Karl J. Nestvold, *News Verdicts, the Debates, and Presidential Campaigns* (New York: Praeger, 1991).

95. This point is made most clearly in cross-national comparisons of the news media; in particular, see Daniel C. Hallin and Paolo Mancini, "Speaking of the President: Political Structure and Representational Form in U.S. and Television News," *Theory and Society* 13 (1984): 829–850.

96. Weaver and Wilhoit, *The American Journalist,* pp. 112–117. These roles were obtained through a factor analysis on ten questions; the interpretive factor was best defined by "provide analysis of complex problems," "investigate government claims," and "discuss national policy," while the disseminator factor was best defined by "get information to public quickly" and "concentrate on widest audience." It is intriguing that a majority of the information disseminator role endorsed the interpretive/investigative role and vice versa, suggesting that these are far from mutually exclusive. Overall, the percentages endorsing these questions appear to be quite stable over time; cf. John Johnstone, Edward Slawski, and William Bowman's 1971 results in *The News People* (Urbana: University of Illinois Press, 1976), p. 230.

97. Weaver and Wilhoit, *American Journalist,* tables 5.7 and 8.6.

98. "Weekend Edition," National Public Radio, January 24, 1993.

CHAPTER FIVE

1. "To understand the political life of a community one must understand the conceptual system within which that life moves; and therefore those concepts that help to shape the fabric of our political practices necessarily enter into any rational account of them . . . To the extent that the investigator stakes out a position on these conceptual contests, and we know about it, he can be said to participate in our politics itself." William E. Connolly, *The Terms of Political Discourse,* 2d ed. (Princeton: Princeton University Press, 1983), p. 39 (emphases in original deleted).

2. This strategy is similar to how some political scientists have considered "feminism," for instance, by focusing on what all feminists would agree as its core, even if some feminists would go beyond that very basic definition.

3. David Easton, *A Framework for Political Analysis* (Englewood Cliffs, NJ: Prentice-Hall, 1965), p. 50. Easton's work is most helpful, insofar as he recognizes that the boundaries around "politics" are permeable, fluid, and changeable.

His painstaking consideration of what is and isn't political, and where boundaries may be drawn for the purpose of analysis, is especially beneficial in comparison with more slippery definitions. Cf. ibid., chaps. 4 and 5, with Robert A. Dahl, *Modern Political Analysis,* (Englewood Cliffs, NJ: Prentice-Hall, 1963).

4. I do not want to get enmeshed in the ongoing terminological battles over the meanings of "politics," "the polity," "government," "governance," and "the state." The latter term owes some of its recent popularity in political science and political theory, at least, to the ambiguous way in which it has been defined. Almost all will agree with a definition of "the state" that contains a neo-Weberian understanding of centralized and rationalized bureaucracies that exercise a monopoly over regulation, particularly over the means of violence and coercion. See, e.g., John A. Hall and G. John Ikenberry, *The State* (Minneapolis: University of Minnesota Press, 1989), pp. 1–2. Yet the boundary between state and civil society has always been difficult to specify, and as such authors admit, the state's power may not emanate from the state itself but from its coordination of other sources of power. Although most authors would see the state as a subset of government, even deleting institutions such as the legislature, others would argue that "the state must be considered as more than the 'government.'" Alfred Stepan, *The State and Society* (Princeton: Princeton University Press, 1978), p. xii. Given the uncertainty of the term and the unclear payoff its use would provide, I will not discuss here the media's relationship to "the state."

5. Take Charles Tilly's definition—following Max Weber in its focus on the control of organized force—as one example: "For any specified population, let us identify the organizations which control the principal concentrated means of coercion; such organizations are *governments.* In any particular population there may be several governments operating—or none at all. To the extent that such an organization is formally coordinated, centralized, differentiated from other organizations, and territorially exclusive, it is a *state,* but many governments are not states." Tilly, "Revolutions and Collective Violence," in Fred I. Greenstein and Nelson W. Polsby, eds., *Handbook of Political Science,* vol. 3 (Reading, MA: Addison-Wesley, 1978), pp. 501–502 (emphases in original).

6. Bert A. Rockman, "Government," in Vernon Bogdanor, ed., *The Blackwell Encyclopedia of Political Institutions* (New York: Basil Blackwell, 1987), pp. 257–260 at 260.

7. Theodore L. Glasser, "Journalism's Glassy Essence," *Journalism and Mass Communication Quarterly* 73 (1996): 784–786.

8. Gans, *Deciding What's News,* p. 92.

9. On the formulaic quality of the news, see esp. Darnton, "Writing News and Telling Stories"; Phillips, "What Is News? Novelty without Change" and Gans, *Deciding What's News,* chap. 2.

10. See, in particular, Paul H. Weaver, "Is Television News Biased?" *Public Interest* 26 (1972): 57–74; Hofstetter, *Bias in the News;* and id., "News Bias in the 1972 Campaign."

11. Hofstetter, "News Bias in the 1972 Campaign," p. 5, is acute in operationalizing these three forms of bias, noting that one can identify situational bias if different events are covered differently across modalities; structural bias if the same events are covered differently across modalities; and political bias as any residual difference, particularly between news outlets that use the same modality.

12. Gans, *Deciding What's News*, chap. 2.

13. Gans's speculation (ibid., pp. 68–69 and 204–206) is reinforced by historical work that documents the shifts during the Progressive Era. See, for instance, Schudson, *Discovering the News;* and McGerr, *The Decline of Popular Politics.*

14. Gans, *Deciding What's News*, p. 44.

15. The best indications of the increasing negativity of the news is in Patterson, *Out of Order.*

16. The two classic statements on congressional norms in the prereform era are Donald R. Matthews, *U.S. Senators and Their World* (Chapel Hill: University of North Carolina Press, 1960); and Ralph K. Huitt and Robert Peabody, *Congress: Two Decades of Analysis* (New York: Harper and Row, 1969).

17. See, in general, Gans, *Deciding What's News*, esp. chap. 5; Altheide, *Creating Reality;* McManus, *Market-Driven Journalism;* and Edwin Diamond, *Behind the Times*, rev. ed. (Chicago: University of Chicago Press, 1995).

18. Gans, *Deciding What's News*, p. 81, and chaps. 4–5, passim.

19. See the discussion of "phase structures" in Fishman, *Manufacturing the News*, chap. 3.

20. Gans, *Deciding What's News*, chap. 6.

21. Cook, *Making Laws and Making News*, p. 169. Tuchman used a similar term ("negotiating newsworthiness") to discuss the ongoing bargaining within news organizations; see her *Making News*, p. 31.

22. For an overview of this literature in social psychology, see Dean G. Pruitt and Peter J. Carnevale, *Negotiation in Social Conflict* (Pacific Grove, CA: Brooks/Cole, 1993).

23. P. H. Gulliver, *Disputes and Negotiations: A Cross-Cultural Perspective* (New York: Academic Press, 1979), p. 70.

24. Grace Ferrari Levine, "Learned Helplessness and the Evening News," *Journal of Communication* 27 (1977): 100–105; and "Learned Helplessness in Local TV News," *Journalism Quarterly* 63 (1986): 12–18, 23.

25. Jay G. Blumler and Michael Gurevitch, "Politicians and the Press: An Essay on Role Relationships," in Dan D. Nimmo and Keith R. Sanders, eds., *Handbook of Political Communication* (Beverly Hills, CA: Sage, 1981), pp. 467–493 at 485.

26. Timothy E. Cook, "Domesticating a Crisis: Washington Newsbeats and Network News after the Iraqi Invasion of Kuwait," in W. Lance Bennett and David L. Paletz, eds., *Taken by Storm: The Media, Public Opinion, and U.S. Foreign Policy in the Gulf War* (Chicago: University of Chicago Press, 1994), pp. 105–130.

27. Tuchman, *Making News*, p. 21.

28. Fishman, *Manufacturing the News*, p. 125.

29. On the social organization of the newsbeat, see, in particular, Sigal, *Reporters and Officials*, chap. 3; and Fishman, *Manufacturing the News.*

30. Tuchman, *Making News*, p. 152.

31. John Taylor, quoted in Martin Gottlieb, "Dangerous Liaisons: Journalists and Their Sources," *Columbia Journalism Review* 28, no. 2 (July/August 1989): 21–35.

32. Gans, *Deciding What's News*, p. 141.

33. David L. Protess, Fay Lomax Cook, Jack C. Doppelt, James S. Ettema, Margaret T. Gordon, Donna R. Leff, and Peter Miller, *The Journalism of Outrage: Investigative Reporting and Agenda Building in America* (New York: Guilford Press, 1991).

34. Ibid., p. 21. Note their conclusion that for a story to develop once it has received the journalists' attention, it must be credible and do-able, both of which hinge on the cooperation of official sources, or at least the presence of official documents. Ibid., pp. 207–208.

35. Ibid., chaps. 9–10.

36. Sigal, *Reporters and Officials,* chap. 6; Gans, *Deciding What's News,* chap. 1; J. D. Brown, C. R. Bybee, S. T. Weardon, and D. M. Straughan, "Invisible Power: Newspaper News Sources and the Limits of Diversity," *Journalism Quarterly* 64 (1987): 45–54; and Dan Berkowitz, "TV News Sources and News Channels: A Study in Agenda-Building," *Journalism Quarterly* 64 (1987): 508–513.

37. These generalizations are drawn from the numerous good studies of the difficulties that nongovernmental political actors have in getting into the news on their own terms. These include David Paletz and Robert Dunn, "Press Coverage of Civil Disorders: A Case Study of Winston-Salem, 1967," *Public Opinion Quarterly* 33 (1969): 328–345; Edie N. Goldenberg, *Making the Papers: The Access of Resource-Poor Groups to the Metropolitan Press* (Lexington, MA: D. C. Heath, 1975); Molotch and Lester, "Accidental News"; and above all, Gitlin, *The Whole World Is Watching.* A recent "how-to" book is also a fine outline of the many obstacles that social movements face in using the news; see Charlotte Ryan, *Prime Time Activism: Media Strategies for Grassroots Organizing* (Boston: South End Press, 1991). At one point, Ryan seems to suggest that not much can be hoped for: "Victory is seldom such that the challenger frame achieves equal status to the dominant frame; more commonly, it is that the challenger frame did not allow the dominant frame to hold sway uncontested" (p. 70).

The best account of the media strategies of organized interest groups is Kay Lehman Schlozman and John Tierney, *Organized Interests and American Democracy* (New York: Harper and Row, 1986), esp. chap. 8, although the discussions in Jack L. Walker, Jr., *Mobilizing Interest Groups in America: Patrons, Professions and Social Movements* (Ann Arbor: University of Michigan Press, 1991), on inside and outside strategies are highly instructive.

38. Ryan, *Prime Time Activism,* p. 157. This is also a theme in Goldenberg, *Making the Papers.*

39. *World News Tonight* (ABC), *CBS Evening News,* both August 5, 1991.

40. Daniel C. Hallin, *The "Uncensored War": The Media and Vietnam* (New York: Oxford University Press, 1986); W. Lance Bennett, "Toward a Theory of Press-State Relations," *Journal of Communication* 40 (1990): 103–125.

41. Molotch and Lester, "Accidental News."

42. Regina Lawrence, "Accidents, Icons, and Indexing: The Dynamics of News Coverage of Police Use of Force," *Political Communication* 13 (1996): 437–454.

43. Gaye Tuchman, "The Newspaper as a Social Movement's Resource," in Gaye Tuchman, Arlene Kaplan Daniels, and James Benét, *Hearth and Home:*

Images of Women in the Mass Media (New York: Oxford University Press, 1978), pp. 186–215.

44. Gitlin, *The Whole World Is Watching*, chap. 2.

45. Soloski, "News Reporting and Professionalism," p. 215.

46. Gans, *Deciding What's News*, p. 157. His term for "production value" is "product consideration," but it is much the same thing.

47. See, respectively, McManus, *Market-Driven Journalism*; Penn Kimball, *Downsizing the News: Network Cutbacks in the Nation's Capital* (Washington, DC: Woodrow Wilson Center Press, 1994); and Diamond, *Behind the Times*.

48. Sigelman, "Reporting the News."

49. Darnton, "Writing News and Telling Stories," p. 190.

50. Quoted in Epstein, *News from Nowhere*, pp. 4–5.

51. In general, see Kerbel, *Edited for Television*.

52. Michael Schudson, "When? Datelines, Deadlines, and History," in Manoff and Schudson, eds., *Reading the News*, pp. 79–108 at 84, 98–99 (emphases in original).

53. A good place to begin is the pathbreaking work of Roger C. Schank and Robert Abelson, *Scripts, Plans, Goals, and Understanding* (Hillsdale, NJ: Lawrence Erlbaum Associates, 1979). See also the highly approachable book by Roger C. Schank, *Tell Me a Story: A New Look at Real and Artificial Memory* (New York: Charles Scribner's Sons, 1990).

54. John Robinson and Mark Levy, *The Main Source: Learning from Television News* (Beverly Hills, CA: Sage, 1986), chap. 7.

55. See, e.g., Akiba A. Cohen, Hanna Adoni, and Charles R. Bantz, *Social Conflict and Television News* (Newbury Park, CA: Sage, 1990).

56. Quoted in Cook, *Making Laws and Making News*, p. 50.

57. "The first specific task in conceptualizing an investigative story is to identify the possible characters and story line. In thinking about their initial information, reporters ask: [W]hat sad stories can be told? Who are the villains? The victims? From this assessment, reporters may see the kernel of an exposé. Alternatively, the absence of a sense of personal drama may lower the salience of a story." Protess et al., *Journalism of Outrage*, pp. 211–212.

58. Thus, a memorial tribute on the editorial page of the *New York Times* to one of its legends, Harrison Salisbury, recounted an anecdote about him by beginning, "A great journalist can take the most unpromising subject and turn it into page-one news." "A Salisbury Scoop," *New York Times,* July 11, 1993, Focus sec., p. 18. Likewise, Darnton described a reporter who told him that his proudest moment at the *Times* was when he went to cover a fire, only to discover that it was a false alarm, at which point he whipped up a story on false alarms. "He felt he had transformed the humdrum into 'news' by finding a new 'angle.'" "Writing News and Telling Stories," p. 187.

59. On presidential press conferences, see, among others, Cornwell, *Presidential Leadership of Public Opinion*, pp. 142–207; Jarol B. Manheim, "The Honeymoon's Over," *Journal of Politics* 41 (1979): 55–74; Michael Baruch Grossman and Martha Joynt Kumar, *Portraying the President: The White House and the News Media* (Baltimore: Johns Hopkins University Press, 1980), pp. 241–248.

60. Particularly strong portraits emerge from Timothy Crouse's classic

participant-observation in the Nixon White House in *The Boys on the Bus;* and Mark Hertsgaard's interviews with White House officials and reporters in the Reagan administration, in his *On Bended Knee: The Press and the Reagan Presidency* (New York: Farrar, Straus and Giroux, 1988).

61. Hess found in *The Washington Reporters,* "Capitol Hill is the dominant location of news gathering" (p. 48).

62. Cook, "The Negotiation of Newsworthiness."

63. For a recent consideration of the state of the literature on this hypothesis, see a special issue of *Political Communication,* "Journalism Norms and News Construction: Rules for Representing Politics," 13 (1996): pp. 371–481, coedited by W. Lance Bennett and myself.

64. See Hallin, *"Uncensored War";* and the essays in Bennett and Paletz, eds., *Taken by Storm.*

65. Jonathan Mermin, "Conflict in the Sphere of Consensus? Critical Reporting on the Panama Invasion and the Gulf War," *Political Communication* 13 (1996): 181–194.

66. For a fuller analysis, see Cook, "Negotiation of Newsworthiness."

67. I have borrowed the term "failed event" from Kiku Adatto's invaluable work on the 1988 presidential election campaign. See Adatto, "Sound Bite Democracy: Network Evening News Presidential Campaign Coverage, 1968 and 1988," Research Paper R-2, Joan Shorenstein Barone Center on the Press, Politics and Public Policy, Kennedy School of Government, Harvard University, 1990, reprinted as part of Adatto's *Picture Perfect* (New York: Basic Books, 1992). In the Tower case, Bob Schieffer for CBS noted, "The President went to the Pentagon to shift the save-Tower campaign into high gear with a high profile show of support," and then he added a soundbite from Vice-President Quayle: "I do believe that in a certain period of time as things go, the numbers keep dwindling." Andrea Mitchell sarcastically narrated the footage for NBC by saying, "The president of the United States just happened to drop by the Pentagon to see his disputed nominee for the Defense Department at work—a carefully arranged photo opportunity," before turning to the debate on the Senate floor. *CBS Evening News, NBC Nightly News,* both March 3, 1989.

68. *CBS Evening News,* February 2, 1989.

69. Gitlin, *Whole World Is Watching,* chap. 8.

70. Ibid., passim, and esp. pp. 25–31. Gitlin himself does not argue that such a cycle occurs, given that these phases empirically overlap considerably. Nevertheless, as a general model of the interactions of social movements and the media, it holds considerable promise, and the evidence to date from other social movements seems to fit this model as well.

71. See Gitlin's discussion of the front-page feature by Fred Powledge in the *New York Times,* and the lengthy two-part "outtake" on CBS, produced by Stanhope Gould and reported by Alexander Kendrick, in *Whole World Is Watching,* respectively, pp. 35–40 and 85–89.

72. My thanks to Douglas Arnold and Michael Schudson for pushing me in this direction.

73. Happily, there has been an outpouring of strong work in recent years on the political party system and the interest group system in the United States. The following sections draw on this literature. Two outstanding overviews, and su-

perb theoretical contributions in their own right, on parties are Leon D. Epstein, *Political Parties in the American Mold* (Madison: University of Wisconsin Press, 1986); and John H. Aldrich, *Why Parties? The Origin and Transformation of Political Parties in America* (Chicago: University of Chicago Press, 1995). More focused inquiries, that persuasively challenge the "decline-of-party" school generated in voting behavior studies and note the increasing activity of parties as organizations and within other institutions, include Cornelius P. Cotter, James L. Gibson, John F. Bibby, and Robert J. Huckshorn, *Party Organizations in American Politics* (New York: Praeger, 1984); Paul S. Herrnson, *Party Campaigning in the 1980s* (Cambridge, MA: Harvard University Press, 1988); and David W. Rohde, *Parties and Leaders in the Postreform House* (Chicago: University of Chicago Press, 1991).

The three major research projects in the 1980s on the interest group system are all indispensable; they are best summed up in Schlozman and Tierney, *Organized Interests and American Democracy;* Walker, *Mobilizing Interest Groups in America;* and John P. Heinz, Edward O. Laumann, Robert L. Nelson and Robert H. Salisbury, *The Hollow Core: Private Interests in National Policy Making* (Cambridge, MA: Harvard University Press, 1993).

74. See Aldrich's discussion of the political party as an "endogenous institution" in *Why Parties?*

75. Epstein, *Political Parties in the American Mold,* p. 7. In his chap. 6, Epstein, having rejected terms such as "quasi-governmental," "State agency," "governmentalized," or "quasi-public," turns to "public utility," which "suggests an agency performing a service in which the public has a special interest sufficient to justify governmental regulatory control, along with the extension of legal privileges, but not governmental ownership or management of all the agency's activities." Ibid., p. 157.

76. Walker, *Mobilizing Interest Groups in America,* pp. 29–33.

77. Speaking of the party as a single institution should be easily accepted, given the common and imitative ways in which parties evolve, and given the scholarly consensus on a historical succession of party systems. I might expect more resistance to the idea of the interest group system as an institution. Although space and time prevent me from going into much depth on this point, it is worth remembering how E. E. Schattschneider in *The Semi-Sovereign People: A Realist's View of Democracy in America* (New York: Holt, Rinehart, and Winston, 1960) sketched the overall bias of what he termed the "pressure system," or how Walker, in *Mobilizing Interest Groups in America* (pp. 10, 14), argued, "The larger interest-group system has a relatively stable structure within which associations maintain identifiable roles and ideological positions . . . The interest-group system provides a mechanism in an increasingly complex society through which emerging issues and ideas can be offered up as possible new items on the national political agenda."

78. This point is perhaps best made by the comparison of American and Italian television news reported in Hallin and Mancini, "Speaking of the President." Another good indicator of this tendency is a comparative analysis of television coverage of the 1984 American presidential election campaign and of the 1983 British general election. Whereas fully 69 percent of British election stories fell into the "straight/descriptive" or "mixed" categories, only 44 percent of Ameri-

can election stories did so; 9 percent of the British stories were judged "deflating" and 5 percent "reinforcing," compared to 34 percent and 22 percent of the American stories, respectively. In other words, American television campaign news distinguished itself from its British counterpart not only by greater negativity but also greater positivity. See Semetko et al., *The Formation of Campaign Agendas,* table 7.6.

79. Reporters' patronizing attitudes toward—and unwillingness to learn more about—their audiences are well described in Darnton, "Writing News and Telling Stories"; Gans, *Deciding What's News,* chap. 7; and Burgoon et al., *World of the Working Journalist,* chap. 5.

80. Protess et al., *Journalism of Outrage,* chap. 3 (quote is on p. 82).

81. Patterson, *Out of Order,* presents the best information on the rising negativity of the news media. Elsewhere, a team of authors, including myself, showed that the coverage of candidates during the 1992 election campaign was significantly more negative in journalist-initated stories. Whether journalists initiated the story also was the most consistent predictor across media of the tone toward the candidate; Just et al., *Crosstalk,* p. 111.

82. Shanto Iyengar, *Is Anyone Responsible? How Television Frames Political Issues* (Chicago: University of Chicago Press, 1991).

83. Quoted in *USA Today,* June 7, 1995 (emphasis added).

84. Kernell comes to a similar conclusion, though he refers more to the impact of speechmaking than to the impact of newsmaking (and of the search for news stories). See Kernell, *Going Public,* esp. chap. 8.

Part Three

1. Cater, *Fourth Branch,* chap. 1.

Chapter Six

1. Richard E. Neustadt, *Presidential Power: The Politics of Leadership* (New York: John Wiley and Sons, 1960).

2. Good examples include Ralph K. Huitt's essays reprinted in Huitt and Peabody, *Congress: Two Decades of Analysis;* Matthews, *U.S. Senators and Their World;* Richard F. Fenno, Jr., *The Power of the Purse: Appropriation Politics* (Boston: Little, Brown, 1966); and John Manley, *The Politics of Finance: The House Committee on Ways and Means* (Boston: Little, Brown, 1970).

3. The classic account of bargaining justices is Walter F. Murphy, *Elements of Judicial Strategy* (Chicago: University of Chicago Press, 1964). On the distance of Supreme Court justices from the news during that period, see David L. Grey, *The Supreme Court and the News Media* (Evanston, IL: Northwestern University Press, 1968).

4. Schattschneider, *The Semi-Sovereign People;* Peter Bachrach and Morton Baratz, "Two Faces of Power," *American Political Science Review* 56 (1962): 947–952; and Peter Bachrach, *Theory of Democratic Elitism* (Boston: Little, Brown, 1967).

5. The first and best example is Anthony King, ed., *The New American Political System,* rev. ed. (Washington, DC: American Enterprise Institute, 1990

[1978]); but see, more recently, Kingdon, *Agendas, Alternatives, and Public Policies;* and David M. Ricci, *The Transformation of American Politics: The New Washington and the Rise of Think Tanks* (New Haven: Yale University Press, 1993). While these theses have not been as prominent since the mid-eighties, the theoretical shift can be seen elsewhere. For instance, public choice theories, that stressed equilibrium only when it is "structure-induced" suggest a disorderly political world that political actors attempt to control, often in vain. A good place to begin here is Shepsle, "Institutional Equilibrium and Equilibrium Institutions."

6. Heinz et al., *The Hollow Core*, p. 371.

7. This point is derived from Aldrich, *Why Parties?* esp. chaps. 8 and 9. It is true that Aldrich points out how the greater national organization of parties makes for more ideological similarity within the party, but he implies that one cannot predict the outcome in any given case: "Politicians are just as autonomous in office as they are in elections." Ibid., p. 292.

8. The case for the media contributing to contemporary political dispersion has been best made by conservative observers such as Samuel P. Huntington who classifies the news media as an "oppositional" institution comparable to Congress in *American Politics: The Promise of Disharmony* (Cambridge, MA: Harvard University Press, 1981); or more fully, by Austin Ranney in *Channels of Power* (New York: Basic Books, 1984). Those who see the news media's role as the effect of dispersion often point to the abrogation by political institutions of their role—such as political parties in the presidential selection process—and point to the otherwise empty public sphere. See Patterson, *Mass Media Election;* and Hallin and Mancini, "Speaking of the President."

9. This point has been made in some pioneering comparative work on television journalism. Jay Blumler and Michael Gurevitch, for instance, were participant-observers in the BBC during the British general election of 1983 and in NBC News during the American presidential election of 1984. (See their "The Election Agenda-Setting Roles of Television Journalists: Comparative Observation at the BBC and NBC," chap. 4 of Semetko et al., *The Formation of Campaign Agendas.*) Blumler and Gurevitch found a number of differences, most particularly with American news being more "participatory, generalist, affective, pragmatic, skeptical, and autonomous" (p. 59). They speculated that a number of system-level influences produced this difference, not simply the means of ownership (public in Britain, private in the United States), or journalistic and political cultures, or degree of campaign professionalization, but also "the strength of the national political system, relative to its media system, which tends to frame their respective agenda-setting responsibilities and capabilities differently" (p. 60).

Such conclusions fit with the arguments of Hallin and Mancini's comparison of American and Italian television news, "Speaking of the President," whereby the public sphere is already quite full in Italy with multiple political parties, whereas its comparative emptiness in the United States likewise invites journalists to fill the vacuum. Hallin has more recently hypothesized that "relatively weak institutions of political debate may well be a necessary condition for the development of the kind of highly active journalism that characterizes, especially, American television." *We Keep America on Top of the World*, p. 6.

10. This point is best made in the work of Louis Fisher. A good introduction is his "Separation of Powers in America: Theory and Practice," in Robert L. Utley,

Jr., *Principles of the Constitutional Order: The Ratification Debates* (Lanham, MD: University Press of America, 1989), pp. 131–149. More fully, see Fisher, *Constitutional Conflicts between Congress and the President* (Princeton: Princeton University Press, 1985); and Fisher, *The Politics of Shared Power: Congress and the Executive,* 2d ed. (Washington, DC: CQ Press, 1987). Garry Wills, in *Explaining America: The Federalist* (Garden City, NY: Doubleday, 1981), chaps. 11–13, also notes the multiple rationales that Hamilton and Madison evoked for separation of powers—not merely the much-vaunted "checks and balances" but also the efficiency of dividing labor and the legitimacy it imposes by requiring accountability of one institution before another.

To be sure, each institution may have sole authority to use particular powers in this shared process (e.g., the House's monopoly over initiating tax laws, the Senate's confirmation of presidential appointees, the presidential veto, and the judiciary's right to review laws for their constitutionality), and judicial conservatives such as former Chief Justice Warren Burger and Associate Justice Antonin Scalia have been working to establish clearer barriers between each of the three branches. But even those who see the theory of the founders as focusing primarily on inefficient checks and balances have noted that the *practice* of the three branches has been toward overlapping functions and greater interdependence.

11. This point is made nicely in Mark A. Peterson, *Legislating Together: The White House and Capitol Hill from Eisenhower to Reagan* (Cambridge, MA: Harvard University Press, 1990), chap. 1, which develops what he calls "a tandem-institution" model of legislating.

12. Neustadt, *Presidential Power,* p. 33. Of course, whether the founders intended that is still open to dispute; see note 10, above.

13. *Youngstown Steel* v. *Sawyer* (1952), 343 U.S. 579 at 635.

14. See, e.g., Cater, *Fourth Branch,* p. 17; as well as Bernard C. Cohen, *The Press and Foreign Policy* (Princeton: Princeton University Press, 1963); and Francis E. Rourke, *Secrecy and Publicity: Dilemmas of Democracy* (Baltimore: Johns Hopkins University Press, 1961).

15. See, e.g., Martin Linsky's survey of federal executive policymakers: 63 percent said positive coverage would make action on an issue in their office or agency easier, versus a slightly larger number (68 percent) who said negative coverage would make action more difficult. Similarly, only 50 percent said positive coverage would galvanize outside support, whereas 66 percent said negative coverage would undermine outside support. That much having been said, however, 79 percent said positive coverage would "increase your chances for successfully attaining your policy goals regarding the issue," compared to 71 percent who said that negative coverage would decrease those chances. Linsky, *Impact: How the Press Affects Federal Policymaking* (New York: W. W. Norton, 1986), appendix C, question 3a, p. 236.

16. These functions, of course, supplement the traditional governmental aims of propaganda and publicity in shaping and mobilizing public opinion, which I reviewed in Chap. 2.

17. Linsky, *Impact,* p. 82.

18. J. L. Austin, *How to Do Things with Words,* 2d ed., ed. J. O. Urmson and Marina Sbisà (Cambridge, MA: Harvard University Press, 1975), pp. 6–7. For a wonderfully pithy introduction to his argument, see J. L. Austin, "Perfor-

mative Utterances," in *Philosophical Papers* (Oxford: Clarendon Press, 1961), pp. 220–240. It is true that Austin probed the distinction between performatives and statements only to discover that we could not say that the latter were not also actions. I reserve the category of "performative" here for actions that could not have been taken except by such statements. Others commonly make similar moves; see, for instance, G. J. Warnock, "Some Types of Performative Utterance," in Isaiah Berlin et al., *Essays on J. L. Austin* (Oxford: Clarendon Press, 1973), pp. 69–89, esp. 87–89.

19. See Stephen Hess, *The Government/Press Connection: Press Officers and Their Offices* (Washington, DC: Brookings Institution, 1984), chap. 6. Although Austin concluded that it was a vain effort to distinguish the performative from mere statements by particular verbs, his lists of potential candidates make for instructive reading; see Austin, *How to Do Things with Words,* pp. 148–164.

20. Austin suggested several tests for figuring out a performative; the most pertinent are when one cannot say "Does he really?" and when the act could be accomplished without saying anything. *How to Do Things with Words,* pp. 79–80.

21. Gaye Tuchman, "Objectivity as Strategic Ritual," esp. at p. 665.

22. See, in particular, Mayhew's argument that advertising, credit-claiming and position-taking take precedence over building coalitions and legislating in his *Congress: The Electoral Connection.*

23. Austin, *How to Do Things with Words,* pp. 14–15. Stated somewhat differently, the power of performative political language depends upon the speaker's faithful adherence to appropriate rituals whose meaning is shared with the audience; for the importance of ritual in contemporary American politics, see, among others, Murray Edelman, *The Politics of Symbolic Action* (New York: Academic Press, 1971); and David I. Kertzer, *Ritual, Politics, and Power* (New Haven: Yale University Press, 1988).

24. Indeed, given that journalists wish to display their independence from political actors without overtly ideological criticism, they have an interest in pointing out how and when the latter's stage-managed performances have gone awry. Kiku Adatto found numerous examples of what she called "failed events" in her study of the three broadcast networks' coverage of the 1988 election campaign: "Sound Bite Democracy," republished as part of Adatto, *Picture Perfect.*

25. This argument is well made in Kernell, *Going Public.* Of course, under such circumstances, making such news may be a way of persuading themselves and/or others that they've accomplished something rather than as a means to accomplish something; a variant of this contention appears in Roderick P. Hart, *The Sound of Leadership: Presidential Communication in the Modern Age* (Chicago: University of Chicago Press, 1987).

26. See, e.g., the questionnaire results in Linsky, *Impact,* appendix C; or the elite interviews in Patrick O'Heffernan, *Mass Media and American Foreign Policy: Insider Perspectives on Global Journalism and the Foreign Policy Process* (Norwood, NJ: Ablex, 1991), passim. One of Linsky's findings, reported in *Impact,* p. 237, indicates, moreover, that policymakers are paying attention to the media as the latter affect their job; in responding to the question, "To what degree did you rely on the mass media for information about your policy area?" 31 percent of the policymakers responded "very much," with another 39 percent

saying "somewhat." The survey then asked a similar question about "parts of government outside your policy area"; the response was again 38.8 percent saying "somewhat," but now only 15 percent answering "very much." This tendency to concentrate on news about one's own policy domain or agency is undoubtedly exacerbated by the practice, now common in the White House, agencies, and even some congressional offices, of circulating an internal compendium of news clips that press officers deem to be relevant to their jobs. See Hess, *Government/ Press Connection,* pp. 41–42.

27. Matthews, *U.S. Senators and Their World,* p. 206.

28. Schattschneider, in *Semi-Sovereign People,* was the first to demonstrate the power of setting the agenda. The most influential recent consideration of policy agendas is Kingdon, *Agendas, Alternatives and Public Policies.*

29. Shanto Iyengar, Mark D. Peters, and Donald R. Kinder, "Experimental Demonstrations of the 'Not-so-Minimal' Consequences of Television News Programs," *American Political Science Review* 76 (1982): 848–858; and more fully, Iyengar and Kinder, *News That Matters.*

30. David E. Price, "Policy Making in Congressional Committees: The Impact of 'Environmental' Factors," *American Political Science Review* 72 (1978): 548–574.

31. Schattschneider, *Semi-Sovereign People.*

32. See Molotch and Lester, "Accidental News," pp. 235–260.

33. Ibid., p. 237.

34. I make this point in some detail with the case study of Representative Don Pease's attempt in the 100th Congress to renew a federal unemployment program. See Cook, *Making Laws and Making News,* chap. 6.

35. Kaniss, *Making Local News,* chap. 7.

36. See, e.g., Cook, *Making Laws and Making News,* pp. 125–129.

37. See also my discussion of "issue spokespersonship" in Timothy E. Cook, "Press Secretaries and Media Strategies in the House of Representatives: Deciding Whom to Pursue," *American Journal of Political Science* 32 (1988): 1047–1069.

38. The process is similar to one Bruno Latour and Steve Woolgar noted for scientists who sought credit, not for its own sake but to reinvest it to obtain the monetary resources necessary to allow them to continue playing the scientific game. See Latour and Woolgar, *Laboratory Life* (Princeton: Princeton University Press, 1978), chap. 5. Another comparison is how companies develop a "brand name" for a product, as Shepsle suggests in "Institutional Equilibrium and Equilibrium Institutions," p. 71.

39. Neustadt, *Presidential Power;* however, the various writings of Neustadt since that time do see a growing centrality of the media image of the president.

40. E.g., James W. Dearing, "Setting the Polling Agenda for the Issue of AIDS," *Public Opinion Quarterly* 53 (1989): 309–329.

41. David P. Fan and Lois Norem, "The Media and the Fate of the Medicare Catastrophic Extension Act," *Journal of Health Politics, Policy & Law* 17 (1992): 39–70.

42. See, in general, Hess, *Government/Press Connection.*

43. See, e.g., Deborah Sontag, " 'Partial Birth' Just One Way, Physicians Say," *New York Times,* March 21, 1997, p. A1.

44. My thanks to Kathleen Stephens for making this point based on her own experience as a foreign service officer in Korea.

45. Robert M. Wachter, *The Fragile Coalition: Scientists, Activists, and AIDS* (New York: St. Martin's Press, 1991), p. 120.

46. Linsky, *Impact,* p. 94.

47. This is one reason that we may be better off talking about "agenda-building" rather than "agenda-setting." The most impressive account of how repetition and expansion of news coverage can build an agenda from scratch is Gladys Engel Lang and Kurt Lang, *The Battle for Public Opinion: The President, the Press, and the Polls during Watergate* (New York: Columbia University Press, 1983).

48. *White House Bulletin,* May 12, 1992, p. 3. My thanks to Nancy Mehlman for calling this article to my attention.

49. Edwin Diamond, Adrian Mann, and Robert Silverman, "Bush's First Year: Mr. Nice Guy Meets the Press," *Washington Journalism Review* 12, no. 1 (January/February 1990): 42–44; and S. Robert Lichter and Richard E. Noyes, "Bush at Midpoint: In the Media Spotlight: Bad Press by Default," *The American Enterprise* 2 (January/February 1991): 49–53. Probably a more accurate understanding would be to see the Bush presidency seeking to distinguish itself from its immediate predecessor by having a carefully managed media operation that stresses the appearance of *not* being carefully managed.

50. Philip Selznick, *Leadership in Administration: A Sociological Interpretation* (Evanston, IL: Row, Peterson and Company, 1957), pp. 62–63.

51. Of the three branches of government, the media strategies of the presidency have received by far the most attention—partly because of their presumed increasing importance, but also partly because they provide a useful source of quantifiable data that can be used to compare and contrast presidents. The historical sweep of presidents and publicity is best captured by Tulis, *The Rhetorical Presidency.* On the linkage of media strategies and governing strategies, the place to begin is Kernell, *Going Public.* The strategic use of mass communication on presidential approval is best studied in Lyn Ragsdale, "The Politics of Presidential Speechmaking, 1946–1980," *American Political Science Review* 78 (1984): 971–984.

One should not neglect the fascinating studies by students of rhetoric, who have devoted considerable attention to presidential speechmaking as an adjunct to, a substitute for, and the quintessence of action, although their willingness to elide definitions of power also makes them a bit problematic. See esp. Hart, *The Sound of Leadership;* Karlyn Kohrs Campbell and Kathleen Hall Jamieson, *Deeds Done in Words: Presidential Rhetoric and the Genres of Governance* (Chicago: University of Chicago Press, 1990); Carolyn Smith, *Presidential Press Conferences: A Critical Approach* (New York: Praeger, 1990); and Barbara Hinckley, *The Symbolic Presidency* (New York: Routledge, 1991). Mary E. Stuckey suggests an interesting role for the president, which, unfortunately, she does not adequately develop in her *The President as Interpreter-in-Chief* (Chatham, NJ: Chatham House, 1991).

The four major studies of the institutionalization of the media operations of the presidency are Cornwell, *Presidential Leadership of Public Opinion;* Grossman and Kumar, *Portraying the President;* John Anthony Maltese, *Spin Control:*

The White House Office of Communications and the Management of Presidential News (Chapel Hill: University of North Carolina Press, 1992); and the work of Karen M. Hult and Charles Walcott, reported in "To Meet the Press: Tracing the Evolution of White House Press Operations," paper delivered at the Midwest Political Science Association, Chicago, April 13–15, 1989; and in "The Evolution of Presidential Writing: An Organizational Analysis," paper delivered at the American Political Science Association, San Francisco, August 30–September 2, 1990.

In addition, there are studies of individual presidential press operations—the best of which is undoubtedly still Timothy Crouse's acid description of the Nixon White House in his *The Boys on the Bus*—and multitudinous memoirs by White House correspondents, press secretaries, and communications directors.

52. Tulis, *The Rhetorical Presidency;* Kernell and Jacobson, "Congress and the Presidency as News in the Nineteenth Century." Mel Laracey, in a thought-provoking series of papers, has argued against these claims on the grounds that presidents in the nineteenth century usually had party organs that could speak for them; but while this is an important point, Laracey is not able to suggest, as he might like, that presidents have always "gone public," because while the party press might well represent the president's point of view, it was rarely noted as such, and presidents themselves maintained distance from publicity.

53. Good sources include Schudson, *Discovering the News;* Juergens, *News from the White House;* and McGerr, *The Decline of Popular Politics.* See also my discussion in chap. 3.

54. Neustadt, *Presidential Power,* p. 6.

55. On cycles in the presidency in general, see Bert A. Rockman, *The Leadership Question: The Presidency and the American System* (New York: Praeger, 1986), chap. 4. Cycles of governance are best outlined by Paul C. Light, *The President's Agenda* (Baltimore: Johns Hopkins University Press, 1981). The cycles of presidential popularity have been much bruited in the literature, with James A. Stimson's article, "Public Support for American Presidents: A Cyclical Model," *Public Opinion Quarterly* 40 (1976): 1–21, being the most outspoken advocate of the inevitable decline of presidential popularity over the term. Although the dynamics under Stimson's model are highly questionable, largely untested, and probably wrong, his basic observation that popularity does fall over time has been unchallenged; see particularly Samuel Kernell, "Explaining Presidential Popularity," *American Political Science Review* 72 (1978): 506–522. The most thorough examination of the connection of news to presidential popularity is to be found in the work of Richard Brody and his collaborators; for a synopsis, see Brody, *Assessing the President: The Media, Elite Opinion, and Public Support* (Stanford, CA: Stanford University Press, 1991). For reasons that should be clear to any reader of chap. 4, I am highly doubtful of Brody's contention that the media merely condense real-world information into usable form, but the evidence of the impact of the cumulated tenor of news upon presidential popularity can (and should) be examined independent of that conclusion.

56. For historical accounts see Cornwell, *Presidential Leadership of Public Opinion;* Juergens, *News from the White House;* and Kernell, *Going Public.* This

is not to say that only activist presidents aggressively court the press; the example of Calvin Coolidge's innovation with the media alongside a limited policy agenda proves as much.

57. Memo from Moyers to Kintner, April 8, 1966, quoted in Grossman and Kumar, *Portraying the President*, p. 82.

58. The amount of speechmaking in and of itself has increased only little since Truman, but the lengths of the speeches and the amount of travel have gone up dramatically. Cf. William W. Lammers, "Presidential Attention-Focusing Activities," in Doris A. Graber, ed., *The President and the Public* (Philadelphia: ISHI, 1982); Gary King and Lyn Ragsdale, *The Elusive Executive: Discovering Statistical Patterns in the Presidency* (Washington, DC: CQ Press, 1988), chap. 5; and Hinckley, *Symbolic Presidency*.

59. Foote, *Television Access and Political Power*, table 7.2.

60. Ragsdale, "Politics of Presidential Speechmaking."

61. On the latter point, see esp. Paletz and Vinegar's experimental study comparing responses to a Nixon speech with and without the journalists' interpretations: "Presidents on Television." On the increase of equal time for the opposition, see Foote, *Television Access and Political Power*, esp. chap. 5.

62. Quoted in Gustav Niebuhr, "Books on Faith Are a Comfort, President Says," *New York Times*, October 4, 1994, p. A17.

63. These results are derived from Hart, *Sound of Leadership*.

64. Kernell, *Going Public*, chap. 2.

65. Hult and Walcott's figures, showing a gradual rise and then a huge jump under Nixon, include staffers in the Office of the Press Secretary and the Office of Communications. See Hult and Walcott, "To Meet the Press," table 1.

66. Daniel C. Hallin, ed., *The Presidency, Press, and the People* (La Jolla: University of California, San Diego, 1992), p. 170.

67. See Grossman and Kumar, *Portraying the President*, pp. 83–84, for a variety of estimates in 1976 and 1977.

68. Two book-length journalistic accounts shed light on Clinton's press operations, although one is more sympathetic to Myers (Jeffrey H. Birnbaum, *Madhouse: The Private Turmoil of Working for the President* [New York: Times Books, 1996], chap. 4) and the other is more critical of Myers and praising of McCurry (Kenneth T. Walsh, *Feeding the Beast: The White House Versus the Press* [New York: Random House, 1996], esp. chaps. 9 and 13).

69. This point is best made in Hult and Walcott, "To Meet the Press."

70. See Douglas Jehl, "After White House Shuffle, Most Old Hands Stand Pat," *New York Times*, September 24, 1994, p. 9; Burt Solomon, "With a Smoothie Behind the Podium . . . The Press Cuts Clinton Some Slack," *National Journal*, June 3, 1995, pp. 1352–1353; and John Aloysius Farrell, "Meet the Press Secretaries," *Boston Globe Magazine*, April 7, 1996, pp. 12–13, 21–28 at 27; as well as Birnbaum, *Madhouse;* and Walsh, *Feeding the Beast*.

71. Hallin, ed., *The Presidency, the Press, and the People*, p. 15. Note that this was rebutted by Larry Speakes later in the forum; ibid., p. 30.

72. Quoted in Grossman and Kumar, *Portraying the President*, p. 92.

73. The best history of the Office of Communications is Maltese, *Spin Control,* although, by its almost exclusive reliance upon presidential documents, it

may exaggerate the *effect* of the office in managing the news (in spite of its misleading subtitle).

74. Memo from Haldeman to Herbert Klein quoted in Maltese, *Spin Control,* p. 110.

75. 1979 exit interview with Rafshoon, quoted in Maltese, *Spin Control,* p. 161.

76. Hertsgaard, *On Bended Knee,* pp. 35-37.

77. These are, of course, the ways in which Selznick discusses, in *Leadership in Administration,* institutional mission and institutional embodiment of purpose, his two critical tasks for leaders. These fit Witherspoon's conclusion from her fine study of internal communication in the White House where one "communication competency needed by chief executives . . . is the ability to provide clear directions to staff about a president's expectations." Patricia Witherspoon, *Within These Walls: A Study of Communication between Presidents and Their Senior Staffs* (New York: Praeger, 1991), p. 230. Such "clear directions," it should be noted, can come either from within the White House, as Witherspoon stresses, or from the media's version of what the president wishes to pursue.

78. Kernell, *Going Public,* chap. 5.

79. Richard E. Neustadt, "Presidential Leadership: The Clerk Against the Preacher," in J. S. Young, ed., *Problems and Prospects for Presidential Leadership in the 1980s,* vol. 1 (Lanham, MD: University Press of America, 1982), pp. 1-36 (quote is on p. 15).

80. The evidence here is, of course, far less abundant than at the federal level; for an overview, see Alan Rosenthal, *Governors and Legislatures: Contending Powers* (Washington, DC: CQ Press, 1990), pp. 24-27.

81. Thad L. Beyle and Lynn R. Muchmore, "The Governor and the Public," in Beyle and Muchmore, eds., *Being Governor: The View from the Office* (Durham, NC: Duke University Press, 1982), pp. 52-66. See also Coleman B. Ransone, Jr., *The American Governorship* (Westport, CT: Greenwood Press, 1982), chap. 3.

82. This conclusion rests on two unpublished research papers done for classes of mine, one by Sally Kay Mitchell on "new South" Mississippi Governor Ray Mabus's attempts to push education reform through the good-old-boy legislature, and another by Tom Dupree on Connecticut Governor Lowell Weicker's strategy, as an independent, of passing a state income tax. Massachusetts Governor William Weld, a Republican facing an overwhelmingly Democratic state legislature, provides another good example; see Scot Lehigh, "Stagecraft as Statecraft: Weld Molds His Message," *Boston Sunday Globe,* May 5, 1991, p. 1. Governors, too, may be taking a page from presidents by taking increased advantage of asking television stations to preempt their regular schedule to deliver the equivalent of an Oval Office speech; see Alessandra Stanley, "Governors Facing Fiscal Troubles Take Their Cases to the Airwaves," *New York Times,* July 22, 1991, p. B2.

83. Center for Policy Research, *Governing the American States: A Handbook for New Governors* (Washington, DC: National Governors Association, 1978), p. 85.

84. In the executive, see Grossman and Kumar, *Portraying the President;* Hess, *Government/Press Connection;* and David Morgan, *The Flacks of Washington: Government Information and the Public Agenda* (Westport, CT: Green-

wood Press, 1986), p. 34. I make this case for Congress in *Making Laws and Making News*, chap. 4.

85. See Blumler and Gurevitch, "Politicians and the Press," p. 485.

Chapter Seven

1. The study of public information officers has been blessed by several important studies that end up charting the development across departments and agencies over time, starting with James L. McCamy's pathbreaking study from the 1930s, *Government Publicity: Its Practice in Federal Administration* (Chicago: University of Chicago Press, 1939); and followed by Dan D. Nimmo's *Newsgathering in Washington: A Study in Political Communication* (New York: Atherton Press, 1964), an examination in the early months of the Kennedy presidency of public information officers and their journalistic counterparts. The most recent studies include Hess, *Government/Press Connection*, an excellent participant-observer study in the State Department, the Pentagon, the Transportation Department, and the Food and Drug Administration; Morgan's *The Flacks of Washington*, an update of Nimmo conducted in the Reagan presidency; and the collection edited by Lewis M. Helm, Ray Eldon Hiebert, Michael R. Naver, and Kenneth Rabin, *Informing the People: A Public Affairs Handbook* (New York: Longman, 1981), which includes many case studies and short essays by a variety of public information officers.

I also recommend, for discerning studies of single departments, two on the State Department, despite their age: Cohen, *The Press and Foreign Policy;* and William O. Chittick, *State Department, Press, and Pressure Groups: A Role Analysis* (New York: Wiley-Interscience, 1970). The Pentagon's press operations desperately needs some dispassionate study outside of the context of war and crises. Typical of the literature are J. W. Fulbright's *The Pentagon Propaganda Machine* (New York: Liveright, 1970); and Juergen Arthur Heise's *Minimum Disclosure: How the Pentagon Manipulates the News* (New York: W. W. Norton, 1979), which are both serviceable but hortatory. A more useful recent collection is Loren B. Thompson, ed., *Defense Beat: The Dilemmas of Defense Coverage* (New York: Free Press, 1991).

2. See, e.g., Chittick, *State Department, Press, and Pressure Groups*, p. 42: "The fact that the State Department has trouble reaching the public with its own publication, speaker, and conference programs has forced the Department to rely more and more upon the manipulation of the private media . . . in order to get its story across . . ." As Chittick goes on to say, congressional restrictions on direct propaganda only compound this tendency.

3. Hess, *Government/Press Connection*, p. 17.

4. Cook, "Domesticating a Crisis."

5. Graham Wilson, "Are Department Secretaries Really A President's Natural Enemies?" *British Journal of Political Science* 7 (1977): 273–299.

6. This dilemma is greatest for vice-presidents who must seek visibility in order to be taken seriously but who have no portfolio beyond whatever presidents give them. As one assistant to Vice President Walter Mondale noted, "The job becomes a challenge when you're trying to get the Vice-President at least some notice. Sometimes, you're between a rock and a hard place. You want to keep

the Vice-President alive and visible, but you don't want to threaten the President. The best stories become the 'team player at work' kind." Quoted in Paul C. Light, *Vice-Presidential Power: Advice and Influence in the White House* (Baltimore: Johns Hopkins University Press, 1984), p. 89.

7. William Safire, "The Bush Cabinet," *New York Times Magazine* (1990).

8. See, e.g., Neil A. Lewis, "Energy Secretary Used Fund to Monitor Reporters," *New York Times,* November 10, 1995, p. A1; and H. Josef Hebert, "A Strategy for O'Leary," *Boston Globe,* November 16, 1995, p. 3. The latter story outlined how one consultant crafted a " 'communications plan' that mapped out in detail how O'Leary's status could be elevated within the Clinton administration and become a 'household name' to the public."

9. This is one conclusion that could be drawn, e.g., from Lincoln Caplan's contrast of the almost beatific public role of Clinton's attorney general, Janet Reno, versus Reno's poor internal reputation for managing the Justice Department. See Caplan, "Janet Reno's Choice," *New York Times Magazine,* May 15, 1994, pp. 40–46, 51, 70, 81.

10. The term "golden triangle" comes from Stephen Hess, "The Golden Triangle: The Press at the White House, State and Defense," *Brookings Review* 1 (Summer 1983): 14–19.

11. See Lester Bernstein's review entitled "Spokesmen Without Influence," *New York Times Book Review,* January 13, 1985, p. 10.

12. Lewis M. Helm, "Agnes: The Politics of a Flood," in Helm et al., eds., *Informing the People,* pp. 205–217; and Hess, *Government/Press Connection,* chap. 5.

13. Helm, "Agnes," p. 207.

14. Ibid., p. 211.

15. Hess, *Government/Press Connection,* pp. 55–56.

16. Quoted in Chittick, *State Department, Press, and Pressure Groups,* p. 185.

17. See, e.g., ibid., table 5.2, item 26; and table 5.8. Note that while the policy officers and information officers surveyed agree with each other that information is an instrument of policy, as contrasted to the reporters and leaders of nongovernmental organizations who disagree with them, policy officers are far less committed than information officers to the use of information in democratic processes.

18. See, e.g., Hess, *Government/Press Connection,* pp. 26–28. As far back as 1964, Nimmo, in *Newsgathering in Washington* (p. 64), noted, "Reporters tend to regard the information officer as important to them only if the information officer is first assigned tasks of responsibility within the agency or department. An officer without responsibility is expendable."

19. See, e.g., Linsky, *Impact,* p. 126: "Compared to the other policymakers, the public affairs people are professionally disinterested in the substance of the policy, except with regard to its communication aspects. That gives them some degree of distance in looking at the implications of what is being proposed. Part of their job is to perceive what the public reaction will be." Chittick, *State Department, Press, and Pressure Groups,* p. 170; and Morgan, *Flacks of Washington,* pp. 35–36, come to similar conclusions.

20. Morgan, *Flacks of Washington,* p. 36.

21. Herbert Kaufman, *The Administrative Behavior of Federal Bureau Chiefs* (Washington, DC: Brookings Institution, 1981), pp. 71-73, found that the six bureaus he studied ran public relations offices that relied only infrequently on the bureau chiefs themselves. On the contrast between the short durations of presidential appointees and the lengthy tenure of civil servants, Hugh Heclo's description of the executive branch in *A Government of Strangers: Executive Politics in Washington* (Washington, DC: Brookings Institution, 1977), still has not been bettered. Heclo's account also brilliantly outlines the difficulties at the middle-management level of distinguishing between presidential appointees and civil servants.

22. McCamy, *Government Publicity*, pp. 221-227.

23. Quoted in Chittick, *State Department, Press, and Pressure Groups*, pp. 31-32, where the entire account of Dumbarton Oaks may be found.

24. Hess, *Government/Press Connection*, p. 68.

25. Ibid., p. 73. This section relies on Hess's indispensable description of State Department briefings, in ibid., chap. 6.

26. See, e.g., Heise, *Minimum Disclosure;* and Robert Sims, *The Pentagon Reporters* (Washington, DC: National Defense University Press, 1983). Although Hess, in *Government/Press Connection*, estimated thirty-four reporters to be regulars once one includes reporters for specialized publications such as *Aerospace Daily*, he had earlier suggested, "The press corps at the White House, State, and Pentagon—mirroring the news values of the mass media—can be thought of as a ratio of 4:3:1." Hess, "Golden Triangle," p. 15.

27. Quoted in Heise, *Minimum Disclosure*, p. 110.

28. A cottage industry has cropped up of studies about the Gulf War and the media. Two journalists' books that vividly describe the censorship, pool systems, and briefings in Saudi Arabia are John J. Fialka, *Hotel Warriors: Covering the Gulf War* (Washington, DC: Woodrow Wilson Center Press, 1991); and John R. MacArthur, *Second Front: Censorship and Propaganda in the Gulf War* (New York: Hill and Wang, 1992). Most critiques of the censorship, however, make it sound as if the reporting would have been dramatically different had there not been such systems in place, which, I have argued elsewhere, is a problematic assumption. In addition to my article in Bennett and Paletz, eds., *Taken by Storm*, also see the articles therein by William Dorman and Steven Livingston, and by Robert Entman and Benjamin Page.

29. Sims, *Pentagon Reporters*, p. 51.

30. See, e.g., Terry M. Moe, "The Politics of Bureaucratic Structure," in John E. Chubb and Paul E. Peterson, eds., *Can The Government Govern?* (Washington, DC: Brookings Institution, 1989), pp. 267-329; and Cathy Marie Johnson, "New Wine In New Bottles: The Case of the Consumer Product Safety Commission," *Public Administration Review* 50 (1990): 74-81.

31. This is the major conclusion of Brent Fisse and John Braithwaite, *The Impact of Publicity on Corporate Offenders* (Albany: State University of New York Press, 1983). In a number of case studies, the financial impacts of adverse publicity were mixed. However, "With regard to non-financial impacts, we have a much more consistent picture of publicity stinging the company—through loss of corporate prestige, loss of prestige in the community for top management, trauma for executives in facing cross-examination about the scandal, distraction

of top management from normal duties, and decline in employee morale." Ibid., p. 233. Fisse and Braithwaite also note that although the companies will explain their side of the story to journalists, they rarely engage in a countercampaign.

32. Connecticut Public Radio, local news, April 24, 1995.

33. My thanks to Greg Leo, who served as public information officer for the INS in the early eighties, for recounting this story.

34. Steven Greenhouse, "In New Political Climate, Saving U.S. Foreign Aid Isn't Easy," *New York Times*, February 19, 1995, p. 18.

35. Steven Erlanger, "Albright Struts across a World Stage, Radiating Star Quality," *New York Times*, February 24, 1997, p. A9. See also Steven Lee Myers, "Secretary of State Sells Foreign Policy at Home." *New York Times*, February 8, 1997, p. 6.

36. The examination of Congress and the media has lagged considerably behind the presidency. Highly useful studies of the days before the congressional reforms of the 1970s include Dorothy Hartt Cronheim's indispensable work, "Congressmen and Their Communication Practices," unpublished Ph.D. dissertation, Ohio State University, 1957; and Robert Blanchard's anthology, *Congress and the News Media*, which includes Blanchard's own survey of Capitol Hill correspondents. Stephen Hess's books, *The Ultimate Insiders;* and *Live from Capitol Hill! Studies of Congress and the Media* (Washington, DC: Brookings Institution, 1991), are crucial for their wonderful evocation of Capitol Hill and for their correctives to speculation about media domination of Congress. My own book, *Making Laws and Making News,* was the first book-length consideration of the House; references to articles on Congress and the media can be found therein. A more recent work that confirms some of my conclusions with different data— surveys of top staffers in House offices—is Karen M. Kedrowski, *Media Entrepreneurs and the Media Enterprise in the U.S. Congress* (Cresskill, NJ: Hampton Press, 1996).

37. See, e.g., Michael J. Robinson, "A Twentieth-Century Medium in a Nineteenth-Century Legislature: The Effects of Television on the American Congress," in Norman J. Ornstein, ed., *Congress in Change: Evolution and Reform* (New York: Praeger, 1975), pp. 240–261; id., "The Three Faces of Congressional Media," in Thomas E. Mann and Norman J. Ornstein, eds., *The New Congress* (Washington, DC: American Enterprise Institute, 1981), pp. 55–96; Ronald Garay, *Congressional Television: A Legislative History* (Westport, CT: Greenwood Press, 1984); and Cook, *Making Laws and Making News,* pp. 24–30.

38. See Lynda Lee Kaid and Joe Foote, "How Network Television Coverage of the President and Congress Compare," *Journalism Quarterly* 62 (Spring 1985): 59–65.

39. I discuss this in more detail in Cook, "Press Secretaries and Media Strategies in the House of Representatives." See also David W. Brady, "Personnel Management in the House," in Joseph Cooper and G. Calvin Mackenzie, eds., *The House at Work* (Austin: University of Texas Press, 1981), pp. 151–182; and Hess, *Live from Capitol Hill!* pp. 62–68, and table B-11.

40. See, among others, Susan H. Miller, "News Coverage of Congress: The Search for the Ultimate Spokesman," *Journalism Quarterly* 54 (Autumn 1977): 459–465; Charles M. Tidmarch and John J. Pitney, Jr., "Covering Congress," *Polity* 17 (Spring 1985): 463–483; Hess, *Ultimate Insiders,* passim; Cook,

"House Members as Newsmakers"; and James H. Kuklinski and Lee Sigelman, "When Objectivity Is Not Objective: Network Television News Coverage of U.S. Senators and the Paradox of Objectivity," *Journal of Politics* 54 (1992): 810–833.

41. Cook, *Making Laws and Making News,* pp. 81–89; Hess, *Live from Capitol Hill!* esp. pp. 68–76. Both Hess and I found that the popular presumption that current members of Congress are preoccupied with local television is greatly overdrawn, despite the increased presence of local broadcast reporters on Capitol Hill. I found that House press secretaries generally saw local television as useful to their job only as the district overlaps with a television market, while Hess, through a nonrandom sample of various local news broadcasts, found television news about or from members of Congress to be scarce.

42. Burdett A. Loomis, *The New American Politician: Entrepreneurship, Ambition, and the Changing Face of Political Life* (New York: Basic Books, 1988). I found in 1984 that Democratic House press secretaries' ratings of the value of national news outlets were most powerfully predicted by what I termed the goal of "issue spokespersonship," which, in turn was positively affected by members' seniority, membership on a policy committee, the press secretaries' ratings of the importance of ambition to their jobs (allowing the member to run for higher office), the lack of overlap of television media markets with the district. See Cook, "Press Secretaries . . . ," tables 2–4. Hess, although he is less convinced than I about the importance of the national media to members of Congress, presents evidence that the activity level of a typical House office's media operations grows with seniority, peaking at six to nine terms, and falling off thereafter. See *Live from Capitol Hill!* p. 75, and table B-13. The perceived benefits from the national media and levels of activity may be somewhat different from more general attitudes toward using the media in the legislative process, to judge from Kedrowski's 1991 survey of top congressional staffers, where such attitudes (what she called "media entrepreneurship") were significantly higher among younger, more liberal, and Democratic members, but where there was no relationship with seniority. In other words, at all levels of tenure (over and above age, party, and ideology), members of Congress seem to agree that the news media *can* work beneficially to accomplish policy goals. Kedrowski, *Media Entrepreneurs,* table 3.4; the four questions she uses to measure "media entrepreneurship," and their frequencies, are indicated in table 3.1.

The pattern for the Senate is less clear with seniority, probably because, as Hess shows, media activities are dependent on the electoral cycle, increasing as the election approaches and gradually declining to the fourth year of the term (*Live from Capitol Hill!,* table B-10). Moreover, Hess indicates how one media outlet, the op-ed page, is "the domain of the policy committee member" (ibid., p. 95).

43. Compare Mayhew, *Congress;* and Richard F. Fenno, Jr., *Congressmen in Committees* (Boston: Little, Brown, 1973), p. 1.

44. Richard F. Fenno, Jr., *Home Style: House Members in Their Districts* (Boston: Little, Brown, 1978), esp. chap. 7. The "two arenas" term comes from Thomas Cavanaugh, "The Two Arenas of Congress," in Cooper and Mackenzie, eds., *The House at Work,* pp. 56–77. Cavanaugh's interviews with members and Fenno's observation of the quickness with which newly elected House members enter a "protectionist" phase of home style, whereby they maintain rather than

expand their constituency relations, both indicate that reelection is largely viewed as necessary but onerous. Useful theoretical considerations combining these various approaches include R. Douglas Arnold, *The Logic of Congressional Action* (New Haven: Yale University Press, 1990); and Glenn R. Parker, *Institutional Change, Discretion, and the Making of Modern Congress* (Ann Arbor: University of Michigan Press, 1992).

45. See, e.g., Robert H. Salisbury and Kenneth A. Shepsle, "U.S. Congressman as Enterprise," *Legislative Studies Quarterly* 6 (November 1981): 559–576; and Loomis, *The New American Politician*. A good overview of the reforms of the 1970s is Leroy N. Rieselbach, *Congressional Reform* (Washington, DC: CQ Press, 1986).

46. See in particular Steven S. Smith, *Call to Order* (Washington, DC: Brookings Institution, 1990).

47. See in particular the essays in Roger Davidson, ed., *The Postreform Congress* (New York: St. Martin's Press, 1991); and Barbara Sinclair, *Legislators, Leaders, and Lawmaking: The U.S. House of Representatives in the Postreform Era* (Baltimore: Johns Hopkins University Press, 1995).

48. This story is based on Michael Katz, "Hunger Panel Gone, Chairman Plans to Fast," *Chicago Tribune,* April 2, 1993, p. 21; Richard Blow, "Life in the Fast Lane: Rep. Hall's Hunger for a Noble Cause," *Washington Post,* April 16, 1993, p. B1; John Dillin, "Congressman's Fast Challenges Indifference to World's Hunger," *Christian Science Monitor,* April 16, 1993, p. 2; Colman McCarthy, "A Congressman's Taste of Hunger," *Washington Post,* April 20, 1993, p. D15; Linda M. Harrington and Michael Katz, "Actors Back Democrat's Hunger Fast," *Chicago Tribune,* April 20, 1993, p. 12; Kenneth J. Cooper, "House's Ex-Hunger Panel Chief Finds His Fast Is Bearing Fruit," *Washington Post,* April 24, 1993, p. 3; "Celebrities Join Ohio Congressman in a Fast," *New York Times,* April 25, 1993, p. 27.

49. Joe S. Foote, "The Speaker and the Media," in Ronald M. Peters, Jr., *The Speaker: Leadership in the U.S. House of Representatives* (Washington, DC: CQ Press, 1994), pp. 135–156. On the greater newsworthiness of the Senate and senators, see, for instance, Hess, *Ultimate Insiders,* passim, and Cook, "House Members as Newsmakers."

50. Arnold, *The Logic of Congressional Action,* pp. 72–74.

51. The most famous account of this act is, of course, Jeffrey H. Birnbaum and Alan S. Murray, *Showdown at Gucci Gulch* (New York: Random House, 1987).

52. For further thoughts on the rise and decline of Gingrich's linked media/governing strategy in 1995, see my "Revolution and Evolution," *Media Studies Journal* 10, no. 1 (Winter 1996): 15–22.

53. See Cook, *Making Laws and Making News,* chap. 6. Little wonder, then, that the top congressional staffers surveyed by Karen Kedrowski in 1991 saw the media's role in the policy process as most powerful in "setting the agenda" and "framing the terms of debate," considerably more than "influencing interest groups" or "generating floor support" with even less for "moving bills in committees" or "generating support in the other chamber." Kedrowski, *Media Entrepreneurs,* table 4.1.

54. The Supreme Court's relationship with the news media has also been the

least studied of the three branches. For years, the only available book devoted to the topic has been David L. Grey's now outdated account, *The Supreme Court and the News Media*. Since that time, most of the accounts have been content analyses of coverage of the Court and its decisions, and there have been virtually no scholarly investigations of the Supreme Court press corps, its Public Information Office, or the media activities of the justices themselves. That situation has been rectified by Richard Davis's very fine *Decisions and Images: The Supreme Court and the News Media* (Englewood Cliffs, NJ: Prentice-Hall, 1994), to which this section is indebted.

Justices rarely write memoirs themselves, law clerks are sworn to secrecy, and even reporters on the beat have rarely revealed much about their daily grind, with the salient exception of CBS's former law correspondent, Fred Graham, in his memoir, *Happy Talk: Confessions of a TV Newsman* (New York: Norton, 1990). Besides Davis's work, the best published work on courts since Grey is for lower courts, most notably Robert Drechsel's *News Making in the Trial Courts* (New York: Longman, 1983).

55. Davis, *Decisions and Images*, p. 66. For a vivid description of law reporters and the Public Information Office at the time of the retirement of Justice Lewis Powell, see Ethan Bronner, *Battle for Justice: How the Bork Nomination Shook America* (New York: W. W. Norton, 1989), pp. 15–19.

56. Linda Greenhouse, "Telling the Court's Story: Justice and Journalism at the Supreme Court," *Yale Law Journal* 105 (1996): 1537–1560 at 1540.

57. See, e.g., Chester A. Newland, "Press Coverage of the United States Supreme Court," *Western Political Quarterly* 17 (1964): 15–26; Stephanie Greco Larson, "How the *New York Times* Covered Discrimination Cases," *Journalism Quarterly* 62 (1985): 894–896; Richard Davis, "Lifting the Shroud: News Media Portrayal of the U.S. Supreme Court," *Communications and the Law* 9 (1987): 43–59; and two papers by Elliot E. Slotnick, "Television News and the Supreme Court: The Case of Allan Bakke," delivered at the American Political Science Association, San Francisco, August 30–September 2, 1990; and "Television News and the Supreme Court: 'Game Day' Coverage of the *Bakke* Case," delivered at the Midwest Political Science Association, Chicago, April 18–20, 1991.

58. Anthony Lewis, "Problems of a Washington Correspondent," *Connecticut Bar Journal* 33 (1959): 363–371 at 365, quoted in Grey, *Supreme Court and the News Media*, p. 19.

59. Greenhouse, "Telling the Court's Story," p. 1559.

60. See esp. Davis, *Decisions and Images*, chap. 5.

61. The locus classicus for this view is, of course, Murphy's *Elements of Judicial Strategy*. A nice recent empirical demonstration of this point is Perry, *Deciding to Decide*, who concludes that justices' decisions on granting certiorari fall under two different processes, depending upon whether the justice cares strongly about the outcome; if not, he/she follows a more jurisprudentially inclined model.

62. William Rehnquist, *The Supreme Court: How It Was, How It Is* (New York: William Morrow, 1987), p. 98, as quoted in Davis, *Decisions and Images*, p. 17.

63. Allan P. Sindler, *Bakke, DeFunis, and Minority Admissions: The Quest for Equal Opportunity* (New York: Longman, 1978), p. 292.

64. Kristin Luker, *Abortion and the Politics of Motherhood* (Berkeley: University of California Press, 1984), chap. 6.

65. "In order for the Supreme Court to persist in influencing the behavior of actors in the political system who may not be under a strictly legal obligation to act, it seems imperative that the Court *continue* to generate the impression that its determinations result from calm deliberation and the application of esoteric rules of law." Richard M. Johnson, *The Dynamics of Compliance: Supreme Court Decision-Making from a New Perspective* (Evanston, IL: Northwestern University Press, 1967), p. 149 (emphasis added).

66. Murphy, *Elements of Judicial Strategy*, p. 95.

67. The examples that come most readily to mind are those where the Court, faced with the possibility of massive disobedience in the case of a split decision, worked hard to build a unanimous decision, such as *Brown* v. *Board of Education* (1954), which declared segregated schools to be unconstitutional, and *U.S.* v. *Nixon* (1974), where the Court was ordering a president to turn documents over to a lower court.

In addition, in the 1960s, following controversial decisions on defendants' rights and on school prayer, there was a boomlet of studies on how and whether Supreme Court decisions obtained compliance from law enforcement officers and from school officials, ably summarized in Stephen L. Wasby, *The Impact of the United States Supreme Court: Some Perspectives* (Homewood, IL: Dorsey Press, 1970). Those who were affected generally learned about the decision from the news, as Johnson found for school officials and others in the small rural twin villages he studied in *Dynamics of Compliance*. Moreover, the news provides a base of information, even when it is supplemented by more professional education programs, as in the variety of responses in the four Wisconsin cities studied by Neal Milner in *The Court and Local Law Enforcement: The Impact of Miranda* (Beverly Hills, CA: Sage, 1971).

Public opinion about most Supreme Court decisions is often scanty, but again, the amount of media coverage and individuals' news habits are key. From a 1989 survey in St. Louis, Liane C. Kosaki and Charles H. Franklin studied predictors of awareness of five decisions, all of which had been on the front page of the *Post-Dispatch* and had led the television news. Their most intriguing finding is that, in the cases of the three decisions that did not receive follow-up coverage, attentiveness to news media was crucial, whereas with the two more salient cases (the flag-burning case, *Texas* v. *Johnson*, and the *Webster* abortion case), such attention made no difference. In the absence of continuing coverage, in other words, Court decisions that are momentarily in the spotlight tend to disappear from the public's mind. Kosaki and Franklin, "Public Awareness of Supreme Court Decisions," paper delivered at the Midwest Political Science Association, Chicago, April 18–20, 1991.

68. Quoted in Kenneth S. DeVol, ed., *Mass Media and the Supreme Court: The Legacy of the Warren Years*, 3d ed. (New York: Hastings House, 1982), p. 139. Brennan himself practiced what he preached, most notably in a 1985 speech at Georgetown University (released by the public information office of the Court). Brennan took issue with then-Attorney General Edwin Meese's argument in favor of judicial interpretation by returning to the founders' intent as "little more than arrogance cloaked in humility"—a soundbite that made it to the front

page of the *New York Times*. See Stuart Taylor, Jr., "Brennan Opposes Legal View Urged by Administration," *New York Times,* October 13, 1985, p. 1.

69. This section relies upon Newland, "Press Coverage of the United States Supreme Court"; Johnson, *Dynamics of Compliance;* and Grey, *Supreme Court and the News Media,* chap. 4. Another study of the response to *Schempp:* William K. Muir, Jr., *Prayer in the Public Schools: Law and Attitude Change* (Chicago: University of Chicago Press, 1967), does not analyze the media's role in the town he studied, but his before-after study comes to similar conclusions as the less rigorous study by Johnson.

70. Quoted in Johnson, *Dynamics of Compliance,* p. 70.

71. Elliot Slotnick and Jennifer Segal found, in their analysis of network news coverage of the 1989–1990 Supreme Court term, that even with the coverage of what they term "leading cases," 80 percent of the stories focused on the stages of oral argument (23 percent) and decision on the merits (57 percent). Slotnick and Segal, "Television News and the Supreme Court," paper delivered at the American Political Science Association, Chicago, September 3–6, 1992, p. 18. Davis (*Decisions and Images,* p. 75) quotes Rita Braver, then covering the Court for CBS: "This is the only beat in the country where you know what you're getting. The way the Court works they tell you what cases they're going to take, and they tell you what days they're going to argue them on."

72. Drechsel, *News Making in the Trial Courts,* chap. 5. Compare esp. tables 5.3 and 5.5.

73. Quoted in Mitchell Tropin, "What, Exactly, Is the Court Saying," *Barrister Magazine* 14 (Spring 1984): p. 68.

74. Slotnick and Segal, "Television News and the Supreme Court," p. 20. Of the twenty-two oral argument stories, Scalia was mentioned in ten, considerably more than the runners-up, O'Connor (six), Blackmun (four), and Kennedy (three).

75. See, e.g., David O'Brien, *Storm Center* (New York: W. W. Norton, 1986), pp. 263ff.

76. Quoted in Davis, *Decisions and Images,* p. 27.

77. Note, for instance, how Davis, in the acknowledgments to *Decisions and Images,* points out that he received considerable help from Toni House, the public information officer of the Court, despite her strong disagreement with his basic thesis that the Court uses a media strategy to assist its authority.

78. Ibid., p. 9. Davis concluded that most Supreme Court correspondents had had off-the-record sessions with a majority of the then-current justices and had engaged in them with some justices during every term. Ibid., p. 120.

79. Linda Greenhouse, "Rehnquist Joins Fray on Rulings, Defending Judicial Independence," *New York Times,* April 10, 1996, p. A1.

80. Thus, in the spring of 1994, Ted Koppel and Nina Totenberg conducted an interview on ABC's *Nightline* that was specifically called "A Conversation with Justice Blackmun." That same year, when visiting Sacramento, Harry Smith, on the *CBS Morning News* (May 10, 1994), interviewed Justice Anthony Kennedy in the backyard of the house where Kennedy spent his childhood. Although Smith's co-host, Paula Zahn, commented approvingly at the end of the segment that this had been a "nice conversation" and a "rare opportunity to chat," Smith did have a chance to ask the justice not only about his youth, the responsibility of being a judge, and whether he liked his work, but also whether being part of

the moderate wing of the Court must have been a disappointment to President Reagan, who had appointed him.

Chapter Eight

1. E.g., Neil Postman, *Amusing Ourselves to Death* (New York: Viking, 1985).

2. This is an important theme convincingly outlined in W. Russell Neuman, Marion R. Just, and Ann N. Crigler, *Common Knowledge: News and the Construction of Political Meaning* (Chicago: University of Chicago Press, 1992). Another good study that comes to a similar conclusion about the possibilities of learning from television vs. learning from newspapers, but from a very different methodology, is Jeffery Mondak, *Nothing to Read* (Pittsburgh: University of Pittsburgh Press, 1995).

3. See, in particular, Doris A. Graber, *Processing the News: Taming the Information Tide* (New York: Longman, 1984); and Robinson and Levy, *The Main Source.*

4. Recent studies of public broadcasting have concluded that since the Public Broadcasting Act of 1967 the tendency has been clear toward an increased support by private sponsorship (or, in the euphemistic vocabulary that public television and public radio prefer, "underwriting") of businesses rather than governmental grants, and a concomitant skittishness about controversial issues or programming. The extent to which commercial and private broadcast news differs, in terms of the subject matters and sources, is actually quite small, although there are considerable differences in format and style. See, for instance, Marilyn Lashley, *Public Television: Panacea, Pork Barrel, or Public Trust?* (Westport, CT: Greenwood, 1992); William Hoynes, *Public Television for Sale: Media, the Market, and the Public Sphere* (Boulder, CO: Westview Press, 1994); Thomas Looker, *The Sound and the Story: NPR and the Art of Radio* (Boston: Houghton Mifflin, 1995); and Philo C. Washburn, "Democracy and Media Ownership: A Comparison of Commercial, Public and Government Broadcast News," *Media, Culture and Society* 17 (1995): 647–676.

5. This notion is borrowed from writings of Thomas E. Patterson. See, for instance, his *Mass Media Election,* chap. 14.

6. See, for example, the rationale enunciated by Ted Koppel, "Koppel on the Interview," in Ted Koppel and Kyle Gibson, *Nightline: History in the Making and the Making of Television* (New York: Times Books, 1996), pp. 145–185 (quote is on p. 146).

7. For instance, Benjamin Page has recently analyzed the contents of the editorial page of the *New York Times* during the build-up to the Gulf War, including unsigned editorials, op-eds, and letters to the editor. Having documented that the *Times* can only publish around 3 percent of the letters it receives, Page found that the stands taken in the letters actually tended to be more dovish than the *Times*'s editorial stance on the Gulf crisis, suggesting an attempt to provide some balance but along the lines of the standard pro-and-con division of "the" two sides of the story. See Page, *Who Deliberates?* esp. pp. 19–20, tables 1 and 2, and p. 41n.32.

8. James Ettema and Theodore Glasser, "Public Accountability or Public Relations?" *Journalism Quarterly* 64 (1987): 3–12.

9. The notion of the "public sphere" has become increasingly influential in political communication circles. The term gained prominence in the work of Jürgen Habermas, who developed it most fully in his 1962 book, translated into English as *The Structural Transformation of the Public Sphere: An Inquiry into a Category of Bourgeois Society,* trans. Thomas Burger (Cambridge, MA: MIT Press, 1989). A good introductory volume is Craig Calhoun, ed., *Habermas and the Public Sphere* (Cambridge, MA: MIT Press, 1992).

Habermas's public sphere is a space of public deliberation constituted by discussion about common concerns and autonomous from both the state and the market economy. This notion—combined with his dictum that the press is the "public sphere's preeminent institution" (*Structural Transformation,* p. 181)— has made for a little cottage industry. While I have considerable difficulty with Habermas's later rationalistic notions of "communicative action," I do find the public sphere to be a useful conceptual ideal toward which to aspire, and the comments in this conclusion may be viewed with that in mind. In some ways, the conclusion to Just et al., *Crosstalk,* is implicitly Habermasian, in calling for an expansion of talk within and across categories of participants in a presidential campaign. For useful forays in political communication that focus on the public sphere, see, e.g., Nicholas Garnham, "The Media and the Public Sphere," in Peter Golding, Graham Murdock, and Philip Schlesinger, eds., *Communicating Politics: Mass Communications and the Political Process* (New York: Holmes and Meier, 1986), pp. 37–53; Peter Dahlgren and Colin Sparks, eds., *Communication and Citizenship: Journalism and the Public Sphere in the New Media Age* (New York: Routledge, 1991); and Hallin, *We Keep America on Top of the World.*

10. Jeffrey Abramson, F. Christopher Arterton, and Gary Orren, *The Electronic Commonwealth: The Impact of New Media Technologies on Democratic Politics* (New York: Basic Books, 1988), chap. 2.

11. This, for instance, is a theme of McChesney, "The Internet and U.S. Communication Policy-Making in Historical and Critical Perspective."

12. See, e.g., Abramson et al., *The Electronic Commonwealth.*

13. This comes from a presentation by Todd Gitlin, "Glib, Tawdry, Savvy, and Standardized: Television and American Culture, and Other Oxymorons," at a conference cosponsored by the Joan Shorenstein Center and Home Box Office at the Kennedy School of Government, "The Future of Television," Harvard University, February 8, 1993. It is reinforced by Doris Graber's presidential address to the International Society of Political Psychology, Vancouver, British Columbia, July 1996, which makes many of the same points in greater detail.

14. New York: Cambridge University Press, 1991.

15. There has not yet, to my knowledge, been a systematic study of the content of all cable stations, but Bill McKibben's fascinating essay, *The Age of Missing Information* (New York: Random House, 1992), provides an initial insight. McKibben collected all of the video disseminated over the cable system of Fairfax, Virginia, on the day of May 3, 1990, and examined it in its entirety. In addition to its mind-numbing repetitiveness, McKibben also found that much information was simply not present anywhere, which he contrasts (rather poetically) to the information he obtained while camping out by himself in the Adirondacks.

16. This next section is based on research conducted for me by my research assistant Zachary Cook; we both thank Ethan Zuckerman, of Tripod, an Internet content company based in Williamstown, Massachusetts, for his thought-provoking observations.

17. This useful phrase comes from John Simons, "A New Online Odyssey," *U.S. News and World Report,* July 15/22, 1996, p. 85.

18. For instance, on-line services such as America Online, faced with losing customers to the Web, have sought to distinguish their products with unique content and have entered bidding wars for content providers; see Jesse Kornbluth, "Who Needs America Online?" *New York Times Magazine,* December 24, 1995, pp. 16–19, 36, 40; and Jared Sandberg and Bart Ziegler, "Web Trap," *Wall Street Journal,* January 18, 1996, p. A1.

19. It is, however, not beside the point, particularly when one considers the exponential increase in digital space used up by pictures and video, which could easily clog the system when access is cheap. See Charles C. Mann, "Is the Internet Doomed?" *Inc. Technology,* no. 2 (1995): 47–54.

20. Julio Ojeda-Zapata, "The Internet's Vanishing Freebies: Veterans Mourn the Rise of a For-Profit Mode," *Washington Post,* November 13, 1995, bus. sec., p. 15.

21. This story is told best by, among others, Bagdikian, *The Media Monopoly;* Underwood, *When MBAs Rule the Newsroom;* Kimball, *Downsizing the News;* and McManus, *Market-Driven Journalism.*

22. William Glaberson, "Miami Herald Plans More Cuts in News Staff," *New York Times,* October 12, 1995, p. D6.

23. For instance, my former student, Karin Meitner, has written a superb analysis ("Rocking the Presidency," unpublished seminar paper, Williams College, 1994) comparing the entirety of the famous MTV show where President Clinton was asked whether he wore "boxers or briefs," against the coverage thereof, and found that the news focused on the boxers-or-briefs question even though the show as a whole was issue-oriented, serious, and substantive.

24. Howard Kurtz, "Money Talks," *Washington Post Magazine,* January 21, 1996, pp. 10–15, 22–25 (quotes are on pp. 12–13).

25. Hanna Fenichel Pitkin, *The Concept of Representation* (Berkeley: University of California Press, 1967).

26. Public journalism is usually traced back to the early days of the 1992 presidential campaign, when the *Charlotte* [NC] *Observer* polled readers to find out which issues the paper should highlight in its election coverage in order to provide a counterweight to the usual horse-race mentality of most political reporting. Although the trend is too new to have attracted significant scholarly attention, the first book-length overview of public journalism has been published: Arthur Charity, *Doing Public Journalism* (New York: Guilford Press, 1995). Charity's book is something of a celebration of public journalism but nicely captures the presumptions behind its practice, and I have relied heavily on it in this section.

27. Charity, *Doing Public Journalism,* p. 2.

28. For instance, the Kettering Foundation, Pew Center for Civic Journalism, and the Poynter Institute have all been key players in supporting public journalism.

29. The list comes from Charity, *Doing Public Journalism,* pp. 161–164. On the difficulties of figuring out how to cover local news in a large metropolitan area, a good source is Kaniss, *Making Local News.*

30. Most of the considerations of the First Amendment focus on freedom of speech rather than freedom of the press, even when they are packaged as works on "mass media law." The best exception, although I do not always agree with its conclusions, is Lucas A. Powe, Jr., *The Fourth Estate and the Constitution: Freedom of the Press in America* (Berkeley: University of California Press, 1991).

31. The most famous interpretation is that of Levy in his *Legacy of Suppression,* wherein he concludes that the founders had a constricted understanding of freedom of the press, only proscribing prior restraint but saying nothing against such punitive measures as seditious libel, breach of parliamentary privilege, and the like. Levy's work created a cottage industry of its own that forced him to revise somewhat his original thesis (and rename his revised book, *Emergence of a Free Press*). Much of this debate hinges on the extent to which one should consider legal theory or press practice, but either way the evidence is equivocal. Two major critiques of Levy that are informative without being wholly persuasive are David A. Anderson, "The Origins of the Press Clause," *UCLA Law Review* 30 (1983): 455–541; and Smith, *Printers and Press Freedom.*

32. "My enterprise is not the history of freedom of the press, but the history of the language that became the press clause of the first amendment." Anderson, "Origins of the Press Clause," p. 462.

33. Ibid., pp. 464–466 (quotes are on p. 465). Anderson also shows that the first phrase was incorporated into Madison's first draft of the Bill of Rights; see ibid., p. 477.

34. The initial cases ruled that news organizations, in their guises as businesses, were not exempt from regulation, such as labor laws or antitrust; see *Associated Press v. National Labor Relations Board,* 301 U.S. 103 (1937); and *Associated Press v. United States,* 326 U.S. 1 (1945). More recently, the standard citations include *Branzburg v. Hayes,* 408 U.S. 665 (1972; no constitutional right to refuse to disclose names of confidential sources); *Pell v. Procunier,* 417 U.S. 817 (1974; no constitutional right of access to prisons); *Zurcher v. Stanford Daily,* 436 U.S. 547 (1978; no constitutional exemption from police searches of newsrooms); and *Herbert v. Lando,* 441 U.S. 153 (1979; no constitutional right to prevent those suing for libel to investigate journalists' thought processes).

35. Potter Stewart, "Or of the Press," *Hastings Law Journal* 26 (1975): 631–637 at 633 (emphasis in original).

36. Ibid.

37. Ibid., p. 634.

38. Ibid., p. 635.

39. See in particular the "uneven influence" of a structural understanding of freedom of the press considered at length in Vincent Blasi, "The Checking Value in First Amendment Theory," *American Bar Foundation Research Journal* (1977): 521–649.

40. Stewart, "Or of the Press," p. 634.

41. This last point is the theme of Timothy W. Gleason, *The Watchdog*

Concept: The Press and the Courts in Nineteenth-Century America (Ames: Iowa State University Press, 1990).

42. William W. Van Alstyne, "The Hazards to the Press of Claiming a 'Preferred Position,' " *Hastings Law Journal* 28 (1977): 761–770.

43. This theme is best developed in Lee C. Bollinger, *Images of a Free Press* (Chicago: University of Chicago Press, 1991). Bollinger did note that one strand connected with the autonomy and independence of the press is almost entirely evoked with print media, whereas the "secondary image" of a press officially regulated in order to safeguard public discussion is almost solely to be found in cases on the broadcast media, but he went on to say that, particularly with the decline of the "scarcity" rationale for regulation of broadcast media, the possibility for the two to instruct beyond their particular modalities is strong.

44. See *Federal Communication Commission v. Pottsville Broadcasting Company,* 309 U.S. 134; and *National Broadcasting Company v. United States,* 319 U.S. 190 (1943). This origin myth is repeated time and again in broadcast regulation cases; see, e.g, *Red Lion Broadcasting Company v. Federal Communication Commission,* 395 U.S. 367 at 375–377.

45. *Red Lion v. FCC,* p. 388.

46. Ibid., p. 390.

47. See, for instance, the section of White's opinion that indicates "more serious First Amendment values" that this case does not touch, including, e.g., "the Commission's refusal to permit the broadcaster to carry a particular program or to publish his own views; . . . government censorship of a particular program; or . . . the official government view dominating public broadcasting." *Red Lion v. FCC,* p. 396.

48. *Miami Herald v. Tornillo,* 418 U.S. 241 (1974). Burger's majority opinion had been preceded by another by the then chief justice who ruled that CBS was constitutionally permitted to refuse to sell political advertisements; in *Columbia Broadcasting System v. Democratic National Committee,* 412 U.S. 94 (1973), Burger focused on the importance of "journalistic discretion of broadcasters in the coverage of public issues" (ibid., p. 124), but even there he pointed to the intent of Congress, not the demands of the First Amendment, to "permit private broadcasting to develop with the widest journalistic freedom *consistent with its public obligations.*" Ibid., p. 110 (emphasis added).

49. Moreover, as Bollinger adeptly recognizes, *Red Lion* and *Tornillo* used divergent vocabularies. In *Red Lion,* "the Court not once refers to the broadcast media as the 'press,' or to broadcasters as 'journalists' or 'editors.' In the idiom chosen, broadcasters are referred to only as 'licensees,' 'proxies,' and 'fiduciaries,' or as the holders of 'monopolies' capable of exercising 'private censorship.' " Bollinger, *Images of a Free Press,* p. 72.

50. *Telecommunications Research and Action Center v. Federal Communications Commission,* 801 F.2d 501 (1986), cert. denied, 482 U.S. 919 (1987), quoted in Donald E. Lively, *Essential Principles of Communication Law* (New York: Praeger, 1992), p. 246.

51. For the FCC's ruling, see the excerpts in Lively, *Essential Principles,* pp. 246–252. Of course, if the appeals court was correct that all news media operate under scarcity, the *Red Lion* logic could apply to print media as well

rather than presuming that *Tornillo* must then extend to broadcast media, as the FCC assumed.

For the record, it is worth noting that the Supreme Court has not yet abandoned the scarcity logic when it comes to broadcast media. In *Federal Communications Commission* v. *League of Women Voters of California*, 468 U.S. 364 (1984), the Court specifically held back from reconsidering the scarcity approach, at least until "some signal from Congress or the FCC that technological developments have advanced so far that some revision of the system of broadcast regulation may be required." Ibid., p. 377 n.10. Instead, the *Red Lion* precedent was quoted to justify how "those who are granted a license to broadcast must serve in a sense as fiduciaries for the public" (ibid.), a phrase in turn cited in the Court's decision supporting minority set-asides in broadcasting, *Metro Broadcasting, Inc.* v. *Federal Communications Commission*, 497 U.S. 547 (1990) at 566–567. The scarcity approach was not extended to cable (and not overruled either), but a kindred notion was used to uphold the constitutionality of cable regulation in the *Turner Broadcasting* case. Justice Anthony Kennedy's majority opinion specifically held back from considering economic scarcity but continued to focus on "the unique physical characteristics" (p. 639) of broadcasting as necessitating a particular approach. Cable, by Kennedy's logic, was regulable in a way that print was not. Still, by focusing exclusively on the technology necessitating a "bottleneck monopoly power" (p. 661), Kennedy's opinion has the feel of an endgame to it. We should think twice before turning to either scarcity or bottlenecks—particularly if print media are thereby excluded—for the basis of a news media policy.

52. *Grosjean* v. *American Press Company*, 297 U.S. 233 (1936) at 250 (emphasis added).

53. See, e.g., *AP* v. *NLRB*.

54. *AP* v. *U.S.*, p. 20. In the same case, Justice Felix Frankfurter's concurrence went yet further, suggesting that the institutional position of the press in politics meant that it was more than just any other business, requiring an even greater necessity for regulation—a sentiment that Frankfurter had already developed in cases regarding the rights of broadcasters.

55. See Powe, *Fourth Estate and the Constitution*, chap. 8.

56. The initial cases on rights to information dealt with—listed chronologically—being able to receive handbills from a Jehovah's Witness going door-to-door, hear a labor organizer's speech, get magazines in the mail from Communist countries without having to request each one from the Post Office, find out about contraception, privately possess obscene films, or interact with a Belgian Marxist denied a visa to the United States. See, respectively, *Martin* v. *City of Struthers*, 319 U.S. 141 (1943); *Thomas* v. *Collins*, 323 U.S. 516 (1945); *Lamont* v. *Postmaster General*, 381 U.S. 301 (1965); *Griswold* v. *Connecticut*, 381 U.S. 479 (1965); *Stanley* v. *Georgia*, 394 U.S. 557 (1969); and *Kleindienst* v. *Mandel*, 408 U.S. 753 (1972).

57. As law professor Lucas Powe nicely points out, "That the case was purely a listeners'-rights decision was dramatically illustrated by the lack of a willing speaker. The plaintiffs who brought the suit wanted to *hear* comparison-price advertising." Powe, *Fourth Estate and the Constitution*, p. 249 (emphasis in original).

58. *Virginia State Board of Pharmacy* v. *Virginia Citizens' Consumer Council,* 425 U.S. 748 (1976) at 756 and 757n.15 (emphasis added).

59. For instance, Justice White, in the majority opinion in *Federal Communications Commission* v. *WNCN Listeners Guild,* 450 U.S. 582 (1980), specifically interpreted that his language in *Red Lion* did not mean "that the First Amendment grants individual listeners the right to have the Commission review the abandonment of their favorite entertainment programs." Ibid., p. 604. Likewise, the Ninth Circuit Court of Appeals denied the attempts of readers of the *Seattle Post-Intelligencer* to assert a First Amendment right to challenge the Newspaper Preservation Act that enabled the paper to merge its operations with its competitor, the *Seattle Times.* See *Committee for an Independent P-I* v. *Hearst Corporation,* 704 F.2d 467 (9th Circuit), cert. denied, 464 U.S. 892 (1983).

60. As this book went to press, an intriguing statement of this concern came in a concurrence by the newest Supreme Court justice, Stephen Breyer, in a rehearing of the *Turner Broadcasting* case after it had been remanded to lower courts for additional factual information. Breyer's vote gained attention, partially because he had replaced Harry Blackmun, who had sided with the majority in the original 5-4 decision. But while Justice Kennedy's majority opinion centrally emphasized how the 1992 Cable Act was constitutionally acceptable inasmuch as it sought to preserve economic competition, Breyer found a different logic, saying that, "whether or not the statute is properly tailored to Congress' purely economic objectives," the First Amendment interests of the cable operators needed to be counterposed to another First Amendment concern to protect the range and quality of information available to citizens. Breyer's willingness to emphasize the latter, and to point out that the act "strikes a reasonable balance between potentially speech-restricting and speech-enhancing consequences," is worth considerable attention. *Turner Broadcasting Company* v. *Federal Communications Commission,* March 31, 1997 (Legal Information Institute and Project Hermes). Available: http://supct.law.cornell.edu/supct/html/95-922.ZC1.html [April 25, 1997].

61. Cass Sunstein, *Democracy and the Problem of Free Speech* (New York: Free Press, 1993), pp. 30–31.

62. Ibid., chap. 3, passim.

63. Four lines of precedent are pertinent here. One refers to differential taxes on the media. Another, closely related, examines whether exemptions from certain regulations can be legislated differentially by size. A third suggests that for the news media to qualify for extra benefits, they may have to engage in certain behavior (as long as that is not content based). A fourth notes how government can provide subsidies contingent on the recipients' not engaging in certain speech. A good overview is Benjamin Lombard, "First Amendment Limits on the Use of Taxes to Subsidize Selectively the Media," *Cornell Law Review* 78 (1992): 106–138. C. Edwin Baker's final chapter, on the constitutionality of taxation and regulation of advertising, in *Advertising and a Democratic Press* (Princeton, NJ: Princeton University Press, 1994), also has a useful discussion of the following cases.

First, in the *Grosjean* case cited above, the Court overturned a Louisiana tax that applied only to large newspapers. This decision hinged on ascertaining a legislative intent to penalize critics of Senator Huey Long, but it reaffirmed that newspapers were subject to generally applicable taxes. The legislative intent test was superseded by the Court's decision in *Minneapolis Star & Tribune Co. v. Minnesota Commissioner of Revenue*, 460 U.S. 575 (1983), which struck down a Minnesota use tax on the cost of paper and ink products that exempted all but a handful of newspapers. Justice Sandra Day O'Connor's majority opinion concluded that the tax violated the First Amendment in two ways: it was limited to newspapers, and it applied only to a small subset thereof without justification, which opened up possibilities for abuse even in the absence of legislative intent to act against the newspapers. The Court extended this logic in *Arkansas Writers' Project, Inc. v. Ragland*, 481 U.S. 221 (1987), which struck down an Arkansas law that allowed certain outlets (i.e., "religious, professional, trade and sports journals") to avoid paying a sales tax, thereby discriminating by content as well as targeting only a few magazines. But differential taxation was salvaged by the case of *Leathers v. Medlock*, 499 U.S. 439 (1990), upholding a new Arkansas law that extended the sales tax to cable television services while exempting print publications as a whole, given that (in contrast to the previously annulled laws) the tax was generally applicable, was not applied on the basis of content, and affected a large part of the media. The criteria in *Leathers* thus provide the bounds on differential taxation.

Second, O'Connor's majority opinion in *Leathers* specifically drew on two paired decisions from 1946—*Mabee v. White Plains Publishing Co.*, 327 U.S. 178; and *Oklahoma Press Publishing Co. v. Walling*, 327 U.S. 186—which, as she wrote, "do not involve taxation, but . . . do involve government action that places differential burdens on members of the press." *Leathers*, p. 452. *Mabee* and *Walling* concerned newspapers that sought in Court the same exemption from the Fair Labor Standards Act that Congress had awarded to small weekly or semiweekly newspapers (i.e., where their circulation was less than 3,000 and mostly within the county of publication). In each case, the Court held that, in contrast to the *Grosjean* test of a deliberate attempt to penalize certain newspapers, Congress had simply exempted small newspapers "to put those papers more on a parity with other small town enterprises" (*Mabee*, p. 184). Benefits awarded on the basis of limited circulation can then be denied to those news outlets with wider or larger readerships.

Third, the Court decision that decided the constitutionality of the Newspaper Publicity Act of 1912 (see Chap. 3 above), that required daily newspapers to reveal their circulation, indicate who owned it and the labeling of advertisements as such when they resembled news, ruled that, as long as it did not exclude publications from the mail altogether, Congress not only had the power to "favor the circulation of newspapers, by giving special mail advantages, but . . . the authority to fix a general standard to which publishers seeking to obtain the proffered privileges must conform in order to obtain them." *Lewis Publishing Company v. Morgan*, 229 U.S. 288 (1913). To be sure, more recent cases, most notably *Hannegan v. Esquire, Inc.*, 327 U.S. 146 (1946), have made clear that the second-class privilege cannot be conditioned on the postmaster general's content-based conclusion that the publication refers to "information of a public character" or otherwise contributes to the public good. Presumably, if content is not the gauge for the postal subsidies, they can be targeted at only a certain class of periodicals.

Fourth, although these cases have involved freedom of speech rather than freedom of the press, the Supreme Court has suggested numerous times, starting with the case of *Cammarano v. United States*, 358 U.S. 498 (1959), that government is not under a First Amendment obligation to subsidize equally all speech activities. In *Cammarano*, the Court upheld the Internal Revenue Service's regulation denying tax deductions for lobbying activities, reinforced by *Regan v. Taxation with Representation of Washington*, 461 U.S. 540 (1983). The Court has been skating on judicial thin ice, given the content discriminations that may arise here, most notably in the 5-4 decision (*Rust v. Sullivan*, 500 U.S. 173 [1991]) that upheld the constitutionality of the so-called gag law that prevented clinics that received federal money from offering information about abortion as one possible form of birth control. Moreover, it is not clear that the same logic would be applicable to the press, given the Court's decision in *Federal Communications Commission v. League of Women Voters of California*, 468 U.S. 364, which invalidated a section of the Public Broadcasting Act of 1967 that forbade stations receiving public broadcasting funds from "editorializing." But if one were to meld the caution from the media taxation cases with the broader principle from *Cammarano* that not all speech activities—and by extension, not all activities of the press—need be equally subsidized, there are interesting and useful opportunities for governmental action.

64. This point is well made in Justice O'Connor's dissent in the *Turner Broadcasting* case. The majority opinion by Justice Kennedy upheld the "must-carry" provisions of the cable regulation act passed by Congress in 1992 over President Bush's veto, but O'Connor argued that the effect is to favor channels that must be carried at the expense of others that would be denied access. She noted, "Content-based speech *restrictions* are generally unconstitutional unless they are narrowly tailored to a compelling state interest," (emphasis added) and continued, "While the government may subsidize speakers that it thinks provide novel points of view, it may not restrict other speakers on the theory that what they say is more conventional" (pp. 680–681).

65. Leo Bogart, "Shaping a New Media Policy," *The Nation*, July 12, 1993, pp. 57–60 at 58. The policies administered by the FCC at least have an easy place to track them down. For a recent excellent compendium of the laws and regulations facing newspapers, see Simon, "Newspaper Regulation, Policy and Taxation."

66. See, e.g., Jeremy Tunstall, *Communications Deregulation* (New York: Basil Blackwell, 1987); and Horwitz, *Irony of Regulatory Reform*.

67. This information comes from *CQ Weekly Report*, February 3, 1996, pp. 290–291; and February 17, 1996, pp. 413–416.

68. In addition, the proposal preserved previous restrictions to periodicals above a certain amount of editorial content and with a large list of paid subscribers. This section is based on "Reclassification Splits Industry," *Folio*, May 1, 1995, pp. 24–26; Edmund L. Andrews, "A Publishers' Slugfest over Postal Rates," *New York Times*, November 13, 1995, p. D1; Victor Navasky, "Postal Stampout," *The Nation*, November 27, 1995, pp. 653–654; Debra Gersh Hernandez, "Postal Fight Projected for 1996," *Editor & Publisher*, January 6, 1996, pp. 28–31; and Laura M. Litvan, "Postal Changes Raise the Stakes," *Nation's Business* (June 1996): pp. 32–34.

69. For instance, Michael McBride, a lawyer for the *Wall Street Journal*,

claimed, "This debate isn't between big and small; it's between efficient and inefficient," while Victor Navasky, publisher of the *Nation,* argued that the subsidies were "what the Founding Fathers had in mind when they supported second-class mail." Both quoted in Andrews, "Publishers' Slugfest," p. D3.

70. For instance, compare Robert M. Entman, *Democracy without Citizens: Media and the Decay of American Politics* (New York: Oxford University Press, 1989); with Stephen Lacy, "The Effects of Intracity Competition on Daily Newspaper Content," *Journalism Quarterly* 64 (1987): 281–290.

71. See, e.g., Patricia Aufderheide, "After the Fairness Doctrine: Controversial Broadcast Programming and the Public Interest," *Journal of Communication* 40, no. 3 (1990): 47–72.

72. Linda J. Busby, "Broadcast Regulatory Policy: The Managerial View," *Journal of Broadcasting* 23 (1979): 331–341.

73. Indeed, such a proposal surfaced in 1987, when Senator Ernest Hollings introduced a bill that would have assessed a 2 percent tax on the sale price of television and radio licenses upon their transfer. Not surprisingly, the broadcast industry lobby went into high gear, and the proposal was defeated. See Hoynes, *Public Television for Sale,* pp. 170–171. A similar proposal by Senator Larry Pressler, who chaired the committee overseeing telecommunications reform in the 104th Congress prior to his defeat for reelection in 1996, did not gather much momentum.

74. J. H. Freiberg, *The French Press: Class, State, and Ideology* (New York: Praeger, 1981), p. 171, quoted in Robert G. Picard, *The Press and the Decline of Democracy: The Democratic Socialist Response in Public Policy* (Westport, CT: Greenwood, 1985) p. 111.

75. See, e.g., McManus, *Market-Driven Journalism,* chap. 1.

76. The best consideration of the impact of the NPA is Busterna and Picard, *Joint Operating Agreements.*

77. For some particularly thought-provoking discussions of possible policies, see Robert Picard, "Policy Implications," in Picard et al., eds., *Press Concentration and Monopoly;* Baker, *Advertising and a Democratic Press;* and Bogart, "Shaping a New Media Policy."
Investigating the communication policies of other democracies is also fruitful. See, for instance, Anthony Smith, "Subsidies and the Press in Europe," *Political and Economic Planning Broadsheet,* no. 569 (1977); Robert Picard, "Patterns of State Intervention in Western Press Economics," *Journalism Quarterly* 62 (1985): 3–9; and Picard, *The Press and the Decline of Democracy,* chap. 5. Smith, for Western Europe, and Picard, for the same countries but adding Iceland, Canada, and the United States, both show in some detail that all Western democracies have some form of "state intervention." For instance, beneficial taxation, postal rates, and government advertising in newspapers are nearly universal. What is most intriguing about surveying the various options outlined, particularly in Smith, "Subsidies and the Press," is the range of possibilities that can assist news outlets while being content-neutral, referring instead to such criteria as circulation, ratio of advertising to editorial space, distribution in more than one province, etc. Although such ideas might be doubted on the basis of the United States as an "exceptional" political system, Picard, "Patterns," table 3, shows through a factor analysis that the United States' patterns of interventions are similar to a

number of European countries such as the German Federal Republic, Denmark, and Switzerland.

78. For instance, Picard proposes that tax incentives could be crafted to help smaller papers to compete with large metropolitan dailies, such as investment tax credits to help lower barriers to entry. "Policy Implications," p. 200. Baker (in *Advertising and a Democratic Press*) quite ingeniously suggests that direct grants could be given to newspapers on the basis of high circulation, the proceeds having come from a tax on advertising, thereby producing a subsidy going from high-advertising, low-circulation newspapers to high-circulation, low-advertising counterparts. Elsewhere, as in France and Sweden, direct subsidies have been awarded to newspapers with low advertising (as compared to editorial) content; the fact that such a subsidy is content-neutral can be aptly seen by the two newspapers in France that were the first recipients of aid, the Catholic right-wing *La Croix* and the Communist *L'Humanité*. Smith, "Subsidies and the Press," p. 15.

79. Again, see Baker, *Advertising and a Democratic Press*.

80. See, e.g., Thomas Patterson and Robert McClure, *The Unseeing Eye* (New York: Putnam's, 1976); and Just et al., *Crosstalk*, chap. 6.

81. This latter point was initially (and nicely) made by Robinson, "Three Faces of Congressional Media." In my study of media strategies in the House of Representatives, I did find that C-SPAN was primarily of benefit to members and their press secretaries to the extent that it helped them woo either the national or local media; see Cook, *Making Laws and Making News*, table 4-2, and pp. 93, 97–99. Nonetheless, as the viewership becomes narrower amidst the proliferation of channels, such attempts to reach a single "best" medium will probably begin to fade.

82. Jerry Gray, "1-Man Crusade over Lobbying Ensnares a Bill," *New York Times*, November 4, 1995, p. A1.

83. Richard L. Berke, "G.O.P. TV: New Image in Appeal to Voters," *New York Times*, January 30, 1994, p. 20. GOP-TV also bought time on the Family Network to air nightly live shows during the 1996 Republican National Convention, modeled on the broadcasts of the major networks, complete with anchors in the skyboxes above the convention hall and reporters with headsets roving through the delegates. Although the production values were still a bit creaky, the ability to package a message of mobilization is a genuine potential.

84. This is, incidentally, one of the conclusions in Just et al., *Crosstalk*, regarding the role of the political information environment in the 1992 presidential campaign.

85. Thomas Rosenstiel, in the *Los Angeles Times*, calendar sec., November 27, 1988, p. 28.

86. Quoted in Pollard, *The Presidents and the Press*, p. 48.

INDEX